Slow Travel

ALSO BY MARTHA BARRON BARRETT

Maggie's Way

God's Country

The Grazer

Invisible Lives

Slow Travel

Two Women of a Certain Age—
and Modest Means—
Leave Home

A Travel Memoir
by
Martha Barron Barrett

Photographs by
Sandra Taylor Lawson

Slow Travel
©2014 by Martha Barron Barrett
All rights reserved

Published by Piscataqua Press
A project of RiverRun Bookstore
142 Fleet St
Portsmouth, NH 03801
603-431-2100

info@riverrunbookstore.com
www.riverrunbookstore.com
www.piscataquapress.com

Visit the author at: www.marthabarronbarrett.com

ISBN: 978-1-939739-21-6

Printed in the United States of America

For my children

BRENT JAMES ELIZABETH

With thanks and love

Wanderer, there is no road,
the road is made by walking.

—Antonio Machado, Spanish poet

CONTENTS

Preface

A boutique on the Octagon in Dunedin, South Island, New Zealand.

"So, you're on your own then?" The shopkeeper sounded surprised and uncertain. "Not from the cruise ship? No tour?" She focused on our white hair. "No husband saying what time you have to be where?" We smiled and shook our heads. "You mean like girls' night out?"

"Well, not exactly ..." Sandy and I had been together for twenty years. "We're wintering-over, be in New Zealand three months. "

"Everyone zips in and out in two weeks. Both islands."

"We like slow travel," I said. "See something one day, think about it the next."

The woman extended a small open box of Cadbury chocolates. "Good on ya', ladies. I only wish I could tag along."

TO HUNKER OR STRETCH?

Maine Cottage

WEDNESDAY MAY 9: *Maine cottage*

I'm sitting at my computer in the addition, designed and built by Sandy and me — with the help of three books and Pinkham's hardware store — and grandly dubbed the South Wing. No wallboard covers the sheathing boards, so the wind, now riding a howl and spewing a white-capped chop out from the mouth of the Narraguagus River into open ocean, overrides the noisy blast of the electric heater. On rainy mornings like this I stare at a wall of green tarp. The windows we used had formed the wall of a sun porch that was being torn down and they leak.

No view except a mental one of me stutter-stepping along the edge of life styles. On one side is a gradual slope leading to hunker-down comforts, on the other a tangle of puckerbrush hides unknown terrain. Ahead an ever-narrowing path tunnels into old age.

I'll be seventy-four in September. A decade ago that would have indicated it's time to make a plan for living ten more years. I don't think that's prudent now; twenty years may be more realistic. Rather amusing that in this capitalistic era where numbers are god, we have to be so vague about something so definite, so irrevocable as the end of the path. Nevertheless, my peers and many who are twenty years younger are making a best guess how to plan their future, choosing versions of the familiar or the puckerbrush of change.

WEDNESDAY MAY 16 Sandy, my partner for twenty years, and I returned yesterday after spending four days at our 1890s in-town house in Portsmouth, New Hampshire, a four and a half hour drive away. That tall, blue house is the lynch-pin in our decision making.

Although we expected to do a two-day round trip with Sandy's woodworking machine tools, we ended up watching baseball games on TV while flooding rains poured down: ten inches in thirty-six hours. We'd already made the three-story house perfect for the renters. Summer renters for three to six months is how I've kept the bills paid since I purchased the house in 1984. But child of the Depression that I am, I'm wary that this economic up, up, up can't last forever. My mother's hand still grips mine as she hurries me to the other side of the Pittsburgh street that fronts the stock market, in case, I believe, it falls again—crashes with good men jumping from windows. Not that I hold stocks, but potential renters do.

Sandy and I sat pretty much paralyzed, eating breakfast at Friendly Toast, take-out chowder from the fish store, dinners bought at the Fresh Market deli, while monitoring the water oozing up through the concrete cellar floor and eventually flowing out the drain. Now it seems we will, minus the distractions of TV and restaurants, be tethered to fireplace and electric heater in this way-downeast coastal village of Milbridge. Sandy will complete a set of nesting tables in her semi-heated shop that perches on the ledges above the cottage; and mornings I'll continue to write in the green glow of the wind-pummeled tarp.

No view is bothersome, but even if we could afford their efficient preciousness, Anderson windows would jar the 1930's simple, make-do ambiance of this seasonal home. Fifteen years ago we, high on bravado, had taken an electric saw and recycled the salvage frames into seven one-or-two pane windows to hang horizontally on hinges inside screening nailed between the trim boards. They swing inward and upward to hang from what look like meat hooks secured to the rafter stringers, allowing us—on rare and marvelous summer days and nights—three sides of wraparound outdoors. Since we also sleep here, it's like tenting with a roof. A multitude of paperbacks pressed on shelves between studs complete the campish decor. Outside lie two brief terraces, then ledges, ocean and islands.

THURSDAY MAY 17   Fog. Juncos chatter under the deck in a domestic spat over nest-building, I rarely look at myself from the outside, put myself into a scene, but when writing a journal for others to read it seems necessary to acknowledge the frayed sleeves of my ancient red bathrobe and the belly that has taken a growth spurt. I'm like a teenager, not at all certain where my body is headed. But my mind, once it progressed beyond those fierce battles with the cultural norms of the 30s, 40s, and 50s—including my mother's tight observance of "what people will think—" has remained settled in living from the inside out.

Perhaps aging will breed opinionated crotchetiness, but I cannot ingest the new philosophies. I have let crystals, past lives, future lives, visualization, feng shui, ghosts, spiritualism in general float by. And even though my white hair falls into a ponytail, I firmly reject "old hippie." To the contrary, I spent America's cultural revolution raising three children and teaching in a skirt and tiny heels.

Now, Sandy, sixty-six, and I feel the pressure of rising food costs, upkeep on the Portsmouth house and future vagaries of the body. What should we be doing at the moment to arrive at the right spot to enjoy the rest of our precious lives together?

Living longer is new territory. I imagine that people now enjoying or enduring their nineties did not plan for them, probably blink every morning in a state of surprise. A wonderful short story describes an old woman who lives alone, waking to chest pains. Aha, she thinks, at last. She makes a cup of tea, pulls up the quilt, and waits. Eventually she dozes off and upon opening her eyes feels fine. Sighing, she gets up and makes the bed.

For us, so far, brief, random discussions and small decisions have wiggled out from daily living, making my writing these journals "on pulse"—as May Sarton described her yearly books on aging—seem apt for me. A daily record to catch the details, the shifts and changes before they solidify, became foreshadowing of a known end. Perhaps Sarton's style is comfortable when pulse does literally assume a more dominant role as the years dwindle down to a precious few.

FRIDAY MAY 18 Thick fog. Great for reading, but conscience will also demand attention to bills, banking, etc.

Either I'm growing feeble, or this electronic world has shoved more into our laps instead of less—it's not for our convenience, as those cheery machine voices insist. Cash hidden in the mattress might still be the way to go. But if we were to sell the Portsmouth house, we'd be depending on interest to pay taxes here and for winter quarters, a situation that would make capital rather sacrosanct. Perhaps we would find tending several hundred thousand dollars of cash from a sale as burdensome as renting the house seems now.

Living lightly, in my case, is rooted in a heritage of Scot parsimoniousness and the Great Depression. It flowered with the voluntary poverty I embraced after leaving private-school teaching and my then husband Chuck. Realistically, my $8,000 a year teacher's salary could also be filed in the voluntary poverty category. Quitting the day job for the writer's life in my midforties was, however, a true adventure in reducing overhead and pinching pennies.

Is it time to cash in that now quite valuable Portsmouth house and live it up a little? The vicissitudes of the body may visit any day. Also, Sandy complains more and more about upkeep we can't afford to hire out, increasing the drag of our own efforts to maintain and improve. But I don't think she agrees that not owning property will give us a higher discretionary income. Cutting loose requires going against some strong cultural norms, and Sandy is quick to acknowledge her tight and tidy suburban Boston values.

"Owning" seems to be a hot capitalistic item, but even owning a condo has certain fixed disadvantages: maintenance fees that creep or leap upward, and property taxes that do the same.

SATURDAY MAY 19   These rainy forty-something degree days bring practical thoughts about actually living here. For example: Would it be possible to run baseboard heating off the propane water heater in the kitchen? Or on the more esoteric side: If we sold the Portsmouth house, how about following the sun for several months? Instead of spending $5,000 for a ten-day tour, we would establish ourselves in a vacation rental in, say, a country in the southern hemisphere. We have done short-term renting twice in the United States: three months in an Albuquerque apartment after I finished *Invisible Lives,* and three in a nice Spokane house as a Visiting Writing Professor. We liked the comfort of being rooted and the excitement of exploring, which could be as stimulating as climbing in the Sandias, or as bland as walking around our top of the ancient volcano neighborhood in Spokane. And very inexpensive compared to "traveling."

Neither of us has taken the time to go online and see if this living overseas short-term idea would work—too many variables to make more than a wild guess. And shivering in May does not bode well for the shoulder months of March and November. Insecurities about water inflow and outflow, reasonable warmth, and the steep rise of our dirt driveway hover.

Sandy will take the idea of heating off the hot water tank and ground it in reality: I am air--Libra; she is earth--Taurus.

FRIDAY MAY 26   An e-mail from my son Jim last night--he had put my childhood Lionel train cars on eBay in the afternoon. "$250 in bids so far," he wrote. "Promising." Just now I looked again--$800! And nine days to go. Much more than enough to buy a comfortable chair for my shrinking frame in a Portsmouth apartment—another alternative for winter living.

The sun looks iffy, the sea calm. Unless a good breeze comes by nine, the black flies will eat me alive while I plant my salad garden.

SATURDAY MAY 27 The Lionel trains are up over $1000.

MONDAY MAY 29 Im-pulse--Malcolm Gladwell's "blink"—could be defined as long-held beliefs swiftly applied to a new situation. Awareness of those beliefs can provide clues to future decisions. An important clue in my case comes from an underlined sentence in a well-worn copy of Anne Morrow Lindbergh's *Gift From The Sea*: "I mean to lead a simple life, to choose a simple shell I can carry easily—like a hermit crab." That philosophy sent me, at forty-three, teenage daughter by my side, in search of land on the Maine coast. Twenty years later an environmentalist culture would describe it as a desire to live lightly upon this earth.

Shed the rest and live lightly here in a small gray-shingled summer cottage? Could I?

WEDNESDAY MAY 31 Still and gray, low 40s. Back to turtlenecks and wool. Yesterday the iMac started snapping. Sandy dusted off the fire extinguisher, checked the pressure gauge. A techie in Bangor confirmed a possible electrical fire and "thought"—foreboding word—he could save the data. Now what? Fix or chuck?

A laptop would be essential if we did extended overseas time. But deciding which one looms as a huge, unpleasant task.

THURSDAY JUNE 1 Started taking apart sink area. The thirty-plus-year-old porcelain is worn to an implacable dirty gray, so last fall— living lightly has its limits—we brought back a new acrylic one from tax-free Portsmouth and stored it under the bed in Sandy's room.

Computers don't fit my guidelines for cottage upgrades. Fall a few years behind and whack—nothing is usable. Having written my first novel on an electric typewriter using carbon paper and white erasure strips, I am a fervent worshiper of the word processor, and e-mail is heaven compared to the interruptions of phone calls. Technological inertia, however, is a mighty weight.

FRIDAY JUNE 2 Being severed from the computer umbilical cord continues to be unsettling; TV withdrawal never is.

My definition of old, old age is a stack of books, a rocker, and a window with a view. That's why I don't want to die mid-stride and miss it. I want the joy of my own bed-sit, breakfast on a tray, a cane to get me to that rocker. No chores, no guilt, just books and gazing and napping.

MONDAY JUNE 5　A fitful sky after two days of downpour.

The final total on the train sale was an amazing $2,000 after fees were paid. A definite push toward a new computer. I try to keep $3,000 in an interest-bearing account for medical emergencies. Like a $1,400 dentist bill last winter. I save money by having no premiums on a supplemental Medicare policy. Insurance goes against my grain anyway: rates are fixed to sustain their no-risk profit.

After the Medicare deduction, my monthly Social Security pay is $500. Freelance teaching yearly gross is $6,000, plus $4,000 as my half of the gross summer rent on the Portsmouth house which Sandy and I own jointly. But prices on everything have surged. Even with no car payments or mortgages, $16,000 is barely scraping by. But I live in extraordinarily beautiful places that I share with a person I love deeply.

Some financial impetus for lifestyle adjustment comes from those fears about changing economic conditions. If no reliable summer renters appear we would have no funds for $5,000 of property taxes, over $400 of insurance, and what if the furnace, roof, whatever has to be replaced? Renting an apartment would be less risk. I think.

TUESDAY JUNE 6　A couple days ago Sandy slipped on the mossy slime of the shop deck and went down hard; Schoodic, the cat, was launched from her arms onto the ledge, fortunately bewildered, not running. Then last night in bed she turned, froze in breathless pain. She did not appreciate my attempts at cutesy distractions, so we lay in the dark holding hands; eventually she relaxed and discovered she could get up after the first stabbing pain subsided. Broken ribs?

In Portsmouth we are minutes from a good hospital and doctors we know. Here, there is a volunteer ambulance service and a small hospital fifty miles away. The doctor in town has a sketchy reputation. And overseas would certainly be even more iffy. Son Jim says there is a clinic in the Argentine town where he has bought a fix-up casita, but he's never heard an ambulance siren. If anything were seriously wrong, he told me, he'd take a plane home.

Medical. Another variable to throw into the mix.

MONDAY JUNE 12　I first saw Sandy in the teacher's room at a high school where I was substituting. The white golf shirt and navy sweats with a broad white stripe told me the role she played. Her bare arm on the table was brown and beautifully curved. Months later as she served me a plate of chicken, I saw behind the rosy cheeks and flashing smile a bit of hostess-concern in her blue eyes, a look familiar from my mother who had died that fall, eight days before my father.

I was there in Sandy's 1834 brick schoolhouse home for an interview. A first-class lesbian bar and restaurant had opened in the heart of town, and I'd suggested to my editor at a Portsmouth weekly that I write an in-depth article. Two weeks, I thought, would do it, but fascinated by the duality of the lives lesbians led, I was still interviewing two months later. I had to assure the women I talked to that composite characters would be used to hide identities. As a local teacher, Sandy was taking a big chance. Two years later Sandy and I would be traveling across the country, together, interviewing women for my book, *Invisible Lives*.

This morning on my way back from the bathroom at 3:30 the sea was pale and still, edged by low dark islands. Above, against a crystal-blue sky, shone the delicate, hopeful morning star. This far north and east first light comes early. I warmed a mug of milk and sat at the table by the picture window. The first faint chug of a lobster boat eased into the silence. Its running lights moved down the bay to the open sea; a smaller one followed. All lobster boats are calm, steadfast, and brave.

Milk finished, I tiptoed across the worn pine boards back into the South Wing and our bed where Sandy and Schoodic slept, white heads sharing the same pillow.

SUNDAY JUNE 25   After ten days away woke cozy with my love. And Maine strawberries and bagels for breakfast.

MONDAY JUNE 26   If I lived alone, how long would the events of the writing conference — an outgrowth of my adult classes here and at the University of New Hampshire — and my ex-husband Chuck's eightieth birthday party churn voiceless in my mind? Who but Sandy would have been interested? One of the most painful things about my marriage was that Chuck always had secrets that kept him distant. I remember thinking: If only he would sit down beside me, ask, How are you? and really mean it ... I suppose he didn't dare to.

Got acquainted with new Mac iBook — found Microsoft Word. I'm in business.

TUESDAY JUNE 27   I'm aware now that aging sucks up time and energy so subtly that one day I may just wake up and say, I don't want to travel, I don't want to face moving out of the Portsmouth house, I can't, I won't, and miss whole gobs of living.

Should I give up teaching? Can I pay my daily expenses without that income? Am I ready to forego the excitement of the people? Bonds with diverse adult writers over twenty-five years have enriched my life, both those I've known only through five or ten weeks of their essays, and those who have become close friends.

WEDNESDAY JUNE 28   The cocoon of drippy fog remains. Even if the neighbors on either side were in residence I would not notice. Shut windows muffle all sounds, from boat motors to the backyard calls of robin parents and babies. If I lived alone here, my mind would tend to travel outward to coming guests, family concerns, perhaps a hopeful romance, but Sandy and Schoodic are a stable base: one I can in imagination push off from and then return for lunch.

WEDNESDAY JULY 5   Thank goodness the fog lifted for the weekend so that my eldest son, Brent, his wife, Kath, and their three teenagers were not captive to chairs, couches, and beds with books and cards, but could spread to deck, lawn, and ledges. Seemingly out of the blue, Kath had remarked, "You two are so symbiotic with this place."

FRIDAY JULY 7 At last, true summer—not quite bare feet, but close—and time for some usual days. In-the-moment days that move along in a regular beat: dum, dedum, dedum. Waking at five to sunlight and coffee. A morning of writing, an exercise walk, the annoyance of marketing a screenplay. Lunch on the rocks. Afternoon in the garden. Wine at five on the lawn. Cooking and eating. Red Sox on radio and reading till nine. The march of the ordinary—I love it.

SUNDAY JULY 9   Yesterday Sandy and I had a rare tiff. Our estrangement simmered as we drove an hour and a half to an outdoor farm lunch. On the way back we could chat about the event and the people, but I went to bed at seven and pulled the covers over my head. Others may claim this kind of tension lays bare the hard core of art, but I feel battered and dull.

SATURDAY JULY 15 A barefoot morning. Over the years people have asked us: Which place do you really like best? If you had to choose, would it be Milbridge or Portsmouth? Although the Portsmouth house is perfect in size and location, its winter comforts and the town could be enjoyed from another venue; there is no other place like this cottage, where indoor and outdoor are knit into such a magnificent whole. Only 120 shore-front feet, but a universe in itself: a mile east lies the low sleeping-woman hill of Trafton Island; Dyer Island and Foster's rim the bay to the north; to the south, Pond and Jordan's Delight float on open ocean. I could never part with this, our natural habitat, where we breathe with Gaia in the ebb and rise of earth's forces.

THURSDAY AUGUST 10 Yesterday I sorted a new package of photos selecting some to send out as postcards. The one of Jim, my bachelor son, making pancakes in the Portsmouth kitchen on Christmas morning brought an unexpected lump to my throat. How can we even think of selling the kitchen that Sandy and I designed and built? Am I out of my mind?

MONDAY AUGUST 14 We won't be able to complain there was no summer in 2006: this series of incredible days should suffice. Nevertheless, for the past month I've been on a seesaw that anguish has occasionally tilted to the ground; the growing possibility that my thirteen-year-old grandson's girlfriend will succumb to leukemia; my daughter Bett forced to take out a restraining order against her out-of-control ex-husband; this morning's phone call from a close college friend that her husband's untreated prostate cancer has spread to his bones — too late for any cure.

Lately, I rush to gloomy, even horrific, conclusions. Does having lived so long, heard so much, cause this? Or is it a subconscious awareness of my own demise?

On the high side of that seesaw was Saturday, another brilliant showcase day. Skirting the tourists in Arcadia National Park we enjoyed our ritual haunts — a picnic on top of Cadillac Mountain, ice cream in Bar Harbor — then a dinner/theater evening to celebrate, along with eighty other friends and family, a student's eighty-eighth birthday, evidence, I'd say, of her very rich life.

Yesterday, Sunday, I had what I call a flat day. I moved slowly between deck, rocks, garden, back bedroom, South Wing. Today the flatness lingers around the edges, curling me inward.

WEDNESDAY AUGUST 16 While I lay on the narrow back porch, thighs pulled up over a no-longer-flat stomach, searching the trees for the newly-fledged, endlessly chipping robins, I noticed that the massive green of summer is slightly tarnished, more penetrable.

Autumn has begun its slow, sometimes erratic creep. The grasses dry so early they don't really count, but the reds and oranges of the weeds and the submissive droop of the birch leaves are telling, as is the sprinkling of copper-coin leaves in the rock maple. So it begins.

I could never bear to think this would be the last time I would be a witness to autumn here, but I can deal with thinking of never going back to a winter at the Portsmouth house. With the recent switch to a buyer's market it will probably take longer to sell, but that is okay: we could probably use two winters to properly dispose of all the possessions there. Like the family quilts that an expert said were museum quality.

THURSDAY AUGUST 17   A college friend, one of us four "Bal Gals," had a fall walking on oceanside rocks. My body and mind feel braced for more bad news and questions swirl: How long will Audie's Paul live? Is there bleeding in Burnsie's brain? Making a habit of this kind of thinking might foster rampant timidity: I might fall on the rocks; Sandy might have some unknown raging cancer.

A fearful bunker-type mentality would surely affect plans for this next twenty years.

SUNDAY AUGUST 20   Our options were cut yesterday when I figured in the impact of property tax increases in both Milbridge and Portsmouth: we have to sell. Five months of rent money cannot cover even those bills, let alone $600 of insurance, plus maintenance. A cold winter of oil bills could put us in debt.

We have to find out prices for renovations here, and how much being a resident would reduce—or raise—property and capital gains taxes. Then once back in Portsmouth get a price range on the house and look at what's available for rentals.

WEDNESDAY SEPTEMBER 6   High clouds from a far-out-at-sea hurricane, stiff wind from the east.

Have made progress with New Life planning. Jim, my middle child who is here splitting a year of kindling for us, says he'll be happy to stay with us in Portsmouth for November and December to get our salables on eBay for pre-Christmas auction. We have no idea how much we have to sell.

The *Times* had an article about online brokers taking only 3% commission and that fits right in with my idea of showing the house myself. I've done it for renters for twenty years and the only goof-up was when a real estate agent muscled her way into the deal. No love lost there.

We three also talked visas and travel insurance. Jim, who left Wall Street to become a full-time sculptor, will stay at his fix-up casita in Argentina until spring. So long.

WEDNESDAY SEPTEMBER 13 Yesterday was a Holiday For Us Day. Up to Canada by ferries and back Route 1 at twilight.

Trips like this remind us why we would prefer to do our overseas traveling from a fixed spot called home. It is not entirely age, but also our fondness for refection that makes this desirable. We can ruminate on what we have experienced in familiar surroundings, chewing over moments that would otherwise be lost in gulps. I have never been one to dive from one thoughtful book to another, or one TV movie or program into another. A full experience, to my mind, requires playback to examine nuances, different slants, and plug in ideas worth keeping.

When we were forty-eight and fifty-five, newly partners, we traveled New Zealand for five weeks, moving almost every day; a couple months later we were on a wild trip the length and breadth of the United States interviewing lesbians for *Invisible Lives*. Today that would flatten us. And would what we plan now be unthinkable at eighty and seventy-three?

FRIDAY SEPTEMBER 15 Nights in the 50s, days in the 60s preserve the illusion of summer, but by late afternoon yesterday when Sandy and I gathered with friends for wine at one's hilltop home, the sun lit only the far view of bay and islands.

The conversation turned to travel and eventually to the need to make our cottage more comfortable in the shoulder months. Sandy said that her workshop quickly became unusable, prompting both Sue and Jean to offer space for her to work. They would like us as voting residents participating on committees and boards. Well, who knows? But it is good to have friendly support to alleviate shuddering visions of cramped, cold living. Must talk to our nearby year-round neighbors about how they keep our common road clear, and call a respected, local sand and gravel man for ideas on a new septic system.

WEDNESDAY SEPTEMBER 20 Donny came over yesterday and after a lot of tramping around the premises gave us the good news that our present septic—grandfathered in with this house—could probably handle a washing machine. Wow. Try it, he said, and if you have problems call. Good Maine philosophy: if it ain't broke, see how far she'll go and then fix 'er. An engineer, others had told me, would suggest a $7,000 leach field and $2,000 for a new tank—and if they needed to pump it out back ... Fortunately, I've never had the money to do that. An "Indian burial mound" is just too disruptive for our narrow seaside lot. I prefer crossing my fingers and living lightly.

We've now determined an order for improvements: plastic gutters in the back—maybe this fall. Although I love the wooden ones, they do take work. Next, calling the carpenter who's been doing new underpinnings next door for a consult on ours.

Donny suggested the only way to stop crawling under the house to fuss with pipes in cold weather was to put them up in the house. To which Sandy quickly remarked, "That wouldn't look very pretty." "It don't," he said. "But they just built these old camps too low to the ground." Raising the cottage is something we won't do anything about. Today I'll call the gas man regarding propane heaters.

THURSDAY SEPTEMBER 21   After yesterday's talk-fest I relish today's silence, that semi-alert somnambulist state of people who live together in close quarters. But I suppose interactions with others keep us lively. Like the pair of grebes—winter residents of the cove—who were joined by another couple at daybreak and thus reinforced began a haughty patrol. Their skinny, long necks and raspy voices sent the thirty-some young male eiders steaming out into the bay.

MONDAY SEPTEMBER 25   My birthday: seventy-four years on this earth. I woke at sunrise, marveling that my body has held out so well so long. Still pain-free and eager for the day.

Last evening while eating dessert in Jean's dining room, she offered us the gas wall heater that she has never used. "Be out of my way when I paint." Progress.

THURSDAY SEPTEMBER 28   A grebe-eider truce was established late yesterday. Two pairs of fully adult eiders came in, and this time one of the males approached the grebes and conducted negotiations so successfully that one grebe has begun hanging out with a batch of young eider males. Score another good point for interaction with strangers.

MONDAY OCTOBER 9 Dave stopped by to take a look at our underpinnings. Over the years we've heard a wide range of fanciful, incomprehensible, expensive solutions, but Dave poked around, said the sills looked good—to Sandy's surprise and my nod—and the fix would be to simply jack the house up a bit and straighten or replace the old concrete pillars. His guess at cost was "under $1,000." With visible reluctance he put us on his spring list: he's looking for work easier on his back—like inspections. Overall, he agreed with Donny Ellis that the roof line looked good. So, the good news and the good weather continues. Like a turtle we move steadfastly toward our new life while carrying this domicile on our back. The load is light, however, compared to the Portsmouth house.

TUESDAY OCTOBER 10 All of the traps in the cove have been hauled; November is a month of storms: rough sailing and damaged gear. The grebes, who now number fourteen, and eiders, diminished to groups of about the same number, seem to get along all right, but prefer the company of their own kind; like the so-called snowbirds from here who go south for the winter. The loon, a true loner, occasionally amuses himself by herding the others around.

FRIDAY OCTOBER 13 A heavy, dark morning and I woke late with a tied-down feeling. I recognized it from long stretches here with fog or rain or cold making the outside—our real living space—uninhabitable. When allowed to build up with no tangible relief ahead, this sensation of being trapped would, I suppose, result in either a mad dash for the car or agoraphobia. What will happen next year if we are faced with an extra off-season month or more without a city house to go to? And if the South Wing is shut off, a third less space. Well ... Spring is traditionally ax murder time in Maine as cabin fever rises to unbearable levels. The solution is probably always having a trip or two in mind.

THURSDAY OCTOBER 19 *Portsmouth House*

    I reside now in a tall blue house perched on a high hill above the Piscataqua River, although the sight of the water is obscured by layers of houses, none built in the last one hundred years. This one is 1890s—the mahogany furniture of our parents' homes fits well. The house to our right is early 1800s, the left 1600s. Portsmouth is ranked by some, along with Charleston and Annapolis, as America's best example of a colonial town. I'm still hard by the Atlantic Ocean and Route 1 is even closer: the towers of the drawbridge to Maine rise outside my north window. I, once again, face east as I work, my desk angled toward the clock and steeple of the South End Meeting House. I love it.

Sandy applied for and received a $125,000 Elderly and Low Income reduction on the assessment of the house by the city. I, however, have the asset of the Maine cottage,

Bett, who lives twenty minutes away, has given us the name of the Realtor she used and says if she figures a what-we-can-sell-for price will not pester us with follow-up calls. Too often Realtors have noticed our rental ad in the *Herald* and phoned. Excited whisper: "I have this couple with me in the office now, really nice folks, and they have to start back to Boston by four. If they could just have a peek—" I have no trouble with an unapologetic "No."

SATURDAY OCTOBER 21 Heading off to see a model two-bedroom apartment this morning. I think success will come with acquiring an attitude of excitement toward leanness. Towels, for example. What do we need beyond our new monogrammed sets and one other? Certainly not the dozen we leave for renters. And we must get hardened to the fact that those towels will be trash. Hard after a lifetime of viewing them as excellent rags.

The sun is brilliant following yesterday's hard storm. Scraping the front of the house for painting beckons.

The cottage in Milbridge seems far away, tucked in a summer world.

TUESDAY OCTOBER 24 Telling people of the plans to sell and spend winters in foreign lands makes it more believable. It also serves as word-of-mouth advertising and outside pressure to prevent total relaxation and enjoyment of life as is.

THURSDAY OCTOBER 26 Swirls in my head: the unfamiliar rat-a-tat of in-town noise, the fact that Bett is in the same room, albeit a courtroom with her ex-husband; and the visit of a real estate agent this afternoon. She will appraise the house at what? $250,000? $350,000? $500,000? I have no idea.

FRIDAY OCTOBER 27 I could not believe it when the real estate agent drove up in a blaring red, white, and blue Re/Max car. If she weren't Bett's friend, I'd have told her to just keep moving. We'll get her estimate next week, but I'm more determined than ever to do the sale myself.

MONDAY OCTOBER 30 The eastern sky is clear and still; early morning is quiet here in the South End of Portsmouth. Commuters to Boston slip off in the dark; the retired emerge later, brisk and casually well-dressed. We breathe self-satisfaction here.

However, a neighbor who usually rents one half of her duplex through the local newspaper, is concerned. "Twenty-seven rentals, just in Portsmouth," she said. "I've gone to Craigslist, but no calls yet."

Guess the real estate market has cooled. Of course, it may adversely affect our selling price. But we don't feel greedy. More money would create more interest to spend for travel, comforts in Milbridge, and relief from some of the strict discipline imposed on eating out and thermostat settings. But since our original planning was for $250,000, we are bound to feel we are rich with anything over that.

WEDNESDAY NOVEMBER 1 Transition month is over; now come the settled city days. But will they ever be truly settled this time around? Perhaps the heightened air of "Can we pull this off?" will subside when more questions are answered. The big one, the sale price of the house, will come in this afternoon.

THURSDAY NOVEMBER 2 The news on the sale price was good. We will be able to follow through with our new life plans. I think we have covered our bases for events that cause downswings in interest, upswings in rental prices, and medical emergencies. In fact, having no house would work to our financial advantage in the latter case: Sandy will own no house and I will only have one, no extra house for some institution to seize. But there is time before it will go on the market—March?—to get more solid info.

It was odd that we did not feel more elation when Julie said $469,000 as a base. That is $150,000 more than the '04 figures that set us on this course in the first place. Perhaps we doubt her judgment. So with our evening DVD, we had our usual cider and popcorn, not champagne and ribs. Perhaps when the sale goes through, we'll have what we call a Prairie Star restaurant night. We were renting in Albuquerque where—after receiving the call that HarperCollins had bought the paperback rights for *Invisible Lives*—we ate quail as three waiters hovered and the sun set red across the Rio Grande. Don't hesitate: dance when the harvest is in.

FRIDAY NOVEMBER 3 When I joked about being half-millionaires, Sandy called me on it. I assured her we'd change lifestyle gradually: new underpants every two years instead of four, perhaps a degree or two up on the thermostat. In Macy's when I suggested she could afford those $40 jeans, she looked as though I'd gone out of my mind. I agree, it will take time.

The selling situation right now seems similar to falling in love. We're at a point where the disease is not yet incurable, that edge before the plunge when you are still willing to dig for possible areas of incompatibility and be firm about the hazards of them. I need to sit down this weekend with calculator and old work sheets and apply hard reality, not fudge the possible pitfalls. Better to break it off before commitment moves are made.

Will the IRS booklet on home sales still give the same deduction formula for renter/owner occupation? What will those who know far more than us say about long-term interest rates? Can I successfully advertise and show the house myself? What will be the sale price by spring—down another 5 percent? How will my personal budget look without teaching income?

MONDAY NOVEMBER 6 An unease tightens my stomach today, as though there is too much to do for time available and yet, in truth, that is not the case at all. I must not let the worry worm into my system. There is a long haul ahead and no reason for panic—or even hurry. Some slow deep breathing is in order.

WEDNESDAY NOVEMBER 8 The idea of residency has morphed from a question to an acceptance that indeed, we will be citizens of Maine, not New Hampshire, for several years. Other decisions may end up in the plus or minus column, but there is the relief of: that's one settled.

I may remain housebound today, perhaps go off for a bedroom read and nap this afternoon. This house with its abundant privacy, noiseless carpets, large dim rooms is a luxury I will never enjoy again. But twenty years of it is certainly more than most people ever have. My life has overflowed with the comfort of beauty.

THURSDAY NOVEMBER 9 Lately, I've gotten several reactions to our travel plans that at first seem to question my mental balance, then shift to an attitude of: "You're a better man than I am, Gunga Din." Audie's husband used the actual quote. Another friend's husband has announced that, personally, he will not fly overseas again: too much hassle. A new acquaintance, who is accustomed to flying to her native Holland twice a year, thinks traveling now "is just too exhausting." Her husband said he admired our spirit, but a raised eyebrow signaled the unspoken caveat: you may be sorry.

These are people near my age, and I do wonder if I've still got it to make even the first plane. Let alone the second or third. Certainly, we'll not do as we did in 1987: rise here at 3 a.m., drive to Boston's Logan Airport, spend twenty-four hours in a plane, land at Auckland, tour the city with a local, catch a flight for Christchurch, walk around town, have a drink in an upscale bar, a spot of dinner, and at dark curl up in a B&B bed. Never happen.

I suspect, however, that the toughest part may be the tension involved in "making the first plane." It has been a decade at least, since I've been on a plane. Back when son Jim worked for Continental Airlines I flew standby, domestic and foreign, for years. Now, despite desire and will, I may have anxieties that never occurred to me then.

Habit and familiarity surely have an impact. For example, we usually only drive into Boston once a winter and Sandy—who, as a native, always takes the wheel—makes a huge deal of it. But once we've done it, we're ready to go again the next week. I'm not one to anticipate the worst. Shakespeare's quote about the coward dying many times, the valiant only once, was a real hit in the weekly series I hung in the bathroom for my kids to stare at. I firmly believe it, but I also firmly believe in listening to your body. I could never run down dark steps to catch a subway train at my age—I know and respect that but this morning we did not hesitate to tackle the job of moving an old box spring and mattress down two flights of narrow stairs and into the car.

The disgust about flying that I hear expressed concerns security measures and cost-cutting airlines and the sheer volume of people who fly in the 21st century. We'll see.

TUESDAY NOVEMBER 14 It's been awhile. Immediate concerns have shortened my writing time—especially the job of getting items ready for Jim to eBay. He flew in from New Jersey yesterday.

In the midst of all this rooting about in nostalgia, we have been talking New Zealand, and Sandy's been reading a neighbor's *Frommer's South Africa*. Gives a lift of excitement to all this backward gazing.

THURSDAY NOVEMBER 16 Sandy and I have spent many hours down in the cellar and up in the third floor storage room. Jim stays glued to a dining room chair and computer for twelve hours a day. He has suggested living here for a couple summer months if the house hasn't sold yet, take over the showing etc. instead of calling in a Realtor. Since he sold his wonderful Jersey City condo, he rents apartments here and there: "My life is in storage. I visit it occasionally."

We are still unsure about the conclusions the Feds will make concerning principal home/rental status. Asking them would only trigger an immediate red flag on our income taxes. Let sleeping dogs lie. Probably, we need an accountant.

MONDAY NOVEMBER 20 Sandy and I talked gently in bed this morning about supporting each other during this upheaval, which according to some experts can lead to heart attacks, cancer, whatever ... I know that my heart attack in 1994 was directly related to piling on things that had to be done by a certain deadline: roofing Sandy's shop, having her furniture moved in here from storage—she had sold her house in the spring—the day after we arrived for the winter, and preparing a book party for Bett which was also a this-is-our-place-now house warming. That sense of being out on an unsupported limb must be avoided.

For a year after my hospitalization any guests at all made my hands sweat and we did cut back. Our internist, Dr. Diane, said my blood had a propensity to clumping: "Good stress," she said, meaning fun things. "can kill you, too. " In the two months prior to the attack, I could literally feel my heart lurch at moments of overload, and I should have asked for—demanded, perhaps--more understanding support from others. To do that, however, would have necessitated a sea change in my own attitudes: hard work never hurt anyone, and pride in being competent, unruffled, efficient in any circumstance which fostered Martha/Mom can handle anything. Wrong—all wrong—at sixty-two. Our bodies pay for our mind's blindness.

I am determined to come out of this change whole without the aftereffects of paranoia, cancer, or blocked arteries that friends have suffered from managing overload with a stiff upper lip. In '94 the blocked tiny feeder vessel healed almost immediately, but like paper that has been balled and wrinkled, fault lines remain—and I am seventy-four.

Part of my Health First plan is to keep Sandy's mindful support.

I'll extend the information to the children, maybe over the Thanksgiving table. We'll see. I am aware, however, that opening one's life to such an enormous change is like a nation going to war: outside forces, collateral damage cannot be internally controlled.

FRIDAY NOVEMBER 24 I arrived for Thanksgiving in gold and black striped rayon pants and a black turtleneck strewn with my mother's pins and necklaces, wrists ablaze with her bracelets. Nineteen-year-old Tee whispered to her mother, "Mam's gone bling." My mother was a lady, never, ever bling, but she would have smiled and twinkled watching the family denude me.

This morning I'm in a flat zone. Jim arrives from Oklahoma this afternoon.

WEDNESDAY NOVEMBER 29 Yesterday, we taped the boxes of thirty-eight eBay items and talked about these Christmas surprises for people nation-wide, mostly mid and far westerners. Of course, some "gifts" will detour through antique stores, but a lot of the addresses were just folks. The only departure that tugs at my heart is the old sidesaddle I never used; it's the unrequited dreams that linger.

FRIDAY DECEMBER 1 I have been gradually pushing Sandy to decide about a knee replacement. Last winter I supported delay, but now for her just a walk around town is hurtful. Not pill-gulping pain, but she takes stairs more slowly and the collapse of her right knee is ever more obvious. Who knows how quickly really bad will happen.

This morning I urged her to make an appointment with an orthopedic doctor here, now, to see what he/she would opine about surgery. "You are not going to have much fun in New Zealand in the state you're in." I have been reluctant to use that as a blunt instrument, but I fear she is in the grip of the paralysis of analysis, questioning what doctor and where—Boston? Portsmouth? Bangor?

SATURDAY DECEMBER 2 Sandy sent for her passport yesterday. She also made an appointment Monday for an appraisal of her knees.

MONDAY DECEMBER 4 7:30. The slew of drops under the still orange streetlights resembles snow more than rain. For all practical purposes winter is upon us.

Yesterday we decided to hire an accountant. I cannot understand how the IRS deals with depreciation on a house. The gobblygook wording in the pamphlets allows a great deal of wiggle room around the word "allowable." I need an experienced, knowledgeable answer as to what Sandy and I should put on our 2006 return.

An accountant is a good idea for many reasons, however. As I told Bett, "Either Sandy or I is liable to suffer dementia any day now, maybe both of us, so someone needs to be familiar with our business." She asked if there were imminent signs and if I had answered honestly, I would have said that of late, I am forgetting a lot more than ever before—from words, to phone messages, to numbers on eBay. I've seen stress affect friends this way, some for months, one for a year. Every spring during the last two weeks before moving ourselves to Milbridge, Sandy and I alert each other by saying, "I'm getting dangerous." This means the mail may be in the refrigerator, summer clothes green-bagged for winter wear, the cat locked in the pantry.

TUESDAY DECEMBER 5 "Getting fussed," my mother called it. My father never seemed to get fussed, a demeanor I admired and preferred for myself. But once a mind is full, spillovers cause "stress," in today's lexicon. Could age shrink the brain, resulting in a higher frequency and amount of spillover? Is that why at some point people become ever more attached to routine, fearful of change?

Yesterday, a local orthopedic surgeon, said that Sandy's knees needed to be done before their collapsing made surgery and recovery more difficult. We don't want that. She did some thinking while I was at class last night and told me over coffee in bed this morning that she wanted it done immediately so there would not be a conflict with her recovery and the house sale. Questions of which doctor and what hospital remain. Doctor experience and hospital infection rates have to be considered—carefully—somehow.

Full moon last night. In the wee hours I cracked open the blinds in the bathroom, revealing thin lines of tree branches like calligraphy brush strokes across it. I thought of the Wyeths and titled it December. I will, however, feel more ho-ho-ho when classes are done.

WEDNESDAY DECEMBER 6 Bursting week. Classes Monday and Tuesday; tonight, granddaughter's band concert plus picking Jim up at the bus terminal; tomorrow a book reading downtown; Friday meet writers for wine as usual; Saturday appears free and Sunday morning a reading/talk/book signing by Barack Obama, who may or may not become the first black president of the US.

In 1984 I had one-on-one interviews for the local weekly with the entire field of seven Democratic presidential candidates. Wouldn't I love to sit down with this man.

THURSDAY DECEMBER 7 My sluggish brain is seemingly expanding against my skull and facial bones. It could be a cold; my grandson has one. Probably just blood being nudged into sleep-narrowed vessels by two cups of black coffee. Or the gel I put in my eyes for glaucoma acting weird.

Getting physical might help. I'll put on my paint clothes and prime this north window frame. The house painters can't come until spring.

MONDAY DECEMBER 11 Sandy is once more leaning toward a Boston doctor and hospital for her knees.

TUESDAY DECEMBER 12 The ten-minute drive to deposit Jim at the bus station shone rays of enlightenment on our derailment. When I first heard he had to catch a 5 a.m. bus, I thought—no way. And last night when I came home tired from teaching, I was tempted to agree with Sandy that I should just stay in bed and she'd drive him over: pulling up the covers and turning to the wall had great appeal. But at 4:15 when Jim's stocking feet padded down from the third floor, I easily swung out and up to fetch coffees.

The frosted car windows, the darkness, the bags hoisted into the trunk were reminiscent of leaving for New Zealand from this house almost twenty years ago. We spoke of this on the drive home and decided that being all packed and on our way there again would be wonderful. More and more we appreciate the lightness to come when the house is gone from our lives.

Besides having the material weight lifted is the knowledge that standing in the same doorway offers the same view, the same slant on people and events. Change sparks imagination—demands it really. For example, a metal sculpture of a cavalier set on my bookshelves twenty years ago was, I felt, in the right place. No other ever occurred to me until I was carrying it back upstairs after Jim examined it for eBay, and then, without thought, I placed it on the sill of the narrow stair window. Cats had knocked off every other decoration placed there, but this five-pounder was secure. He sits there now, boots crossed, mandolin and sword at hand, in a slant of morning sun and I think: perfect.

I've been telling people we are "going adventuring" and I'm beginning to wholeheartedly believe it.

MONDAY DECEMBER 25 It is afternoon, but I just checked e-mail. Among the responses to e-mail address change and Jim's links to online house sales, was a Deanna CarePage. It has been a long struggle for this thirteen-year-old; we kept a candle burning in a window for months. This time the news was heartwarming rather than heartbreaking. That miracle of her receiving new bone marrow—and life—from her brother was certainly the most deeply touching event of the year. Right down to the basics of giving, receiving, and rejoicing in our brief encounter with being alive on this planet.

Sandy and I looked through our new poetry book this morning to find a reading we could enjoy after our presents in bed. Nothing but downers. Where are the hallelujahs? I asked. Isn't sheer joy also a part of woman's life? The rising to the music of triumph.

Sandy's card wished us "adventures and outrageous pleasures" in the coming year. That's where I'll place my bets, too.

FRIDAY DECEMBER 29 My view is a tableau of sunlight, spotted with the red, lime, and blue coat colors of children pulling their adults toward the doors of the Children's Museum. An unexpected lump hurts my throat. The corners of this house where my grandchildren's voices hide will belong to someone else. Twenty years of my life. I was fifty-four years old when I bought it. Brent, fifty-two now, is me then, but my children had been long gone from the nest and I was ready for a new partner in love. This house has been truly ours, Sandy's and mine. I trust that closeness of "ours" to remain wherever we are.

SATURDAY DECEMBER 30 Twenty degrees and snow clouds hover.

We started sorting Christmas decorations—mostly Sandy's—yesterday: what to keep with us, give to her siblings, or toss. I guess this is our first true packing-up-the-house job and I am strangely eager to see things go. Perhaps because I will lose Sandy's help when she goes off to Boston for her knee replacement.

Our decision to sell spurred her decision, but, of course, the qualms remain, niggly now, but which I'm sure will inflate to overwhelm like balloons in the Macy's parade. Only absolute preparedness will allow me to relax enough to pursue my usual methodical pace through all this, and contrarily, only a nose to the grindstone attitude will lead to that preparedness.

Saddam Hussein was hung before dawn. Strange reminder of lands that coexist beyond mine.

TUESDAY JANUARY 2, 2007 The cottage would be a different world. Winter days passing with no yellow hi there! from another house or boat, only us perched like a lighthouse above a stormy sea. Here, no matter what time of night I wander from bed, the narrow east window is a panorama of twinkling orange blobs from the Navy Yard across the river; the dark of the stairs and hall is gray like a half-opened eye, thanks to the streetlight outside. And this morning the round, lighted face of the Meeting House clock shines against black-turning-blue heavens. The comfort of community.

Yesterday morning we scanned vacation rentals, stretching boundaries to include New Zealand. It didn't look promising until we checked foreign exchange rates and sliced 40 percent off the prices. Immediately that little place set back from the Pacific shore, twenty minutes out of Dunedin, became it. US $65 a night is certainly within budget, and the memory of bluff oysters and the hope of penguins put us right in the photo of chintz chairs with rainforest birds singing outside.

Hunker or stretch? An item in the *Herald* noted the possible expansion of a local group that offers extended home-care so the elderly (boomer generation?) are not unwillingly forced into an institutional setting. The average cost of home care services for Portsmouth clients is $1,000 a month as opposed to $4,000-$12,000 for the latter. Its emotional appeal lurks in the sacrosanct word home, but as a friend said of her aunt in Vermont: Thank goodness she sold her home and moved into an apartment. Every winter she endured a cold house, afraid of the oil bills. Now heat is included in her rent and she jacks it right up there. Loves it.

I wonder how many repairs she had let go, too. Clinging to the old out of fear and habit can make for dismal, even dangerous living. But the more options for us old folk, the better. We, like all groups, should never be boxed, labeled. and pigeon-holed.

THURSDAY JANUARY 4 Brain-groggy in spite of a clear slate ahead all day. Yesterday in Boston soaked up my reserves, although it was a highly successful trip. We like both hospital and surgeon, and the operation date—February 15. Just got an e-mail from Kath:

"You are booked at the Hotel Bradford for Valentine's Day..." I am fortunate to have generous love, not duty love, from my family.

A month and a half to ready the house for the market. Enough, I'm sure, to keep to a steady plodding pace. Sandy is over in Kittery at the Bose store looking at iPods. I find it magical how she can lose herself in music, attend to every note. That and the morphine button will get her through the awful pain. I would need books: words, not notes, form my escapist narrative.

TUESDAY JANUARY 9 The #2 Realtor's visit was unsettling. She scanned the whole house with a practiced eye for detail: good as well as bad to be sure, but we aren't accustomed to hearing about problems. Renters don't care about that antiquated fire-alarm system, asbestos on the cellar pipes, leaky windows, and ancient furnace. This agent's message is: today's buyers either expect perfection is already there, or the money to make it perfect is deducted from the price. Because Sandy and I have contributed almost all the labor for our twenty years of improvements, the costs have been minimal. But cast perfection in terms of hiring out and it's huge. Glitz is in, make-do out. I can see a buyer thinking: I'll have to put $100,000 into this fix-up. So take the first Realtor's $490,000 top price down to $390,00 and we have a lot less play money. This #2 agent will be back on Saturday with a price and suggestions on what we can do to keep the asking price up. I had been thinking in terms of small things: new sink, new counter top stove burners, painting the north side, not of tens of thousands of dollars. Scary.

And the winter bills pour in. Thank goodness I have $1,275 in student checks to throw in the checking account today. And it is a crisp, sunny day for a walk. Yesterday at our Portsmouth exercise club, I weighed in at 143—less than I thought and a short time with the weights and walking the track made my tummy tighter and my shoulders straighter.

WEDNESDAY JANUARY 10 Green tea and a bright blue sky. Streets still bare of snow.

The price of the house is even less important than I thought. A sale price of $470,000—the top we could expect—would at four percent interest yield $18,800 a year for our New Life. A sale price of $400,000—the low-- at 5% interest would yield $20,000. So interest rate—which is absolutely beyond our control—is more important than $100,000 as far as life style is concerned.

Now, down the road in terms of buying into assisted living

housing or a nursing home or building a wing on somebody's house, $100,000 is huge. Money is nothing except in relation to something else.

For example: if we sold in May at $400,000 and invested at the current 5 per cent, we'd be banking almost $2,000 a month in interest, $12,000 by October. If we clung to a higher price, we'd probably have to lower it by $20,000 in order to proceed with winter travel plans. Meanwhile—if we didn't rent—taxes, utilities etc. for six months would cost maybe $5,000 borrowed at 10 per cent interest. So when I casually say, "We can afford to wait for our price," we really can't unless we rent for the summer.

Hiring a Realtor might bring a quicker sale, but she'd cost us $20,000.

One sick grandson and another coming for a last visit at his Mamar's before returning to college fill today: the latter tugs at my heart.

FRIDAY JANUARY 12 Pressing dirty-gray clouds, but I think they hold rain, not snow.

Have been reading about "staging" your house. White space is in. An outline, a glimpse: a dining table, a desk, a bed is enough to suggest a room's possible use to a buyer. Probably a far-reaching effect of the need to interrupt TV shows for commercials, which accustoms viewers to muted white space. Fragments will do: in short stories, electronic communication, speed dating   Zip,   zip. Minimalism is art.

But, Sandy pointed out this morning, how do we live in white space? Good question ...

MONDAY JANUARY 15 Am worried about the mounting deductions from gross sale price. If our net has to be $400,000, will the asking price be unreasonable?

We are not just selling a house, we are establishing a fund to see us through the next ten or twenty years.

A pick up just spread a narrow tan sand path of safety down the middle of the ice-coated street. I suppose that's a metaphor for the Milbridge cottage: the safe path for worse coming to worst. I must keep that in mind.

TUESDAY JANUARY 16 It seems I am doomed to never live in a generous style. The #2 agent came in at $100,000 less than the first one. And now that I'm forced to give those figures some real dimension, they are closer to $150,000 lower. And she may be right. She is experienced, knows the area, and really goes after the details of the house, which #1 did not. I'm calling #3 today.

Of course, agent's philosophies may be only a part of the problem: the market is way down and still sliding. On the front page of the Sunday *New York Times* was a story about the crash of condo renting in big cities.

The ice still holds us fast and single numbers are expected tonight.

WEDNESDAY JANUARY 17 Harried is one word for the way I've felt since 4 a.m.. Mostly, by the idea of negotiating a sale. If I can't do that, then part of this carefully constructed New Life plan is in jeopardy. Mistakes that carry huge penalties bring on sweaty palms—immediate and temporary—and a tight stomach—delayed and long lasting. Computers, insurance companies, governments, and driving lost can initate this I'm-in-over-my-head condition. Plus diarrhea.

Over the phone #3 said: Wildly over pricing is the worst mistake a seller can make. But the perfect house next door that was listed at over half a million did sell. However, the people who bought it and wildly overpriced their Portsmouth condo haven't been able to sell even with a reduced price. So …

At noon the temperature is barely zero, but the wind has subsided and the sun looks warm although I'm sure it isn't. The tap water this morning was so cold it made my back teeth ache, a reminder of how life in the cottage would be if it ever came to wintering over. One icy safety net, for sure.

THURSDAY JANUARY 18 Feel more normal today, but probably shouldn't. What we heard from Agent #3 yesterday was radically different. Maybe we will be better off doing our own marketing. At the very least we wouldn't be having dilettante multilisting agents representing our property. The order-out lifestyle so much in vogue is not all it's cracked up to be.

Agent #3 is quite blunt about a quick sale. "The first offer is the one you should take." And it sounds like she means regardless of the money offered. "The offer you will accept six months later will be lower." If there are no offers in the first two weeks, she said, the price is too high.

She also believes that any time is the time to sell—even the dead of winter. So taking into account her thirty-four years of experience, the date we go on the market can be relaxed a bit, probably the last week, rather than the first week of March. And by then we'll be more prepared for two weeks of blitz, or silence. Of course, a silent phone has been common during renting season these last few years. We have to go around muttering, "It only takes one," to keep from sagging into a tick-tick-tick mentality that is truly hard on our dispositions.

Whoops, here comes the oil truck—this means more big bucks.

FRIDAY JANUARY 19 Yesterday we visited the nearest storage facility, which turned out to be excellent. Today the plan is to go room by room listing the destination of each item. The memories of the basement-to-attic clearing of my parents' house, done in three frantic days by grieving family, are not pleasant: the choices were the dumpster in the driveway or the moving van. I'm sure at some point we'll be reduced to that.

MONDAY JANUARY 22 Solid sleep last night, yesterday an extremely mellow Sunday. I'm ready for the week. I wonder if many people are conscious of what they lost when "the seventh day" became zip-zip like the other six. Sandy's farmer friend used to say, "Sundays are for taking out splinters."

TUESDAY JANUARY 23 This old city is draped in gentle white. Twenty-two years ago my first grandchild was born here.

My ancestor-imposed "have to get this right the first time" cultural attitude was shaken last Friday when, in departing our downtown writers gathering, a woman said, "Well, if when you are done traveling, Portsmouth is too expensive, you can just go someplace else." Yes, we could. I don't have to guess right about uncontrollable events.

However, I was raised to believe that taking chances— "flyers," they were called—where money was concerned was irresponsible, possibly fatal.

Another woman defined what Sandy and I are doing as bold. Bold. Hunker or stretch?

WEDNESDAY JANUARY 24 Agent #3's opinion is in. List at $399,000, but use $374,000 for figuring tax on depreciation, interest to live on, etc. The hard figures sound reasonable and her attitude that nothing needs to be fixed up in order to sell fits with ours. She was excited, however, about Peter doing railings out front, considers him a Portsmouth treasure.

She confirmed a possible six to seven month wait for a sale. And was adamant that one should never rent while a house is being shown. I think we will go ahead with a March for-sale listing. The borrowing from the home equity account has already begun. We paid back $1,000 to the city for 1987 repair and sent an $800 check to Heritage Storage for an indoor unit for six months which gives us the seventh month free. At 10 per cent interest we may have to consider dipping into our own savings that gives us only 5 percent. So, much will depend on when we sell.

Tomorrow is Sandy's pre-op day and there has been a subtle shift of sub-surface anxiety to that concern. More hugs, more awareness of the preciousness of simply being together, day and night. That feels right, whereas tightness due to the sale is probably me taking myself too seriously. Trying for control instead of letting it flow. I suppose that will become easier when the big decisions are made. And they are—day by day.

FRIDAY JANUARY 26 Yesterday at New England Baptist was a pillar-to-post rat race—X-ray to blood work to cardiologist, to whatever, and finally to register the exact date and time: February 12 at 6:30 a.m.. Both knees at once, four to six hours, epidural anesthesia. We like the doctor, we like the hospital, we are content.

The other side of the coin is a hard and fast deadline: seventeen days left for Sandy to help with stripping down the house for showing. After that both she and I must be free to concentrate on her recovery.

Ice-etched windows emblazoned with sunlight. Eight below.

Hot milk has done its soporific trick of giving us good nights of sleep. Wednesday it was 4 a.m. when I brought warm mugs up to bed, and we never woke until eight, an unheard of late hour. Last night it was about 1 a.m. when Sandy offered to go down. After drinking I read, slept soundly until six.

MONDAY JANUARY 29 January has been thin and bleak like a parsimonious Yankee; the street is whitish and the cracks, clogged with salt, add a bitter, dry touch. Unpaved ground in yards and parks seems threadbare, patched with ice. Winter drought.

Our home, too, is losing its lush warmth. The dining room table, mahogany, Duncan Fife, is gone, sold for $40. It's replacement, Sandy's round table, mahogany, Empire, seems to float on the

Oriental rug — more ornamental than an anchor for a family.

Bare bones outside and in.

WEDNESDAY JANUARY 31 Yesterday was not a good one. An overnight house fire made our asbestos-removal man homeless; and our furniture was refused by the Salvation Army. Talk about low man on the totem pole ...

In retrospect, however, I have to agree with what our neighbor said with obvious surprise, "You're on schedule."

LATER

On Jan 31, 2007, at 8:16 PM, Brent & Kathleen Barrett wrote:
Hi everyone,

I wanted to let you know that Kathleen had some potentially bad news from her doctor today. She has been having some neurological symptoms lately in her legs and went to her PCP to get it checked out. The doc ordered an MRI which Kathleen had on Monday and today the doc called back with a preliminary diagnosis of MS. Kathleen will be having a brain MRI tomorrow and we are going to a neurologist on Friday when we will probably get the definitive diagnosis.

We are doing well, although it has been an emotional day, especially for Kath.

I will let you know when we have more news, but don't hesitate to call if you want to check in.

Love, Brent

FRIDAY FEBRUARY 2 10:25 AM Of course, what was future yesterday afternoon is now past for Kath and Brent: their present is sitting in a neurologist's waiting room. 10:35. I can see them walking into the office, greeting the doctor, sitting down, listening.

The voices I'm hearing in my present time are those of men in the cellar in hazmat suits, or perhaps it is a talk show on radio. Their saws rasp against the pipes. Now they are pounding on the pipes — I wonder why. My radiator is actually trembling.

It is almost 11:00. How long do specialists take to decide a person's fate?

From: MARTHA BARRETT
To: Brent & Kathleen Barrett
Sent: Friday, February 02, 2007 7:05 PM
Subject: Re: Kath

What glory hallelujah!!!!!!!!!!!!!! news I received from Sandy in the Library Lounge. Now what do we do to get this transverse myelitis virus to leave our marvelous woman alone? Sign petitions? Act up? Vote libertarian? Whatever--we're with you, Kath. Love Mom

Reply:

Amen and amen! It has been a whirlwind of a week; I'm exhausted and exhilarated at the same time. It has left me feeling more blessed than anything. love, Kath

MONDAY FEBRUARY 5 Yesterday, except for a brief walk for the Sunday *New York Times* and a sub from Moe's for Super Bowl eating, I did nothing of any lasting value. Marvelous. And after Tee—she and boyfriend Matt were down from UMaine Saturday—said she wanted the maple bedstead and two dressers the Salvation Army rejected, I feel the big clearing out is complete. Brent will pick them up when they bring a U-Haul for the organ.

WEDNESDAY FEBRUARY 7 The oldest antique in the house—the furnace—has sure been getting a workout. But the skies remain staunchly clear of precipitating clouds thanks to the swooping jet stream. In fact, it looks excellent for the Sunday trip to Brent and Kath's, the Monday drives to and from the hospital along Route 9, and even on Tuesday when I return to home, hearth, and a lonely kitty.

Sandy did another cellar-dump run yesterday and another is planned for today, plus a storage-room trip to put some furniture destined for Milbridge in the small storage room we also rented. Oddly enough, or maybe not so oddly, my spirits are light. In fact, lightening the house lofts them ever higher. Of course, the fact that my family is happily taking so much furniture has boosted this lift-off effect.

THURSDAY FEBRUARY 8 Before we were even out of our bathrobes a man from the oil company was here to fix a slow water leak in the pipe to the hall radiator —caused by all that banging last Friday—and turn the valve Sandy couldn't budge in order to replenish the amount of water in circulation. The pressure had fallen almost to the shut-off point. At wind chills below zero that is not a comfortable idea. Cost: $75.

The photo on our computer desktop is one of comforting hope: two fat robins silhouetted in the backyard tree, red breasts slivered with sunlight.

I certainly can't put in hours of physical work, but my body is operating sufficiently and without aches and pains. Sandy, despite her crumbling knees, still carries the heavier part of loads, even on stairs.

FRIDAY FEBRUARY 9 Three days left before Sandy becomes a true cripple—temporary, thank goodness.

MONDAY FEBRUARY 12 *New England Baptist Hospital*
Diary Notes: 10:30 AM. S could be out of surgery in 30 min.—or 1 1/2 hours. My corner by the window of the now full waiting room is secure. Joanna Trollope's *Second Honeymoon* is absorbing. I am not worried—just waiting, eating ginger snaps.
11:45. Dr. Reilly came in—all went well. Proud she was awake the whole time.
Evening. Saw her in her room b/w 3-4—pale but OK. Am back at Brent's for night.

TUESDAY FEBRUARY 13 *Portsmouth house.*
Diary Notes: Good 11 hours of sleep. At Room 423 at 11:00. Empty! ICU for night—nausea. Brought back to room—very groggy from drip. Saw first exercises—not standing yet.

LATER. Home in Portsmouth by 5. She called at 7:00—pain in back of leg—clot? Ultrasound tomorrow. Very tired, but pleased I functioned so well.

WEDNESDAY FEBRUARY 14 *Diary Notes:* San called sounding so good at 7 AM, but nausea struck again when doc decided she needed more than Tylenol. So it was bad day again. Plans for rehab also went wrong—don't know where she will be now. It will be another very fragmented night. Foot+ of snow

THURSDAY FEBRUARY 15 Bright sun on pristine white; plows working. Neighbor shoveled strip from steps to street. I'll tackle car at noontime.
Spec notes for house that I wrote yesterday look good. Listing price $402,000. Will settle for $380,000 if no Realtor taking 5 percent. More work on marketing this morning.
Sandy's 6:30 AM call lifted me from "down in the dumps" to my normal "go for it" attitude.

FRIDAY FEBRUARY 16 Now that Sandy is on her way to rehab over in Woburn MA, near her brother and sister-in-law, I am a blob. And intend to stay that way, even if it means not driving down there tomorrow. I know my limits.

MONDAY FEBRUARY 19 Clear, five degrees, wind.

Still secure in my wonderful office. My father's bureau is gone, however. Had a few sad moments on Saturday trying to cram underwear and socks in Sandy's lowboy—the drawers are not nearly as deep

Today, I plan to start getting rid of my business by clearing the tall wooden file cabinet. Twenty years of wonderful UNH teaching and my own writing, including folders of ideas, both fruitful and failed.

TUESDAY FEBRUARY 20 In the street below the trash truck just growled and swallowed; my past is in its belly.

That isn't, of course, the only past of mine that has been mechanically digested, leaving mostly non-material remembrances. The first and most wrenching was at age twelve when we moved and I left behind my persona of woods and fields and country school tom boy. But, as would be the case thereafter, the new me that emerged was worth all the who-am-I-now?

WEDNESDAY FEBRUARY 21 Today I talked to a former neighbor, an old hand at renting and selling in the South End, and she advised: "Craigslist—and put a sign in the window." I'm also going to add some art work to my handouts and create a mailing list.

Twenty-three days until the first potential Showing.

THURSDAY FEBRUARY 22 The east has only a strip of pale yellow to show for daylights arrival, but I'm going to press on with the living room painting.

Tomorrow I will drive to Massachusetts to pick up Sandy and begin my dotage, as we refer to my doting on her during her convalescence. What are the connections between doting, duty, and dotty?

In my daydreams—living alone for two weeks promotes them—all this Late Capitalistic Consumer Economy preparation will prove unnecessary when a simple knock on the door—or perhaps just a phone call from California—results in a full-price offer.

WEDNESDAY FEBRUARY 28 I was shocked to see I had written nothing here for almost a week. Too busy doting for reflecting. It was all ups, however, until Monday night when a roaring infection took up residence in my left eye and cheek. I had one last winter caused by a blocked tear duct, but nothing like this. Even today it's a boa constrictor wrapped around me.

When I do look back, I am proud that I set off for Woburn on a sunny Friday morning with not a qualm about the more than two hours of Route 128 traffic. The Sandy I fetched home was much more mobile and pain free than I thought possible. Her medical people all have the same opinion. That was a huge help when three days later I suddenly became a shivering lump of pain. She, of course, could not drive me to my ophthalmologist, but Bett came in from Exeter by 7:45 a.m. I believe this intense pain was my first acquaintance with the desire to simply shed my body.

Little advancement toward a ready-to-show date—now only twelve days away--and taking care of this plugged tear duct may wipe out even more of my body and mind. It might have to be put off.

Saturday my last Getting Published Seminar was as good as it gets. What a way to go out of business. I'm turning it all over to Bett who started her career in publishing/editing in Manhattan right after college.

THURSDAY MARCH 1 Mother's birthday—and March comes in like a lamb. Almost feels like the house should be going on the market today, but the *Herald* says three days of ice and snow coming up. Facing a weekend of that, I would hesitate to advertise even a rental.

Woke at 4 a.m. in such face pain that Sandy had to go downstairs on her crutches—she is quite expert—to get graham crackers to coat my stomach for four ibuprofen. Woke at seven feeling better, but Sandy assured me I looked no better. I have a second appointment with Dr. Turner at 11:30; his reaction to this prolonged agony will be interesting. He is a man of few—or no—words, so I will have to dig for information.

FRIDAY MARCH 2 Yesterday when I told Dr. Turner, "But I feel so lousy," his reply was, "Of course you do, you have an infection." He's right, I sure do. Today, however, I've cut back my dosage from four to two ibuprofen. That figures: I bought 250 yesterday.

Sleet gusts against the window; a couple of inches of snow has fallen. What ancient wiring connects our get-up-and-go to weather?

Temperature today has barely made it over zero and the wind at forty mph is attempting to knock the top off the house. Sandy's physical therapist has come and gone. Always gives strong praise for Sandy's improvement, making her strive even harder to be a poster child of knee operation recovery.

Just had a pleasant conversation with a receptionist at Mass Eye and Ear Hospital; all set for appointment with Dr. Aaron Fay on April 6 regarding an operation on that blocked tear duct. Feel relieved. Why is it events do not arrange themselves in nicely spaced time frames, or do we only note overload?

WEDNESDAY MARCH 7 I do believe there is a lay-low hormone or something that keeps a sick human curled in the cave—at least of no danger to others on a mammoth hunt. As Bett e-mailed, "Yes, wouldn't it be horrible if you had the urge to garden this week?" Below zero and winds still grip us.

THURSDAY MARCH 9 I did leave the cave yesterday. Dr. Turner had said I have an upper respiratory infection not connected to my tear duct infection. I immediately rubbed on the Vicks, took aspirin, and drank orange juice. It's always better to know. And childhood remedies come packaged with memories of a mother's forehead kisses and an "all better in the morning." Isn't that what mothers promise?

And speaking of mothers, I am finding the disposal of goods, particularly parents' possessions, is draped with as many ritualistic euphemisms as death.

SATURDAY MARCH 10 Today is bookshelf day. Plan to start by packing the ones I'd like to have with me to the end, so to speak. Good grief, what is the criteria for that?

SUNDAY MARCH 11 My chest is tight with waiting again. Barbara the partner of Kathleen, my longtime Baltimore friend, seems close to death.

LATER. Barbara died at 10:25 a.m.. Fifty-five years old. Kathleen e-mailed: *Her body finally whumped her spirit.*

She closed with: "Take care of each other." Certainly that was the hallmark of their relationship. Barbara struggled with myasthenia gravis for twenty years.

Another weight added.

WEDNESDAY MARCH 14 Flipped from the physical to the mental side of this move yesterday by calling my lawyer's office. Tom, an acquaintance since the early 1980s, will handle the legal side of this perhaps over-the-top undertaking of mine.

SATURDAY MARCH 17 Got a definite lump in my throat last evening at the beauty of the nor'easter as viewed from an upstairs window: the streets, narrow beds made-up with snow, the pitched white roofs, swirls and bursts across our antique porch light. But this morning as the plows began their beeping, blinking work, I reconciled myself with thoughts of warm New Zealand rain, a sun-room lounge, a pile of books—NO HOUSEWORK.

This has been a winter without the daily joys of the town I love; I've been in a tunnel, burrowing away, with progress, yes, but no real light.

Yesterday, I drove Sandy to her Boston post-op appointment with the threat of the storm overhead and back again in the actual beginnings of it. And, surprising even to myself, I did it with the confidence of thirty. A twenty-minute nap restored me completely and I have hopes that my weeks of battling lassitude are over.

Of course, Sandy's release to normal living is a boost.

MONDAY MARCH 19 E-mail last night informed me that a friend whom I've known since 1973 when I bought the Milbridge cottage and who later became a neighbor here in the South End has an illness she may not survive. That would, as they say, be a blessing. Parkinson's disease created a long, sad ending for a feisty feminist.

WEDNESDAY MARCH 21 Almost noon and only twenty degrees, but the sun is beating down on the still huge piles of snow/ice. It is the first day of spring. So? What does that signify this year? My conclusion: the end of winter. No look forward, just a huge sigh at the passing of November, December, January, February and half of March.

THURSDAY MARCH 22 My friend died this morning.

Warm spring air has arrived. Off with the third floor draft door and plastic kitchen window.

FRIDAY MARCH 23 A shot of pressure-panic last night had me downstairs at 3 a.m. writing on the calendar for April 6: Put Sign Up. Easter weekend, but that can't be helped. It might even work to our benefit. I am discouraged by the tackiness—and even immorality—of the For Sale By Owner Internet sites that are framed with foreclosure listings and sub-prime mortgage ads that cause those foreclosures. Of course, there are some really tacky Realtors too.

Having Tom as a lawyer should remove those fears, empty one compartment of a brain that feels like a stomach too full of meat and potato.

SUNDAY MARCH 25 Lazed through my Sunday walk for the *Times*. Lots of people on the streets, sitting outside in Market Square with coffee, smells of breakfasts brunches floated freely—and free. This winter has been much too serious.

TUESDAY MARCH 27 My friend's memorial is going to be at UNH, scheduled for the same day as Barbara's in Baltimore which I am already committed to. Some May evening when there is promise of a good sunset, Sandy and I will drive the mile down the peninsula to her Maine cottage with a thermos of coffee, sit facing west on the deck and raise our cups to twenty-five years of memories.

FRIDAY MARCH 30 One of the three Realtors said she would represent a buyer for 2% of the selling price. That would be $7-$8,000. A price we would, I think, be willing to pay. But we'll give it a couple weeks or so on our own.

My legs are holding up well; they probably do a 3,000 foot mountain every day.

THURSDAY APRIL 5 After a solid night's sleep, I feel tired to the core. Plow snow is piled in front of the house and the five-day forecast is grim with snow, rain, cold. We decided to delay putting the house on the market. I'm trying to adjust to a puttering rhythm without staggering into total collapse.

Yesterday's trip to Mass Eye and Ear resulted in an appointment for an outpatient operation on June 5 with a follow-up visit on the fourteenth. Memorial service in Baltimore April 29; grandson Nate's graduation in western Pennsylvania May 12; writers' conference the week of June 17. One reason people may not make big life changes is that their schedule is too busy.

And so much for the illusion that we'd have a spring of sitting around waiting for the phone to ring.

FRIDAY APRIL 6 It's only a month shy of a year since I began this journal. Then the idea of stretching and living lightly was mere air — a possible working philosophy. Since then, and especially the last five months, there has been much concrete grit and little air. That goes for both the physical and all the mental — more like math than poetry.

SUNDAY APRIL 8 Fast, high clouds against a delicate April-Easter blue. Almost noon and probably not above freezing. Our first true Sunday in at least two months. Even though we are slam up against the selling part of this adventure, a huge calmness and relief has come with the house being so close to perfect.

THURSDAY APRIL 12 The dread of self-sell has passed. I found that the *Portsmouth Herald* runs an excellent site for only $99 a month which gives an owner-seller equal listings with the agents. And I am sure we can present our house better than any of them could.

SATURDAY APRIL 14 It was hard to nail up the sign. Both of us were tense and irritable, but it is done.

We actually had a showing later in the day: young couple from Boston looking for a weekend place so they could get their two-and three-year-old daughters to beaches etc. A pleasant learning experience all around. Another couple from the western part of the state called, but we had neighbors coming for wine and besides, I was exhausted from the diverse activities of the day.

MONDAY APRIL 16 I moved in luxurious slow motion, prepared for calls that never came: it rained and nor'easter storm warnings were up. This morning we have house-shaking winds and heavy rain.

Sandy has a lot of her old energy back and we plan on going to our gym. I feel heavy-shouldered, slouched by too much housework. Bit of water in our clean basement.

FRIDAY APRIL 20 The blue of the sky is less tentative and the slant of the sun more direct. It will be a grand weekend for house selling. Already a family is coming at 12:15 today. Yesterday, we were watching the news and having wine when Sandy reported that the man and woman driving a Volvo had stopped to pick up a leaflet and now were out of the car really looking the house over; they called later with questions.

Whoops, just had a phone call from them and they decided that $402,000 was more than they can pay. So that is that. But very considerate of them to call.

We are used to the roller coaster of renting, so this is no surprise, but it does illustrate on-pulse reactions. Fast, slow; excitement, downer; plateau, plateau ... Words inform, but also trigger expectations: for example, the subtext of last night's call for a showing was: big weekend ahead! Prepare for a bid! And today's was: you've priced it too high.

SATURDAY APRIL 21 The twenty-first suddenly seems late in the month, as though plans for May should be well underway. In truth, May will depend on what happens in the next ten days, and the trick is to enjoy those ten days as not only a fact-finding mission for future plans, but rather for themselves, for the soft greening-up of spring. But the silence of the phone is harsh, not easily dismissed.

We are still struggling with getting our ad on Craigslist. Computers can make one feel so stupid.

TUESDAY APRIL 24 Have done a total of five showings with another scheduled for 5 p.m. I find they are absolutely exhausting, but certainly my optimism is high for a purchase & sale agreement in a few weeks. Every viewer has been local, as close as a block, as distant as Boston. I remember Realtor #3 mentioning "pent-up demand," and that is certainly what we're seeing. Of course, most of those one hundred plus flyers taken have gone to serve pent-up curiosity and illusions of living in the South End of Portsmouth.

WEDNESDAY APRIL 25 Had my first broker-buyer showing this morning. Realtor #2 had lined up a series of tours for some returning South Enders and they were in a hurry. Went through as fast as the "I gut houses" woman. They were qualified cash buyers, primed and informed by an agent, and most important: this agent expected no remuneration from me. It was buyer pay all. Very different from what Realtor #1 explained to me. I guess the system can't be generalized. Maybe those other Realtors who contacted me thought I knew that I would not be asked to pay—should I re-contact them and ask?

FRIDAY MAY 4 We are having a run of perfect spring days and four hours spent on backyard improvement shows. This piddley picking-up stuff that we are forced to do every day only sustains the status quo: I have never been fond of work that does not improve.

No calls since Tuesday, and in this height-of-buying-season-good-weather week that is disturbing, but worse is the lack of second visits. I did expect one call back, maybe two, but face-value assessments can be so wrong. The most amazing example I can recall from renters was when the husband was signing a deposit check in the living room and the wife was in the dining room on the phone setting up another appointment.

This selling process stirs a low-level excitement akin, I suspect, to gambling. I noticed it strongly when we had items on eBay: the compulsion to check prices was ridiculous. Now I recount flyers in the box and hits on our dotcom listing, neither of which has—as far as I know—resulted in one tour. I suppose this compulsion, this addiction to risk taking, had some evolutionary value. Hunters, as well as those content to stay by the water hole, were necessary. Capitalism feeds at the same trough.

MONDAY MAY 7 That subterranean rumble of death was reinforced on Friday by the arrival of an e-mail entitled More Sad News. Kathleen's mother had died the night before. How horrific to lose your partner and then your mother.

Speculations following deaths and near deaths, I assume, protect us against being blindsided and whacked silly when tragedy occurs close to home. Carolyn Chute wrote about people who were constantly being surprised by life, and how their ensuing frantic scrabble of action frequently led to more troubles down the road. Fine line between head-in-the-sand and constant worry that we all-knowing humans tread.

FRIDAY MAY 11 May 8, the day I began recording this adventure, passed without notice. No matter, I could not assemble congruent points of what this year has been like. As with all history that wishes to avoid exaggeration and making heroes or fools of people, daily details render the only honest telling. The current detail is the phone has not rung for six days. Total, absolute nothing to hang hope on.

SUNDAY MAY 13 A thought reorientation has been necessary: no phone calls from buyers is normal; a call extraordinary. I'm sure I'll learn to live with it. And long-range plans have taken on a longer aspect. Assuming three months from listing to acceptable bid puts us in mid-July with a probable closing the end of August.

Therefore, renting the Milbridge cottage the last two weeks of June and the first two weeks of July seems appropriate.

Yesterday, Sandy declared that she was moving her birthday from the twentieth to the thirteenth—today. I cooked a stupendous veal, tomato, shallot, Portobello mushroom dish and a side of huge artichokes; she made a lemon meringue pie.

WEDNESDAY MAY 16 Monday I e-mailed 130 letters with photos advertising the Milbridge cottage for rent. All of them friends, family, writing students. Two of the weeks are already taken: $1,000 toward our June 1 Portsmouth biannual property tax bill of $1,500.

Even when away from the house we are conscious the phone might ring. Bracing oneself, that tight stomach and hunched shoulders posture, feels unhealthy and yet evolution-wise we must have been built for that. Maybe our present-day illusion of control exacerbates stress; sunrise to sunset living is rarely practiced. We don't float, we dig in our heels and plan, face forward and expect to win. Rolling with the punch is difficult from this stance.

I remind myself, however, that rather than an abyss yawning, there is another path: ordering out. That is, signing up with a real estate agent.

FRIDAY MAY 18 My pulse this evening is charged with the excitement of seeing Nate graduate tomorrow. My darling Nathan William, first child of my first child. Also, my first flight in many years adds a few tingles.

WEDNESDAY MAY 30 Any anxieties over flying alone simply faded into pleasure. Of course, there was Sandy at Manchester Airport, almost-cousin Newt at Pittsburgh, but still—I loved it.

And even though the Milbridge trip involved four days of driving and go-go-go at the cottage, we're refreshed and satisfied that it is camp-pristine for renters. All four weeks are booked.

The house tours I gave before and after that trip—both arranged by brokers—seemed quite promising and I thought they might call Tom for the P&S packet, but no. Perhaps now that I am more comfortable and actually enjoy showing the house, I exaggerate their interest. The facts are: one viewer, a lawyer, had four horses; and the Kittery man had a daughter with whom he didn't want to share a bathroom. People who have not yet committed to boarding their rural life are not ready to buy, and divorce-riven people are unpredictable.

SATURDAY JUNE 2 One side of the duplex around the corner is listed at $460,000. A $50,000 difference and they have no parking either. That should lay to rest the niggle of our price being too high. Amusing that the agent there is the same one who told us overpricing was the worst mistake.

The painter who has been pounding in a new shingle under the flashing is now washing the window in front of me. Ordering out can be wonderful. Time for lunch.

MONDAY JUNE 4 Sometimes I pick up a phone just to hear the dial tone.

Several days ago I had read aloud to Sandy a passage from *Timothy; or, Notes of an Abject Reptile* by Verlyn Klinkenborg.

Wet, foreign light of a cold, manicured country. Every direction showed the human in the landscape. Fields stitched together by hedges. Lanes overlooked by yew and elm and lime. District of gates and stiles and paths. Country tended as closely as its sheep, fat as its flocks.

For thirty-five years I have moved back and forth between either a manicured Philadelphia suburb, or Portsmouth's closely tended city style and a make-do, live with nature, "It's just a camp" style. Will being a legal resident of rural Maine change us? Will we go native, wear unwashed mackinaws and boots, say Ayah, and overflow with chatter at the novelty of another human face?

THURSDAY JUNE 7 The first breath-holding day. The cause was a phone call from Realtor J. who had brought Kittery Mike—divorced with daughter—to see the house the morning before we left for Milbridge, over two weeks ago.

"He's still considering your house," she said, the thrill of hope undisguised.

In minutes her assistant arrived in sandaled heels, pressed capris and silver convertible to pick up a buyer's package. She turned and flashed a thumb's up sign as she left. I remained unaffected. I liked him and he is my first choice, but having an agent will—as she and I had agreed—mean 2.5 per cent off the price. But then Mike may offer $400,000, not the $375,000 I would expect from yesterday's twenty-something prospect. But …but …but …

My nose is healing from Tuesday's tear duct surgery. It wasn't painful, but a drive to Boston at 5 a.m., general anesthesia for a two-hour operation, and a night awake taking care of it has left me a bit soggy.

FRIDAY JUNE 8 The call came shortly after nine. Mike had made an offer on the house. I called: "Announcement! Announcement!" down the stairwell to Sandy and son Jim. No leaping or dancing, even after the Realtor had come and gone and we had a genuine bid in our hands. Finally, Sandy and I had smiles and hugs in the kitchen, but mostly the mood was serious. I did, however, shout out at one point, "It worked. Our plan worked." That is still sinking in. A year of mulling, plotting, researching, taking the bit in my teeth and doing. It worked.

SATURDAY JUNE 9 A limbo day after all the bangs and crashes of Friday. Realtor J. faxed the bid ($375,000) to Tom at two. Tom's assistant called us to say he was looking at it and would call us. He did at six just as we were to start cooking dinner. Tom used the agent's form, not his own, which was written for people without such help. He discussed changes to it and we took his advice. Sandy sat beside me with her copy while I talked and listened and then let her in on what Tom suggested. He is adamant on not filling out a disclosure form, which the Realtors love and Tom says is not required by law. He said too much knowledge is assumed and could come back to haunt the seller. For example, do we really know the lot is .038 acres or is that just what the city records say? I agree with him.

On price, he said, we must focus on what the buyer is willing to pay. Unless the Realtor said to us: "He will not pay a penny more than he has offered," there is room to negotiate. So we will write in 397,000 and he will come back with 380,000: down 5,000 for us, up 5,000 for him. Next we say, 393,000 and they offer 385,000. We go down to 390,000, and they come up to 388,000 and we accept. That is just what we want: enough above our base price to pay the Realtor $10,000, and another $3,000 for painting.

It is a ritual dance that we hope goes as it should; the same result as my thought of splitting the difference, but takes longer. And Mike wants to close on or before July 20: the day before we had planned to arrive in Milbridge. So, perfect on that. This week I can work on clothes, under the eaves stuff, and books. We dare not disturb any of our staging, which has become a bland shell of what home used to be. A disposable commodity.

If somehow this deal falls through, we may be in for a long dry spell. Our number of online hits is stuck in the 150s, so I figure that source has run out. The phone did not ring today with the financial boy wanting a buyer's package. The *Herald* said mortgage rates have risen again. A selling price of $10,000 less is probably equal to living costs here into autumn. If this deal with Mike doesn't go through, I'll play with the figures. He's traveling on business, so we have until Monday noon to send our counter offer with a price of $397,000.

SUNDAY JUNE 10   Time dangles in a willing suspension of belief.

MONDAY JUNE 11   Last night the town clocks echoed each other. First, the one on the Children's Museum — the 1863 Meeting House — clanged abruptly, two quick strikes; a half minute later, soft and resonant, came double bongs from the tall spire of North Church in Market Square. I was still awake to hear the succession of threes. Like a watchman's cry of "All's well," these punctual, metal, public voices bounce across the sleeping roofs — gabled, mansard, federal — of this old seaport. And, it being mid-June, trickle into breathing bedrooms.

The solidifying form of the end lurks. Good days, good decades.

TUESDAY JUNE 12   I dressed, walked to town, rode the elevator to Tom's office and put my initials on the agreement to sell at $397,000. It was hot and the procedure not calm. Sandy's presence was necessary and she was thirty miles away delivering the antique china cabinet to her sister.

At breakfast we had agreed that if the counter offer was $385,000 or over, we'd take it. Although the deadline we gave was Thursday at noon — Mike is in Hawaii — conceivably the phone could ring with an answer from the agent at any moment.

I think I have an infection in my left eye.

THURSDAY JUNE 14   It is now 10:40 a.m. I have the phone on my desk and its ring made my heart jump--diminishing minutes to deadlines can do that. It was a survey about FedEx Kinko who created our For Sale sign. Now there are seventy-nine minutes left. My mouth is dry.

LATER   At one I called Realtor. Seems Mike "was willing to put up with no parking for 375, but ..." He then asked her "for more info on house #3." I said we would "certainly be satisfied with 385, which is true. She said it was only 6 a.m. in Hawaii — she'd get back to me.

LATER. Inconclusive talk among Sandy and Jim and me about accepting counter-offer of 380. Silent phone all afternoon. A friend took us out to absolutely marvelous dinner at Café Mediterranean. Returned to no blinking light on phone and sinking feeling: we've lost him. No doubt he's trying a bid on House #3.

FRIDAY JUNE 15 Awake last night with thoughts of calling and saying, "We'll take 375." Pressing, globby waves of failure are not fun.

Three minutes until nine now and Jim has been on phone since 8:30. I will resist urge to ask him to get off—for a while anyway.

I am encouraged by my attitude of: okay, when's the next showing?

I hear Sandy talking to someone outside—is it agent with new offer?

LATER Realtor J. called. Mike has not bid on #3, but is undecided about this one. We go off to a graduation party for Nate with hopeful hearts.

LATER. Three messages on machine. One of them agent. Mike is bidding on #3. Might get back to us if that doesn't fly. Well, forget that.

SATURDAY JUNE 16 Mind spewed early-waking ideas. One really brought some calm: if it doesn't sell by August, we could put it up for rent until next April and proceed with our travel plans. Rent money would not be much different than living on interest. And we would avoid the terrific utility costs. Thinking along those lines must, however, include the idea that the housing market will probably be worse next year.

Another thought was reduction in price. Perhaps a significant one that we could hold firm to. Dropping to $385,000 would probably cause new interest.

An Open House may be necessary.

Sunny and muggy with lots of pollen. All this sneezing and blowing is hard on that left nostril and eyeball. Found out the trouble: a filament is threaded through the new opening they bored in my nose and comes out in the corner of my eye.

THURSDAY JUNE 21 A surprise farewell party by conference writers, both attendees and alumni, brought many questions about my future and I was proud to say what is planned. To move on and outward: learning, feeling, lightly embracing this planet. With Sandy adding her loving presence.

Would I do it without her? Travel with a child, a grandchild, a friend? Probably, but without the deepest whole-person fulfillment I have ever known.

WEDNESDAY JUNE 27 Too hot, too hot. High 90s predicted again for today. It absolutely exhausts me. Fan on high in bedroom all night. For thirty years I've had the summer coolness of Milbridge.

Sandy and I took containers of cold pasta salad to Haven Park, one hot block away, and ate under the huge oaks while watching the tide go out on South Mill Pond; good breeze too. This morning I again woke exhausted.

We are preparing new flyers: 350 plus of the old have gone out. Different photos, bits of different text and a different price. Reports from Maine and the nation indicate that May sales were down 15 percent from '06. I don't think that is true here. Have had two Realtor calls: one, a personal buy and sounds fishy, the other genuine. A Dover Realtor at 2 percent appointment at 3:30 this afternoon. Somewhere, I must find the emotional ginger to do that. I will serve iced tea with lemon and ginger root, that should help.

THURSDAY JUNE 28 The changes made to the marketing scheme have raised my spirits. Probably a mistake to think change is progress, but we humans face forward, so moving in that direction makes sense for us. Standing still or walking backward is not our biological style.

FRIDAY JUNE 29 Temperature in the 60s—I'm a new woman. Yesterday I was mostly a puddle without a mind.

I do notice, however, that if, like now, there is no showing on the horizon, I am restless. Same sort of hormonal influence, I suppose. Humans are such excitable creatures.

SATURDAY JUNE 30   High-time selling season is half over.

Bought twenty-five inch, wheeled, pull-along suitcase, a wonderful deep red—and, because the price was so good, a small matching bag to also check-in, for shoes probably. With all of Kohl's discounts, the total cost was eighty some dollars. So my sporty red and Sandy's classy black stand side by side in the living room like ready-to-board companions. Sandy looked up New Zealand rentals this morning …

Called back that person, possibly a bottom-feeder Realtor, who wanted to see photos, but other than that, silence. No hits on new ad. But it is a blessedly cool, blue and gold summer day: slept with a blanket last night.

MONDAY JULY 2 Sun and low humidity; Bett will come in after lunch.

LATER. 9:30 p.m. Bone tired. Tomorrow we sign papers at 12:15; house inspection at 4:30; closing July 20—seventeen days away.

TUESDAY JULY 3 It all happened so fast. Phone rang at 10:35 a.m. just after I shut down computer. It was Realtor J. Mike was with her: the inspection on House #3 had turned up things he didn't want to deal with; when could they come over for a second look? Eleven, I said. I'm sure my voice was flat. They arrived promptly and I waved them on through; Sandy and I sat in the living room trying not to listen to the murmurs. Much of the day was spent that way, sitting, trying to think and not think.

They left in fifteen minutes without any commitments, no comments really. We ate lunch in the yard: Sandy talked about hiring a singer for a friend's sixty-fifth birthday party here on Saturday; I speculated about Mike's intentions. We agreed that at this late date we could not be out by July 20 and went inside. The phone was ringing: they were sitting in her car outside the house.

The ensuing kitchen conversation revolved around a closing date of July 20. We declared, questioned, listened, moderated. Finally, J stated that the buyers of Mike's house "would not be happy with a delay." I questioned the feasibility of inspections, loans, etc. in two weeks' time. J was firm as she explained Mike's credit, bank approval, her contacts: "Yes. It will be done." His wife was arriving the next day—no, she was not involved in the buying. His business headquarters are in Utah; his wife's in Colorado. Hmmm. I'd like to meet this daughter—the one who will bear the burden of Daddy's house.

The kitchen conversation ended with my saying, "Give us a few hours," and their quick departure. Sandy started cutting the grass; I settled inside with clipboard and calendar. The phone rang: J wanted to give us the complete picture. "Your house is #1, he is not bidding on #4. He accepts the $385,000 price. But if you can't meet July 20 closing, he will go to #4."

A wheeler-dealer for sure. He likes to win. But we will win too— our price--if we get out in eighteen days. #4 is not an idle bluff—this is a man who has visited seven or so different countries on business in the last few weeks. Snap. Snap. Snap.

I went outside and told Sandy I thought we could do it, but we needed Brent's van and two strong people to drive to Milbridge on the 14th. Sofia, our last renter in the Maine cottage, checks out that day at 10 a.m. Called Kath. She said there would be a way, but Brent was under a lot of stress at work. Long days and his promotion hanging, twisting him in the wind, as they say.

Bett arrived while Kath was giving Sandy the recipe for ice cream cake for Saturday's party. We sat in the yard with tea and talked. The phone rang, but it was a hang-up before I reached it. I brought it outside and the mundane talk continued and I announced I was calling to say: We can do it. It's a deal. Sandy agreed. I called J's cell phone and left the message.

In the yard the conversation continued, but the listening was palpable. Bett went off to town and returned: still no callback.

It had been an hour and a half and I voiced my concern. Had Mike said to hell with it and gone off to #4? Then Cousin Mary called with her recipe for ice cream cake and mentioned that she had tried to call before. So that was the hang up. Big relief.

At about 4, J called. She congratulated us and I said I was glad it had worked out. I didn't feel any bounces of joy. But we all hugged and Sandy poured white wine in the absence of champagne. Then we changed and walked downtown. Had a mixed hors d' oeuvres dinner in Portsmouth's finest—window table looking out on the tugboats.

In the night I woke with tears seeping from the corners of my eyes.

WEDNESDAY JULY 4 Last night we sat side by side on the bed watching the fireworks through the leaves of the box elder. Booms and flashes, the falling decorations of red, white, blue, gold, green, silver seemed to be for us. Celebration and farewell. Deep satisfaction and poignancy.

The day was a blur of contract explanations by J and signatures, a quick house tidy-up, then a chair in the yard next door while inspectors and new owners—wife seems nice—roamed cellar to attic for an hour and a half. We did not expect glitches, but who can ever be sure? J called at six—clean bill of structure and safety. Next event bank appraisal.

We ate, made a run to the grocery for egg carton boxes, watched a *Foyle's War* DVD, and climbed tired and complete to our bedroom.

THURSDAY JULY 5 Rain in the night. Such a nourishing sound and smell through the open summer windows. Sleep was broken, awake for good shortly after four—definitely a nap day. The clouds are snuggly, although the morning will not be, with its demands of errands and packing for storage. Feel we must keep pushing against the tide, or float back downstream into the shallows of mundane ordinary. It will get progressively harder as we ravage what is left of our comforts. I keep the dream of waking on the South Wing of the cottage handy where I can call it forth to give a happy ending to these two weeks.

It is funny how that huge check means nothing at this point.

FRIDAY JULY 6 Mover can do us Wednesday the eighteenth. $775 is the estimate for from here to storage.

On Tuesday Sandy's brass bed and mattress and my antique cherry drop-leaf dining table go to Milbridge with Jim and Nate in Brent's van; Wednesday, moving day; Thursday, pack car and clean—walk-through at 5; Friday, closing at 9 a.m. and then drive north.

I do get a lump thinking of that final good-bye, and I assume I'll cry buckets, but the most wonderful part of this place—the partnership that bloomed and set deep roots—will simply move on. Divorce from a house is quite different than from a longtime love.

CHASING THE SUN TO NEW ZEALAND

I have always been skeptical of the claim that travel broadens the mind. It depends on how well equipped the particular mind was in the first place. Plenty of well-traveled minds are also nicely atrophied.

--Penelope Lively, English writer, <u>Oleander, Jacaranda,</u>

She went traveling, but her mind stayed to home.

James W Balano, Ed., Downeast Maine adage: <u>The Log of the Skippers Wife</u>

Wainui Beach

New Zealand

MONDAY JULY 23 *Maine cottage*

We are in residence here by the Gulf of Maine. Soft clouds sit motionless, a shield against the blare of blue and gold. Sea vacant of swells; intense silence. A Portsmouth summer, we discovered, is polluted with noise: by day from construction, by night from surround-sound air conditioners. And the months of exposure to strangers — in the house, outside taking flyers, on the phone asking questions — lowered my tolerance, scraped it to the bone in that final week.

I feel like Timothy, the abject reptile, wanting to dig that shallow, snug place in the earth and doze. In ten days I'll feel differently. But right now, it's a struggle. Much to organize in the cottage, loose ends dangle in Portsmouth.

TUESDAY JULY 24 A true turtle day: drips and fog and blessed silence.

I think when Sandy first saw actual figures on how much interest the sale money would bring in before December, she began to believe that our life would be both secure and more comfortable. No good having money if we can't relax and enjoy it. We are, we tell each other, reasonably rich.

WEDNESDAY JULY 25 During those last eighteen days in Portsmouth I lay awake some nights with a tight chest wondering if tomorrow night I would be in the ICU. Here with the cool, utter darkness and nothing-but-nature sounds, sleep is an eight-hour coma.

That first turn-around trip to Portsmouth for the twenty foot ladder adjusted my mind to a new dimension. Signatures and money, mere flat paper, had swelled to life-size reality when I saw those gutted rooms. It is no longer our house. It is Mike and Maggie and daughter Kristen's house.

Sandy was tying the extensions ladder on the car when our neighbor asked, "Are you happy?" "Yes!" I shouted, startling even myself. That is gone, this new life is upon us; two guide books to

New Zealand, already ragged with yellow post-its lie on the bedspread beside me.

A fallow mind is a blessed one.

TUESDAY JULY 31 Did not find a dream rental in Dunedin, the city at the south of the South Island, online yesterday, but we will get 20 cents off every NZ dollar. I will try the Dunedin chamber of commerce site today. We would like to spend our first month of the three out on the bay with a store nearby and daily bus into town. A clean kitchen, a deck, an indoor flush, and a bedroom with a door are also must-haves. When traveling there twenty years ago we had good luck with the chamber. Much of what I saw yesterday sleeps five to nine people in a definite holiday setting: we don't need that. We are wintering-over people.

FRIDAY AUGUST 3 Wednesday afternoon I forced myself to lie on the chaise in the sun, read a book, and tan my sock-lined ankles. My subconscious still believes that I must not do this, that I must work or else. But I stayed, little by little lowering the back of the plastic chair until I was flat, sprawled, dozing . . . occasionally half opening my eyes to study the patterns of leaf shadows on white birch bark, dancing ripples on water, way out to the taut line between sea-blue and fog-gray, a white sail swung behind Trafton Island. Another harbor neighbor for the night.

Rearrangements of furniture have moved my computer into my bedroom where distances between wall and bed, and dresser and bed, and even the foot of the bed and this table are measured in inches. My writing muse has, however, after doubts and pouts, also moved in and made herself comfortable.

Ah—there's the sun, finally breaking the high fog and gleaming on fat whorls of needles on the spruce outside the window. It's after nine, but still time for a tub of wash to dry.

Only one job still presses with a do-it-now-and-do-it-right insistence and that is the distribution of money.

THURSDAY AUGUST 23 Bett's birthday. Called and repeated her birth story. "A girl—thank God." Doc: "What's the matter don't you like boys?" "I have two. Now, my girl. I can quit."

Our money all in CD's. One 60 month at 5.48% and a 12 month at 5.38% with the Credit Union. A 5 month at Provident Bank at 5% and $16,000 in Money Market for easy access—taxes etc. Jim checked and both places have sound investments, plus federally insured at $250,000. Sigh of relief. Worry free which is better than higher interest.

OCTOBER 1 Guests are gone, summer cottages vacant, all is calm on this autumnal coast. I think I have purchased round-trip tickets to New Zealand: Boston to Auckland December 31; $2,187 apiece. The local travel agent was almost 50 percent more, so although I really don't trust this new virtual world, I went with Orbitz Travel and chose flights that will give us a whole afternoon in San Francisco, a quick trip in from the airport. Will be a nice break. No middle-of-the-night stops in Hawaii anymore — thank goodness.

MONDAY OCTOBER 22 January bed-sit secure! E-mail from Geraldine McLennon in Dunedin, New Zealand, late last evening. We are quite giddy, like a couple of teenagers. Not only does it intuitively feel like the right spot, but the price is so good. NZ$410 a week or $1,640 for the month, which is US$1,300, and we had been hopeful to make our budget of $2,000. Transport from Dunedin Airport will drop us at the door. We are one hundred yards off George Street. Joy abounds.

My Internet searches, interrupted by a trip to the Gaspe Peninsula, company, and scrabbling preparations for the coming cold, have been a cautious daily plod, further slowed by fears of slip-of-the-finger-on-keyboard mistakes, of scams, of misunderstandings, and the dial-up systems agonizing waits. No wonder that today I startle both Sandy and the cat with outbursts of: "It worked!"

In metaphor: life has burst through the brown paper wrapping of age and grabbed me in a full-Monty embrace.

THURSDAY OCTOBER 25 Must move ahead on December rental in Portsmouth where we have doctor, lawyer, accountant visits and all the Christmas stuff with friends and family. I'll check Craigslist and put an ad in the *Herald* next weekend. Should be time for absent NH beach-house owners to think that one month of rent is better than nothing. All agencies have No Pet, especially no cat, prohibition. That would mean leaving Schoodic with Barbara, our down-the-road neighbor who is keeping him for the winter. I'd like him with us for as long as possible.

Another raw, cloudy day and the living room gas wall heater has been on one panel since seven this morning, maintaining probably sixty-five degrees. I work here in the east bedroom warmed by the same oil-filled heater I used in my Portsmouth office — seventy is my sitting comfort level. Dunedin in mid-summer—January—will be fifties at night and low seventies during the day. I should take a jacket for evening, but maybe buying a new sweater there would be more fun.

SATURDAY OCTOBER 27 Switched my ad search in the *Portsmouth Herald* to Furnished Apartments instead of Winter Rentals and came up with a one-bedroom in Exeter, where both Bett and Sandy's friend Elaine live, that says one cat okay. Will call later.

LATER. Rental was already taken. Rain.

MONDAY OCTOBER 29 Low twenties this morning. As we drove Schoodic the fifteen miles to his vet appointment the world was brilliant and fragile, crystal waiting to crack. We kept the water spigots dripping last night—the outflow pipe will not freeze until temperatures constantly remain below freezing—and a portable electric heater on beside the kitchen pipes; the gas heater cast a warming glow into the living room and bathroom. Schoodie slept in front of it until about three when he snuggled into our down comforter.

THURSDAY NOVEMBER 1 Did some more calling yesterday afternoon and I think we got a live one, an apartment building on the water in Hampton Beach which stays open all winter and does rent by the month. The price, $1,296 including the NH percent tax, is over budget, BUT he will accept a cat, male, neutered. So we are excited. Did not follow up on any others.

MONDAY NOVEMBER 5 I raised the dark green window shade at what our newly turned-back clock said was five-fifteen; a blast of cold air rushed in. We sipped steaming coffee and talked as the moon waned, Venus dissolved, and lobster-boat lights flickered seaward. Off the ledges lobs of foam from Saturday's storm bobbed like frosty eiders.

This is the first month of our new life. New because I've never stayed in the cottage through November. Our space has been reduced to the kitchen, one ten by eight foot bedroom, and the twenty by fifteen foot living and dining area now cluttered with the printer, boxes of freezable from shop and shed, and a wooden rack hung with drying clothes. Dust from constant fires and Schoodic's long hair coat everything. Sunny outdoor days have been a delight, but when Saturday's pouring rain and high winds condemned me to a total indoor experience, I got pretty fidgety. Something will have to be done.

Waking to no power Sunday morning was a minor inconvenience: our main heat and cooking sources are gas. The water pump in the well needs electricity to start, but we had a gallon of bottled water, and our dipping well provides plenty for bucket-flushing the toilet. We plugged an older phone directly into the wall connection—cell phones are pretty useless here—and our dial-up Internet server brought such essential trivia as wave height--over thirty-three feet off Jonesport—and some e-mails from the kids. No TV is normal here, and the bold-coast surf show on our hi def plasma screen--that is, the big picture window—was absolutely spectacular.

No trees or even limbs down in the forty mph gusts. No sleep lost. Quite fun, in fact.

FRIDAY NOVEMBER 9 Sunny day, but by twelve-thirty our whole yard was gray with shadows—the sun barely skims the southern horizon now—and four hours later the windows were painted pitch black: this section of eastern Maine geographically belongs in the Canadian maritime time zone.

I got my exercise by cleaning leaves from the gutter-ditch I dug years ago to keep water away from the squatty concrete triangles that support the house. When I first summered here in 1973, I, perhaps inspired by childhood memories of Pittsburgh river floods, would lie in bed imagining that the tide might not stop rising, would lift this little gray house right off those triangles, and it and I would go floating out to sea.

Given the fact that I'll be here only three more weeks, it is hardly a true test of my oft-stated sentiment: "I like the early dark," which to me means guilt-free reading. My parents believed sunrise to sunset was work-time.

THURSDAY NOVEMBER 15 Ever since I realized that indeed we could simply move our groceries from here to our Hampton apartment, I've had a strange lightness of spirit. How odd. In mulling it over, I concluded it has something to do with continuity. That is, a flow, rather than a cut-off deadline, and—this just came to mind—we don't even have to be perfect in our packing: we will be back here the last week in December to leave Schoodic at Barbara's. So what's the big deal?

Has age—perhaps wisely—robbed me of the relaxed confidence

that I can pull things together at the last minute? Is all this extensive planning age related? Or normal for anybody? Hard to tell.

What about dependency on routine? Is it crazy to be flouting that truism of aging? In an e-mail yesterday a writer friend, also seventy-five, wrote: *So nice to hear from you! Yes, you are toughing it up there in Maine on the ocean in a summer cottage ... But, I bet you like the challenge! It wouldn't be for everybody, but once in a while it is nice to be "measured" by circumstances. When the electricity goes off in the winter I immediately go in "war" mode: be ingenious and make the best of it.*

Her reference to war mode is not a simple cliché: she was seven when the Nazis marched into her Dutch town.

MONDAY NOVEMBER 19 Hard frosts are a nightly occurrence. Enough to warrant scraping the windshield this morning. Even on sunny days the curled brown leaves on the woodland floor remain tipped with frosty highlights. Sixteen this morning, but the house warmed quickly to the sixties — could go to the eighties if we chose — and there was no wind.

I am walking a half hour every day; I even hike the house to test the fit of the light-hikers I bought in Ellsworth. Still looking for a slip-on type for the plane and town walking.

More reading in travel guides to decide where to spend our second month.

MONDAY DECEMBER 3   *Hampton Beach, NH*
Wind beats against the vinyl siding of our Ocean Air apartment building, and I can't tell whether the rumble of water is from surf on the beach — two short blocks away — or the dishwasher. The computer sits at one end of a peninsula that houses the dishwasher: the sliding doors to the balcony are at my right ear.

The kitchen and sitting room combined must be about twenty-five feet by twenty-five feet; all is modern and extremely pleasant. Kitchen has full-size brand name appliances and quality wooden cabinets; everything is sparkling clean. A big-enough bedroom and fine bathroom with washer and dryer. Two TVs.

A walk yesterday morning to the Royal grocery on H Street revealed a subdued, muted tourist village. The pizza, photo, subs, ice cream, fried dough shops on Ocean Boulevard are boarded up; the Casino Ballroom and concert shell face a wide deserted beach, beyond which the Isles of Shoals levitate on the horizon. A sure sign of this impending storm.

We feel we escaped rustic just in time: a foot of snow and very high winds are forecast for downeast Maine.

The closing of the camp ritual went smoothly, as did the five-hour drive. I was quite bouncy with pleasure at the quality of our apartment and the fact that phase one—November at the cottage, and phase two—December rental in New Hampshire—both are exceeding expectations for pleasure. The underlying emotion: it worked!

WEDNESDAY DECEMBER 5 Our first pink and green sunrise here at Hampton Beach; snow covers the black pavements and roofs and ubiquitous cars with clean and white. If the wind has lost its bite, perhaps a walk on the beach will happen. Can't arrive chalk-white in midsummer down under.

Drove the twenty minutes to Heritage Storage and swapped "For Milbridge" green bags for "NH Winter" sheets, towels, and warm town clothes.

FRIDAY DECEMBER 14 Big snow created winter wonder in beach land. No time to walk and enjoy, however. Follow-up letter from lawyer—a young woman in Tom's firm—advises us to resolve questions and proceed with trust before we leave. Both of us having simultaneous-death wills would complicate things. And there is the niggle that Medicaid would go after Sandy's life-estate in the cottage. Should there be a private, verbal agreement?

We have some time this weekend to work on it, but I do want to get a travel outfit comfortable for a thirty-hour trip.

SUNDAY DECEMBER 16 Whipping, slapping, white-out blizzard, and I do believe that low-tone rumble is surf on the sand. An inside, curl-up-comfy Sunday for sure: Patriots football and a DVD. Sandy signed us up for Netflix before we left Maine.

FRIDAY DECEMBER 21 Walk on Ocean Blvd. Black sky over steel-blue ocean, sporadic spurts of cold spray rising over orange snow-fence plastic. That water has to be cold: the temperature has been under thirty-two almost every day this month. According to the Internet, Dunedin weather today: "18 C (64F) max. 12 C (56.6F) low. Fine. Some high cloud. Warm northerlies."

Definitely time to chase the sun down under.

TUESDAY DECEMBER 25 A week from today we land in Auckland. I'm eager to be in the plane, off the ground, contained with only Sandy and some luggage. Preparation time has seemed very long.

Perhaps I am affected by these halcyon days of December. A hundred and fifty years ago loaded ships, having waited days in Portsmouth Harbor for this break, would hoist sail, maybe bound for the South Pacific.

FRIDAY DECEMBER 28 Waiting for call from MetLife re: buying CD, waiting for call from lawyer re: imminent will signing, waiting to leave for Maine with Schoodic.

SUNDAY DECEMBER 30 2007 Later we will check for snow update, but the other breath-holdings are over. We are pared to the bone— just us and fifty pounds of stuff. Schoodic, along with all of his possessions, is safe in "winter camp" at Barbara's. Bett has come and collected leftover food. Sandy is out dropping off the car at her sister's. In tonight's wee hours I will drape my passport bag around my neck, dress in my travel suit and beige/orange beach shoes, fasten my fanny pack around my waist, put on my Moosehead Lake Polartec jacket, hoist the computer case strap over one shoulder and carry-on bag over the other, extend the handle on my twenty-five-incher, slide the matching sixteen-inch bag on top of it, and roll down the hall, bump down the stairs, out the door, and heave-ho into Gary's Jeep. Off into the dark of night just like we dreamed.

MONDAY DECEMBER 31 Airborne Thirty-six thousand feet, sunshine on clouds, heading west, living in the moment at last.

We had woken at 2 a.m. to rain that didn't turn to snow until Gary had the Jeep warming outside Ocean Air. He tapped on our door, carried the luggage downstairs, and stowed it. He drove us carefully over the fast-filling back roads to Newburyport, refused any offer of payment, and carried the bags into the small C&J building set in the middle of a vast, now solid-white parking lot. In fifteen minutes there were a half dozen of us; the bus arrived exactly on time—amazing. Driver Sue shoved our big bags into the belly and we, with the help of a lady behind us, found an overhead for my small red bag and our black and brown carry-ons, leaving us in the front seat with the computer on my lap and Sandy's big pack between her knees. It seemed like a lot of luggage, but by the time we fumbled through the Logan check-in and completed the bin and socked-feet routine of security—Sandy's new knees guaranteed her a pat-down while I guarded our worldly goods—we were slinging straps over our shoulders and striding out like, if not pros, at least not in need of assistance to the elderly.

And we are not hungry or thirsty. In the 3 a.m. silence of our Hampton kitchen I had eaten a hard-boiled egg and half a bagel, then at eight on the tethered plane half a Kittery Bakery scone. Above the clouds at 9:30 I bought a $5 United breakfast of very good cheese, yogurt, crackers, a few grapes, and cantaloupe. One wedge of cheese, an apple strudel, and biscotti are packed away for later. Coffee and water are free. So far, so good. I'm dozy but not tired, and not dead asleep like a lot of the passengers. On this, the day before one of the busiest flight holidays of the year, the plane is about two-thirds full. Many rows have empty middle seats, but our request for a window and aisle seat did not work: a young actor is by the window; he and Sandy, however, have talked up a storm.

We rolled down a cleared runway on time—United defeating its bad reputation—and we are due in San Francisco early, a few minutes before noon. But that will be mid-afternoon for us and I'm wondering if we will have the energy to make a trek into town. However, in the bathroom just now I felt twenty years younger, a savvy stand-by traveler—thanks to son Jim being an airline employee—maybe even way back to thirty-five years younger when I squatted on train toilet seats and wondered if indeed the bottom of the bowl still opened onto the tracks. Will NZ prove to be a fountain of youth?

Last night we were wise to walk a couple of blocks down Ocean Boulevard to the Breakers Lounge in the Ashworth Hotel. The quiet plushness of the 1940s decor was soothing, a pause in the tick-tick-tick of the last few days, and, fittingly I downed a huge cheeseburger while watching guests of a certain age carefully make their way toward the elegant dining room while others hooked their three-inch heels over the rungs of a bar stool. My frequently unreliable innards found it perfect.

Subject: WILD BLUE YONDER
To: Family

GREETINGS EARTHLINGS—*On this the really far-out beginning of my new life. Sunshine on cloud-tops, ventilation wind roaring, halfway across the US, Iowa perhaps where primary candidates are rushing about. We were treated to Huckabee and McCain on TV as we waited to board.*

WEDNESDAY JAN 1--or 2?   *I think the sun arrives here 18 hours before you all.*

The land of the recent earthquake is beneath us — the east coast of the North Island — we will land in Christchurch — middle of South Is. in about an hour. One more flight and bus and we are done. Very pleased that we have "been measured by circumstance" over the last 30 hours and not been found wanting. Even ate gourmet Mexican in Union Square, San Francisco.

LATER. Out the west window are snow-capped mountains — a vacant land, newly born.

WEDNESDAY JAN 3, 2008 *Dunedin, New Zealand*

Since arriving we have showered, had tea on real china with Geraldine and Ross in their dining room, been driven by Ross, the former police commander here, on a tour of the city, eaten eggs Benedict with salmon in a pub four doors down the hill, slept nine hours straight, and now at noon are ready to set off to find someplace wired to the Internet — a café or maybe the library?--and a bank to change money. It was a holiday yesterday so the shuttle driver took us to the casino — a real trip!--to get enough to pay him.

FRIDAY JANUARY 4

To Family:
Ten-thirty a.m. here. Sun up about seven. I just came in from the east-facing patio outside our bed-sit door where we had breakfast, then a loll-back, eyes shut in sun with an under-bite which will do a fine tanning job. A breeze rattled the palm fronds and an occasional bird twittered. I have arrived.

I had been reassured of sanity when I found my Polartec jacket in the bathroom among last night's clothes heap, but my billfold still has not turned up.

LATER At the Common Room we discovered that we could receive e-mail, but not send it. We switched to their Mac, told the family we had landed. About then I began to get nervous thinking what a lost billfold might mean. If a thief got hold of it he/she might have already maxed out the one credit card. If misplaced, it must be in the shuttle van we took from the airport: Sandy and I had been pooling US dollars to pay the driver NZ$35 each plus tip. The fewer the passengers, the more each one paid.

Nervous became high anxiety as we dodged through shoppers,

tourists, backpackers and struggled up the nearly vertical London Street; I called the van driver from Ross's phone. No, he did not have it, nor had it been turned in by any of the load of eleven people he had transported after the next flight, but he would go to the garage; I should call him again at ten p.m. He strongly urged that I call the casino.

Ross joked, "You stopped at the casino before you came here! You couldn't wait?"

I knew I could not have left it there because I had never taken out my billfold: Sandy had been holding our fare in her wallet. I called anyway and after listening to my story, security said, "I believe we have it." Thank you! Thank you!

Ross offered to drive us right down to the casino and as we hurried in Sandy said, You did remember to bring identification ... No, I had not. But when we stood in front of the desk, one man looked at the lettering on my polo shirt, said, "Milbridge, Maine. You are the one." We all broke up in laughter, mine a bit overwrought.

Sandy later remarked, "No better place to lose money than at a casino crawling with security." No need to cancel the card and of course the money—only $27--was all there.

Back to the patio sun. Air heady with roses and the spire of Knox Church rising against the hill across the bay.

SATURDAY JANUARY ? Sandy switched the monitor screen photo from the empty, cold expanse of Hampton Beach to a green hillside pitching precipitously toward the harbor bay—the only guard rail four strands of barbed wire. Across the blue water the city of Dunedin, population 120,000, nestles under blue-green hills.

From our two comfy beds and my seat at this large desk, which also holds the TV, a huge window brings us light and garden flowers. Two steps down is the entrance hall leading right to a large bathroom; straight ahead the kitchen that completes the L around the patio also has a picture window. Overall our bed-sit has a British 1950s feel: the electric heater has a cozy setting. At night the steps make the bathroom trip a cautious one, especially since I am still stiff from the flight and the exertion of carrying groceries up London Street.

But yesterday we found the steepness of our street could be worse, much worse. The corner a half block above us is not the top, only halfway; two roads branch to the right, one snakes up in switchbacks, the other ends in long, steep stairs. The one to the left toward town pitches down at such an angle that I had to grab the metal handrail to slow my descent: we will not be coming home that way.

The supermarket, Count Down, is new, big, well-stocked, busy, and only about a ten-minute walk. The center of town, the Octagon where Bobbie Burns sits in homage to all things Scot, is perhaps a fifteen-minute walk, but all is level once we are on George Street. Since I'm almost finished with Lloyd James, *Mister Pip*, I must return to the library there—a bustling, modern place. I will give them fifty dollars and at the end of the month they will return about $42 to me: charges are based on use. Better than Portsmouth where I had no choice but to pay $40 for six months. I should have added books to my budget.

Yesterday, Sandy discovered we did not need a $70 computer adapter. From here on I'll write all prices in NZ dollars, 20 percent off US. A simple $14 plug-in will do because the Mac has a built-in international converter or something. God bless the Macs; in twenty-five years I have never had to purchase one extra.

The weather is akin to early July on the coast of Maine and the *Otago News* promises two more "fine" days. We will not, however, dash off to see the penguins, but rather enjoy patio sun, garden, and birds, and a walk to town center to check for arriving e-mail—we still are unable to send for some unknown reason. The Common Room offers coffee—short blacks and long whites are popular—and the pleasant bustle of travelers. The i-SITE visitor's center is on the Octagon, a large green space with eight short commercial streets for spokes. Dunedin is New Zealand's fourth or fifth largest city so we'll surely find items we chose not to bring in suitcases, such as hand lotion and nail polish remover

A turn left on George Street would bring us to Ortago University, and, I think, the Black Caps cricket match against Bangladesh. Perhaps we will get to some harness racing out near the beach one of these days. But as yet, tiredness lingers in my bones, and Sandy's too. It's been quite a week.

SUNDAY JANUARY 5 Barack Obama won Iowa. Iowa—a black man—a miracle. What a weekend in New Hampshire it must be; I wish I were there to flaunt my big Obama Coming Soon button.

Already my hands are no longer pale, but rich with color, brown, thank goodness, not red. After we read in the newspaper that depletion of the ozone layer in Antarctica has resulted in a 40 percent higher rate of UVs here, Sandy has insisted I apply her SPF seventy strength prescription—it's over the counter here—cream to my nose several times a day. I did and today I look healthily, not foolishly, burnt. I also bought my first ever roll-on protection for arms and legs.

Yesterday, after Geraldine remarked that we looked like tourists as we set off in our sandals and bright colors, we did a tourist thing and toured the University of Ortago. It was designed to be a copy of Edinburgh University: the architecture is gray stone and Gothic, complete with a square bell tower righteous against the sun-sharp heavens.

The campus green, lush with giant ferns and palms, is, however, more indicative of the east coast of Northern Ireland than the cold bleakness of Scotland, yet the overall geography of this island presents the wildness and loneliness that the Scot soul seems to crave. Now at 9:45 on a Sabbath morning we wait to hear the bells. There have been none for early masses—perhaps Catholics are still barred from town—but down in the Octagon Plaza the grand Church of England church stands, although as Sandy noted, Bobbie Burns' broad bronze back is turned to it. Yesterday we stepped into Knox Presbyterian Church and stood under the vaults and struts of the incredible wooden ceiling. Above the pulpit are two sets of organ pipes, one tall and brass, the other short, thin, and silver; I suppose we'd have to attend a service to hear them. The stained glass windows depict geometrics as well as medieval and biblical scenes; the walls are stone but the brilliance of the windows and the wealth of warm wood certainly obviate any sense of pomp. Ostentation was—as John Calvin taught—a bad thing, a sign of popishness. Ah, the bells have begun ... a rapid, hasty bonging, a call to get up and get to it. Now they have slowed, softened, faded away.

The temperature yesterday reached a high of 21 C (70 F), last night a low of 14 C (58F). We feel at home, but when I glance at a calendar that says January the momentary confusion knocks my brain about.

MONDAY JANUARY 7 Rain on our roof at five a.m.; now at eight it's just wet. Our conical hill across the bay is soggy green, but not obscured by the gray-black fog that came in around dinnertime last evening. Although we have the electric heater on the cozy setting now, 30C (85F) is predicted for this afternoon. As Ross said, "The only predictable thing about our weather is that it is unpredictable." So, as in Maine, I am wearing my Polartec jacket and fuzzy sweats, which at noon will be changed to rayon pants and long-sleeved shirt, and no doubt for teatime on the patio I'll be in shorts.

Very excited about a bus tour ($145) south through the Catlins, a truly wild place, to Invercargill and returning along a high cliff coast, which includes the possibility of an overnight and three meals at a sheep/deer farm ($125) along the way. Yesterday at the i-SITE Sandy got more details on the Twilight Tour out the Ortago Peninsula to see the rare yellow-eyed penguins and albatross ($125), and this morning while looking up temperature conversion in *Rough Guide*, I stumbled on what looks like a much better deal that would satisfy both of us.

I don't feel in great physical shape yet, however. November and December we had minimal exercise, and it is taking some effort to pull out of the drag imposed by the long trip. Lugging groceries and the computer around will have us pretty tough in another week, assuming the westerlies keep it cool enough, so we don't just sit and pant and drink beer.

Living month to month in different domiciles takes a certain amount of not only adjustment, but time spent on daily domestic duties. Having a host and hostess thoroughly orient us in generalities and specifics has been invaluable; a similar language and currency likewise. Nevertheless, we do have to buy groceries every day, cook, wash dishes, make beds, and in general care for ourselves instead of bolting from motel rooms to breakfast spots. It is easier than camping, however, and Geraldine says she is responsible for the weekly washing of our towels and sheets. We use her machine for our clothes, and yesterday, once we figured out how the clothespins work, successfully hung them on the metal lines attached to a swivel post. Differences here are amusing, not irritating.

While in the Common Room using their Internet service, I heard a teenager say, "Yeah-yeah-yeah," just like my grandson, Blake. By living day to day like ordinary folks, we pick up on the culture. Yesterday we ate strawberries dipped in chocolate sauce, thanks to overhearing a local in the supermarket asking and being directed to the little cartons set in a kaleidoscope of gorgeous local fruits. The Summer Sale signs in almost every window tempt me to look for a sweatshirt and lightweight pants. We are not on Vacation or Holiday, we are wintering-over.

The sun has found a slit in the bunched clouds. Off we go.

TUESDAY JANUARY 8 At ten last night it was still quite light outside, and I crawled between the sheets feeling like a child sent to bed while other kids are outside playing. I woke, not at six, but seven, padded to the bathroom and back, clicked on the electric blanket and slept soundly for another hour. Coffee, made in a plunger-style glass carafe, and some of Geraldine's raisin bread — she uses a machine just like ours — while waiting for my eye drop gel to absorb took another hour. It is 10:15 now; 4:15 yesterday afternoon in New Hampshire.

Chopper blades beat as another rescue helicopter moves precisely to the roof of the hospital. There are one or two of these landings a day; then later we read in the paper about climbing accidents, motorcycle crashes, near drownings, all the risk stuff that Kiwis pride themselves on.

One week in residence. Time to take stock. Body. It has a different feel: can do leg stretches without calf pain, feel taller, a little lower back pain when fingers touch the patio concrete — softer bed, I think. Mind: even keel after a couple of upsets yesterday: an e-mail from Barbara saying that Schoodie was off his food; another was a rude encounter with owner of Common Room. Got lucky, however, by finding the door to the Old Settler Museum in the nick of time to miss a hard shower. The exhibits compelled me to start Michael King's *The Penguin History of New Zealand*.

Body again. I've got the water situation under control: tap is okay for coffee and tea, drinking has to be bottled. This is not a new problem for me; a trip to Europe before the world-wide prevalence of bottled water had me swigging paregoric every morning

My first butterfly — bright yellow — just fluttered past the picture window. Sun is zapping the mist from "our hill" across the bay. I still have my snugglies on, but Sandy is heading for the patio in new Capris. We each bought a pair for $10 in Posties: the boutique store prices are outrageous. Food prices are, however, what we notice most. Eight dollars for a gallon for milk, $8 a pound for coffee, surely exceeds our $100 a week food budget, perhaps doubles it. The thin NZ bills fly from our wallets. We will see what the Lodge in Nelson comes back with for availability and price in February. For this wonderful place we are paying the same as in Hampton, NH.

On TV news last night — after sports and shark bites and killed climbers — we actually saw New Hampshire. A wavy line of what looked like five blocks of people waiting to see Barack and Hillary debate.

I'll join Sandy on the patio for muesli cereal and local nectarine.

The apricots are in, the red-right-through strawberries continue. Bliss.

WEDNESDAY JANUARY 9 Had some bad news yesterday both from Barb and Schoodic's vet; he has stopped eating and drinking. The vet said a large blockage of crystal were easily removed from his urethra and he *is now getting some IV fluids as well as indwelling urinary catheter so we can make sure his bladder stays small for a while. While this can be life threatening, Barbara brought him down in time and I think he will make a complete recovery. I plan to keep him for several days*
...
   My immediate response was: he's under such stress at being left, abandoned if you will, that this might recur. Or he might be so depressed he just gives up. Sandy has returned from city center, reporting that the Common Room was not open, so we have no new news. GG.C a half block away at the bottom of our hill will open fairly soon, so perhaps we'll have a response from the vet as to cause.
   Sandy took our computer since part of her mission was to check our bank accounts online and see if indeed our CD money had gone into our checking accounts and thence into MetLife CD. We are reluctant to do this at GG.C because they do not have wireless and Jim cautioned us about ever doing banking at a café. Too easy for someone to get into it. We really have no choice: Geraldine has offered her computer, but we need wireless—don't we?
   Geraldine took us through her 1934 story-and-a-half home yesterday. It was a B&B when they bought it in 1985 ($138,500). The house is sheathed in double-brick, the roof is concrete tiles and flat iron; our annex is rough-cast plaster over timber; the low boundary walls and paths are plastered concrete. Many interior architectural features were familiar from my childhood: casement windows decorated with diamonds of leaded glass; the massive railing edging the broad staircase where heavy-framed ancestral portraits—Ross's from New Zealand, Geraldine's from Wales and England—hung on small-design wallpaper. Our quarters are converted from a 1940s concrete block air raid shelter that also echoes the America of my youth.

THURSDAY JANUARY 9 A load was lifted with e-mails from both Barbara and Jenny the vet. Schoodic's kidneys and blood tested out fine and although Jenny said he was quiet all day, when she stopped to talk to him he talked back. We could just picture him, his little mouth going, "I'm fine. Let me out of this cage. Now." Jenny says crystals can be caused by stress, but usually heredity and diet have more to do with it. He will go on a prescription diet for six weeks, then a special one for life. She is sure that will prevent any future problems which, of course, eases our guilt at leaving him and mitigates any thoughts of having to return to save his little life. E-mails from Bett and Kath concluded he was heart sick/wanted extra attention.

At a wool shop downtown we got into conversation with the saleswoman after Sandy asked, "Do you have to kill the possum to get the hair?" Possum and merino sweaters are the rage here. The answer was, Sadly yes. She asked where we were from, weather etc., and told us to avoid Nelson—much too hot, adding, "And it is supposed to be an above average heat summer. Finally, she asked with a bit of awe, "So you two are on your own then?" We laughed kindly at that ingrained idea that without a male, women are alone, and nodded. "So, you can have a bit of fun without someone saying, we have to be here or there now." You mean, I thought, like girls night out, but was rather charmed by her puzzlement. She gave us some under-the-counter chocolate—the Cadbury factory is around the corner—and waved us out, saying how glad she was to see two women off doing what they like.

I guess we are not only role models among our friends at home, but are having a bit of an international impact. I sense New Zealand may be in general a male-first society. After all, a hundred and fifty years ago white settlers were just arriving to turn the land of the Polynesian hunter-gathers into a vast pasture; farming usually means a sharp division of male-female work: the exhausted male at the table waiting to be served by the equally exhausted female.

New Zealand hangs like a dagger at the bottom of the globe; Dunedin, poised over Antarctica, clings to the edge of the blade. Last night winds sawed away at this low concrete house like banshees loosed from the depths of unknown seas and today they continue, a reminder that this is a wild land, subject to any violent whim of nature land. We will not be venturing halfway out the Ortago Peninsula to Portobello today. Perhaps a tour of the old Victorian mansion, Olveston—an extremely steep climb to the Royal Terrace above us—will suffice.

SATURDAY JANUARY 11 Another spotless blue sky with no wind rushing about. Yesterday we did take a bus to Portobello and were thankful for sporadic, cooling bursts of it as we strode ever up on the road to the university aquarium.

Those two kilometers comprised the walk of a lifetime, not for cliffs, or mountain precipices, or jungle, but the expansive freedom of pasture, sea, and far mountains. Slopes of golden grain undulated beneath the northeast breeze; shorn sheep stared, while geese marched across thick green grass. The dirt road curved and wound upward beneath our steps. With all senses fully engaged, the biblical "I lift up my eyes to the hills from whence cometh my help" chimed in my head. When a tourist van or car invaded with noise and dust, I would pause and stare like a native shepherd.

We had fortified ourselves for the walk at an 1880 restaurant, I with a curry chowder of baby sea creatures: mussels and shrimp with bits of clam, squid, and octopus, which I viewed live in tanks a bit later. Sharks and whales, octopus and colossal squid abound in New Zealand waters; fossils of even more ancient creatures remain in Antarctic ice.

The half-hour bus ride each way on the peninsula road was thrilling/terrifying/lovely—take your pick. A narrow two-lane road carved from the base of vertical hills curved continuously along the edge of the harbor's three-foot seawall. No guardrail, only a two-foot wide strip of grass between macadam and over the edge. That this amazing ride was not even mentioned in any tourist material I read is proof that such roads are commonplace in this uncoddled land.

Am taking a bit longer than usual to get over those exertions this morning; just swallowed a couple aspirin. My body is much stronger, I know, but nevertheless, I am seventy-five. A fact I am not sure Geraldine appreciates. While I was on the patio about 8 a.m. doing my stretches, she bounded up, sure that I would want to go to the far edge of the city, either swimming in the big pool with Ross, their son, daughter-in-law, and infant, or beach walking with her. I made quick excuses of a bit of stiffness from yesterday and that I needed to get cracking on finding a place up in the Nelson area for February. She looked surprised. I could never have kept up with any of them. New Zealanders are fit.

SUNDAY JANUARY 13 Geraldine is what one would describe as "open," emotions illuminate her face, supposedly a New Zealand trait; as is "craggy" for men, and Ross is certainly that. I gleaned "open" and "craggy" from statements made about Sir Edmund Hillary who died yesterday. All NZ mourns their Sir Ed.

We met a number of McLennan children, who are assembled to celebrate a late Christmas, but did not have long enough at teatime to assess them for stereotypic behavior; all except a son-in-law, Paul, are quite lean. Gregor is married to a woman with a Maori mother — the first woman and the first of her race to hold a cabinet portfolio — and a British father, Dennis. Dennis is a nuclear physicist about my age who has traveled back and forth to the US a great deal: on the trip over in '87 I sat next to a nuclear physicist who was returning from a conference in DC and we talked all night. You don't suppose ... But why would he remember me?

In the 90s yesterday, back to Polartec today. Off to city center to library and i-SITE to book a tour to see the yellow-eyed penguins and albatross. We'll pop in stores, probably have tea and a sweet, shop at Count Down, and climb the steps of GG.C to check for news of Schoodic and assess more possible accommodations in Nelson.

MONDAY JANUARY 14 Not a word on Schoodic yesterday. We are filled with silent questions. Is he "home" and happy? If so, why hasn't Barbara written: possibly her computer is down? Has he been kept in the hospital over the weekend? If so, why? Last night I thought of infection, but did not mention it to Sandy. If she hasn't thought of it, why pile on extra worry? Another flash I quickly smother is that he has died and they don't know how to tell us.

Our GG.C will not be open until afternoon when it will be Sunday in the states, but perhaps Barbara will respond to Sandy's "We feel so far away ..." e-mail of yesterday.

Picked up a fat book Motel & Apartment Accommodations at the i-SITE and perused it on the patio with an early beer. Nothing striking there, but did get three good suggestions from an i-SITE agent: check ads in the Nelson Mail on Wednesday and Saturday, which I suppose we could get online; contact Jenny Orchard, who "specializes in finding the best accommodation to suit your needs;" examine website which lists "many self-contained" cottages. The latter is, I believe, the site that came up "Oops" for an agent. Our bed-sit here was listed on the Dunedin i-SITE as "Seville," next to last on the list. Persistence won out.

If we don't get some kind of good response on accommodations today or tomorrow, we will contact Jenny — whose last name, Orchard, is quite apt for the apple-growing center of New Zealand. When we traveled to Albuquerque for several months in '91, we had arranged through their chamber of commerce for a woman to aid us in our apartment search. We were never sure whether she was paid by the chamber, city, tourist bureau, or was supposed to collect from us. But she was invaluable and gave a couple of days of excellent help at no charge.

Lay in bed an extra half-hour this morning finishing *Ellie and the Shadow Man* by Maurice Gee. The settings are Wellington and Nelson and was a good read to boot. May An, a McLennan daughter-in-law, said, "Oh, no, you don't want to holiday in Wellington—too commercial, all businessmen. Nelson is where you want to be. There should be accommodations there, everyone has to go back to work this Monday." Geraldine chimed in with the word "hot," but I'm beginning to think their weather values are different than ours. The TV weather map of the whole country is filled with numbers ranging from 20-30C (68-86F) with nights in the 60s F. Nelson ranges in the mid-80s. Here in Dunedin the sun is extremely sharp, but around every corner is a chilling breeze. If Nelson is humid and still the way it is today that might be a tad warm for us; but New Zealand has limitless access to water and I certainly am willing to pack up my Polartec jacket and not sleep every night under a thick coverlet. Plenty and more of that awaits in Maine this spring.

I wonder if the body-piercing quality of the sun is due to the clarity of the air, or the sun's slant, or perhaps both?

TUESDAY JANUARY 15 Schoodie is safe. I keep repeating it to myself and aloud. The e-mail Barbara sent about bringing him home Friday had been reshuffled onto another page of mail. Our days of anguish were unwarranted, but the overwhelming relief is *that he follows me into the kitchen, crawls into my lap, behaves like Schoodie again.* He is not wild about his new diet food, however. No surprise there.

In my history reading last night I learned that the population of this country is a bit over four million. Not very many and the vast majority of them are on the North Island. This was also true for the Polynesian people, who, as they adapted to the different geography and climate of these vast empty lands, became known as Maori. By the time Captain Cook arrived in 1769, almost all people in the north were settled in groups delineated by family and place; and most were marked by a fortified hilltop, a pa, in case matters got out of balance with neighbors. The whole of the south of the South Island was inhabited by just one tribe that avoided the west coast with its rugged alps, and deep fiords and sounds.

Today this area known as Fiordland is, thanks to tourists who ski and climb, the world-wide image of New Zealand. When Sandy and I arrived in 1987 we spent our first week there, hiking and sightseeing on Milford Sound. On the Routeburn Track two guides led our small international group from shelter to shelter, and carried and cooked our food. If we saw any other people, I don't recall it. Now, I'm told, one signs up a year in advance, and apparently our first night's simple camp has become a tourist destination with numerous rooms and comforts.

Solitude is not something we seek—especially with Sandy determined not to drive, which is fine with me. Consequently, the queries we e-mailed to Nelson yesterday were all to places within the borders of that small town. It will be interesting to see the responses.

WEDNESDAY JANUARY 16   Late yesterday afternoon the Twilight Tour van picked us up out front for our Ortago Peninsula trip ($108).

Descriptive words for it will be difficult to find this morning. But then our many digital photographs will be equally lacking in their ability to convey the wild ride across the interior of the peninsula, and the majesty of the royal albatross in flight.

Travel experiences often come from within. The visual is also the visceral. Just as the smell of a bubbling stew is more than the sum of its ingredients, so too the five senses do not rise naked and merely report; they stream forth from a rich mixture of many like ingredients. I suppose this is what some call a mystical experience. When twilight skittered across the landscape, blackening the deep folds of pastureland and gilding the precipitous slopes of grazing, always grazing, sheep the word stop rose in my throat. As in, Stop, I want to get off here, this is all that could be.

For others I'm sure that would not be true, but for me, for whatever reason—heredity, culture, personal make-up—the space and clarity, the Pacific with its mighty rollers white on blue, deeper even than the sky, always there, over the next ridge, around the next bend, and the edge-of-the-world scene of knee-high yellow-eye penguins moving on big webbed feet, either going down the sharp hill to enter the sea, or returning from it to hurry across the wide sand, across rocky edge and up, up to relieve the partner who has fed young ones larger than itself all day long. It was this amazing coexistence of wildness and human make-over of pastureland that brought me to a standstill, perhaps emotional, perhaps eternal.

We had taken this tour for the express purpose of seeing the rare, the improbable: these penguins and the royal albatross, black wings locked glider like, soaring, banking, tips folding, landing near broody nesters. For seeing the male fur seals, for decades victims of slaughter, waking from a day of slumber and incidental pup-minding, to lurch off into a roiling sea for a night of squid feeding. All of these creatures, whether their times of child rearing are counted in months, as with the penguins and seals, or a year for the albatross, males and females share equally in the continuation of the species. But, our guides informed us, some individuals are better parents than others. Young albatross, first-nesters at about seven years old, need to be encouraged to stay on their nests when a nearby teenage-mate-selection party tempts them to desert. Human minders will even test them with a dummy egg to record which males simply don't show up again after a day of dining at sea. So the tour was far more than sight, awe, and beauty, it was insight into how interconnected we all are: how our planet works.

It also tested our trust in human skill when our young female driver roared the van up and off the main road—scary enough in itself—into breathless up and downs, the motor sounding like a Cessna taxiing, revving for takeoff, landing, slowing, speeding, careening over one-lane dirt roads, defying gravity and belief. We sat, still breathless with the rush, when she paused beside ponds with Australian black swans, inlets with black stilts and paradise shelducks, and finally jumping out, opening the gate into a high pasture without even a track on the long down slope. The constant groan of gripping tires on our four-wheel drive were reassuring yet had me wondering if we were participating in a high adrenaline TV commercial.

Today is another fine one, but we will be content at home: a large breakfast, laundry, washing yesterday's dishes, cataloguing the digital photos, and a trip to GG.C to wrestle with more Nelson accommodation letters. Content to ponder all we saw and did, trying to store it in our fallible brain cells before something equally spectacular takes up the space. But then I doubt anything can; these are sticky ones.

FRIDAY JANUARY 18 *"… the guinea-gold light, and the size of the sky and air that went to the head quicker than gin."*

Purportedly a quote from a mid-1800s letter luring immigrants to New Zealand. Frances Keinzley's *The House of Hogs* is historical fiction, but that description rings true.

In 2008 I can e-mail my New England audience that almost every morning feels like a Canadian high has rushed through, to scour away any moisture or dust between earth and heaven. The gin effect I would describe as psychological buoyancy. The first week or so I would have written to the contrary: Each night I'm thrust so deeply into sleep that surfacing in the morning is a doubtful proposition. That sounds like gin, but probably was the result of adrenaline-laced blood from the journey needing time to flush itself out.

Successful wintering over, we have decided, needs a first stay of at least three weeks to allow for dissipating physical/psychological stress and pure adoration of sun and flowers and foods of summer.

Would it have been better to make arrangements for further travel and accommodations online from the US, sparing me the week-long chore of lining up our next month? We were ambivalent about that, however, thinking that we would make wiser decisions with access to local information. And that has proved to be true. Our bus trip to the north of the South Island is an example. At the visitor center late yesterday afternoon a tired—cruise ship tourists had flooded the town—but game woman unraveled myriad bus schedules through self-knowledge and phone calls to chart us a bus journey that leaves Dunedin February first and arrives in Nelson the evening of Tuesday the fifth. Almost $600 for the two of us. Certainly renting a car would be cheaper, but no fun for Sandy. Paying the high-season rate for staying a place one or two nights was a given.

Our decision to make in-town Nelson our long stay place was based on conversation with locals. And likewise our desire to see the Catlin region to the south instead of going by Christchurch was definitely a local decision. A lot of my searching through accommodation guidebooks—the best of which we picked up at the i-SITE—was conducted on the patio during my usual downtime. In bed after morning coffee, but before rising, was where we made lists of places we wanted to see and that fit comfortably with weather and our age.

MONDAY JANUARY 21 Fine—the favorite word of New Zealand weather folk and ours too. It lacks the hype of a Florida "4 palm day," but suits this land of understatement.

We got used to our plans being looked on with a bit of awe and surprise among New England people, but once here in New Zealand we thought we would be simply tourists among tourists. Not so. Our helper in the visitor center yesterday confessed that the second time she saw us in there she said to a coworker: "How long are they staying?" Yesterday she asked us and was very interested in how we managed a month's stay in Dunedin. Probably the question in the back of most minds is: how can they afford it? We had asked ourselves that when we added and divided and found that our grocery store bill averages $25 a day, $175 a week. I think perhaps the entire trip will come to $15,000. Too early to tell yet. At the end of January we'll do another average of groceries, teas, and dinners out, transportation, tours and entrance fees and accommodations. The latter we know is going from $53 a day to $90 in Nelson, but reduce that by the now almost 25 percent exchange rate and US$50 a day is not bad.

The Saturday morning farmer's market was a real high.

Held adjacent to the huge Rule Britannia train depot, it sported colored tents and gaily dressed people, a welcome relief from the ubiquitous all-black. Welcome, too, was the change from the preciousness of the small organic ones in Portsmouth and Milbridge, where emphasis is on cute little bundles at astronomical prices. Geraldine seems to think that that is true of her hometown one, but we found prices lower than supermarkets and quality better. Raspberries, peaches, a new crispy kind of lettuce, oyster mushrooms grown on a gunny sack, hot dumplings stuffed with cabbage and pork—Sandy went back and bought a frozen five-pound bag—lamb chops, a new kind of local bottled beer, sweets, and to top it all off a huge bunch of deep-colored sweet pea flowers. Next Saturday we plan to take a table there to devour the savory smelling food and rich coffee, but today we skipped home merrily — thoughts only, not feet—with our booty.

Although skipping is not in our immediate plans, on Sunday we became fully aware of how much our lungs, legs, and hearts have benefited from twenty days of living without a car. A very up-hill-down-dale city walk that included long flights of steps was pleasant. not painful.

Living lightly on this planet has become ever more true. No car, no phone feels like the end of a process that started a year ago, when staging our house for showing made leanness a tangible virtue. Camping is, of course, an ultimate, but at our age we do not anticipate a return to that. Learning to cope with less is enabled by a laptop computer that fulfills the necessity—and pleasure—of quick connections to accommodations and the mother country. No desire, however, to talk, so no cell phone, no Skype.

Woke a bit earlier, six-thirty, and slow getting up to speed: groggy, shins a bit achy, cabbage-stomach, but since drizzle is predicted for tomorrow—we watch the 6 p.m. weather for forecasts and aid in pronouncing Maori names of cities—I think we will follow through with a planned bus trip up the north side of the harbor to Port Chalmers where the cruise ships and freighters dock.

TUESDAY JANUARY 22 A long bad news letter from Barbara. We did not get to GG.C until after four, when we returned from a café lunch and a long, exquisitely beautiful stroll, probably four kilometers, along the Port Chalmers harbor and beachfront.

Schoodie is back in the hospital. He did not adjust to his new prescription diet in spite of Barbara's imaginative innovations; has lost of full pound since original weigh-in. He finally perked up a bit with the addition of canned food, but that same day he had great trouble urinating. By four in the afternoon Friday still no clumps in his litter box. Barbara called the vet: Bring him right in. A doc, not Jenny, could detect no blockage; they kept him and he passed urine that night. They assured Barbara they would find some food he would eat that would also be good for him.

GG.C opens about 11:30 — it stays open until two or three a.m. for college students playing games. Fortunately, a young Korean student is now in charge, and opening on time is one of his promised upgrades. We will be there hoping for better news, but neither one of us had a good night's sleep.

I am back to my original fear that our absence is creating intolerable stress; Sandy believes it is a medical problem that has been building for a long time. It may be a combination of both, but what do we do? Even if we raced to his side believing that would fix matters, where would we live? There is a great deal of cold and snow yet to come, making Milbridge with its current plumbing impossible to inhabit. Probably we could go back to Hampton Beach and wait it out there. But to leave here … it seems unthinkable, but I suppose …

A full-fledged rain beats on the patio outside our east windows, and we heard that up in Nelson they are experiencing a drenching, along with gale winds due to a cyclone somewhere to the west. None of that will come this far south, and I'm certainly content in our cozy bed-sit. Almost 10 a.m. and Sandy and I have been sitting in bed — more comfortable than the chairs — catching up on what the *Otego Times* prints about the US and the rest of the world. Sir Edmund Hillary, the conqueror of Mt. Everest, is being eulogized as a symbol of the highest virtues of a New Zealander: a humble, ordinary can-do bloke.

I'll fill the rest of the time until the GG.C opens reading some history and organizing more stays on our way to Nelson. Maybe shopping and a movie this afternoon.

Poor little Schoodie. Our hearts ache for him—and for Barbara. Breath-holding is depleting.

WEDNESDAY JANUARY 23 And there was no end to it, no e-mail from Barbara. I sent her one and looked for a reply at the end of our-hour session. Still nothing. It is 3:30 Tuesday afternoon in Milbridge now, but to imagine what is and has occurred is not a positive act. The range of possibilities is too broad and we do not have the knowledge to narrow it down.

While I was making the bed, the thought: what if it were one of the grandchildren—today is Nate's twenty-third birthday—gave me a bit of perspective. When people said, "New Zealand ... so far away," distance seemed irrelevant, but the impulse to rush to the hurting person's or pet's side is strong. "If we could only give him a hug," Sandy says wistfully. His photo looks out from our tiny travel clock, and our voices break when we try to answer "What time is it?" with the usual: "Schoodie says ..."

THURSDAY JANUARY 24 An e-mail from Barbara. Schoodic is still at the vet's, but she reports that Jenny assures her that this is but a bump in the road, he is in no serious danger. Huge sigh and shoulder slump. Last night I dreamed of his big feet padding downstairs and his white fluffy self trotting into the room, a belief that he will not die but be waiting for us when we come home.

At the visitor's center in the plaza we bought our bus tickets from Invercargill to Nelson, and just in time. One bus had only six seats left, but I think they are small, maybe vans. Outside from a phone booth with a door, we dialed the 800 numbers for Tower Lodge Motel in Invercargill and Beach Front Hotel in Hokitika on the west coast. If space is available we will call the Lake Hawea Motor Inn in Wanaka tomorrow for a two-night stay. A place out on the lake with peaks against the sky sounded like a good change from city streets.

But we have enjoyed Dunedin immensely, finding small delights like the extraordinary hot chocolate in both Everyday Gourmet and the Art Museum Café. Kevin, our Korean friend at GG.C, now offers us tea at every visit, a welcome gesture. Organizing our three weeks in February has taken a great deal of time. Fortunately, I rather enjoy it, but I imagine it would drive others to distraction. Another fortunate is that we have been dealing with extremely courteous people eager to oblige; a Kiwi character trait perhaps. I don't think we could have done it from the States: one, because although our *Rough Guide* and *Frommer's* give the information in words, working out the schedules and making reservations would have been an expensive, perhaps impossible chore; two, we needed the information given in *AA Regional Accommodations Directories and the Jason's 2008 Motels, Apartments & Motor Lodges* book which covers all of New Zealand. Having these books in hand and talking to the excellent people at the visitor's center assured us of getting what we wanted, once we knew what that was.

January is the busiest tourist month because of the local vacations, and things will get easier in February, although not necessarily in price. Now that I know more about the details of how to go about the process, planning for our last six weeks doesn't look so daunting.

Magnificent cloud shows yesterday. Two new New Zealand fiction books from the library.

In our gallery crawling part of the day, we had a conversation with a man who, when I asked, gave us some valuable information about gemstones in Hokitika. Then since it was cloudy, windy, and cool, we went to the movies in the Octagon, a classy theater with plush armchair seats wide enough to set my box of popcorn beside me. Death at a Funeral had me laughing out loud—hard. A different kind of day that would have answered last night's pub mates question of "Dunedin for a month? What do you do?"

The broad answer is we live along and enjoy feeling like guests who have no responsibilities beyond food procurement and personal cleanliness—two loads of wash this morning, but Geraldine will be in to change our beds.

FRIDAY JANUARY 25 Bobbie Burns's birthday. We are going to a celebration held on the green dominated by his statue—even though it was his nephew who was mayor of this city. Those Scot bloodlines certainly were evident in the couple we met in The Bog last night, where we had gone to shake off a discouraging online search for a reasonable weekend accommodation in Wanaka. One side of the pub's upper level is a continuous booth-type seat, so that when we sat down these folks were our near neighbors. Typical of the Scot-Irish in my family, they were friendly and garrulous: one Scot dictionary defines it as *oncomingness*. At the end of lamb stew—Sandy—and my bangers and mash we knew quite a bit about each other. They live an hour and a half drive north in the rural part of Otego Province and left us one of their son's cards: recreation director for Abel Tasman Park across the bay from Nelson, a prime factor in our choosing that destination.

LATER. An e-mail from Jenny. Schoodic is not healing. She expects to have to do an operation to remove his male parts tomorrow morning.

We read this in the Internet café by the Octagon and were still staring stunned when a cannon boomed and everyone jumped. Oh, yes, Bobbie's birthday celebration. We plodded numbly across the street, raised a dram of malt, ate crackers with haggis, and joined the crowd in singing "Auld Lang Syne". We barely held it together as we stood at the base of the everlasting stone steps up to St. Paul's cathedral, watching people slowly ascend to attend a service for Sir Ed; two kilted men piped them in.

By almost silent consent we boarded a bus to the Botanical Gardens. We ate by the windows looking out onto the last brilliant splotches of roses, then climbed to the hilltop, a feat we had thought impossible on our first visit. A solemn day.

SATURDAY JANUARY 26 Almost 9:30−3:30 yesterday where Schoodie is−and no word. Sandy went over to use Geraldine's computer while I stayed in bed with a last bit of coffee. I could not believe it. Our minds still race in silence, careful not to allow ourselves to spill into weeping. I did, in the silence of the night, go to him. Did touch his little body, look in those understanding blue eyes.

Best stop that or I will crack. And how do we know ... He might have started urinating yesterday and they didn't do the operation. Jenny might be waiting until he is out of recovery and his signs are tested. He might be in doubtful shape, in pain without hope, so ... Going on in silence seems best. We won't go to the farmer's market, but wait here in case there is a call. Then see if our GG.C is open at 11.

LATER. SCHOODIC CAT. We stared at the monitor, eyes grasping words for the split second transition to understanding: Your Schoodic is doing well. .... The surgery went very well. As he was coming off anesthesia, I expressed his urethra, and "pop" out came a stone that ... unable to get out while his penis was on! So I am pleased, and suspect his urinary problems to be resolved. We will keep ... over the weekend ...Monday ... Barbara will ..."

My eyes went wide, then shut, but it took some time for the brain to slide off high alert.

MONDAY JANUARY 28 Only three days left to play. Our finances looked good, so we took advantage of one more brilliant day and joined a bus tour out to the castle on the peninsula.

I'm cribbing some help from books by New Zealanders to describe what I often fail to find words for.

From Ghost *Net* by Lynn Davidson: "The weather here is a religious experience . . . It's huge, extreme and absurdly beautiful."

The Carpathians by Janet Frame: "... undusty trees, the huge blossoms from the blossom-tree pinning the corsages against the sky, the golden, newly washed and oiled spring flowers."

WEDNESDAY JANUARY 30 Cool and cloudy. Wearing my new plum-colored merino and possum sweater—NZ$205. A made-in-New-Zealand, not-on-sale purchase in a tourist boutique on the Octagon bought mostly with Christmas money.

On our tour bus to Lanarch Castle Monday, a casual conversation with a couple from Auckland resulted in their definite pronouncement that we should spend March on Waiheke Island, a half-hour ferry ride from the city. At last a place that sounded right to us. After doing book research I went online yesterday morning and discovered it is geared to the rich and famous; however, there were a couple of cottages that offered the possibility of meeting our $85 a night top price. We will have our fingers crossed when we go online this morning: both for that and for word from Barbara that Schoodic is home safe and well. We expected to hear that yesterday, but have avoided any worry talk.

On our list of Things To Do before leaving Dunedin was haggis and a dram at the railroad station restaurant. It was before dinner hours, but the hostess remembered us from a previous try and brought an hors d'oeuvre plate with a few oat crackers and a half-dozen fingers of haggis along with the whiskey of the day. A plus to that treat was the Scot bartender in a kilt coming over to discuss the two hundred and thirty different single malts and over one hundred blends of whiskey that tower above the bar. He had told us this bargain whiskey, "Will get you to the same place."

THURSDAY JANUARY 31 At six we will walk across our patio, down the concrete steps, and knock on Geraldine and Ross's kitchen door. Tantalizing smells of dinner have been emanating for quite a while now, and we anticipate a most pleasant evening. Earlier I watched Geraldine root about in the garden and toss young potatoes in her bucket.

Our schedule north to Nelson is set. Friday: tour bus along the south of the South Island, an overnight in Invercargill; Saturday:

another bus north to Lake Wanaka; Sunday: a rest day in Wanaka by the lake; Monday: a bus across the South Alps to the west coast with an overnight in Hokatica; Tuesday: long bus ride along the coast and east to Nelson at the top of the South Island.

Open luggage is everywhere in this lounge/bedroom, waiting for those final bits to be packed when we return from dinner. We'll probably get up at 5:30 a.m.; the Bottom Bus will be out front at seven. What an easy take-off compared to the one from Hampton Beach with Gary hustling us through the swirling snowy darkness into his Jeep at what--4:30? Tomorrow it will be light and the birds will sing, and I will have a feeling that has persisted for days now: this will not be a permanent farewell. After all, Sandy said, there are our eighties to consider. And since last week the bus stops right outside this house, 21 London Street, Dunedin, NZ.

LATER Geraldine's dinner was in the grand New Zealand tradition—with many children and spouses around the table— beginning with Ross pouring Scotch whiskey and serving a bit of haggis, through a table loaded with vegetables and roast lamb and ending with their rich dessert, pavlova. "Something she doesn't do for everyone," her Maori daughter-in-law assured us.

SATURDAY FEBRUARY 2 *Invercargill*
Yesterday Geraldine waited on the sidewalk with us surrounded by two big wheeled bags, three small ones, a pack, briefcase with laptop, a lunch box, and me draped with my fanny pack and Sandy with her purse. At eight, parked beside the in-town hostel waiting for backpackers to get themselves organized, Sandy and I, by now into the laid-back mode, found a Starbucks for coffee take-away. Finally our green graffiti-painted Bottom Bus headed south with four of us oldies among twenty plus kids. They were well-mannered and the driver was excellent on history and geography of this rugged, isolated Catlin Mountain country.

Under cloudy skies the bouncing bus wheeled along the edges of coastal inlets and outlets. Unfortunately, the heavens let loose just before our long hike up a wind-lashed trail out to a lighthouse and magnificent view; thank goodness for Gore-Tex hikers and Eastern Mountain Sports raincoat.

In New Zealand when the driver says, "We'll get out for a walk here," it lasts at least twenty minutes, and walk is a Kiwi understatement, as was the term wet. At other stops the kids lunged off to find young sea lions at play, or waterfalls draped in thick green, or changed into bathing suits and charged into an inlet where small Hector dolphins swam, or investigated a bit of ancient geology, or whatever. As the day progressed I lagged farther and farther behind, happy to stroll and watch raindrops splash on fronds or winding jungle streams. Going at a fast clip from point A to B was never my style: twenty years ago on the Routeburn Track to Milford Sound, Sandy and I were always last into camp.

It was after six when we were dropped at the Tower Lodge Motel in Invercargill.

SUNDAY FEBRUARY 3 *Wanaka*
Yesterday as we traveled north from Invercargill, the true drama was in the sky. The land rose from coastal plain into low hills that grew into the Eyre Mountains, over which clouds tumbled as though a cloud-making machine on the other side of a stage cutout was spewing a variety of mare's tails, cirrus, puff balls up and over. Then through the bus's broad windshield appeared miles of the empty blue-green waters of Lake Wakatipu, in places a mirror for ever higher mountain ranges and now thick roiling basket loads of sheet clouds which tumbled into their deep cavities. This morning the clouds are broader, some gray, over this little lakeside resort, and earlier a helicopter beat its way north over the sharp blue strip of Lake Wanaka; perhaps a climbing accident rescue, more likely sightseeing around Mount Aspiring.

Last night was cool and breezy, so I'm in heavy sweats and Polartec, but on the sidewalks below it's all short sleeves, short pants, flip-flops, the women in beach-top mode. The men's chests remain covered with the ubiquitous T-shirt, although a flash of bare brown occasionally rises from the skateboard and bike park.

Our studio room is timbered right up to the tall peaked ceiling that slopes to the sliders and covered balcony; between the sleeping area and sparkling stainless steel bathroom is a tiny, clever space for cooking and clean up. Obviously a brand new renovation for only $130 a night, an upgrade bargain in this crowded summertime town. Last night, a Saturday, the waterfront was jumping, particularly at the Speights Ale picnic table restaurant, mostly kids, and we walked beyond to eat quietly at Thai-Siam; I have enough rice noodle vegetarian for lunch today.

Saturday our bus didn't leave Invercargill until 1 p.m., giving us time for the lovely Queen's Garden and the Southland Museum, which was my introduction to the four sub-Antarctic volcanic islands: there were fascinating exhibits on shipwrecks and their use as watch stations for German ships during WWII. A map with

Antarctica at the center and the tips of New Zealand, Africa, and South America encircling it prompted a Malcolm Gadwell blink experience. Those are the places we plan to visit! The circumference of the sixty degree parallel, aptly named the screaming sixties, was small, focused on that white of ice, but the forty, the roaring forties, caught this South Island of New Zealand and a great deal of Argentina, but missed South Africa, our goal next year.

WEDNESDAY FEBRUARY 6 *Nelson*
It is good to be arrived, which occurred at 5:30 yesterday after a hang-on-to-your-seat ride over the switchback roads and plunging down hills of Murchison and Hass Pass. Once more the bus was a small Atomic with only four passengers: Sandy, myself, the "Frenchman with an Irish accent," as the bus driver dubbed one of the young men who told us he was from New Caledonia — wherever that is, we thought. We had left Wanaka on Monday with more people, but lost most of them at the Franz Josef and Fox glaciers which reach up into the Southern Alps. We disembarked in Hokitika.

This was another stop I was a bit concerned about. We had signed up for a "standard" room in the old Southland Hotel; after all, it was just an overnight so we could shop for jade in the morning. Well, after wrestling bag and baggage into the reception area, we knew we had arrived in the pricy, new Ocean View section. The dining room offered three choices for a three-course dinner and fronted on a deck, beyond which palm trees wafted above the wide beach and Tasman Sea surf. To our joyful amazement the woman behind the desk told us we would be "more comfortable over there," at no increase in price. "Over there" was a studio on the beach with every comfort, including my first glass shower on a tile floor. The four-star rating continued with dinner of blue cod, preceded by a Thai pumpkin soup with a kick, and followed by pavlova which we lingered over on the deck among the beautiful people. Worth every penny. We strolled the sunset beach in awe of the Tasman's thundering series of five consecutive sets of breaking waves, and amused by sculptures of driftwood, stones, and grasses. Indeed, this west coast was, at least for this moment, a tropical paradise.

Our Nelson motel on the highway appeared at first sight to be quite a comedown. But again, our hosts took one look and upgraded us from a studio to a two-bedroom at the same $90 a night, a real help since we are booked for two weeks. Downtown, a ten minute walk, lacks the excitement of Dunedin, but a chic resort-type restaurant served reasonable and excellent pizza. When the morning sun rose over the high hill of trees and lighted our "apartment," we were more than satisfied. Sandy has returned from the laundry room with a good report, plus two small plunger coffee makers and promise of free early morning newspaper delivery.

This afternoon at four our Sky-equipped TV will carry a rerun of the Super Bowl. We already know the sad outcome, having heard our Patriots and the Giants last touchdown calls on the radio, thanks to the bus driver who knew we were fans. So there we were, hurtling through a dripping rain forest, hearing a Kiwi announcer relate the football upset of the century.

Almost ten o'clock. Sandy has the bedroom upstairs and I'm down here with plenty of space to myself. Time to unpack and settle in.

THURSDAY FEBRUARY 7 The wall heater is still on cozy, but the sun is now coming in our east-facing windows, our only windows. Yesterday we did a bit more of a walk about the town than we planned, but an honest to goodness ice cream cone revived us enough to shop and carry home a roasted chicken, beer, and milk; potatoes, broccoli, and fruit; and the omnipresent paper towels.

We had wondered what "room serviced daily" might mean. Well, about eleven in bustled two women with little carryalls of cleaning supplies: they replaced all our towels, emptied the trash, and wiped down the stainless steel kitchen counters and shower. Will there be a day for linens? Carpet sweeping? I'm not complaining.

FRIDAY FEBRUARY 8 We had arrived in Nelson Tuesday evening in time to see Hardy Street and eat; Wednesday and Thursday have passed in making a leisurely acquaintance with Trafalgar Square, Cathedral Hill, and a glimpse of the riverside. Unlike Dunedin where we simply marveled at change: at sun and warm, flowers and sky, the explosive rush of the toilets and our hosts bringing sweet breads, we can now look beyond and compare this residence and atmosphere with that. And of course, our energy is not compromised by the enormity of our US to NZ flights, only a few days of change and bus sitting. I think we can now adjust to two-week stays instead of a month, if that allows enough uptime to see the unusual and enough downtime to polish toenails, do the laundry, browse for a new used book, read the daily paper in bed with coffee, and enjoy slow talk.

Even now, although our first week has passed—today is the

farmer's market from four to seven and tomorrow the arts and crafts fair in Trafalgar Square—we, having learned our personal rhythm of travel, have no plans yet for exploring Abel Tasman and Golden Bays.

Yesterday we found a new Internet café. We need to see if Jenny has sent a report on Schoodic who, on his visit for removal of stitches, was found to have a mild infection. Also, plans are not firm for March. A friend told us, "Your travels will succeed if you can easily adapt to Plan B." Adaptability is easier now because we can envision different situations with more certainty and compromise with equanimity. Our one-and two-night stays helped with this, as did the reality of unforeseen natural wonders and experiences that so easily replaced the charm of the familiar. I guess that is what adventuring is all about.

Here at the Admiral's Motor Inn, the computer faces a painted concrete wall; the open slider behind me has ushered in bright morning air to dissipate the coolness of night, the cicada's song and the rushing whine of Friday traffic. The traveler's trade-offs.

SATURDAY FEBRUARY 9 I want to write June as the month: this morning feels like a Portsmouth summer weekend. And we are setting off on a not dissimilar errand: a farmer's market.

The one we went to yesterday involved a long walk, a cab home. Good veggie buys and for dinner a to-die-for plate of smoked salmon ravioli that had to be carried across the road to the Founders Beer Garden—no food served there on Fridays—where lines of locals ordered giant mugs of powerful ales, and drank and reordered. What fun. This morning's in-town market is "world renowned" for its arts and crafts. We'll see what we find.

SUNDAY FEBRUARY 10 To my mind the reputation of yesterday's market is much overstated. Actually, I liked the Dunedin one better, more excitement, more variety, although I did find a sweater for Bett. A young woman, who emigrated six years ago from Germany, raised the sheep, sheared their gray, or brown, or off-white, or black wool, carded and spun it—then knit the sweater. It still has the lanolin and is heavy and snuggly—just what Bett wants. I said it was too big, and the woman—slight like Bett—modeled it. Perfect fit. I walked away from the $200 price and then came back and said, "I have to have it." The woman hugged me and we giggled together. I will mail it soon, while it is still so cold in New Hampshire.

Last evening the weather woman told us today would be "...

soaking rain from six to two," adding, "a good morning to lie in." We obeyed, eating shortbread and a huge peach from the Friday market and studying local maps. Once we understood the Abel Tasman Park layout, we wondered whether to stay here for a third week or try for a place up there.

Dinner will be lamb leg chops, corn on the cob, and a salad of goodies from the Friday market.

MONDAY FEBRUARY 11 When I used the ATM Saturday I was amazed to see how much money remains in my checking account, and I haven't even switched my $500 from savings in. Is it not having a car? Nor those monthly winter utility bills? We have used a couple of taxis and pay Internet fees that average $5 a day, but that's it. Should we be splurging on accommodations? Or at least loosening up a bit? Be a shame to get home and find out we didn't take advantage of some things we could have afforded: like Waiheke Island.

In a used book store I told the shop fellow (bloke?) that I wanted something by a New Zealand author and set here. He gave me Peter Wells's *Lucky Bastard*, a 2007 paperback for $15, originally $28. I knew that books were expensive here and had brought some used ones ordered on the internet at home, but this personal contact way is better. And I never would have found, for example, Kelly Ana Morley's dark but excellent *On An Island With Dire Circumstances* about young contemporary women, Maori and white.

Geraldine, for one, thought I spent much too much time journal writing and reading when I could be out doing. I consider reading and contemplating essential to understanding.

TUESDAY FEBRUARY 12 I can't believe it. The Auckland agent, Sarah, that I've been online with for Waiheke rentals, agreed that the studio was too out of the way and too small for a long visit. She suggested two other detached places: one a restored bach—short for bachelor, aka guy, place—and the other a renovated house. Both in the village and with hefty discounts for long stays. Yeah, yeah, yeah, I'm thinking and hit the availability box. Both were available all of March. Incredible.

We studied all the features: the bach is fine; the house superior. Where were these places when we were looking and looking? Was Sarah holding them back for the "right" tenants? I replied that we would like figures for a month's rental and if we couldn't afford the house, we'd take the bach. I just can't believe it.

We had been ready to ask about staying here another week, but now plans for a boat trip to Abel Tasman Park are in the works for tomorrow. Rain is predicted to set in Thursday.

Also, we need to sit down and decide where we want to go on the North Island so we can find accommodations for ten days.

The women Linda and Bev (pronounced Beev here) will be in to do a big servicing job in about an hour, so we may take our computer down to McDonald's and see if we can do our banking.

The sun has come out, the traffic is zipping; Sandy, having finished her social hour with the family who owns this place, is now hanging out the wash.

THURSDAY FEBRUARY 14 E-mail from Barbara we read yesterday:

Schoodie had a check-up yesterday, Mon, and he has come along so well, he came home without his Elizabethan collar... [Put on to keep him from worrying his surgery stitches] *Jenny thought it was time for him to start cleaning himself again. Well, to my surprise, he had decided to remove his feeding tube last night, with all his cleaning and preening! So he had another visit today to have the feeding tube put back in place. (It is the easiest way to give him his meds.) Except that, he had been doing great, and he seems to like some prescription crunchies very much.*

First power outage ... Next snow, tomorrow ... I've gotten a wicked bad cold ...

Of course, we need a final sign off from Jenny as to his present and future, but that is niggling compared to the weight we have been carrying.

The Abel Tasman National Park trip was accomplished in fine style yesterday. Sandy, a veteran hiker, has been scheming over the best way to do this: go out by bus and stay overnight? Go halfway by bus and then by water taxi? If we were kayaking people we might have chosen that mode, and if twenty years younger probably would have been tenting. At seventy-five and sixty-seven we chose the cruise boat—capacity twenty-five—where, along with the rest of the above sixty group, we sped seventeen kilometers across the Tasman Bay and then bobbed in and out of the tropical green coves of that tall-hill coast of gold sands, granite and basalt caves, and rocky pop-ups. We landed at Awaroa Lodge at the northern point of the park and immediately made for the trailhead. Sandy, who had originally thought of doing the entire walk, about eight hours at Kiwi speed, had settled for a small section, the Sky Walk that circled in back of the lodge. The woman at reception said, "Nice walk, about forty minutes. Bit of an up at the beginning, but the views are worth it."

The bit of an up—an almost vertical path carved into tall steps— would have stymied anyone not trained on London Street in Dunedin. However, lunch on a bench overlooking a bay of breathtaking beauty put punch back in my legs and we gained the top. The rest of the hike, filled with deep bush and bird song, took an hour and a half and ended on the deck of Awaron, a determined to be international upscale lodge. We people watched, grateful for the mostly ice lemonades clutched in our sweaty hands. No time on the beach to even test a toe in the water, but right up the gangway to power down the coast and across the bay through "a bit of a roll." At least it was not "lumpy," as our taxi driver said that sea could be. Ah, the land of the softened modifier.

Still in fine fettle we walked the riverside path to town with a California-no-accent American woman. A "mountaineer for decades" was how she described herself: she and her husband, "into our sixties now," had just come off bushwhacking where the forest had proved to be "unexpectedly dense" and powerful rivers ran chest high. She said that on one crossing "I fell and hurt my coccyx, but haven't been to a doctor yet. My husband says we're just out of shape, but to me it's getting older and …" I restrained an emphatic, judgmental nod.

SUNDAY FEBRUARY 17 Slider open to sun, cicadas, speeding tires. After a brunch of eating up the camp food—fried egg on top of fresh green beans on top of toast—we will be off for walk, botanical gardens, museum, and Internet: hoping for a response from a B&B in Napier, the city rebuilt in art deco after a leveling earthquake. We gave up on a stay in Wellington because that is the opening weekend of their music festival—which I discovered by accident in a new brochure. There'll be no bargains there.

The huge impediment has been Waiheke Island. After we informed so-called agent Sarah that we would take the bigger house, she dropped off-line. Every day we went to town prepared to deposit $3,000 in Holiday Homes Ltd. Account and found no message. Thursday I sent a Heywhatsup, but no reply on Friday. I called their Auckland office from our room phone—too late: office closed from 4 p.m. until 9 am Monday. I was ripped and began to wonder if Sarah was indeed an agent or if someone had a scam going. It had seemed too good to be true that two cottages would still be completely free during March, and now our hopes for a pure month of island living are dashed. But we know there are many beautiful options out there, it's mostly that we had such expectations. I guess that's what fuels inflexibility and perhaps rashness. Perhaps the loss of $3000.

On Monday at nine the first call I'll make is to Holiday Homes to see if the mess can be straightened out; next alternative is a call to the visitor center on Waiheke to see if they have a person who handles such situations; third is dialing a travel agency whose business card I picked up in town yesterday. I have no experience of that kind and spent some time puzzling over the money angle before thought dissolved into watching a movie on Sky TV. I wonder if engaging a travel agent for South Africa might be a good idea. I know they steer a client to those who give them   the   best commission, resulting in higher costs, but perhaps for Africa, time and money well spent.

A price war is occurring among in-country airlines here, so we also have the option of getting anywhere for between $60 and S100. The backpacker's bus fare for the two-hour ride to Picton Tuesday will be $24 apiece, that plus accommodations, plus ferry, would make the plane fare cheaper. We would miss, however, the thrill of steep hills, marvelous scenery, and the driver's commentary, miss exploring   Picton   and   the   gorgeous   four-hour   trip   out   of Marlborough Sound and across Cook Straight.

MONDAY FEBRUARY 18 No success on calls to Waiheke. Reread printed copies of Sarah's e-mail; she certainly sounded legitimate.

Nelson has proved to be an eat-out delight. We expanded Dunedin teas to lunches and a great Turkish kebab take-away last evening—will try a new Thai place tonight. The most memorable lunch was the Boat Shed at the end of a long walk past shipping terminals and some elegant apartments. It was worth the exertion: a truly elegant-casual deck with an expansive view of harbor and sky. Our inspiration had been hearing of green-lipped mussels and we were more than satisfied. Each platter must have held three dozen of the plump, succulent verdant-shelled goodies steamed in wine and garlic with homemade garlic bread; eat as we would, we still took home a dozen and a half. They are farmed here, started far out in the harbor and then brought in to mature.

With a fish pate starter and a wine for Sandy, the bill came to $67. And on the way out I purchased two choker-style paua necklaces, made by the chef's wife with attention to detail and different from any I have seen.

Have been clocking eight to nine hours of good sleep and now we cast ourselves to the fates of the rented bed for forty more days.

Ah well ...

TUESDAY FEBRUARY 19 It is almost 9 a.m. and the heat of day is just beginning to sear through the east windows. We are packed, Sandy has gone to reception to take care of yesterday's phone bills. We are heading for the B&B in Napier out on the east coast, but Waiheke remains if and when. Feelings of both inertia and excitement about new places swirl the air: pleasant memories of Nelson and wonderings about ten or so days of skidding from place to place. Must shed the soft nightie and press myself into bra and waistband.

SATURDAY FEBRUARY 23 *Napier*

On the high-perched deck of The Green House on the Hill. A phone call netted us the only three days open until mid-March in this *Rough Guide* recommended spot.

Napier is a busy little city with on-going England/New Zealand cricket matches. Tomorrow is their Long Lunch, which I believe is the day they set picnic tables on the beach in a long line and people pay $30 apiece, I think, to eat while the locals walk by and watch them. At least that is the impression that Ruth, our host here, gave yesterday as she drove us out to another local eating adventure: the Mission Winery lunch.

The day was fine with strong southerlies that occasionally shook the huge canvas umbrellas into sails. The napkins and waitresses came in black and many of the customers had *dressed*. Women, that is. The men, Kiwi and tourist and retiree, all wore shorts—as do uniformed schoolboys. I'm sure the gathering on the vast green lawn and under the grape arbor sheltered patio was quite international, from the very British maitre d' to the pushy folks who railed at him to give them a table in spite of full reservations and a wedding at four. I ordered prawn and Sandy ostrich steaks, which came rare and very tasty: my prawn were sweet and well-dressed—ladies, I guess. Anyway, we shared an excellent chocolate dessert. A memorable meal like the Boat Shed mussels, Le Cafe rack of lamb in Picton, and Beach Front Hotel in Hokitika. All combinations of marvelous food and extraordinary ambiance: the busy harbor, the peaceful harbor, the crashing Tasman Sea, now the vineyards accompanied by the ever-present marvel of the awesome trees and the sky.

This deck looks out over tall treetops and white slanted roofs, the far edge is a blur of a misty green Hawkes Bay, fringed with thick dirtysnowwhite clouds. Sheets, pure white, on the high-altitude laundry rack are occasionally whipped about by an uneasy breeze. A storm slid over Auckland last night and is now moving down the west coast of the South Island. According to the cab driver who brought us back from the winery yesterday this eastward bulge that forms Hawkes Bay is spared most of these systems

Our expectation of a month at Waiheke Island has dwindled to the week after Easter—our last. But we had great good luck this morning at the breakfast table when I told Ruth that our hopes for a beach cottage in Gisborne, a few hours northeast, had come to naught. She scurried—her usual pace—for a book, *Charming Places To Stay*, whipped it open to Gisborne and a B&B right on the beach, dialed the number, and handed the phone to me. I asked Anabelle Reynolds if she had space tomorrow; she said yes and would meet the bus. So there we are, for one night or more, we are not sure; there is a place to eat nearby. That is another constraint of bus touring, we have to be able to walk to restaurants; a more isolated B&B farther up the coast offers meals, but would be pricey, I fear. But who knows, the possibility of B&Bs somewhat expands our options from self-contained cottages and motels, which of course, necessitate a grocery store within walking distance.

The Picton Ferry Link Motel, which had no kitchen, was fine for a couple of nights, but was blasted by traffic. Not the continual rush of Nelson, or the silence-shattering sirens and helicopters of Dunedin, but the continuous day and night hurtle of double trucks heading for the ferry to North Island. The Green House has provided total quiet, not perfect as in Milbridge, but any motorized whining is easily overridden by cicadas and the faint scrape of oak leaves moved by the breeze. We knew cities and towns would be noisy, and indeed our winters in Portsmouth have always had a background hum; but it was in Picton, where a moment of silence was painful with expectation, that I thought—enough. So here high above Napier we have had three peaceful days and nights, and the next B&B should provide the same.

Napier feels surfacey—without depth. Granted, we enjoyed the museum of the 1931 earthquake, the art deco buildings mode, similar to Santa Barbara, and an along-the-beachside look into the tents at the preparations for the simultaneous serving of four courses to six hundred people at the Long Lunch. Pure delight bubbled at the sight of a man trundling the most enormous barrel of Speight beer down the sidewalk on a handcart and women in 1930s garb swinging arm in arm toward that endless line of fluttering white tablecloths. We heard the dinner price is closer to $70 and that the guests dance on the lawns between courses.

Perhaps if we had walked farther or had a car, Napier would have seemed less like a theme park where the wealthy flew in for an event and then flew out. As it was we ended up eating at a pizza spot two nights out of three because there was nothing else nearby. Tomorrow on to Gisborne.

MONDAY FEBRUARY 25 *Gisborne*

"… where the day begins." The sun rose—although its rays did not penetrate the heavy clouds to illuminate this harbor and town—setting in motion February 25's march across the globe.

Anabelle, as she drove us to the top of a tall hill on her host-introduction tour, affirmed that indeed on Jan 1, 2000, the beach below was where the Maori danced in the new millennium; a marvel that Sandy and I had rated Best In Show. So we are here, and I want to stay—two weeks at least. Feeling bone-tired is only one of the reasons, but certainly compelling. We have been careful not to stretch our reserves to the breaking point and thereby have maintained our health and eager enjoyment; it would be foolish to leave this place and put that in jeopardy.

Stowing the contents of our suitcases out of sight in this, the largest bedroom we have occupied since July 17 when we left the Portsmouth house for the last time, would be calming to both body and mind. Best Beach View Gisborne is not only spacious but luxurious, and a huge sky canopy vaults over both hilly pastures and white sweeping surf of the Pacific Ocean. I'm like a turtle poking its head out of its shell.

There are so many things right here that it would be flying in the face of a very generous fate not to stay—no matter the cost—for a generous dose of at home in paradise" time. I'm in love.

TUESDAY FEBRUARY 26 Both tall, narrow windows and the glass door to the shallow north balcony are open to the clear blast of day, and this cool room's white glare is surfeited with the omnipresent cicadas, occasional bird chirps, and the uneven but constant thrum of the Pacific on the long shallow sands. Like the curl of the waves, white, clean, and pure dominates this ample room: white over-the-top rose-sculpted bedside lamps, a thick deep-luxury duvet and triple pillows, and a white spread over an extra cot. Color blares or

soothes from art work varied in size and power; the mirror above
this desk is a handsome gold-framed antique, and the north wall
drapes are a satiny cool blue-green that meshes with the turquoise
marble of the bathroom and its see-through, circular shower.
Annabelle says she applied to be in the guide book *Charming Places
to Stay In New Zealand* and after sending photos was accepted: fees
were not mentioned.

The house—we are on the second floor—is in equally good taste,
but definitely a home laden with family photos and bookshelves,
rich rugs and an air of ease granted by ancestors who had a
comfortable living. Annabelle described herself as a farm girl, but
the image of a rough sheep station disappeared with talk of horses,
of riding to hounds. I should keep in mind that her upbringing
parallels my grandparents in an era when wealth still resided in
land. Not only do volcanoes and earthquakes—the latest large one
here happened two months ago—but lifestyles shout: We are young!

Gradually the effects of what I am sure is water-induced diarrhea
is wearing off; and in an effort to keep it at bay we are picking up
liters of bottled water that Anabelle has agreed to use for coffee and
we for tea in our room. As befits a British Commonwealth land
every room everywhere has had a plug-in water heater for coffee or
tea. Upon arriving at a motel the question asked a guest is "thick or
thin?" or "red or blue?" which eventually an American understands
as, cream or milk?

Our relationship with Anabelle shifted last evening as we sat on
cozy leather furniture in her office-study. "How long can you stand
having us here?" I called as she crossed the threshold, tea in hand.
Startled, she scrambled to recover: "Why, forever."

We had gotten a favorable reply from Flower Haven in Waipu for
the eleventh to the twentieth, so I responded, "Two weeks?"

"Two weeks? Won't you get bored with it?"

With laughs and good-humored quips, the three of us established
ground rules for our fourteen-day partnership. One hundred and
twenty dollars a day—our top-end limit; a daily ride to town and
back every day for lunch and a take-home supper; use of the
washing machine and computer to check e-mails. To search for our
in-between travel accommodations and that impossible Easter
weekend, we'll use the quiet Internet spot we found in town
yesterday.

Our early afternoon walkabout there had pleased us. Thirty to
forty thousand people of a good variety, without the big-time tourist
emphasis of Nelson, but with enough quality stores, restaurants,

cafes to keep us happy. Add to that the ocean. And the beach. And the pure sky and air. And the quiet. The night clouds and moon. The gardens. The New Zealand we have not yet enjoyed. I am very happy to be stopped—right here.

I have come to believe most travels are organized around what to see; key to our wintering-over is where we are living. Instead of point to point: museum, art gallery, mountain café, waterfall with wildlife, our emphasis is the room, the view, the environs.

THURSDAY FEBRUARY 28 If I had to choose a city to rent in for three months, I think it would be Gisborne, a town we only vaguely remembered from news reports of December's earthquake. Its discovery is an accident of planning failure; a Plan B richer than Plan A. Or at least so we believe now.

My children would smile and say, "Well, Mom, you always did look for the tent site perched at the end of the park." City of First Light is emblazoned in circular bronze plaques in the sidewalks. Actually the East Cape is farther out, but seems uninhabited.

Three rivers join the sea here and care has been taken to keep them clear of the commercial and tidy-green with parks of great trees. Although, in truth, all New Zealand towns seem to glory in their magnificent trees.

Yesterday at the museum lunch room Sandy ordered a fresh fruit drink she had heard about, and the waitress told her it is not ripe yet. "It is a winter fruit." Hmm. Fruit ripening in winter instead of, as our New Hampshire banker wrote yesterday, "… the eleventh billion snowstorm." Gives one pause. But, then, isn't this the same as California coast living? My guess is no, but I say this out of ignorance passing as wisdom. Certainly here there is no huge center of population just over the hill forcing a pseudo-reality on the town. The show horse that single-foots along the beach each evening comes from the high pasture rising on the other side of this mostly one-street-deep development that grew one house at a time out of a string of bachs. Anabelle said noisy yellow-eyed penguins used to roost under this place which was once Anabelle's father's bach, his getaway from the farm. Additions were made without any architect's design of what a beach house should be. The room we are in, Sandy has noted, does not have a single ninety degree angle corner. Two hundred years ago the Pacific US was probably like this.

Anabelle is late getting to her church fair—scones are still in the oven—so we will be going to town a bit earlier than usual. Although, come to think of it, we went at 10:30 yesterday. Last night she returned from tennis with her son to find an Asian couple with a surfboard hoping for a room and so has had to deal with setting that room to rights — it is a studio underneath our bedroom and Annabelle's — after cooking a full breakfast for them. Not a relaxed lifestyle.

SATURDAY MARCH 1 My mother's birth date. Woke rested at 6:04 — first time since we arrived — and got some photos of sunrise. At last my upset from the water seems beaten back and zest has flowed in. Although the hour I spent under the sheet napping after my late afternoon shower yesterday might play a part too. We'd had a strenuous day.

Anabelle drove us to the National Arboretum a half hour into the hills, but not as far as the farm where she grew up and later raised her children. Sandy and I walked — sometimes on "quite a bit of up" — for three hours, glorying in the presence of leafy wind, giants of bark and limbs and strength, and from the heights miles of the brown emptiness of former pastures and far mountains. We ate power bars, split an apple, and felt quite content, exhilarated by achievement. Anabelle picked us up in her little yellow car and sped along the winding, narrow back roads to return us to this cool, dim room and our tea. The day was capped by a good meal at the Tsunami Restaurant and a ten-minute walk home in soft twilight; at midnight I stepped onto the balcony where abundant stars overrode the waning moon.

The story Anabelle told us yesterday as she drove through pastureland of cows and sheep drew us deeper into this place. Her grandparents had bought a second farm and built a comfortable house, but when the Depression of the 1930s hit they couldn't keep up the payments and were forced back to the old one. There the necessity of crossing a swaying bridge over the river was not to the liking of the man's newish wife, and off she went to Christchurch. Anabelle's father, an adventurous boy, thought the hinterland quite a fun place. He stayed to raise his family, and as was the custom among farm families, Anabelle's brothers were off to boarding school at nine, and she at eleven. Farm life agreed with Anabelle, and she came back from her OE — overseas experience — and married a farmer; by twenty-seven she had borne three children and her husband, Guy, had developed a brain tumor. He immediately had a vasectomy, but after six years of remission, had it reversed; Anabelle to her great joy became pregnant. However, as the fetus grew, so did Guy's tumor. When Anabelle delivered, Guy was in a room down the hall. They had one week together as a family in hospital and another at home before Guy died. That son, now at university, was the much loved center of their family, and Anabelle stayed on raising steers and sheep for thirteen more years.

On a farm, Anabelle told us, you think constantly about the weather, and until she found a good manager, there were some rocky times. "But on the farm, I never had to wonder what to do with the boys. There was always something. The pool if it was hot."

SUNDAY MARCH 2   Breakfast on the lawn in spite of low haze and a quick sticky breeze. Overnight guests from the southwest of England had already tucked into bacon and eggs, and we rapidly progressed from where have you beens and where are you goings into setting the world on the right course. Took two hours; Anabelle was off to church.

A strong line of blue is stalled in the west, but a walk is promised for afternoon. Not our usual private, quiet Sunday morning; my head is a bit full of talk-noise.

Last night was also different: we got into Saturday night dinner clothes–long purple skirt for me and white pants and black top for Sandy—and Anabelle drove us to Fettuccine Brothers. Delightful ambiance and food and, although I felt a bit stagy, it will be an evening to remember. Particularly when we convinced Anabelle, when she arrived to pick us up, in join us for dessert in spite of her boot-slippers.

Sandy just came upstairs after calling for the last bit of bus information to complete our days until we settle on the ferry to Waiheke Island for our last week. So, this long phase of Internet quests is over; a relief, but satisfaction that it turned out so well. Certainly this B&B is proof of spontaneity being superior. Would we do it differently? That may be a topic on some distant day: now is the time for living in the moment.

No aches from the exertions of Friday, but stomach still a bit irregular. I could hit the bed for a nap with no trouble, in spite of a solid eight hours sleep; perhaps it is the humidity or simply the ease and quiet of the moment. A green tea—which I haven't had for a week or more—seems in order.

MONDAY MARCH 3   With Anabelle's help we are staying fit: yesterday a tall walk—many, many steps—up a hill across the cove, where we could look back to the dot of our B&B. The same view as the large painting in our room. I exclaimed over the cracked glaze finish, asked Anabelle who the artist was where we might see more of her work.. Before we were finished breakfast she had called down the road to John, the artist's husband. However, none hanging in their garden gallery included the subtropical vegetation that makes this country so different. "Talk with Chris about a commission," John advised. With prices of $250 to $1,500, it is worth investigating.

This morning I leaned over the waist-high, clear plastic wind shields on the front lawn, looked skyward, and slowly turned almost 360 degrees. Against a backdrop of myriad shapes and colors the powerful clouds seemed to be reenacting what lay beneath the sea, the slide of the Pacific plate under the Australian, the spreading and thinning of the earth's crust, the 14,000 earthquakes recorded in New Zealand each year. The raw power of this land.

LATER At tea on the lawn this afternoon Annabelle talked more about the farm where she raised her four sons. Contrary to my impression of a lone, small house isolated in the hills, it had been a bustling place with a house for chooks (chickens), other sheds for wool, shelter for the cows, a barn for hay, a huge flower garden with three hundred roses, a pool, a tennis court. The manager and his schoolteacher wife lived in another house near the road.

"There were other houses—we had a nice little road," she said. "One as close as that Norfolk Pine, perhaps a hundred yards away." She asked if we would like to go into the country to the place where she grew up. Yes! Then she teased Sandy about not taking wimps who got carsick on narrow, winding roads. "What an adventure that will be," she said. "We'll take a picnic."

She has never had guests for two weeks before and so we are all on new footing.

TUESDAY MARCH 4 White caps rush and break against the long stretch of high tide foreshore, a continual wild, wet sound; on land, heavy-topped, vertical-limbed trees heave and ho in the strong east wind; palm tree fronds wave frantically. We were further integrated into the household and neighborhood by breakfasting in the elegant dining room and visiting a near neighbor, Mary, who was a friend of Annabelle's mother. We knew the mother was a ranking golfer, but her habit of chipping balls over into Mary's yard added a smile inducing insight into New Zealand women.

THURSDAY MARCH 6 Yesterday was another one of changeable weather. I opened my eyes at six: a strip of acrylic blue paint lay between dark hills and a soft gray-pink sky dome. I dozed and woke to solid gray with the waves sliding like meringue across a giant platter. At night stars had swarmed over the roof and I stayed outside for a few minutes, my bare feet cool on the damp boards of the balcony. I am trying to hold everything with all my senses, absorb where we are here on this Pacific island so distant from what is familiar as home. Afraid, perhaps, that the totality will, like the weather, shift to something else, shrinking these moments into mere photographs, visuals.

Probably my waking today imagining a painter's brushstroke across the hills foreshadowed our evening meeting with the artist, Cris Morrell. The top floor of her house is almost 360 degree windows: sunrise on the Pacific, sunset over the conical hills. We sat on tall stools around a small, circular plastic table and discussed the painting we want. The predilection toward bare feet—due perhaps to Maori tradition, or simply the climate—dictates shoes left by the door, so under the table six feet, some toes polished, some not, almost touched.

FRIDAY MARCH 7 The hills are alive—literally—with green. Instead of parched brown sheets, they are a rumbled bed of life. Just the right rain at the right time, says farmer Anabelle. And the right day for going back into the hills where she grew up. Yesterday, driving home, she had asked, "What kind of pie do you want for our picnic?" Sandy's tentative reply, "Apple is always good," was met with a derisive snort. Realizing that we were in unknown cultural waters, I swam to shore with a neutral: "Give us some choices." "Well, there's a breakfast pie with bacon and eggs. Mashed potatoes—that's more of a picnic pie." "Sounds wonderful," I said quickly.

So it is 9:30: the crust is out of the oven and the filling of mashed potatoes, corn, and goodness knows what else has been poured in. We leave at 10:30. Anabelle is always decisive and prompt. We do what we are told.

Mary visited me in the yard yesterday as I was sunning after a brisk ocean dip. What she told me about her life on an East Cape farm I could have read in a book, a history or a novel, but being here with Mary's blue eyes looking at me created a minimovie—with me as a character—that will be stored in my brain that way. Given a prompt I will be able to see her lean forward, forearms on the checkered skirt that fell over her spread knees, saying, "I loved it," in answer to my question "Did you like it on the farm?" And after twenty minutes or so of telling me details about neighbors and sheep and unspun Maori jerseys worn for so long that chest hair grew through it, she clapped her hands on her knees and stood, saying, "That's the way it is. Things change. Do you like apples?" and handed me a brown bag full.

SATURDAY MARCH 8 This morning tall and slim, bright red beads around her elegant neck, Anabelle said: "I am glad you are seeing us at our best. This is our best."

She was referring to the weather: the clarity, the temperature, the sea seemingly at rest, rolling in lazy bumps, a sonorous easy melody. "The sky. The perfect blue." Indeed. A Garden of Eden day in a paradise without snakes, for millennium without mammals of any kind: a fearless state? Or was there always the shadow of eagle wings?

LATER We traveled through the skinned hills of the vast sheep farms one thousand feet above sea level. Anabelle pointed to an amazing house and the sharp slopes surrounding it. "My brother cleared all that of brush," she told us. He would drive his truck to the top and let loose a mammoth roller filled with water; it would crash downward, crushing small trees and scrubs in its path. The truck's motor powered a winch that would haul it back up, he'd let it go to crack down again, up and down, day after day. The towering piles of brush would then be set on fire. Pumice and ash for fertilizer. English seed for grass. Green pastures. Sheep and lambs and bulls and cows. A typical station with a large house for the pakeha (Europeans), very small ones for Maori shepherds.

Our journey ended on a crest that overlooked the family house and outbuildings. Anabelle pointed out the cut through the hills where she rode her black horse, Flicka, the two kilometers to school, winter and summer. "He and I were the horse people," she said speaking of her father. Her mother, a national champion, designed their golf course—the first hole over their bridge that spanned the river; it is still in use. Once off at boarding school at age eleven, Anabelle would return only three times a year for holidays.

On the highest knoll, a riot of tall white Bella Donna lilies waved against a sky blown free of clouds; three crosses—one for her mother and father; one for each shepherd, completed a living Easter card.

SUNDAY MARCH 9 Last evening Anabelle drove us to an upscale farm where what might be called a Maori/Christian event took place at the top of a high hill that was once a pa, a watch place of a local tribe. We tourists, led by a guide from the lodge, climbed the route an enemy might have climbed, vertically through what has evolved from thick brush to pasture, to new plantings by a more ecologically minded pakeha. At the top we were greeted—challenged—by men in traditional Maori garb who danced with aggressive male cries and movements in defense of their area of trenches and palisades. Once accepted as friends we all rubbed noses—interesting sensation. Just as the sun set a chorus of women in white raised their voices in haunting, ancient songs against a backdrop of color-bursting sky and the vast valley.

Cups of punch and crackers were passed, and my mind drifted to how we would get down. Retracing our steps would mean disaster for a number of our older, mostly Brit party: there must be a gentle track behind the singers. When, however, the singers passed out a single white glove, saying it was "for the rope going down," I imagined several quite wild scenarios; Kiwi standards of safety sometimes defy rationality. The pitch was very steep, the footing rough, the dry grass slippery. The young Maori performers skipped along on their tough bare feet, apparently oblivious to the terror of out-of-condition flatlanders.

LATER. E-mail from Barbara. Schoodic, after passing his Wellness check Monday, had to go back with a urinary problem on Friday. Jenny decided to keep him overnight again. Barbara tried to call late that day, but the office was closed, so she had no further news to send us. She said she had finger, toes, everything she could think of crossed for him. Does not sound good.

We hope for news before we leave at noon tomorrow. Our treasured boy.

THURSDAY MARCH 13 *Hick's Bay, East Cape*
We did leave without any word; an added gap between our personal selves and our travel selves: the ache and the eagerness already engendered by leaving not only a place that has won our hearts, but a person too. Similar to parting with Geraldine and Ross and the roots we had put down in that town, with the added tug of luxurious lifestyle. From eating out a couple of times a year to fifteen days in a row, is a fundamental change.

Schoodic, too, was much on our minds as we rode the courier van up and down the East Cape road—330 km around the entire cape, but we could not deny the excitement of being in Maori land. Not that we saw more Maoris than in Gisborne. There is hardly anyone to see except in a couple of towns where our van scuttled among small houses, delivering parcels. This once-a-day delivery and passenger transport was listed in *Rough Guide*, but one has to be on the spot to appreciate its hit or miss nature.

The omnipresent shorn hills of colonial Britons melded into greener, longer grass that obscured winding sheep paths; then trees thickened the valleys and river sides, eventually connecting those heavy green clumps and lines into a solid mass of native bush.

The botanical park had introduced us to the names and uses of a number of trees. The one to two hundred foot tall rimu pine was used for timber, and its charcoal mixed with oil was rubbed into tattoo incisions. The totara, which usually lives for a thousand years, was for war canoes and its bark for baskets. Many trees flower and produce eatable berries; the tawa, a forest shade tree, for example. Underneath the high canopy are countless tree ferns, including the internationally known symbol of New Zealand, the ponga, whose fronds are silver-white underneath.

Going into this bush of the East Cape and surviving there as the Maori once did is still a fantasy of restless males, as evidenced by Barry Krump's 1982 bestseller *Wild Pork and Watercress*. Today some Maori hope tourist dollars can be coaxed here and those once employed on farms like Annabelle's and Mary's can have jobs and a homeland.

We did not leave Gisborne until almost 2:00, when the driver finished picking up all his many parcels, and impending darkness and mounting gray rain clouds made every mile eastward, outward into the Pacific, more laden with mystery and the sense of barefoot, spear-carrying Maori gliding beneath those giant ferns and lofty trees, their heavily tattooed faces—now called moko art—peering from the shadows.

The courier van was what in my youth was called a rattletrap: old, unkempt, lunging ahead with gears grinding and body swaying. The driver's brother-in-law took over the wheel while the driver himself ate his lunch, and then spent the rest of the trip reading off addresses, dashing up to the doors of those who awaited everything from small packets to a washing machine and finally the cardboard carton of rib lamb chops roughly covered by a piece of white plastic that had sat beneath my feet for almost the entire trip.

But Sandy and I in the three-passenger bench seat were better off than the French college student and young Maori boy behind us on the smaller bench, hemmed in by the brother-in-law's ocean fishing gear and the traveler's own five-foot-tall pack.

For some reason there was no little carryall bouncing along behind us, so Sandy's and my considerable luggage and all the deliveries were squeezed in the far back, some to be unloaded and reloaded at every stop. Another carrier "bus" does the mail. The driver tooted as he passed his own house—his wife Polly is the owner of Polly's Courier Service—and unloaded us at Hick's Bay Motel, the only accommodation on the East Cape. We each paid him $40, an increase in fare of $5 to cover spiraling gas prices.

We barely had time to settle in our pine-paneled room and gasp at the enormity of the view--a wide yellow-green slice of coastal flat land and an endless darkening sea--before the dining room began serving. From the two choices, scallops in beer batter or roast lamb with vegetables, we picked the latter. A blue-haired tourist group of maybe fifteen sat at the view end and local forestry workers—some Maori—at the lounge/TV end.

Intense black silence enveloped our sleep.

FRIDAY MARCH 14 *Waipu Cove*
After a night in Auckland and a bus ride north, we once more woke to the roll of the sea. Not the curve of gold beach as at Wainui, but a flat bay—gray-white this morning—interrupted by sharp, sudden rocky prominences and a 180 degree sky. From our concrete veranda fuchsia blaze on either side of wide wooden steps leading to a strip of lawn and an eight- foot tall hedge of camellias which, now that summer is waning, will, our hosts said, burst into a mass of white, pink, red flowers. Delight envelopes me.

Schoodic is home to his "almost home" from the vet's again. There were no further clues to the cause of this latest plug, only the vagueness of "keep up his food and water intake." No question now that we will go straight home. We have met other travelers whose minds buzz with a variety of concerns for those left behind. For others it is the worry about those at home worrying about them. I do not feel that. Thank goodness.

I feel quite healthy this morning. Frankly, it was a relief to grab a bowl of cold cereal instead of sitting down to a rapturous B&B breakfast, because, although Anabelle offered muesli and milk, we could not resist the freshly cut local fruits and yogurt and breads or, frequently, her poached eggs and bacon. I became uncomfortable with constantly feeling full, never hungry, Convenience, not desire, set meal times.

Although Flower Haven is labeled a B&B in *Charming Places,* no food is offered, but a general store at the bottom of our five terraced gardens, one hundred and sixty-eight steps each way, is geared toward tourist tastes. Sandy has just returned with goodies in her pack, including two liters of water. I dare not try local again, although my most serious bathroom bout occurred in Auckland a half-hour before bus-time due to green-lipped mussels eaten   the night before in a most upscale Thai restaurant.

The Flower Haven house is three stories tall, and our ground floor feels quite spacious: efficient kitchen and clothes washing machine at one end of a dining and lounge room with two comfortable couches; two adequate-sized bedrooms and a new bathroom are down the hall. All rooms open to the east and the cove: the main one has a whole wall of window and slider, and the far bedroom a side door to the south and magnificent sloping pasture, complete with rich brown bull and young steer. This stay will be our northern experience: our most tropical. And it is the only place—outside of Dunedin—where a brief stay in '87 has drawn us back: I never quite got over the surf, the miles of long empty beach— it was early April then—and I gasped yesterday when the dark protuberances of the Hen and Chicks pricked the horizon. Our hosts were driving us home from Waipu, a village really, where we had spent three hours over lunch and seeing a fine settlement museum. In their twelve years of B&B keeping, we were the first to arrive by bus. Shirley remarked, "There, no need to go back there again," but seeing the advancement of new houses I felt Waipu was on the verge of an up scaling to where there would no longer be a need to park one's luggage in the mechanic's garage while sightseeing. Shirley with a sidelong glint of amusement asked if we had noticed that their last name was Flower. I laughed and replied, "Eventually. " "Well," she said, my maiden name was Leaf and I married a Flower." A compatible, New Zealand blending.

The days are still warm here and the nights comfortable: contentment will reign.

SATURDAY MARCH 15 Warm is the forecast: 20C (68F) for the next few days; Dunedin average looks to have been about 15C (60F) lately, so our plan of January there and March here is working well. Certainly we have never been sticky hot and yet still enjoyed what we call beach weather. I don't know when autumn, the Season of Winds, arrives here, but a fragrant breeze seems a constant presence. The rack of clothes dried in an hour.

I may stop back in that gift shop by the beach and—if it is made locally—purchase a stuffed skinny mum bunny clutching a wee baby bunny. For whom? The first great-grandchild? My daughter? Are thoughts of home sliding to the fore? Perhaps making the flight confirmation call yesterday stirred up Final Phase sensibilities.

MONDAY MARCH 17 It was after seven when the sun rose into a china blue sky above the pohutukawa trees at the bottom of the pasture; I imagined their bright red blossoms decorating the Christmas season. With our morning in-bed coffee—door open to the pasture, windows to the sea—we spoke of e-mails retrieved through Shirley's computer last evening: tulips emerging in Portsmouth... our friend Karen's strange flu ... no letter from Barb which must mean Schoodic is home and happy. Two weeks from today we will be heading back to all that. Sandy said flatly, "I don't want to go. Except for Schoodie." A sentiment I can't wholly share: family ties are too strong. "But," she added, "I wouldn't even know where I wanted to settle in New Zealand." That led to a ramble through the pros and cons of South Island, North Island, Dunedin, Auckland, mountains, beaches ...

Yesterday, our hosts—he is a retired Episcopalian minister— invited us to ride with them west across the island to a church do near the Kauri Museum, a place we had hoped to stay for Easter weekend. They dropped us at the museum at 9:30 after an hour's drive; every other farmhouse belonged to a relative. We were introduced to museum's life-like mannequins as Aunt Betty, Cousin Ed, and such, and on the drive back stopped in at Brian's brother's and had tea with living relatives whom we interrupted from peach canning.

The museum was as wonderful as the guide books had proclaimed. The great Kauri trees had fascinated us on our first visit; we'd even driven far north to worship, literally, at the base of one 2000-year-old titan. The museum wood we saw, some of it buried for 300,000 years in swamps, is strong and straight, and the heart unfolds in radiance reminiscent of "the heart of Jesus" business. Gum finding and collecting—either from living trees, or by digging into huge burial sites—was big business a hundred or so years ago. The tree's resin has been used in everything from varnishes to linoleum and in the present day as an art form: after scraping and sanding, a glorious clear gold substance emerges.

The North Island skinnies down here and the landscape is by far the gentlest we have seen. A pencil-thin "metal" gorge road, a short cut, did not have the hundred plus feet, certain-death drop-offs we have gasped at so many times before, but Brian and Shirley had once been scared out of their wits by rerouted highway traffic, first a logging truck and then a bus, careening around the bends at them. Of course, we are more accustomed to left side of the road driving and no guard rails now, but this landscape rolls instead of pitches, trees soften what in the south was especially harsh, parched grass and the sense of intruding into an alien world. Another sign that in this small patch of geography, fresh delights are ever just around the corner.

The longer we stay here, the more we think of these islands in Garden of Eden terms. Especially on a morning such as this when the rocky volcanic projectiles are shrouded in mist, the flat blue sea cut by a wide swath of sun twinkles, the breeze swaying the cinnamon-striped leaves of the flax, the pasture a sweet, luminous green. Nature converges into a benign harmony that, one would like to believe, is truly what a god would want for a dwelling place.

TUESDAY MARCH 18 After I wrote that yesterday, Sandy and I packed a picnic to take to a little cove off the main beach that Brian had told us about. Talk about entering the gates of heaven. Under the thick spreading limbs of Pohutukawa trees wound a shallow tidal stream, where later we would see a white faced shag and a gray heron fishing; I waded across barefoot. A narrow path led up a grassy hill and from the top we looked down on an empty beach, perhaps a hundred yards of curving seashell-filled sand, edged by black rock pushed up in uneven edges that caught the coming tide in pools and strands. The juxposition of such serenity and breath-catching beauty froze my feet. The wash of wind and wave were the only sounds as I gathered scallop shells to take home as ramekins. Did I feel fifty-five again? Yes.

Probably we would return there today—it is an under ten-minute walk—but Sandy has a stitch in her back which signals a strictly at-home day. Will I go down alone? Or will my fear of a slip and fall inhibit me? Fifty-five—no, seventy-five. Although yesterday when Sandy and I hung on to each other's hands and dunked in the warm water—the surf was not nearly as wild as that day in Wainui, then stretched on the bench of the picnic table, I felt like a child, perhaps a teenager, my skin—my soul?-- absorbing the delight of cool water and hot sun.

I have no sense that this is the last time I will ever do this or that. Perhaps if I had a terminal illness, or a partner who did, or I was eighty-five, I might. But not yet, not now, the future still stretches — like New Zealand — crowded with wonders.

WEDNESDAY MARCH 19 Nine-thirty. Brian was just here dropping off the *New Zealand Herald* for us to read and answering some extinct-bird questions I had. He left saying he would later today walk us through the gardens — all five terraces down and up the front — naming all the plants.

Brian, Anabelle, Geraldine, and Ross have given us invaluable insights into this country both past and present. We were their guests, their only concern at the moment, unlike motel folks, who, as friendly and helpful as those in Nelson were, must of necessity slide along on the surface. B&B hosts show their guests the best their region has to offer, but to me the insights into families and communities has been of priceless importance. Lack of a car to go spinning off on our own has certainly added depth to that aspect.

New Zealanders, being the friendly folk that they are, are perfectly willing to chat up visitors from other lands, so quick connections are easy to make. The young man at the general store here who has been to Boston, wondered how the Big Dig had turned out; our host serving breakfast at Hick's Bay had talked of loving Boston. Of course, people remember their visits of twenty years ago as vividly as we remember ours here: each contact brings the pleasure of a mini return visit.

Sometime during the night the wind burst out of the south, scattering our big scallop shells off the veranda into the garden, and the day continues windy and cool, quite autumnal. Must ask Brian if they change their clocks here: would it be fall forward or fall back?

THURSDAY MARCH 20 For the last couple of days I have noticed that I walk with a straighter, stronger body. Can anyone else see it? In Dunedin I began to notice curving calf muscle and now my thighs seemed to have acquired more muscle, arms too; no change in the tummy pouch, however. The tentativeness — elderness — that shocked me in December in Hampton is gone. If I had stayed there, I probably would have accepted it as okay, just a seventy-five-year-old body. Now, that's not acceptable, I don't want to accept it, I want — not a return to willowy youth — but to keep this feeling of condensed competence. But how?

Coming up from the store with bottles of water I noted the different steps from the beach road to our concrete veranda. First, forty-eight of wood covered with plastic matting, fairly shallow with railing; next, thirty-eight walking steps up a steep concrete ramp; twenty-three of horizontal lawn to our wooden gate; twenty-six of long-stride stone to stone up along the garden; twenty-three fairly steep wood covered with wire mesh; eleven shorts up the wide steps to the veranda. One hundred and forty six, not counting the horizontal ones. In Hampton Beach did the ever present paved, flat surfaces negate the unconscious calculations of adjustment I had to make at the cottage?

Last night after a fish dinner at the beach restaurant we climbed home empty-handed — the store had closed — and I was not even breathing hard at the top. Since it took three months to acquire this body, it may be gone in three months, leaving only the knowledge that the capacity is there. So?

I am glad we never set up any plans to phone anyone. It has been a relief to return to our quarters without any expectations of letters, or blinking phones, or notes from a host that so and so called. E-mail, at least so far, has allowed us to communicate without that split feeling of being two places at once.

For nine days Flower Haven has been just that, now off again tomorrow, Friday, for the City Central Hotel in Auckland, where we had spent a night on our way north. In one of those aha blinks we had realized that if all the locals were rushing to the countryside for their end-of-summer holidays, we would spend ours in their city.

EASTER SUNDAY MARCH 23   *Auckland*
The few extra dollars to upgrade from a standard to superior room garnered us a whole wall of windows for this tiny, basic but well-functioning room. At neither the sky-scraping, total-glass ASB bank, nor the church with the square granite bell tower is any Easter activity evident, although at six the full moon posed on one point of the tower turret.

The city is calm, almost empty. I consumed a huge brunch of eggs, sausage, toast on the tranquil balcony of the art gallery, high among leafy branches, singing birds. Instead of climbing up the long steps into Albert Park, we sat on a bench in the shade of the pohutukawa trees writing postcards, then another bench facing toward Queen Street and the Skytower. More entrancing than watching for plummeting city skydivers were the sparrows bathing in the gentle bounce of water falling and puddling on giant stones stacked sixty feet high.

LATER Another fine Auckland meal, this time the Dragon Boat: Chinese, with waiters in black bow ties and a well-dressed Asian clientele. Sandy ate pulled cold duck and pickled vegetables and me a huge plate—labeled "small"—of lemon battered chicken. Yesterday, was Brazilian fare at Wildfire on the Viaduct Wharf—prawns, sooo good—for a late lunch, and at seven, thin crust Spanish pizza.

This city of 1.2 million houses 31 percent of New Zealand's population, but is very manageable. We have walked our neighborhood from the university to the waterfront, and the nuggets of Wellesley, Victoria, Queen, and Vulcan Streets now have, day or night, the satisfaction of the familiar. It is simply a larger small town, sprouting tall buildings and a ground cover of international culture, as well it might. It has the largest Pacific Island population of any city in the world, and after adding other Asians and Maori and 50 percent pakeha, living here would send us homogenous northern New Englanders reeling—to our benefit, probably. And young! People our age are scarce, but then it's holiday time, so the legions of businessmen and women in black are missing.

TUESDAY MARCH 25 *Waiheke Island*
Feel rather unsettled, not lolling with pleasure as I have been in our other recent venues. I fear it is the onset of mental preparation for the big change: a week from today I'll wake in Natick, Massachusetts, a land barely touched by spring. If that's the case, relaxation in the moment may be hard to come by and our week here more a marking-time and gearing-up, than a Whee!

Certainly, transportation for this latest shift was swift and efficient and cheap. Seven dollars for a cab from hotel to ferry, fifteen dollars each for a thirty-five-minute ride packed with Kiwis still on holiday, and a cheerful pickup by our host, Sissel. She also performed an ultimate of service when, after I used her phone to call the ferry about my black Dunedin Library carry-bag which had been forgotten on the luggage rack and got no results, she unknown to us drove down, walked on board that ferry when it retuned on its next trip, and grabbed the bags thereby saving our purchases from the Kauri Museum and our chill bag containing my leftover chicken from the Boat Dragon. I hugged her.

Waiheke itself, though, is a bit of a letdown. I do not see the natural beauty that others raved about, nor the poshness implied with the raised eyebrows and, "Oh, Waiheke ..." Maybe, at last, we have seen the best and geography is on mute. And our accommodation is sorely lacking compared to Flower Haven. Sixty dollars did not cover the basics of water, milk, bread, and wine at the neighborhood store; the microwaved frozen lasagna was positively insipid. Our palates and senses are spoiled rotten.

WEDNESDAY MARCH 26 It is taking more effort this time to feel at home in our surroundings. We walked to the main town, Oneroa, yesterday and were delighted by how easily that half-hour went by, but the town itself discomforted us; over lunch we figured out why. Tourist is writ large over everything. But why should we scorn tourist? We are tourists and everywhere we have gone for three months has accommodated a large proportion of tourists. Do we not consider ourselves tourists anymore? Do we think we live here? Do even Waiheke islanders really live here? Over one thousand commute to Auckland to work every day.

Perhaps, over the last three months we have slid, unbeknownst, into thinking of ourselves as summer people? Self-righteously a bit superior to tourists. We do often identify ourselves to locals as "having been here a month, or "into our third month," thereby separating ourselves from those flying in and out for two weeks. Amazing how hierarchical we are, well, all living things are, I guess: if they don't establish a pecking order, we do it for them: oldest, biggest, most colorful, whatever. By even mentioning, "We've been here before," are we giving ourselves a one-up boost?

Our annoyances with Waiheke may signal that instead of embracing all things New Zealand as we did in Dunedin, we now quantify the best of this and of that. Time to go home? Well … We've heard of continuing snow piles and cold, and I did float in bliss this morning as I dried my hair in the sea-and flower-breeze and still strong sunlight. I will adjust my attitude to treasure every fleck of color and moment of warmth—as we did on first arriving.

THURSDAY MARCH 27 This summer's warmth was discussed in yesterday's *New Zealand Herald*. *It's been a great summer for beach lovers, a painful one for farmers … March has been warm enough to be classed as another month of summer; with a raft of anti-cyclones keeping the weather finer than usual … Water temperatures around the north of the north island had stayed above 20C. …. But rain is forecast for this weekend, probably Sunday and, following next month's anti-cyclone, it will be time for the brollies and beanies …* Kenring, who uses lunar cycles to predict weather, said yesterday that the first week in April would bring an icy blast across the country.

An icy blast is not a nation-wide blizzard; maybe some snow in high elevations—after all, the southern alps make this is an international ski resort—but the worst winter can achieve nationwide is frost. However, as Carol O'Biso notes in *First Light*, it is not the fifty degrees outside that produces goose bumps, but fifty degrees inside. Houses here are not made for winter as we in the northeast US know it: outside water pipes festoon houses, there is no central heat, no insulation, no electric heat in the slabs they sit on: the ground does not freeze. Winds from the south can be brutal to both house and garden, but the standard answer seems to be space heaters—even at outside cafes—duvets and electric blankets; jerseys and gum boots for winter gardening.

Yesterday, we took a bus from our hilltop to the ferry terminal and bought tickets for a one and a half hour bus tour of the eastern part of Waiheke Island, not the far east which has been left to rough roads, sheep, and vineyards. The bus driver did mention, however, that one huge winery out on the tip is planning a restaurant, conference center, and hotel; he sounded pleased about that. Well, to my mind, a paved road out to the end will literally spell the end of pastoral peace. Estate land near the ferry is being sold in twenty-acre sections for prices ranging from $300,000 to "millions and millions." Our tour driver added price tags to everything, including average house costs in each area: $300,000 was, I believe, the lowest. For those on the bus with dreams of island living, he lets them know that every house has its own cistern and septic system which Council—Auckland governs Waiheke—orders cleaned out every three years. Sandy piped up and asked what was done with that waste, and he answered that it was buried way out in the eastern section and it just "disappears." He did add that if the population were 20,000 instead of 8,500, a "proper system" would have to be installed.

We had the tour bus let us off at the Cable Bay Winery— electricity comes here from Auckland through an underwater cable—and as we walked toward the beautiful new winery building Sandy said she was starved. It was almost three and lunch had been sketchy, so I found the restaurant and asked if lunch was still being served. By the time Sandy arrived after photo-taking I was seated at a table for two beside an open wall and a view of the distant Auckland skyline, scattered islands, a hill of green pastures and vineyards and olive trees. White linen napkins were placed across our laps. My $11 glass of merlot was excellent, as were a half dozen rock oysters, $18. As we sipped and ate, a Scotch mist snuck in from the east, and the scene before us dissolved like a movie fade for probably twenty minutes and then returned in glittering blue and gold. Combining nature and food is definitely number one on our Favorite Pleasures list.

FRIDAY MARCH 28 Yesterday we decided to go around the point of land to the next cove via the rocks instead of the road. High tide at Auckland had been at noon, so we thought that by one it would be down enough for at least a try. We discovered that walking on the jagged edges of the rocks resembles a circus stunt without padding or helmet in case of a misstep, but we had our light hikers on and the grip felt safe. Some sort of final-days bravado led us on.

Eventually in order to continue we either had to go up or get wet: Sandy went up, I went down—to my knees. Around that corner we got well stuck by banging surf and waited fifteen minutes for the tide to go down. We kept thinking that each obstacle would be the last one and discovered it was Not, as Anabelle used to say. Not, not, not. When faced with a vertical wall Sandy put her teacher-of-rock-climbing self to work and her new knees took her to the top. Her report: it is not worth the risk to try to get down the other side to Palm Beach, our goal.

We returned unscathed to Sandy Cove and, puffed by our two-hour adventure, simply waded into the Pacific. Delicious, warm, and without the defeating surf of Wainui and Waipu. That all-over slide of tang and smooth will be one of my strongest memories of this trip.

This morning my body was a mass of protests. Get over it, I said gruffly.

SATURDAY MARCH 29 Am waiting until it is time to catch the bus heading over to the farmer's market and then another bus to the olive oil producing plant. Nothing is very far apart on this fifty kilometer long island. Overcast, so my raincoat, not windbreaker, will go in my black Dunedin carry bag.

Well. We are now cared for on the extreme edges of our journey. Sissel stopped by this morning and all is set for a ride down with our luggage to get on the 2 p.m. ferry Monday. And Monday night after a long journey east with the sun, a car with driver will be waiting to take us from Logan Airport to Natick. The latter a gift from "the children."

In Oneroa yesterday I got the e-mail from Bett and replied with flowery prose about the burden lifted from our minds. After Sandy had gotten an e-mail from Barbara that she had called Jim Roy about turning on the cottage water, I went back to check my site once more. About six new letters, one a Panic Time from Orbitz: There has been a significant change in your flights. How to call the US number? What options would there be? How to get back in touch about the car being ordered?

SUNDAY MARCH 30 A day we had dreaded; not necessarily because it was our last day in New Zealand — we had no idea how we would feel about leaving — but because the lengthy, cramped flight loomed. Tight tummy was eased, however, by a morning of warmth blowing in the slider, a sweet from the Saturday farmer's market with our coffee, and even a slice of sun to sit in as we watched little Casper the Ghost clouds bop along.

Friday's panic over the Orbitz e-mail had come out just fine with the assistance of the fellow in the Internet café lending us his mobile phone. Ah well, adventure can be defined as a project with an uncertain outcome.

MONDAY MARCH 31 I slept well last night, probably eight hours plus, so along with some stretching exercises, hydration, and the right clothes I feel prepared to thrust myself into this last phase. Being herded from pen to pen has its own anxieties though: if those giving the directions mumble, speak with an accent, or perhaps don't understand our question, landing in the wrong pen is far worse than merely standing bewildered.

Am I different? Will I look different to others? How can three months traveling in a foreign country not make changes? Perhaps when I get back on home ground I will find out what they are.

In the meantime, bon voyage …

TUESDAY APRIL 8 *Maine cottage* The ground is swollen with rough frost: most of the lattice boards around the foundation are blocked shut. Below freezing last night, but perhaps the warmth of today's sun will melt it down a bit.

Woke clearheaded and with a spot of "I'm where I love to be" in my chest. Jenny the vet called yesterday and said Schoodic had been one of the most difficult cases she'd ever had. She used the word "brave" for him and considering Barbara's description of how crippled he was during that first episode it is a wonder he lived. I'm back to believing he just couldn't cope with us leaving him, and Jenny said that if cats stop eating it is sometimes very difficult to get them started again. Plus a weight drop like his—three pounds—often damages the kidneys. I have told Sandy I will not leave him next week to go south; I fear that feelings of abandonment might yet tip him over the edge. He is still thin and Jenny wants us to monitor his food—at least a half cup a day. A full cup would be better.

WEDNESDAY APRIL 9 Ad-venture, to venture forth as far as New Zealand, makes this cottage and its environs familiar and small. Change stimulates, familiar comforts. Certainly we were deliciously spoiled for those few days at Kath and Brent's home.

The only bad was that my billfold had spilled out on the floor on the United flight from LA. Subsequent frustrating, no-resolution phone calls had an almost miraculous ending when three days later we found an overnight express envelope behind the screen door. Everything there but forty dollars cash.

Another facet of travel: the flaws of home can rise in sharp relief. The noisy, crowded harshness of the LA airport for example. But, as our Polynesian housekeeper at the Auckland hotel loved to say, "TV America so big!"

I e-mailed friends this morning, and under the photo of me sitting on Anabelle's lawn overlooking Wainui beach, I wrote "The golden years? You bet."

At UMaine I discovered that I loved being away, and now in my seventies New Zealand has taught me that I can travel far away and enjoy the changes, that my body will not only hold up, but grow stronger, that I am not old—yet.

MAY 26   *Maine cottage*

Finally worked up the expense sheet for our three months out of country, but found comparisons to past expenditures too difficult to figure accurately. The best I can say is that I've lost about $8,000 in teaching income and $4,000 (one-half) in summer rent from the Portsmouth house and seem to be doing all right on my $500 a month Social Security here in the cottage. Our CDs are averaging 5 percent.

The figures below are in US dollars—20 percent below the NZ dollar—and just my share. Traveling alone would have doubled the accommodations cost, but if we had rented a car instead of using the bus, in theory our transportation would have been cut in half. (Car rental is about $50 day and gas $6-7 a gallon.)

FINANCIAL SUMMARY

December 31-April 1 11 weeks; 93 days
Exchange rate: USD $1.00=NZ dollar $1.20

MBB share of expenses

Accommodations		$3000
Food: Grocery & Restaurants		$2550
Transportation		
Air	$2270	
Bus, taxi, ferry	$576	
Total		$2846
Miscellaneous		
Books	$260	
Museums etc.	$135	
Postage	$182	
Total		$577
Travel Insurance*		$36
Internet Use		$140
Pet Care*		$375
TOTAL		$9524

* American Express
** Not including $2000 vet bills, which was the only billing surprise of the trip.

Life is too full of variables to see how my choice to stretch, not hunker, will play out in the long run, but this first year has been spectacular.

Ross & Geraldine McLennon House, Dunedin

Dunedin hosts, Ross & Geraldine

Bobbie Burns' St. Paul's
Cathedral, Dunedin

Picton Harbor

Anabell Reynolds, host Wainui Beach

Street Music, Gisbourne

Tuatara, Southland Museum, Invercargill

Brian & Shirley Flowers, hosts Waipu Cove

Cable Bay Winery, Waiheke

SEEKING GOLD IN SOUTH AFRICA AND SPAIN

"...the stillness in this ancient continent, the echo of so much that has died away, the imminence of so much as yet unknown."
-- Peter Mattheiessen <u>The Tree Where Man Was Born</u> (1961)

"And so an endless spiral is created: the huntsman – the native with the poisoned arrow, the sportsman with the rifle – deliberately creates danger for himself by attacking the animals, and this danger, his created risk, then becomes the justification for his hunting."
— Alan Moorehead <u>No Room in the Ark</u> (1957)

"'Come quick, I've found his teeth!' .... I turned to look at Mary, and we almost cried with sheer joy ... we had discovered the world's earliest known human."
—L. S. B. Leakey National Geographic Magazine (1960)

Gold Museum, Cape Town

South Africa

WEDNESDAY JUNE 18 *Maine cottage*

I first read those introductory sentences in my mid-twenties, when my mind yearned for, but circumstances limited, more contact with the wide, wide world. Nature, or nurture, or time and place had imbued me with a sense of belonging to this larger sphere. With the desire to know more. See more.

I remember, although I was only four, a crowded Sunday dinner at our dining room table when my Uncle Glenn, home from the 1936 Berlin Olympics, spoke harshly of swastikas and a Herr Hitler to the suddenly subdued, frowning adults; the same relatives were gathered there on December 7, 1941. Pittsburgh became a city engulfed in war: radio broadcasts, newspaper stories, soot from mills, uniforms, rationing, air raid drills. The day after my high school graduation, our high-spirited softball game in the park was interrupted: South Korea had been invaded, our Army was going in. The boys wandered off to lean on cars, puff cigarettes. I studied history and government in college, then turned down a job at *National Geographic* and, like my peers, became enmeshed in the accepted although unarticulated goals of calming and repopulating America before the next war came. In the early '60s, I was thirty-one and my youngest was four; I began teaching social studies in a private school and earned a graduate degree in International Relations. In the early 70s I introduced a physical and cultural anthropology course for our juniors.

Now, I am seventy-six and going to Africa with Sandy. The impossible dream realized.

FRIDAY JUNE 20 My fascination with the mysteries of Africa, that strangest of all lands, simmered for years. A creased green travel folder grew fat with extreme adventures—a tent in gorilla land, a trek by horseback over marshlands, digging in the Olduvai Gorge. Now I'm plotting a cautious foray into the safest, I think, of all places: the touristy south coast of South Africa. A realistic concession to age, African politics, and Sandy's wariness.

What, in these my golden years, is the gold I seek there? Like a gold-rush miner, I, too, hope for riches, not material but abstract. The nuggets I find will be brought home without adding weight to my luggage, and once back I will polish them — whatever they are — into insights.

Seeking gold is inherently risky. Do I crave that part too? To a certain degree, I must. Stretching beyond habitual comfort always necessitates change, new patterns, risk. What if I blunder or fail completely? What if circumstances overwhelm even the most careful planning? Isn't danger for the young? I could rationalize that at seventy-six I'm not putting much of a life span on the line — a decade plus at most. As for my mind, the broader and more experienced it is, the richer those gathered insights should be. But perhaps, too soon, to be buried with me? Alas, the fate of treasures of the mind.

So, beyond the nudge of risk, what else? Knowledge. Not presorted, distorted, by the Discovery Channel, but personal immersion, all senses working to discover my truth, however uncomfortable that might be, however much tourist-marketing mentality will have to be obviated. A third nugget is adventure, a guilt-free fling at what my other life responsibilities — and that thin edge of just enough money to get by on — have constantly curbed. My time for the fun, the footloose and fancy-free, the sheer delight of the unexpected shimmering around the next corner, had to wait until other more work-type experiences had had their day.

Friends ask: But why Africa? Why now? Why South Africa? until I feel besieged. My replies, in reverse order are: Because it's the only place we will feel comfortable living for almost three months; and I will never be any younger, more fit. And Africa because of the uniqueness of its landscapes, plants, animals, and people, proud, black-eyed, with necks, arms, ankles coiled in gold. Thousands of years of gold and — the beginnings of us.

THURSDAY JUNE 26 *Wakefield, NH, writing conference*
Finally found a few minutes to talk with a student whose two children spent their junior college years in Cape Town: she visited twice. Her remarks at dinner the first night of the conference had all been with exclamation points: Oh, you have to go! It is so beautiful! The mountains come right down to the sea! At the safari camp the giraffes browsed the treetops while we sat and watched!

Now on the next to last day I found the chance to probe: "Would it be comfortable for two women traveling together to spend a month in Cape Town?"

She paused, then, "Yes, I think it would. It's a university town and the students find their own rentals there. You can walk to everything."

I was elated. She added, "My son told me not to come alone. And of course, it is not safe on the streets at night."

Another student entered the conversation to remind me that her son is now piloting corporate jets around South Africa.

Mixed signals abound.

MONDAY JUNE 30 *Portsmouth, NH*
A clerk in a travel bookstore said quickly, "I've never been there," then turned back to the shelves, asking, "How long?" "Three months." Silence. Her hands stopped flitting among the colorful spines. "I know," I said. "It's a much more challenging place than last year in New Zealand. That was so easy."

She turned, clicked on a rote air travel spiel: the rapid escalation of prices, the wholesale cancellation of fights—try European airlines, they are in better shape, the hassles fewer. "I'd make my reservations now."

"But if they cancel a flight, a reservation doesn't make much sense." "Well, they'd probably have to get you on somewhere." "At the same price?" "I don't know."

She raised her chin. "Johannesburg has just been named the most violent city in the world."

"I never had any intention of sightseeing in Johannesburg. Cape Town."

She pulled out a couple of Cape Town guidebooks. I shook my head, knowing from experience that there would be a huge selection once we got there. She pulled an *Insight Guide* on South Africa: "Wonderful photos, overview of history, arts ... " I scanned the table of contents and tucked it under my arm. There was no *Rough Guide* on the shelves, only *Fodor's* and *Frommer's*. She looked up the pub dates on the computer and both were '05, no new ones until January. I ended up taking the *Fodor's* because it included trips to Botswana and Namibia. It was a start anyway.

A year ago I had been impressed with her knowledge, her guidance; I wonder if at least some of that was because I knew absolutely nothing.

WEDNESDAY JULY 2 *cottage in Maine*
Had tea with neighbors. Amazed and delighted to learn that another person living on the peninsula has been to South Africa several times and that her son works with an NGO there. Also, an acquaintance e-mailed

information about a Gambian woman who does tours. The list grows.

Took a yellow highlighter to the general info sections in *Fodor's*. Temperature in Cape Town in January will be mid-eighties, not mid-seventies like Dunedin. After two decades plus beside the Gulf of Maine Sandy and I tend to wilt in the eighties, especially if it is at all humid. But a good breeze would make a difference. I also noted that animal sightings are best in October due to large collections at the waterholes. The security warnings were blunt. Reminded me of Manhattan in the seventies.

Must look up the value of the rand against the dollar. Seems the basic prices are cheap anyway.

MONDAY JULY 7 For every exchange of an American dollar we would receive almost eight rand. So if that sightseeing train is R 1,000 a person, that would only be US$125. What a difference an exchange rate makes.

But that's it for a while. I want to dissolve into the beauty and fun of summer here by the sea where my garden already offers lettuce and the earth is leveled for our nine by nine foot utility room, in which our water tanks and pipes are to bask blissfully in controlled heat. A big step toward winterizing.

SUNDAY JULY 20   Brent and Kath and James left this morning. For three days James, at seventeen, threw himself into winning an award for most helpful teenager. His mother was shocked; I grateful.

A pretty flat day for me, and thoughts wandered to a year ago when we numbly signed our house away and then stuffed—with mounting glee—our "millions" in the bank. Being "reasonably rich" has had a learning curve. Not in the sense that we ran out and made ridiculously huge purchases, but the opposite. For me, an incremental climb; easier for Sandy, who at eight moved into suburban Boston's Winchester, and beginning with her first teaching job always had discretionary income for herself. I have a knack for loosening up on vacations, however, and that helped in New Zealand.

The validation of the decision to stretch, not hunker, has been tremendous. Sandy and I are closer than ever, often grinning like fools at each other just because we are so happy. Not that there haven't been pressures in making decisions, but success breeds confidence. Although at times, Sandy—who often speaks what I think—will say, "We could always go back to New Zealand ..."

I'm a longtime fan of Shakespeare's bold Julius Caesar:

There is a tide in the affairs of men,
Which if taken at the flood, leads on to fortune;
Omitted, all the voyage of their life
Is bound in shallows and in miseries.

The flood might be scary, but no way do shallows and miseries appeal. I, particularly at my age, am conscious that the flood is not only money, but health. Maybe by pushing against the parameters that my friends feel and being "bold" I'm hanging on to more than my share of it, but there is no way of knowing that. Money does allow us to avoid doing the really heavy work of building, or taking buses to Kennedy Airport to get a lower airfare—things we've done in the past—and that is probably good for our health too. Dr. Diane nodded when I told her how my body improved with the walking and carrying I did in New Zealand: "Conditioning," she said.

I'm in condition to go for Africa.

MONDAY JULY 28 Definite progress has been made on the utility room: Dave H. laid the new type of flooring complete with foam insulation and Typar. He nailed up some one-bys to show us the roof line, and Sandy just called Ellsworth to order three panels of tempered thermal glass that will form a west wall slanted at forty-five degrees. I guess, with Dave's assurance that he can make them absolutely waterproof, she finally agrees with the design.

For a few days we have been mulling what we've read in the *Grand Circle Tour* book that Sandy ordered online with an eye to possibly jumping on a Cape-to-Cairo tour, giving us a skeleton plan for January, February and March. This morning a friend, who has taken several Grand Circle tours, e-mailed her inner-circle member number for a possible discount.

THURSDAY AUGUST 7 My mind is cloudy as the skies have been for a month. Body too. Both August and I need a good Canadian high to shove this stuff out to sea. My brain is quite unclear about even such trip basics as when and how long. Have not called Grand Circle, but by reading the two books we purchased I'm getting some idea of what safaris, parks, and game preserves are all about. The most exciting news on that front is that a woman my daughter-in-law, Kath, knows who "travels a lot to Africa," actually has a home there—in South Africa—a game farm! Wow and wow! She is there now for a visit but will be back in a few weeks.

The *Insight Guide* says that at least some game farms do take guests; in fact, some are five star in terms of accommodations, knowledgeable guides, care, and comfort. So a couple shafts of sunlight have illuminated my brain's low trough.

Spending lavishly and coming back to the cold of Maine earlier grows as a viable option, and nailing the sheathing board on what we now refer to as the West Wing gives it a concrete shape. The paint on the chipboard floor is dry and ready to receive the water pressure tank, hot water tank. Washer and dryer will arrive this afternoon on a Lowe's truck driven by, we hope, a man familiar with narrow, muddy camp roads.

Everard, the local grave digger, has a trench ready, so after the plumber disconnects all those under-the-house pipes, he can hook the hose from the well up to the new equipment running into what will soon be our insulated, heated West Wing. At seventy-five I can at last discontinue crawling into and duck-walking under this 1930s cottage to do the spring and fall routine of turning on and shutting off the water supply, and on occasion to spot leaks.

SATURDAY AUGUST 16 The plumber and his sister-in-law assistant have gone off in search of a pipe coupling; yesterday they went on a chase around the local hardware stores—all at least ten miles apart—for an I-forget-what. Anyway, electrician, propane dealer, carpenter, and plumber continue to occupy most of our brain cells; and in addition, I have shingles. Physically in pain and mentally prey to alternating waves of chipperness and sog. What causes Shingles to erupt is unknown, possibly stress. Who, me?

Reading the *South Africa Insight Guide*—actually more a zoning out over brilliant photos of animals, flora, and topography—has been a good distraction. Spending the first month in Cape Town has been decided.

A mountain plateau flanked by two oceans, graced with long uncrowned beaches and some of the world's most unique vegetation. ... Weather wafts between pleasant and sublime. ... The howling southwester makes the ... atmosphere one of the healthiest. ... Oldest European settled region ... best shops, hotels, restaurants on the continent. But, like all South African cities, it is a Molotov cocktail of the first and third worlds.

Molotov cocktail? Just a handy stereotype? A personal bias? A warning? Even at www.tourismcapetown.co.za the facts, like total population of the city, percentage of blacks and Europeans, are nonexistent. As I've found with all Internet searches, sites tell you what they want you to know, not what you want—often need—to know and I don't usually take the time to dig and dig. Would that the world could be cleansed of marketing.

So far, online self-catering accommodation descriptions have given only broad hints at price. Using our dial-up Internet connection to find a suitable accommodation will be a tedious process, but I am far more knowledgeable than when I first plunged into this for our trip to the Gaspe Peninsula in Canada and then New Zealand. I do, however, think we will have to engage an agent to map out our second month. What I envision is buses or trains taking us to each of the various geographic areas that span the more northern part of the country—desert, low veldt, bush veldt, etc.— and staying at various locales for one, two, or three days. And if the cost is what I think it is, there will be no third month.

FRIDAY SEPTEMBER 5 Not much has changed: I still have Shingles—itchy now—and the plumber is here again looking for an elusive leak. But a wash done in our beautiful new machine waves in the breeze, and this afternoon Sandy and I hope to install a plastic gutter on the old west side of the cottage. Heavy rain from some hurricane is due Sunday and we want to see how everything works. Son Jim was here for four days and helped Sandy dislodge and remove the heavy original wooden gutter, still sound after almost seventy years, but needing a lot of maintenance that we are tired of doing.

Plans for South Africa have been mere mental blips for the last month. Well, I did check airlines and Dubai now has a flight at $1,700, and a neighbor is coming to talk about her trip, but that is about it. Oh yes, it's time to have Barbara, our cat sitter, over for tea and test the waters as to how willing she is to take him in for another winter. If not, well …

Date: September 17, 2008 9:19:12 PM EDT
Subject: South Africa
Hi Mom,
Had a lovely lunch with Sue who has a wealth of info re: South Africa. She will soon be sending me some info via e-mail which I will forward to you. She does have a good travel agent which she'll pass on. Bottom line … sounds like you can't do the country without a car, she was pretty emphatic about that. Best if we talk, hopefully over the weekend while stuff is still fresh in my brain! love, Kath

THURSDAY SEPTEMBER 18 Photos of Inkasi Game Farm arrived. The first two were of a smiling white woman and her gun and a peaceful, very dead water buffalo. Enough said.

> Subject: *TRAVEL PLANS-MBB USA*
> Date: September 22, 2008 10:05:58 AM EDT
> To: marieke.tucker@flightcentre.co.za
> Hi Marieke,
> My daughter in law – Kathleen Barrett – is a friend of Sue Wiggill and I believe Sue contacted you about my plans to spend (our) winter in So. Africa.
> We have heard from Sue that public transportation is not the way to travel in South Africa; rental car is the only safe way to get around.
> Our tentative plans are: a month in a modest Cape Town unit, a month of unhurried travel across the north, and if we can afford it another month in a smaller town between the western and eastern cape. But we are flexible.
> Sue also warned us of 90-110 F heat and mosquitoes at Inkazi during that time frame. At our age extreme heat and malaria are not on our list of desirables.
> We are interested in the natural wonders of geography, flora (both wild and in gardens) and all fauna large and small and everyday life of people. Comfortable, safe accommodations rather than luxury suit us best. And the company of hunters would be unwelcome.
> At this early stage we don't need names and phone numbers, but more what you think would be a good general plan for us. However, please let us know if immediate reservations are necessary.
> Thank you,

WEDNESDAY OCTOBER 1 Lots of information from Mereike. But the prices! Two or three thousand rand per person a night at game farms and even the Protea chain are six or seven hundred rand per person per night. All that plus car rental and in-country flight for over R 1,000 per person. Of course, we want to be safe, but is five star the only way to do it?

SATURDAY OCTOBER 4 It was one of those translucent New England autumn mornings. As though the stars had dusted and swept the earth and then turned on the big searchlight at a severe angle. Fitting for a breakthrough on housing in South Africa. No hard details on price yet, but I'm back to looking at what we can't afford, just in case … It's a traveler's village right in the city of Cape

Town—separate little houses.

I think I'll make a fire for us to lunch by—not nearly as fascinating as yesterday's on-the-rocks ambiance of surf and two sweet plovers, but a lot warmer.

MONDAY OCTOBER 6 A great stillness comes over the coastlands in autumn. The sea lies motionless, a plate stippled with dark and light currents. The undercover and hardwood leaves shimmer with gold. The sun is silent, there are no clouds, no wind speaks. Small migrating birds cheep as they flit from fir tree to bayberry bushes to the sea rose bushes that edge the two terraces. Eiders, males with splashy white trim and females in nesting brown, murmur to one another as they glide across the cove.

In the shadowy chill of pre-dawn we brought the iBook into bed to see if the Red Sox won or lost, and since the *NY Times* is the homepage briefly scrolled the headlines. European, Asian markets falling, US consumer spending falling, unrest in South Africa. I clicked on the latter. The great intermingling experiment is fourteen years old and Zuma—a volatile figure—waits in the wings to assume the presidency. Whites are "packing for Perth," as the locals call emigration. There is more violence of a particularly cruel type; robberies accompanied by slicing, scalding, garroting. Sandy's reaction: Maybe we shouldn't go. My reaction: Let's hurry to get there before the election.

The Best Western in Cape Town that Mereike, the travel agent, recommended is, I discovered in Fodor's, heavily walled, topped with barbed wire. I ate in a restaurant like that in Northern Ireland in the 80s. Ugly but safe. In South Africa we hope for beautiful and safe.

In our presidential election campaign it seems Barack Obama is playing all the right cards and McCain laying the worst of himself on the table. Thank god.

Wednesday Oct 8 e-mail from Cape Town Village

Dear Ms. Barrett

Thank you for your e-mail!!

There is a 24 hour convenience store in De Waterkant at the local petrol station that supplies the basics like bread, milk, etc. The nearest super market would be at the Waterfront, which is about 20 minutes walk from De Waterkant.

The village is safe in general, although the same rules apply as with the rest of the Cape – don't walk alone after dark, be aware, don't go where you feel unsafe. Furthermore, there is a 24 hour night watch/security patrolling the area.

Your room will get serviced every day in general, although laundry would be charged for. The rates that I quoted you would be the best – the luxury is a bit bigger than the classic, but unfortunately the 1 bedroom units do not have air conditioning. It might get a little hot during the days, but we do have a splash pool that you can enjoy or you can open the windows & doors and let the breeze in.

With regards to 163 Waterkant – that unit is available should you prefer it. It is off the main road and away from the "Bar scene". It has the private patio.

We could also arrange for a airport transfer on your day of arrival/departure. Our service offers a rate of R325.00 for 1-2 ppl in a shuttle bus, or R 395.00 for a private vehicle.

Please do not hesitate to contact me for any further assistance.

THURSDAY OCTOBER 9 The website describes DeWaterkant Village as *"a cultural urban refuge, the authentic traveler's village."* It not only answers our basic needs, but exudes joy. Of course, we can't afford it. Not by any rational standards, anyway. US$140 a night. Whoops, $135: the exchange rate just changed. But still: $2,000 a month apiece. A long-term discount of $135 a week times four is only $270 off for each of us. Now if the exchange rate went up to 9.5, $1,900 is not a huge difference. In fact, about the same as our airfare. Minus $270 for a discount is about $1,600. A lot of money, but what a lark to be in an adorable place, clean and modern, in a safe center-city environment.

It's a drippy day, unlike sparkling yesterday when we walked for two hours around Jordan Pond on Mount Desert Island, then gorged on a popover stuffed with peach ice cream and flowing blueberry sauce. Neither the walk nor the treat seemed to adversely affect my body. Since the rain precludes outdoor chores I plan on spending most of the afternoon here snug in the east bedroom, checking out other options in Cape Town and the possibilities for journeys to wilder and more exotic parts of the country.

Today's front page of the *Times* reports political unrest in the AFC ruling party. "African unrest" and visions of bloodbaths are as linked as lynching and American Negroes. But the only violence against American tourists that I personally know of happened in Central America and Mexico. My granddaughter has taken two long visits to African cities—albeit under the wing of savvy church folk—

with no qualms. Nor did I have any, only envy for her freedom to travel there.

Certainly the loudest sound from the *Times* was the crashing of worldwide stock markets and governments shoveling money into shaky banks.

THURSDAY OCTOBER 21 I woke up thinking—Why not stop off in Spain?

Granddaughter Tee—in for an overnight from UMaine where she is a senior—and Sandy and I sat by the fire last evening and talked about Africa. Two years ago her group had been the last one in Uganda before the area was evacuated. "I knew things were tense, but I didn't know how bad it was. We—the white people—had black soldiers guarding our group, but the Ugandans we could see across the river did not. It made me feel funny." Other incidents she described from a previous stay in Niger and one when she got separated from her group in Uganda sounded more like men-hitting-on-attractive-young-women stories than political/racial ones. "I was most scared in Haiti," she said.

I mentioned reasons why we were having a difficult time getting our stay in South Africa organized: safe areas, transportation, not wishing to stay in luxury accommodations and have to dress for dinner—in general, being tourists in a poor nation. Also how that last month of March was really presenting problems. I'm sure that's what set my brain off on its night's search for options.

When I asked Sandy, "How about March in Spain?" she immediately agreed. Off and on we have mentioned it as a place to visit because neither of us has ever been there and it is reputed to be a great place for a winter home.

The first task was to find out how much airfare would cost with a stopover built in. To my amazement British Airways would do it for about $2,000, the same as the straight round-trip fare. Amazing!

Next I Googled "Spain-Tourism." We saw that Seville and Granada are in the southern part and Googled Seville. There was a brief description, and under accommodations we saw that a three-star hotel costs between 60-100 euros. Checked the exchange rate site: 100 euros = US$128. Still pretty pricey, but perhaps it is headed down too.

The rand is 11.4. Our De Waterkant cottage is down to $105 a night!

FRIDAY OCTOBER 24

NEW YORK TIMES 11:19 AM

STOCKS DIVE AFTER ROUT OVERSEAS
DOW DOWN 500 POINTS AT OPENING

Maybe we should stay in the US. Help our own economy this year.

I e-mailed Cindy, a Spanish professor who has guided students in Spain.

Date: Fri, 24 Oct 2008 08:50:40
Subject: SPAIN-MBB
Hi Cindy,

Hope autumn is fine in your neck of the woods (literally). Now that we've had the cottage a bit more winterized—e.g. all the water pipes indoor—we are truly enjoying the season here. Warm is wonderful.

Our plan has been to head for So. Africa for 3 months this winter, but are finding "safe" accommodations a bit pricey. So I checked w/British Airlines and we could do March in Spain at no extra fare. So...next question where in Spain? We know nothing about the country.

Answer – write to Cindy.

We'd like to avoid: cold and rainy, isolated, risky. A city would probably be most interesting. Any suggestions? Thanks, Martha

On Oct 24, 2008, at 4:57 PM, cindy pulkkinen wrote:

Winterized is good, although nothing seems to matter when you're buried under 12 feet of snow. So, yes ... Spain. Southern Spain, of course. And March ... perfecto. If you're leaning "city" I'd go with Granada ... look for a place in the Albaicin or along the old, winding streets below the Alhambra. The main part of the city (wider, straighter streets) is, like most cities, yuk.

Many more suggestions come to mind, but they're in smaller towns.

SATURDAY OCTOBER 25 Clouds have arrived keeping the temperatures ten degrees warmer and us inside content with domestic tasks. However, about 2 a.m. strong winds and rain are predicted; the sterns of the lobster boats are piled high with traps heading for a winter stacked beside the house.

TUESDAY October 28 Went back to Orbitz to check flights that included Spain. A lot were highlighted ONLY 2 SEATS LEFT" "ONLY 4 SEATS LEFT. Real or mere marketing pollution? But I trudged to the computer after dinner, a most unusual occurrence because when I retired, evenings were labeled For Reading Only. But I suppose travel research is my job now, just as grading papers once was.

I already knew December thirty-first flights on British Airways, which was the recommendation of Kath's South African friend, were $100 cheaper than others in December or January, but there was the problem of a twelve-hour layover at Heathrow on New Year's Eve. Wouldn't every hotel room be booked or at sky-high prices? Arriving at midnight according to our body time and just hanging out did not seem a wise choice for the elderly. So I pulled up Heathrow and investigated booking into an airport lounge—nothing for us peasants—and some hotels that were labeled "Our Secret". They were cheaper but involved a trip into the city.

I quit at 8:30. Time for the World Series game.

This morning I e-mailed De Waterkant to wheedle around about possibly reduced prices for early commitment and long stay.

So it goes ...

Last year the outside pressures had come from troubles family and friends were enduring, this year they are broader in scope: crime and hunger in Cape Town and unstable—to put it mildly— global economies.

Date: Wed, 29 Oct 2008 08:42:36
Hi Cindy, Have peeked at Granada and it seems like a good place for several weeks stay. Could not find what NZ calls "self- contained" accommodations-- — with kitchen that is. Is there a Spanish equivalent?

About how much should it cost? Is a 2 key rating clean and comfortable?

Have sent for a couple used guidebooks thru Alibris, but wanted to make sure we can afford a month there. I know the euro is down some, but ...

Today we will reserve a little renovated Dutch cottage in the heart of Cape Town for 3 weeks — De Waterkant Village. Thanks again, Martha

On Oct 30, 2008, at 11:15 AM, cindy pulkkinen wrote:
What's NZ? One of my friends is in Granada right now (for UNH), so can ask her about this ... whatever-it-is. And the "2 key rating".
Also, in case you haven't heard ... Cape Town is considered one of the most violent cities in the world. Why there ... why now?

LATER. Egad. First an e-mail informs me that Cape Town is number two worldwide in incidents of violent crime, then a neighbor sends over the travel section from the *Maine Sunday Telegram* which extols the wonders of a Cape Town visit, especially now that the rand:dollar ratio is so good.

Evening. Sent an e-mail to De Waterkant asking about credit card downpayment by phone.

TUESDAY NOVEMBER 4 There I was flat out on the braided rug in front of the fire. What an experience. Spent the morning checking flights on Orbitz on a very slow dial-up day. I was trying to book seven flights: Dec 31 Boston to London; London to Cape Town; Feb. 28 Johannesburg to London to Madrid to Granada; March 31 Madrid to London to Boston. Two senior adults for $4,786. It was lunchtime when I finished — tried to book seats too — and submitted my credit card number. Then it needed my Orbitz password which Sandy got a "hint" for and filled it. When I went back a "failed" notice was up.

I e-mailed Orbitz billing people and after lunch they replied with a notice to call. I did. Time passed very slowly as this agent — hired yesterday? — fumbled his way through the list. I even had flight numbers, which seemed to mean little to him. By the time I gave him my credit card number it was fairly dark, and I moved over to sit on the floor where the lamps are and the low fireside table to write on. The agent informed me my buy had failed. The Madrid-London-Boston flight had gone up $450 a person. We tried different times, different dates, split tickets, different airports, different airlines — American Airlines, he said, tripled its rates while we talked. What to do?

I finally told him to just book us to Cape Town and quit. Then I realized that was one-way — very expensive. Should we cut Spain altogether and just come home for March? I said I'd talk it over with my friend and try again in a couple hours. He said everything was going up so fast, that we would lose that price. Then we did. Those flights up $615.

I told him to hang on and I conferred with Sandy who thought we were being railroaded. Back on the phone I said to make the flight from Madrid on the twenty-fifth. That way we save the $1,200 by coming home early. Finally he grasped that I meant saving on hotels, restaurants, etc., not the flight, and put it through. I wrote the confirmation number and that's when I just lay back, flat.

I had done well remembering numbers, something I am usually very poor with. I liked that and the coming home early bit, but could the ticket price actually have risen $615 more a ticket! I did not sleep particularly well.

This morning Sandy assured me that it's only money, then later came down from the shop and said a radio report on South Africa talked of high prices, especially on food. Then I read in the *Times* that the dollar was falling. I did not check the euro exchange. I did not check Orbitz for the cost of flights from Spain to US.

De Waterkant Village is reserving the cottage for three weeks at a ten percent discount. However they will not accept a credit card number over the phone. Bett will fax it to them as security as the credit union recommended.

LATER. Kath sent on a brochure about Sue Wiggill's "Inkasi-Exclusive Wildlife Lodge." I now have Sue's number and she is expecting a call. We'll see. This preparation time seems at least as jumbled and exciting as the trip will be.

THURSDAY NOVEMBER 6 At midnight Barack Obama accepted the job as President Elect of the United States. The relief is a dazed joy.

I should be feeling some dazed joy that we do have airline tickets and a pre-registration for three weeks at 163 Waterkant, but that hasn't crawled from my brain to my gut yet. After lunch maybe.

FRIDAY NOVEMBER 7 I think I was scammed on those plane ticket prices. I'm trying to replace that word with overcharged so that I don't sound so hysterical when I seek reimbursement, a smoother word than revenge. Yesterday I checked Orbitz and there it was the same price as I had started out with. I did not go through the whole process to actually pressing submit, afraid it was perhaps a bait and switch. I called Orbitz.

After the usual junk one has to wade through: delays, tinny Pachelbel Canon, a voice that I could not understand until a callback took the crackle—well, most of it—out of her voice. I met a wall of No, that ticket cannot be refunded. When I asked about their Price Assurance Policy she checked to see if any other person had paid less for that exact list of seven flights. Of course, she was checking only their customers: I should have clicked another button and read the fine print. She gave me British Airways' number and then connected me. All very polite.

This connection was crystal clear and the woman went through the whole seven flights and ended up with the exact same figure— 2,198.91—I had started with. She said she was unable to talk about Orbitz' polices or operation, but she did not indicate that there never had been any change in their prices. She suggested I could go to my credit card company and see if they could or would do anything.

It wasn't until this morning that I realized that if Orbitz paid BA only $2,198.91, I indeed had been overcharged. I will now prepare a letter to Chase Credit Card to make my complaint. Sandy is reluctant to jeopardize our tickets while we are abroad—less than two months to leaving now. I know I can get hung up on justice and fairness and "You can't get away with that!" so I'm moving slowly, checking out all angles and allowing time for my subconscious to work on it.

Next, I have to check over the forms De Waterkant Village sent and make sure it is 163 De Waterkant Street that we are paying for: on the form it just says "1 Classic One Bedroom." That could be any one of many that have no patio and are in the "vivid" (noisy with bars) section. Quite different from dealing with Geraldine in Dunedin, New Zealand. So glad we did the easy country first.

MONDAY NOVEMBER 10 Sunshine for the first time in about a week. And certainly we start off with a lot of new light on our plans, although like the outdoors with its constant wet glow of streaky yellows, tans, reds, and greens nothing has really changed, only become more clear.

An e-mail from De Waterkant Village confirming our 6:45 a.m. shuttle pickup at the airport and asking if we want to reserve a "freshening" room (R 500) until ours is ready about noon, certainly gives sharp detail to our destination.

As did a long phone conversation with Sue Wiggill on Saturday morning. Her enthusiasm for Inkasi Wildlife Lodge—"dream spot," "perfect quiet corner," "lush,"—was contagious. It does sound like my dream place. She described fascinating places to visit, but it was the morning guided walks to see animals, birds, and flowers, and evenings on the veranda watching the animals come to drink that made me gasp. We did talk of malaria and I am not soothed by the "one mosquito bite does not give you malaria" mantra as I would have been twenty-five years ago. Just writing that makes me think I should look for a tough long jacket that those deadly needles cannot pierce for those jungle walks and veranda sits. I am definitely weakening on this point, but will still seek good medical advice.

Sue told us that the plane from Jo'burg was a regular commercial one. Her father lives in a retirement community outside the capitol and would be glad to have us visit for a couple nights and drive us from and back to the airport. I felt as though my mother had just tucked me into bed, recited the Lord's Prayer with me, and kissed my forehead goodnight: someone was going to take care of us.

When Sue asked how long we could stay at the lodge and I said tentatively, "A week," there was a definite pause and then a rush of "But there is so much to see." I immediately said, "Two weeks then."

And speaking of weighing and analyzing, I'm not sure about attacking Orbitz on price scam.

I must slip out into this sun for at least a few minutes.

TUESDAY NOVEMBER 11 Woke up about 4 a.m. when my brain announced that my nagging malaria concern was in mixing the preventative drug, Chloroquine, and psoriasis, a diagnosis I was given for the spots remaining after the shingles ended. Checked it out this morning and finally saw a sentence that said that chloroquine, the most commonly used drug, could exacerbate psoriatic problems. So that's the source of my fears. With further digging I learned chloroquine is not effective against South African mosquitoes. So there. With a different drug I'm fine for Sue's game preserve.

On Nov 11, 2008, at 11:32 AM, cindy pulkkinen wrote:
Hola -
This just in from my friend in Granada ....
I found a website where travelers can arrange to rent apartments short term. I didn't go into the site to see about availability, but I do know that tourists rent apartments all the time.
http://granadainfo.com/aparatmentos.htm

WEDNESDAY NOVEMBER 12 Good grief. Just off the phone with the Bangor Travel Clinic. The malaria pills are easy—a call, a mailing, a $25 fee. But "recommended shots" are another matter. Hepatitis A. $55, typhoid. $70, tetanus $40, adult polio booster $55— or a series of three if never had any. No Medicare help.

How do I know what I need? Who keeps track?

What about side effects? Mixing of drugs? I reminded her I am seventy-six.

I repeat—good grief. More decisions.

THURSDAY NOVEMBER 13 Marvelous list of SA, especially Cape Town, things to enjoy from a man Jim met a couple years ago. It is actually his business. Sandy is happy, wants to do it all.

Wrote to my longtime Portsmouth internist asking her advice on recommended shots. Always a good feeling when decisions become pragmatic actions.

MONDAY NOVEMBER 17 Had forgotten all about finding a place to sleep at Heathrow for the twelve-hour layover. Probably all my stewing about Orbitz scamming me on airline price—must either do something about that or quit bellyaching—slid it to a far back burner. What I tracked down online was almost too good to be true: Yotel cabins. They are off the public area of the terminal and rent by the hour. A compartment with a shower and double bed that converts to a couch by the push of a button, reminded me of the size and efficiency of a hotel room in Hong Kong. Not a bed-tube like Japan or bunk beds with curtains between them like Hawaii twenty years ago. All brand new and sparkling clean. Rent from 6 a.m. to noon is 56 pound—maybe $80 all told. As Jim said, you are having adventures before even leaving home. More like buying coddling, I think; I love it.

Date: November 19, 2008 8:55:59 PM EST
*   Subject: RE: INKASI-MARTHA BARRETT*
Hi there Martha,
*   Sorry I have taken so long to get back to you ... please see my answers under your questions ... .and feel free to call or e-mail whenever.*

*   Love*
*   Sue*

-- — -- — -Original Message-- — — -- — -

From: martha
Hi Sue, The good news is that the anti-malarial pills are no problem, and I guess there is no bad news.
*   Sandy and I fly out of Jo'burg to Spain on Feb 28 and if you still have a place for us at your lodge we'd like to stay there the preceding two*

weeks. For the first part of Feb. we'll be wandering about the Garden Route so whatever date suits your father for a night or two before we fly on to Inkasi will be fine with us. And please give him grateful thanks.

THEY ARE LOOKING FORWARD TO HOSTING YOU - THEY DO STAY IN A SMALL HOME BUT I AM SURE THAT IS NOT PROBLEM FOR YOU ALL!

Since you mentioned a possible discount on rates, I wasn't sure who to contact about firm reservations, deposit etc. Please let us know. We are very excited about being there.

I WILL MAKE THE INITIAL ARRANGEMENTS AND THEN PUT YOU IN DIRECT CONTACT WITH GERARD WHO HANDLES ALL THE RESERVATIONS

A few further questions have come up as we get into more detailed planning and if you don't know the answers that's fine.

How does the medical system work there? In New Zealand it was pretty much a matter of just walking into a clinic or hospital so we did a $15 month American Express travel insurance plan.

MEDICAL IS GOOD AND EXPENSIVE - THE PUBLIC HOSPITALS ARE NOT GOOD THE PRIVATE HOSPITALS ARE THE BEST - GO TO A LOCAL "WHITE" DOCTOR IF NEEDED. OUR FAMILY ON THE FARM WILL BE VALUABLE FOR HELP IF YOU NEED THIS ON THE FARM.

We don't have a cell phone here, but thought we would get one there for emergencies and to be able to call ahead for reservations. Do you have any suggestions for the best deal that would work in the areas we'll be in?

WHEN YOU GET TO THE AIRPORT YOU CAN RENT PHONES FOR THE DURATION OF YOUR STAY - I WOULD LOVE TO SEE YOU WITH THIS SERVICE AS THE PUBLIC PHONES DO NOT WORK. THEY WORK ON A PAY AS YOU GO SYSTEM WHICH YOU CAN PURCHASE ANYWHERE.

IF YOU HAVE A BLACKBERRY THAT IS A WORLDWIDE PHONE. THEIR PHONE SYSTEM IS DIFFERENT TO HERE.

I understand from Fodor's that tipping for services rendered is expected and often done in US dollars — correct?

NO!! YOU TIP IN RANDS

Is bargaining on price for goods common in all situations?

NOT REALLY - ONLY ON THE STREET/ OPEN MARKETS

Thanks much for you generous help. We surely appreciate it.

Warmly,
Martha

FRIDAY NOVEMBER 21 Very cold this week, often with blustery winds. I think if I were looking at a winter of this I might panic and either flee or have a mental implode.

The pressure is lightened on the to-do list for overseas. A letter from Dr. Diane in Portsmouth laid out her opinion on Recommend but not Required shots. Probably will get into securing an apartment in Granada over the weekend. Focus can now shift to moving out of here: Sandy will wheel her big tools from the shop, into the car, and up to Jean's for storage in her shed.

We do remove tools from the temptation of being "borrowed" for the winter, whereas the house is left looking as though someone might return anytime—except for the braided rugs which are replaced with rag ones. In summer if leaving for a few days, I'll put a note on the door telling Jim to come in and make himself at home and that we'll be back soon. Most folks lock up, some to fortress quality, but I think if someone really wants to get in and steal, or do some spray-painting, they'll just take out the door jamb—or a window. The one time I did lock the door, I forgot the key when I returned in the spring and had a terrible time getting in. There is really nothing here to steal—much finer stuff in the cottages on either side—unless it is someone setting up a camp for the winter. Cathryn, down at the end of the point, had that happen once: few pans, knife, silverware, sheets, towels, some cooking spices … Nothing to really get upset about. Like the extremely cold winter someone took a quarter cord of wood stacked out back and even the wood box full of kindling on the porch. If they were cold, I'm glad they had it, and they did leave us a couple days' supply and never entered the unlocked house. A way of sharing that to my mind beats any tiny contributions to high-end, market-driven "non-profits."

FRIDAY NOVEMBER 28 Many issues, some anticipated, some surprises, have arisen and descended in the last month—most to a mere Done written on lists. Tedious to even recall them. Among the as yet undone is contact from Sue Wiggill's Wildlife Lodge confirming that we are welcome there the last two weeks of February; and after two tries by an Alibis bookseller, our 2008 copy of *Fodor's Spain* has not yet arrived. Amazing how equal time expenditure is often required for the big questions and the ones easily solved by expenditure of a bit more money.

Today, tomorrow, and Sunday, however, will be for closing up the cottage and packing for a month of winter in NH, two months of high summer in Africa, and a month of early spring in Spain.

Daunting. But not frantic.

Sunday night forecast is for sleet and snow, but rain should clear the highways to Hampton Beach. With a stop at LL Bean.

WEDNESDAY DECEMBER 10 *Hampton Beach, NH*
Blustery and warm. No trees for the wind to speak through, so it whales itself and thick raindrops against the siding of Ocean Air Apartments. I doubt if the chain link fence whistles, but I'm sure that two blocks away the surf is whacking the sand. Inside our ample first floor apartment it is, for a change, quiet. No laboring of labor-saving machines powered by relentless electricity, but I admit, we fawn over these conveniences after our weeks of hand-to-hand combat against the weather.

We arrived last Monday and it is now the following Wednesday. Ten days of bunched medical appointments which are always routine and always open to outright calamity. Especially when creeping into the back half of the seventies. So there has been some unconscious breath-holding mixed with varying degrees of relief, and this time with gratitude for the professionals I dealt with. Although, I've always had the suspicion that dental X-rays were not quite fair—if he can't find a problem with his pick, I should be able to get away with it—and the cost of them—$144 this trip —is just too much. Reminds me of having to pay for an electrical switch box: what good is something new if no one can see it with the naked eye?

The pace of trip preparations is mixed: a new Capitol One credit card will arrive in a week; reservations secure for Wildlife Lodge line up on the Done side to outbalance some needed clothes and a new carry-on bag.

LATER. Travel nurse available at Dr. Diane's group practice was very thorough.
Immunizations: hepatitis A and B, typhoid, polio booster, tetanus
Medications: malaria, severe diarrhea if needed.
Cost $177, plus medications. I'm writing checks like crazy.

WEDNESDAY DECEMBER 17 The weather looks fairly decent for today. We will meet Sue Wiggill and her mother-in-law, Merle, who lives somewhere near Inkasi, in Burlington Mall for lunch at Dandelion Green. Seems incongruous, but then the whole connection is.

LATER. What a wonderful time we had: Sue is just what one pictures a white South African to be—tall, very blond and beautiful, slim and energetic. At first I thought Merle was feeble, but later it seemed her only problems were her need for a cane, being hard of hearing, and self-conscious about her accent. Afrikaans? It was not a quiet spot. She is sharp, and when Sandy made a wisecrack about the connection between her Catholic upbringing and not being too impressed with the Cradle of Humanity Center, their bond was sealed. Actually, we heard so much information so fast, I had to keep interrupting to slow down the flow in order to take notes. They have relatives all over the country: Sue was raised in Johannesburg and went to university near Cape Town, and Merle had, I think, six children. Merle is going to meet us at some unpronounceable airport and we can follow her into Inkasi; we must rent a car, they say. The way Sue described the drive—"on and on with no signs" made Sandy uneasy. Although I don't really understand much of what transpired, I now have the feeling we will be in good hands with folks who care what happens to us.

When we stepped into the parking lot Sue raised her hand to a smattering of flakes. "Snow! I can't get enough of it!" Sandy and I blinked in wonder, then found it charming. We drove off reeling with the miracle of Sue, Merle, Inkasi.

SATURDAY DECEMBER 20   FEEL LIKE I'M STANDING ON TOP OF THE LAST MOUNTAIN. Found what looks to be the perfect spot in Granada. Wheeeeeeee.

The Broadbill House online photo is of a lush garden patio looking across to the Alhambra. Together we read: *In the Albalcin /Sacromonte area. … in a private street, two bedrooms, permanent wi-fi, washing machine, well equipped kitchen … House is detached, not possible to hear neighbors through the walls. …. one minute away from the nearest bus stop… Plaza Nueva (the absolute center of the city) is only a 15 minute walk … no stairs in the house, but it is necessary to go up 22 steps to get to the house…* I clicked on the calculator: 924 euros for little over two weeks, so under $100 a day.

MONDAY DECEMBER 22 A brilliant, bitter cold morning. Ah, for the flowers of South Africa … Soon. Soon.

Decided to take Schoodic up to his winter camp at Barbara's tomorrow and return in the afternoon. Eight to ten hours is doable if the weather is perfect, as promised. No melting will go on at these temperatures, but the highway will be clear after they work on it today, and, we assume, Route 1 from Bangor to Milbridge. The peninsula road will be passable, and we may be able to hike in to the cottage. Haven't yet located my long purple skirt.

So that will be done in almost full confidence that Schoodie will be happy and not sick to death's door this year. Then we can concentrate on Christmas and final preparations with one long stretch of home time. No real glitches yet, and I'm surely glad I planned on only one check-in bag and a larger carry-on because that's what British Airlines now requires.

LATER *On Dec 22 at 12:40 AM, cindy pulkinen wrote:*
Oh my god ... Albalcin my favorite part of Granada ... envy ... could leave UNH ... take up life of travel again.

FRIDAY DECEMBER 26 The way our new life is scheduled Christmas becomes a blip, not the star of December. That, however, does not dim the pleasure of the family gathering. Every year is different and yet all the basics are the same: Kath and Brent's house wonderfully decorated and filled with warm hospitality. Their three children—both boys over six feet now—hustling to the car and back to bring in packages to spread under an already brilliant feast of presents. Chuck laughing, clothed in some gay holiday costuming. Bett's Blake and Rachel, the youngest at fifteen and thirteen, tall, quiet, smiling at the edges of shifting groups. Tee's boyfriend Evan is a new addition. Love flows in all directions.

Sandy, who has spent the day at her brother's, and I traded stories in bed before sleep. For a few minutes the impending trip was only a background hum and we had a chance to ramble about in fun memories of December at Hampton Beach. We stumbled over the titles of many of the DVDs and forgot the order and dates of lunches with old neighbors, a fancy dinner at Elaine and Priscilla's, the Amare Cantare Christmas concert, the writers' gathering in the Library Restaurant Lounge with the fire and evergreens and Irish coffee. Pie and tea with Bett following an afternoon of cookie baking with the children, writing Christmas cards in front of a football game. Nary a riffle of any unpleasant moments. Amazing—and we are grateful.

SATURDAY DECEMBER 27 Sleet outside, bone tired. The physical and mental relaxation after some broken nights of sleep has brought on an overpowering urge to head back to bed. Maybe as exhausting as anything else is my bravado about the possible difficulties of this trip. Especially Christmas when I tried to soothe children's underlying anxieties. My exit line is now a joke about nursing lion bites. Leave 'em laughing. Much, much to do in the next four days.

LATER. Borrowed this small, light no-hard drive net book from Karen Garrison. I'll owe her $350 if I lose or break it, or maybe most likely, it is stolen. Now that I've discovered that you hit enter instead of return, the beginning of my conversion from a lifelong Mac user to PC has begun. But as Karen said, this is user friendly. Perhaps these teeny weensy keys will be my greatest struggle, but then I thought that about the cell phone buttons when I first saw them.

Now I'll see how my new thumb drive works.

TUESDAY DECEMBER 29 The second load of winter clothes, bedclothes, etc. has been packed in our small storage unit; Sandy has dropped the car at her sister's; Bett will be here in the morning to pick up any leftover food. It will be a huge relief and very exciting to be in that C&J bus heading for Logan. Out to eat tonight at Ashworth Hotel after seeing at 6:00 what we can get for seats online.

LATER. Our travel capsule hatch is sliding toward Close and Lock. Outside new worlds await: inside Sandy and I hold hands.

TUESDAY JANUARY 6 *163 Waterkant Street, Cape Town, South Africa.*

On the edge of Africa. I have much to write about these last few days, but it probably will come as addenda here and there: it is exhausting even to think about. So thought is on hold, physical senses capture each moment.

Compared to Dunedin, New Zealand's crisp dichotomy of burning sun/cool shade, the warm fragrant moistness of Cape Town becomes an undergarment, worn night and day. The filtered light of our high-ceilinged rooms and artful blendings of a decorator's touch contribute to the languid atmosphere, whereas our London Street bed-sit had been haphazard utilitarian, no-nonsense Scot. There we had been in a garden, set back from the street, the sense of community buffered by Geraldine and Ross; here thick walls merely muffle the beat of surrounding life, and although our patio doors are open, that space, too, is guarded by thick twenty-foot high walls, painted yellow and draped with overarching green boughs. Inside is private, sheltered, sprawl-on-the-bed or couch restful and we have taken full advantage of that. The journey seemed very long and it was; jet lag persists, whacking us flat several times a day.

This small alcove off the patio has a bed on which we've piled clothes—only one armoire and no bureaus in bedroom—but a commodious desk accommodates all our paperwork, broad writing space and beyond the open slider a view of the leaf patterns of a Mozambique pink pepper tree dancing on a white iron table and chairs. No indigenous trees remain in Cape Town, our van driver from the airport told us, which, of course, leads to: What was here? And that question morphs to millennia of indigenous Africans and in the last several hundred years the immigrants who imposed their very different needs and desires on both landscape and humans. I know very little now except that 163 De Waterkant is an immigrant house in an immigrant city. Built for Dutch working families in the 1700s and saved from bulldozers in the mid-nineties to be renovated as a community for travelers like us. We know nothing yet of downtown.

WEDNESDAY JANUARY 7 Our first priorities since arrival last Friday have been sleep and food. The latter quest has resulted in some fine wines and meals in the Cape Quarter, an upscale open square of restaurants and shops three blocks away. At the bottom of our steps are the tables of a 7 a.m.-3 p.m. cafe with its pleasant tones of Afrikaans and British and raspy German; the Charles Café, run by the Village, is a block beyond: its breakfasts, with BBC News, are excellent, and out back in a shaded courtyard is a quiet wi-fi hot spot.

All our floors are tile, the walls cream, and the woodwork white; the ceilings are nine feet tall, the walls hung with many mirrors and interesting art. The feeling of spaciousness is African—a stereotypic imposition on my part—and wonder of wonders, furniture comfortable for sitting, napping, or a good night's sleep.

Our leg muscles are stretching to accommodate hillside living, our feet gaining adeptness at navigating undependable sidewalks. Last evening two Imodium made quick work of an impending bout of diarrhea. I have been faithful about drinking a lot of bottled water, but I guess since my outbreak last night I'll avoid tap water even for tea and coffee.

I slept this morning until almost eight and have done little since except to wash body, hair, and a white tropical-weight shirt which hangs on our little line in the patio in the ever present sunshine. A successful shopping expedition yesterday to a supermarket on the waterfront allowed today's luxurious laze of coffee and toast and jam and cold cereal without the need for bra and shoes. Our daily Refresh Service maid has done her thing with the dishes, floor, beds, and bathroom: fluffy clean towels every day. Don't we love it.

THURSDAY JANUARY 8 A normal night—the first in a week. Stopped reading Isak Dinesen's *Out of Africa* at ten. I began it on the flight to London, then on the long jump south read and dozed and read and imagined the continent so far below:

Out on the safaris, I had seen a herd of buffalo, one hundred and twenty-nine of them, come out of the morning mist under a copper sky, one by one, as if the dark and massive, iron-like animals with the mighty horizontally swung horns were not approaching, but were being created before my eyes and sent out as they were finished.

No Cape buffalo on Waterkant Street. Last night I did not go from bathroom get-ups to the front windows to check on activity at the house across the way, where even at 3 a.m. lights blaze and the two white wicker chairs on the sidewalk are occasionally occupied. Waterkant is definitely not only a multinational street, but one where gay men feel at ease.

Woke at 6:30, padded across the cool tile floors to the kitchen, filled the electric water heater with bottled water, clicked it on, and put four scoops of Douwe Gberts Real Coffee in a carafe with plunger poised. According to the package it is a Netherlands coffee, dated simply 1753, with a UK address; locally it is Sara Lee Coffee & Tea in Pinetown, SA. Quite symbolic of the presence of others here. But like the trees—where are the indigenous people?

One week ago a thick snow had fallen and during a lull Sandy's friend Elaine drove us through a Currier and Ives landscape to Portsmouth to catch the 2 p.m. C&J bus to Logan Airport. It arrived at 2:45 amidst a renewed storm. A very slow drive followed. We didn't worry, thinking that it meant only less time to wait if our flight was delayed, so it was a surprise when a hyper British Airlines agent hustled us into a shorter boarding line, saying that the flight was already closed and he hoped he'd be able to seat us together. We grumbled aloud about the bus and snow, and Sandy bluntly told him, "The bus was late—we were on time." A minute later we found ourselves at the Business Class check-in desk where a smiling lady assured us of seating together to London and good seats on our overnight to Cape Town. They were good: first row behind First Class with lots of leg room, but Sandy fretted about being with infants until the little dears proved her wrong by all falling asleep immediately after take-off.

The change at Heathrow (midnight New Year's Eve London time) from Terminal 5 to 4 where Yotel is located took a bit of time, but the room was great and we slept a solid five hours. The overnight flight to Cape Town was a series of naps—followed by, inexplicably, no coffee for breakfast. However, by 8 a.m. South African time we were served a huge breakfast and gallons of coffee in the Village Café. With no Refresher Room available, we wandered—always hoping we were within the bounds of "safe"—up streets and paths until a view of the harbor oriented us. The blast of the noon cannon situated on the Lion's Rump halfway up Signal Hill sent us back down onto the streets where the tall, lean young men in orange vests patrolled. Since then we've expanded our boundaries slowly.

It is now almost ten and heat is creeping in the open courtyard door, always a drowse inducer for me. Sandy has returned from checking e-mail on the computers in Village Reception and taken a load of laundry to the Laundromat—they offer a pick-up service here, but quite pricey. By walking it down the street, we can have a week's worth of underpants and a few shirts and pants done by afternoon. She also has bought us a Vodafone with 200 minutes costing US$50.

FRIDAY JANUARY 9 It rained in the night and I woke wrapped in its lingering moistness. Beyond the tall drapes, their fullness nipped back at the sill, gray clouds, if closely watched, moved from west to east. My mind stepped to the doorway and looked back. Dim, shadowy with a blur of white duvets and cream plaster, even the usual blare of the huge flower prints were scuffed by softness. Am I living this? or dreaming this? or watching a DVD?

Now it's 9:15. The feeding of the trash truck, the grind and sour smell snaps me from the fantasy. Coffee, cool wind from the living room windows, the boiled egg and toast, the shower, those might belong to dreams or movies, but garbage? Highly unlikely. The smell of garbage, like the sight of one of the African security men—all young, all serious, all aware like cats on door stoops—scatters lazy dreams into Here! Now!

Another trash-truck dose of reality, which I should have written in a January 2 entry but got overpowered by other immediate events, happened minutes after landing. I had entered the Cape Town terminal prepared to battle gangs of young blacks for my luggage, my purse, even my life, but instead was greeted with a scene akin to the airport in Bangor, Maine. Our entrance through Immigration and Customs and baggage pickup—in the company of our near-somnambulistic flight mates—was calm and quick, and we gratefully put all our bags in the care of our driver from the Village. Sandy hurried to a nearby ATM machine to get some local currency to pay him. We couldn't manage to operate it properly, so she sped off to another one. I had time to notice a couple of loitering figures and hurried after Sandy to "cover her back" when the cash came out. It did, and she, flustered by the waiting driver, hastened off with me, the slower walker, trailing behind.

At the Village Reception Office when the time finally came for her to produce the Northeast credit card, our joint account where we had deposited enough to pay this last 50 percent of the rental, she could not find it. The more she searched, the more frantic she became. The worst scenario was the possibility of having left it in the ATM. Finally I handed the receptionist our State Farm joint account card.

We had helped wheel our luggage to a locked back room—where I peeled off my knee-high support socks. When we asked directions to the Village-owned Charles Street Café and the nearest ATM, Myra, as we later came to know her, looked around in vain for someone to accompany us to the ATM and paled at our insistence that we would find it alone. "Oh, no. That's where they wait to grab your money. I'll send someone with you after you've eaten." In a tumbled rush—Myra's style—she described the woman who "knows all their tricks. Judo," she added, slicing the air.

Looking, I'm sure, like newly arrived sitting ducks, we stepped warily out into the sun-blaring, flowery streets for our first contact with Africa. Midway through her first cup of coffee Sandy, still absorbed in the hunt, found the Northeast credit card in the bottom of her purse. Sleep-deprived and adrenaline-stuffed is a dangerous combination. So are false assumptions: in New Zealand the airport van driver needed local cash at that moment. In South Africa we had been warned not to use local cabs or buses, so had asked for the only slightly more expensive Village van, not realizing that it and breakfast, computers, and phones would all simply be put on our account there.

LATER. Yesterday afternoon we followed Waterkant Street into Center City. I expected a long stretch of rowdy, fenced playgrounds, blowing trash, resentful black faces, but no, one simply slides down the hill from tidy Village to bustling upscale shopping. I really hadn't known what to expect and was geared for 70s Manhattan, or the Pittsburgh of my youth. Except for young men yelling from the open windows of mini-buses, Cape Town, like St. Nicholas, "soon gave me to know I had nothing to dread."

Our goal was the Gold Museum, starred in *Fodor's.* It was exquisite. Staffed, perhaps organized and operated, by black men it was anything but hokey. The unfolding of the history of gold on this continent took me back to grade school and *National Geographic,* zapped the present-day overriding perceptions of Africa as AIDS, poverty, murderous dictators, and colonial scapegoats.

Our Village is populated by white European tourists and black enablers: waitstaffs, trashmen, security with walkie-talkies, perhaps billy clubs, and women who "refresh" our house every day. In the Waterfront District—a half-hour walk through a variety of neighborhoods—we saw the same cast, except for the handsome black couple seated at our fine-dining restaurant. Inside the upscale mall black women, middle class in dress shopped: and in the supermarket they outnumbered the whites. In Center City the mix was 2009 Manhattan, except here the vast majority is of darker skin; they rule the country, the continent.

Since we arrived the death of Helen Suzman. renowned worldwide for her thirteen years of parliamentary battles against apartheid, has dominated the *Cape Town News* and *Cape Argus* newspapers. Last year in New Zealand it was the death of Sir Edmund Hillary that moved the country to endless eulogies.

SATURDAY JANUARY 10 At 6 a.m. I knelt on the couch and watched the sky through the pepper tree: lemon chiffon where the sun was rising over the bay and the other bits of blue, sponged by clouds pushed onto this peninsula by southeasterlies.

My first African sunrise had been orange-red streaks over the wing of the plane. We had climbed above London in evening blackness, crossed France and the Mediterranean, then flew, an anonymous drone in the sky, over the dark immensity of Africa, on and on. Falling into it would not, I think, have been surprising. With first light I could see beach and surf; before that just glimpses of what I first thought were two electrified villages, but as only blackness rolled on, I thought perhaps were fires.

We were fairly relaxed when we strolled Central City yesterday; enjoyed their tasty version of ice cream in Everyday and discovered an African portraits gallery on Lord Street. I had a long chat with the owner, South Asian, I think, about humanity and found the work of his two local artists fascinating. Sandy and I have talked for years about buying a portrait and each of us spotted a woman—different ones—we'd like in a Portsmouth living room. Milbridge would be a stretch: too jarring, too overpowering.

SUNDAY JANUARY 11 A warm afternoon. I have been on one couch siesta-ing; Sandy reading on the other. After some minutes of staring out through the pepper tree leaves I've deduced that certain trees, their leaves and arrangement of branches have a distinct effect on the quality of light. Do painters use that?

We missed out on buying beer and wine yesterday at the Waterfront supermarket, named Pic and Pay like the one in Portsmouth: the aisle containing same had one of those folding gates, like there used to be on elevators, shutting off each end. The security guard informed us it was past five o'clock. Hmm. Saturday night wildness prevention? Or perhaps a Sunday taboo imposed by rigid Protestant Dutch, a suggestion made by a visiting Brit in the Village cafe. We had gone there after our usual taxi ride home, desperate for a cooling pre-dinner beer. Kenny, the young African day manager, sat with us as we talked, mostly politics: the world, it seems, is waiting for January 20. January 21, Kenny said, Obama will get busy and the world will be different.

Our farthest excursion today was next door for brunch. My avocado, bacon, and Brie sandwich was so huge, I finished the second half at home before siesta, a custom I could learn to love. Probably we will go to a tea spot down near the Cape Quarter in a bit and then pick up something cold at the deli for dinner. We do have some beef stew left from yesterday but it seems warm for that, and both take-out and eat-out prices are so low.

The other day, out on the Waterfront our tea consisted of tricolor ice cream with a few blackberries and raspberries, hot fudge sauce and a filigree honey and sugar decoration on top. About US $4 apiece. And the view was free: luxury yachts passing under the canal bridge while in the background Table Mountain was being laid with a white cloud tablecloth. On our way to the supermarket madness we discovered Hammond Weavers Gallery. An amazing woman-made wall hanging of three African women at sundown— hand woven of mohair—may turn out to be something we cannot live without at the foot of our bed in Milbridge. About US $200. I wore a strand of lucky-seed beads out the gallery door.

Our Village community is subject to sudden musical whims: at noon we had the slapping-on-tall-boots music of four young black men on the street in front of the cafe, now lovely guitar and flute CD from the apartment next door. When we first arrived, there was a band contest far into the evening, and the next day parade music akin to our Philadelphia Mummers; last night it was Happy Birthday from a roof party. It was full moon and I was surprised there was not more commotion—but then maybe they were all at some huge beach party. I had a good view of the moon from the front window and sure enough. that round white face had an African look.

MONDAY JANUARY 12 Last night's bedtime music sounded like a amplified singer from the Waterfront, faint on the still warm air, then about midnight a song blasted right in front of the house—perhaps a car radio? But it all is an experience for us travelers.

Sandy is at reception checking on several places we would like to visit, perhaps one today. The air is clear and seems less humid, but I may soon be closing the glass doors to the courtyard and pulling the drapes against the heat as I did yesterday. I am still in my bathrobe, hair wet from shampooing and body swathed in moisture cream. Necessary with my psoriasis, and even without that it's a good idea since this sun penetrates clothing.

I finished *Thirteen Pennies*, by k. sello duiker, a grim book with little hope for the salvation of a thirteen-year-old black boy on his own in Cape Town. Then in the *Sunday Times* I read of a white Durban couple taking in, adopting I think, a boy of similar circumstances. But, as we know from friends, that is not always a golden answer.

And late in the night I came to the last page of *Out Of Africa*, which has been a great bedside book.

TUESDAY JANUARY 13 Yesterday we rushed off in a cab—we use the company okayed by the Village—to the cable-car station for our much anticipated visit to the top of Table Mountain. From the reception patio Sandy had seen that although misty, the high black cliffs were free from the omnipresent threat of thick white clouds. At 1085 meters (3,600+ feet) at its highest point, it promised cool breezes: and we learned that when strong winds are imminent, a hooter, like a fog horn, sounds a warning and people hurry back to the cable cars for a quick descent: the mountain is then closed.

Ascending, adults laughed and children giggled with delighted surprise at its constant, slow 360 degree revolutions. The modern appearing system was actually built in 1929.

Like most touristy places we've been, there were people, but it was not really crowded and certainly not packed. We ate a recommended Malay Bagel from the cafeteria, then hurried to catch up with a thirty-minute free tour. News to me was that this is almost certainly the world's oldest mountain: six times older than the Himalayas, five times older than the Rockies. The granite and sandstone mass was scraped flat by glaciers and heaved up by tectonic forces, a sizable island until the seas retreated. The sandstone topping, originally silt from rivers, is pocked and worn, feeling more like shoreline than ragged mountaintop, and it supports the richest fynbos vegetation—distinctive for its small leaves-—in the world. The protea, South Africa's national emblem, was the best known of the many colorful blooms we saw as we tramped the easy walkways for a couple of hours. Sandy got a magnificent photo of a yellow and black butterfly on a brilliant red bloom, another of a colorful lizard. However, the pair of dassles, a cuddly creature the size of a big boot whose nearest relative is the elephant, moved, blurring their one and only photo.

Below us the heart of Cape Town lies under the guardianship of this mass of rock. The smaller height of Signal Hill—on whose flank we live—provides double protection for the Waterfront district and harbor, where a huge, weirdly shaped gas container boat floated just beyond a soon to be expanded nuclear plant. Due in the harbor today is a nuclear warship from Russia—protested by peace groups but nevertheless here. New Zealand would never stand for that, but South Africa must, because of its fragile political and economic structure, be pragmatic.

All our conversations with foreign tourists—none American— eventually turn to how Barack Obama will change the world. Yesterday it was an exuberant mid-age Irish couple who slid into the bench opposite as we enjoyed a cooling bottle of a mango drink. We spoke like old friends for probably fifteen minutes and then parted to never meet again, but such are the high spots of travel, and even without photos their musical Cork accents will linger, perhaps for years. As in New Zealand, we seem to be the only female couple on the travel circuit.

Interesting side note. The gay men who are our neighbors pay no attention to us, but perhaps they pay no attention to a) tourists b)

Americans c) the elderly d) anyone without standard male equipment.

THURSDAY JANUARY 15 Both courtyard doors wide open. Southwesterlies broke the hot spell Wednesday night and although they are calm this morning, the humidity is lower and the air light with blossoms. Yesterday on our tour, African Eagle, we saw the Atlantic roiling and crashing off the Cape of Good Hope, and therefore appreciate whence the wild coolness comes. To our north is the Karoo, hot desert, and what I saw of the plants in the Kirstenbosch Botanical Gardens yesterday is enough desert for me. They are fascinating in variety, but viewed in cool, shady comfort is best, I think. If I had not experienced the vast empty silence of deserts in America, I would be tempted, but probably our journey eastward from here will not encompass them. Some tourists who took a tour that dipped into the north told us, "Well, we spent most of our time in the air-conditioned mall, so the heat was not too bad." Well, there. We'll save ourselves for Inkasi.

Our day-long van tour out the peninsula—more on that later—stopped only an hour at the famous gardens and we plan to go back, as much for the scenery as the plants: the 528 hectares (1320 acres) reach partway up the eastern slopes of Table Mountain. Overall they pale when compared to the Dunedin one.

FRIDAY JANUARY 16 A Cape Town morning. Women's voices from the balcony above; French, fast, high-pitched. When I do not understand content, words float like bird song, unprocessed. Out front on Waterkant Street a photo crew is stowing their gear: the lanky blond woman with her blond hair-spray attendant was probably doing a commercial. The winds will be 35-45 km today; Entome will have to dust again, but the swirl of coolness in the open windows night and day is most welcome.

In a low-energy state yesterday, we walked slowly a couple blocks to an Avis Rental. It will cost US$800 for a VW Polo for twenty-one days. We found no other way to wander the coast for three weeks and Sandy is nervous, but she will get her Boston skills in gear and we will make it okay. Have e-mailed to a farm near Stellenbosch—a half hour from here—to see about a room for three nights. If we are paying for a car, we may as well be in the country. The dollar to rand is at 10.01.

Our travel agent Mereike never could get on our page vis a vis accommodations, but she faxed to Village Reception flight forms—

Port Elizabeth to Jo'burg then on to Inkasi for US $800 and a two week car rental—$400. We must take them to a flight center here to have them processed with our credit card. We think a flight center means travel agent.

Since we plan a trip down to the Company Gardens with its parliament buildings and museum and, way at the end, the Mt. Nelson Hotel where we will take tea in grand style, I'm sure we'll find one. Reception has been an invaluable asset: those friendly folk guide us to everything. And perhaps not invaluable, but surely an indulgence easy to adopt, is coming back to a cottage all refreshed by expert maids. In New Zealand we got strong; here we get spoiled.

We certainly did at the Mt. Nelson tea. What an air of elegance that old colonial world held. We tried our best to be elegant too, but in an attempt to hide my psoriasis scarring—I wore ankle length pants—I sat at an awkward angle to my tiny side-table, causing me to pour hot tea water all over it. But our waitress handled that, too, with good-humored elegance.

SUNDAY JANUARY 18 The southerlies today are different; they seem exactly the temperature of the air, around 70-75F. What I feel on my skin is merely motion, no hot, no cold, and if the gust is particularly strong, the wind gives it a voice. Especially in the night.

We have e-mailed for a booking at the farm—vineyard—outside Stellenbosch for Friday, Saturday, and Sunday nights. Here in Cape Town Sandy has arranged for a personal guide to take us on a walking tour of the Bo Kaap area tomorrow. The timing feels good, no boredom, no pressure. Lucky, lucky us.

The tour that we took out the Cape Peninsula last Wednesday had many highlights. Certainly the African penguins were one: bushy orange-yellow eyebrows, huge webbed feet. They were gathered in a large group on the beach while a large group of humans on the boardwalk gawked and clicked. Unlike the setting for the yellow eyed penguins of New Zealand—lonely, windswept, vast—this had a zoolike quality, and yet two breeding pair independently chose this place in 1982. But humans were involved: they had reduced their pelagic commercial trawling in False Bay, allowing anchovies and pilchards, favorite foods, to multiply; they also controlled pelican egg harvesting for food and commercial guano scraping. Now, about 3,000 penguins breed and live here—the only mainland colony in Africa—but they are far from their 1910 population of 1.5 million. This tourist-rich area has profited from their presence, but undoubtedly as both populations increase there will be a clash between the donkeylike bray of these rather smelly penguins and the cultivated sensibilities of rich white-skinned humans.

After many photos by Sandy and hopefully movies by me, we joined the other dozen tour folk for a gourmet lunch of fresh seafood: a type of baby rock fish for Sandy and lagunastina split in the shell for me. What a difference from the frozen stuff they have in the US—absolutely fantastic. We were joined at the table by a bright and interesting woman from northern Japan—a mother of four or five—and her thirteen-year-old son, who both ate pizza. They are staying in one of the miles of luxury rentals and condos that line the highway out of Cape Town: her husband, a professor whose specialty is earthquakes, is here for a five-day conference. She spoke excellent English: a result of one daughter attending university at Christchurch in New Zealand. Other tour bus mates included two young girls, either German or Afrikaner, a young black couple, and three young people from one of the high-rise hotels in Cape Town. As in New Zealand we seldom see or hear Americans.

The high point, both literally and emotionally, was Cape Peak Lighthouse towering 200 meters above the sea. A quick funicular ride and a longer climb up winding stone steps added to the feeling of: Here I am! standing at the tip of this huge continent above the Cape of Good Hope's swirling blue currents, cold from the Atlantic side, warm from the Indian Ocean. In fact, their actual meeting is many miles to the east, but for me this spot has been a geographic life goal, going back perhaps to Miss Wright's seventh grade geography class. Certainly, I recall from somewhere the magnificent tales of struggling sailing ships and many wrecks. Is wanderlust a DNA trait, or inspired by a teacher, a parent, or regular newspaper/book reading?

We walked the cliff paths and there, far, far below us, southern great white whales—spotted by Sandy through binoculars—flipped themselves through the air. Magic. Pure magic.

Later, as our van rolled away from the international photo frenzy at the Cape of Good Hope sign, we saw our first African wildlife— outside of a cockroach in the tub, which Entome neatly dispatched— a magnificent male ostrich watching over his eight teenage offspring, necks bowed feeding. And then, with the wild sea churning beyond, he strode out along the beach, eight feet tall and absolutely imperious. Next, a horde of baboons dashed toward our bus, geared up for tourists with food. The driver announced sternly: "Keep your windows rolled up unless you want seventy pounds of baboon in your lap." He had already advised us: if a baboon wants your cold drink, give it to him—they are strong and aggressive. Unappealing looking creatures with their bare buttocks and messy crew cuts, but the baby riding his mother's back like a cowboy and two small ones wrestling among the rocks brought smiles and the feeling that, indeed, we are in Africa. The miles of gray-looking, flat, harsh, wind-scoured fynbos was new, but the surf at high tide, magnificent as it was, evoked nods of "looks like home."

MONDAY JANUARY 19   Ah, the joy of a guide—a personal guide.

Shireen Narkedieu met us at the Bo-Kaap Museum at 10 a.m. A neat, small woman, forties probably, dark-complexion, fast but very easy to understand English. In her childhood home her three brothers were to speak only Afrikaans, but she was to speak English. Her father felt it was the language of the world and she would make a better living if she was proficient in it. She still lives, along with her twenty-six-year-old daughter, in the house where she was born. Not only has language been a tangle for these people—called Cape Town coloreds or Malays—but how to define themselves.

In the 1600s the Dutch discovered that the indigenous people who inhabited the cape area did not have the skills for the work the Dutch needed done to establish a colony here. So they looked about their far-flung empire, established by the commercial power of the Dutch East India and Dutch West India companies, and brought in laborers from Indonesia, the Malay archipelago, Ceylon, and East Africa to build their houses, grow their food, and repair their ships. Shireen told us that the Netherlands government would not allow them to be used as slaves, so in the manner of many European colonizers they housed their workers in buildings they owned and exerted total economic control over their lives.

Of disparate cultures, languages, religions, and of various body sizes and colors and skills, they were further separated by what amounted to a caste system based not only on those inherent differences, but by job description. As in India occupation became an inherited destiny. Shireen, by now comfortable with our desire to know more than surface clichés, created a most vivid memory when she stopped in the brilliant sunlight where a shabby alley connected to a street of brightly painted houses. "People were ranked," she said, "from high to low in a staggering number of classifications. You can imagine what happened to this system under apartheid when it was very important to decide who was white and who was non-white. It even came down to measuring the amount of curl in somebody's hair." She, without a hat or squint in the blazing African light, ticked off on her fingers the nit-picking divisions. It sounded like Nazis searching for Jews. "But," I asked, "by that time hadn't there been an enormous amount of intermarriage?" Shireen shook her short, neat cap of black-silver hair. "No, and most still don't."

An extra to our tour was tea in a local home. A solid woman in rich Muslim dress, whom Shireen called GG, invited us into her small living room where a table was filled with her morning's cooking: sweets and lightly fried dough stuffed with chicken, vegetables, much more than we and Shireen could eat. A Malay treat for sure. Conversation and laughter flowed easily between the four of us; GG said she had opened her home because she enjoyed talking to different people. Her extraordinarily handsome eighteen-year-old son was headed out for prayers; a midtwenties daughter lives in Saudi Arabia; her husband is associated with an NGO. GG has made two trips to Mecca and has fine, gold-decorated head scarves as symbols of them. Also on display is the exquisite dress her mother wore on returning from her pilgrimage in 1950. Her mother's Chinese dragon tea set and the fact that GG attended the elite St. Paul's School in Cape Town attest to their educated, well-to-do status. All four of us fervently agreed that we needed a world of peace and tolerance.

We returned to the brilliant streets, and Shireen led us farther up the hillside and pointed out the minarets of seven mosques. "Eighty percent of the people who live here are Muslim—that means about seven hundred people per mosque." The tapestry of strong red, lime, and blue painted houses, she said, is the result of the area having been declared a Monument district with strict rules about the exterior of houses. Sandy and I nodded and said we had lived for twenty years in such a district. Shireen cares greatly about Bo-Kaap and has been the impetus behind many improvements for the people. "I've also lived through three World Class Sporting Events. Officials always promise that the average and poor people will be better for it, but it never has turned out that way. All the transportation improvements are to make it easy for tourists—they zip right by the people in desperate need of decent local transportation."

Three children, probably eight to ten, who had been lingering about, approached. "We're hungry," they said, more to Sandy and me than Shireen. We let her deal with them in their own language; they slouched down the hill in the opposite direction from which our guide had pointed them. "I do not give people money," she said.

"I try to get them jobs. Over there is a place which helps people. They would not let them go hungry." "But," Sandy said, "the kids did not go." Shireen shook her head. "They wanted money for something else."

I'm hungry. Sandy, hearing those same words from Entome after she finished cleaning one day, had made her a ham sandwich. When a request for cab fare home followed a few days later, Sandy gave her some coins. When we left, we gave her all our food. On the street one evening a woman came up to us, pointed to her university T-shirt, and asked for tuition money. We could smell beer on her breath. "I come from the East Cape," she said. "People are so poor there. It is terrible." We gave her a few coins. But the man who came banging on our door on a Sunday morning asking for money, we ignored. It did cut deep when he looked in the window at us and said, "You are rich people. You have all this. We don't have anything to eat." The unemployment rate among Africans in Cape Town is 20 to 25 percent.

I was once besieged by small children in a Chinese village, have had hands thrust at me in Thailand, and as a child saw plenty of beggars on the streets of Pittsburgh. Hurtful paradoxes I have never resolved.

WEDNESDAY JANUARY 2 The *Cape Argus* headline   blared: Obama Era Dawns.

I am not conscious of my white minority status here, but am jolted by the sight of normal European types appearing as weird. Not that huge numbers of whites don't populate the paths I tread — Center City, the malls, the waterfront complex — but that black faces no longer require analysis as to their intentions toward me, their economic status, their manner of moving, dressing, speaking. I remember the woman in the drug store who waited on me as white, but I cannot recall the skin color of the young men who helped us print off digital photos. Hmm. Back in the 60s, I served one semester as a long-term substitute in black Philadelphia where a seasoned white teacher insisted he was "color blind." I'm beginning to understand what he meant: blind to the baggage of pigment.

Our route down Strand Street toward Center City yesterday was determined by a To Do list "as long as your arm."

1. Exchange the cap bought at the Gold Museum gift shop. Added a short tour of the oldest "as is" Lutheran church in Africa—1790s? Heard more of rigidity of the later Dutch Reform Church; our guide claimed an influx of German Lutheran soldier-

settlers was responsible for the harshness of it doctrine.

2. Flight Center in St. Georges Mall—air-conditioned! Bought R 90 ebony elephant—with trunk raised for luck—for Blake. Gazed longingly at Lulu's—a delightfully off-kilter woman—watercolor paintings.

3. Information Center for road maps. They had nothing but sloppy tourist ones, but directed us to AA, where we purchased four excellent ones for our travels between Cape Town and Port Elizabeth. Dug for more information about auto travel and found that credit cards only, never cash, are accepted at gas stations. Think it was *Fodor's* that got that wrong.

4. Cab to Waterfront Mall. US$2.50 included tip as usual.

5. Paused in shade—temperature must be high 80s— to listen to five-man marimba group—first one Sandy has liked the sound of. CD US$1.

6. Too hot under umbrellas on wharf, ate inside in AC at the Greek Fisherman— great seafood salad of calamari, prawn, fish, mussels, and a quart of water. Few people about.

7. Pharmacy. Yippee—they gave me a tube, albeit a small one—of ointment for psoriasis without a prescription. If I continue to have to use it, I suppose I can try another store somewhere. Also a new supply of Eucerin body lotion had come in. So excited I forgot— again—baby aspirin and magnifying glass for map reading. Almost US prices: $15 for each item.

8. Digital shop. Sandy was able to have photos put on CD and I to print off about fifty prints to send home.

9. Bubble envelopes and stamps, forget price.

10. Supermarket. Looked for a cooler to carry stuff in car—all too big. But they do sell foil-lined bags and freezies for US$1. So, all set there. Also, a bit of food and drink to last till Friday's leaving.

Called an Excite cab, but he was too slow to beat the gate-closing at 4:00—prevents rush-hour short cutters driving through the mall— and it was a hot ride through traffic. But the driver was older and not hell-bent to get ahead by gunning through skinny openings and racing as fast as possible on every, however short, stretch.

Home at five to beer on the couches in front of the TV watching a skinny black man with an African father become, as Kenny said, "president of the world."

THURSDAY JANUARY 22 We don't see more than snatches of sky from this cottage with its pepper trees both south and north, but the lack of brilliant heat on street and walls and the smell of rain just past lulls us. I am not used to late and intense evenings such as we had at the Gold Museum Restaurant last night. Our first city nighttime venture. At 10 p.m. we were carefully handed into the called-for cab by a doorman, and after the five-minute drive up the hill, the driver waited by the curb until we had climbed the four steps, unlocked the gate, and then door, and stepped inside. A silent reminder that there is a reason behind these actions.

We had arrived about 5:00 for an hour of drumming lessons—quite fun and the leader had a captivating, flashy, exuberant style. Each course of the four-hour dinner spotlighted cuisine from a different part of the continent. We non-tour guests were scattered about at small tables, affording in-depth chats with the young servers: a handsome fellow from Zimbabwe, a freshman at university; the hostess, who does the marketing, speaks eight languages and is studying French—she also plays a fast, mean drum; from Cameroon a man who loved his history studies—unfortunately cut short—and thinks teaching is the greatest occupation in life.

True, their dress and later dance performances as Mali puppets are rooted in the past, but their eyes are on the future, whereas so many of the tourist must-sees are backward looks: Robbins Island and the cell of Nelson Mandela, the museum of the 6th district from which hundreds were displaced, the apartheid museum in Jo'burg. It was a twenty-something salesclerk who first expressed to me that "How bad we've had it" thinking can bind people in a do-nothing status, similar to what, I believe, happened in US racial politics. Many Africans are young, pushing forward rather than nursing a melancholy past, too busy planning and dreaming to tally their stripes as victim. A good counterbalance for them and for the world would be a modern building showcasing the voices and faces of these vibrant men and women who are focused on their hopes and dreams and achievements.

FRIDAY JANUARY 23 Nate was born twenty-four years ago today, and although I may not be maturing at quite the pace he is, these last three weeks have been amazing—not only intellectually but attitudinally.

Our sparkling white VW Jetta is parked across the street and we are pretty much organized for departing by eleven—two hours away. Jitters over setting out on the highways are reduced to a simmer, and as usual, the air of South Africa is balmy and sweet.

JANUARY 24 SATURDAY   *Soverby Farm, Stellenbosch*

We are among ancient trees and showy flowers with grass and the humped earth of the vineyards to walk on; old whitewashed buildings that have a long history of serving useful farm needs have been organized for the comforts of us guests. A giant step into Africa that I truly felt when, in the perfect silence of 4 a.m., I opened the top of our double Dutch door onto a half acre of grassy courtyard and the coolness of near mountains rushed in. The security man strode by, nodded Bowana in greeting. I, wearing my seventy-six-year-old body under a lime green nightie, waved my fingertips, and after a few minutes slid back under the sheet and light merino blanket. A cock crowed at the pre-dawn twilight maybe a half dozen times; I lost count, sleep came so quickly. At five cows lowed: I am on a farm in Africa.

Yesterday, we arrived—without any bad road moments—about noon. The receptionist showed us to the only room that had been available: the Honeymoon Suite. What a hoot—our first exposure to four-star luxury. Immediately we decided that if they served lunch here we would partake. We waited, dallying, luxuriating in boland (highland) air and sipping wine at a linen-set table in deep shade. After an hour and a half, what we thought would be a simple salad arrived on huge platters: smoked chicken, mango, bacon for Sandy, smoked salmon on tiny potato cakes for me. Tomato and cucumbers, diced small; lettuce abundant and crispy; dressing delightful.

We walked along a dirt road to ponds and vineyards that stretched to the vanishing point, then retired to blissfully nap on the honeymoon bed beneath fine white mosquito netting—"just for show." we were told. Cookies had been placed on pillows, and on small oriental rugs new terry cloth slippers, each pair threaded with a fresh rose. Later, we and the sparrow-like bird Sandy had made friends with had tea on our brick patio, admiring tree specimens we quite possibly will never name.

Sandy braved—not only must she drive on the left, but shift with her left hand—the short drive to a supermarket for cheese and ham and bread and milk. She chose a bottle of chenin blanc, and we ate on the patio accompanied by cicadas' shrill song and sunset-colored mountains jagged against a darkening sky. Will three nights be enough?

TUESDAY JANUARY 27   *Abalone Guest Lodge, Hermanus*

Now we are in Hermanus—recommended by a woman at Soverby Farm— overlooking a misty sea and asking, Will two nights be enough? We still do not know how these next two weeks will play out, and perhaps that is the next step. If the clouds hang with us, this is a lovely place to be: big second floor corner room, on one side gardens and stark gray mountains, on the other wide gray sea sweeping into a cove. Five-star features abound, including wireless! in a lovely lounge setting downstairs next to the breakfast room. The light rain seems to have ended and we will set off on the cove walk. And, oh yes, the workmen are once more banging and crashing on a new building outside the windows.

WEDNESDAY JANUARY 28 This place will spoil us rotten. The room has the same lightness as Annabelle's in New Zealand last year, the same tasteful touches of luxury, but much larger overall because of a dressing room with large closets off the quite elegant bath. It is, however, the people "caring" for us that is so above and beyond anything I have experienced. While we breakfast quite grandly, someone makes our bed; while we are off walking and lunching, someone cleans our room and bath; while we are off in a restaurant dining, our bed is turned back, windows shut, and soft lights on. I wish that just once in her life my mother could have enjoyed this, but back then the economic gap between ordinary white-collar folk and travelers was an impossible canyon.

There is no stuffiness, no arrogance, no putting on airs by either staff or guests. The Brits who come here for a week every year are part of the ordinary set. Lisel and her assistant cook the eggs and bacon for our breakfast and chat amiably with us and other guests. In short, we fell into this niche, and fit. When I traveled with Chuck in Asia, five star meant bowing and tipping, uniformed people rushing to open doors and being snappish to underlings, and guests seemed to be placed in a hierarchy from Somebody to Common. Perhaps it is the difference between B&B culture and hotels.

We speak of returning some November to watch the whales.

THURSDAY JANUARY 29 A nook on the west side of Abalone Lodge. Deep shade most welcome after breakfasting on the east side in a brilliant sun that saturated garden and sea, watching what they call Champagne mist that edged the far side of the cove, rose into ever present mountains; now, a stick roof and the rush of a fountain provide freshness. Beyond a splash pool and lounge chairs are the enclosed parking lot and the main street into town. Sandy has just left on her first solo drive to attend to an ATM withdrawal and probably a stroll about.

We have not "done" the town of Hermanus yet, only enjoyed three quite different dinners: wharf-side upscale, harbor-side Italian, and around the corner at Ocean Beach a skillet of fish and chips in the company of locals. Excellent food and descending prices down to last night's US$3.50 for the grilled delight. Returning to our room, our cup runneth over when we found a bottle of local red blends, two glasses, and a glad-to-have-you note from Lisel and tea—we had extended our stay until Monday. It is in all ways a perfect spot for us right now, especially the seaside beach walk that provides an antidote to a lot of days of sitting and eating rich food. The construction crews are more interesting than annoying.

At the vineyard farm we did amble about a bit, and did town strolling in Stellenbosch and back in the hills of Frankschhoek. The latter proved to be our favorite. It was a Sunday and the small village was filled with Africans in their go-to-meeting best, requisite tourists, and local shop and restaurant folk. I asked permission from a group of the former, sitting in the open back of a pickup truck, if I could take a photo. Delightful laughter rose as they primped and arranged their poses. Would have loved to join them in the ride to wherever, but we stuck to the accepted route of a tea and sweet in the shade, then shop sampling. My favorites were a sculpture gallery and a bookstore where I took the best from a bin of South African fiction that the owner was saving for the big May festival. What a feast of women writers.

Frankschhoek is isolated from the route of the hurried tourist by a steep mountain pass, which Sandy took in stride to the beat of a new African woman's CD. I was entranced by the beauty and scared silly by how close she drove to a "breakdown" lane frequently occupied by cyclists and pedestrians. Of course, most of the Africans do not have access to cars, so bikes or feet are their only way to get around in this thinly settled bit of near wilderness. It was only logical that halfway up a very steep hill one man would be resting in the slender shade of a guardrail, bike propped beside him, but in my nervous state I saw a crumpled body sideswiped by an American tourist. We joked about putting a sign in the window: Beware! American tourist! But, of course, as Sandy says: Doing it is the only way to get better. It is hard, however, for such a confident, competent driver to be a beginner again. Yesterday's half-hour trip to tiny, rural Stamford, a striving art center where we met a young Philadelphia student who had taken a course from a lacrosse player that Sandy knew, was not up to a fun drive rating, only a more relaxed one. The fear factor, however, is much reduced.

On the subject of fear, Hermanus seems obsessed with it: Armed Response signs are everywhere; properties are always gated and walled. Our set of keys is clunky and heavy: number one bleeps open the gate from street to parking lot; two takes us through a tall blue gate onto the grounds; three opens the front door if we return after 8 p.m.; four opens our room and the doors to the side balcony and of course, locks us in for the night. Being on the second floor we have the luxury of opening a couple of slider windows on the east side, and that breeze and the fan keep us comfortably under the duvet all night. (The phenomenon of Champagne mist, caused by spin drift being ripped from the tops of surging, breaking waves steaming into the bay, creates dampness, but fresh air is worth it.)

Because of this constant awareness of danger! I am even annoyed by Sandy's use of the in-room safe. I fear that like a kid tired of Mother's warnings, I might do something deliberately foolish just to get that monkey off my back. Maybe I have always tilted toward the risky. A friendly staff member told us to beware of pickpockets, of theft followed by further violence because that is "unfortunately, common behavior among our blacks." "Here?" I asked. "No, there haven't been any incidents in Hermanus yet, but you never know..."

Could all this fear mongering be simply a means of white control: lock them out? Or possibly a ploy by some political parties to keep alive the blacks-as-victims mentality? Or commercial marketing for these thousands and thousands of security guards, for electronic gates and secured houses, for wall builders and armed response services, manufacturers of razor wire and so on and on? When I talk to tourists about this puzzle, like the young Australian couple this morning, they admit to "being scared to death" by pre-trip news reports and publicity, but are now wondering if it hasn't been drastically overdone. The Aussie woman said, "The world is dangerous. I wasn't going to sit at home forever." The man admitted he never would have come without her insistence. When questioned, white locals either sigh and say it is unfortunately necessary, or raise an eyebrow and lower their voice to a whisper as though they know of unimaginable terrors. Rather, I imagine, like pre-Civil War southerners in America whispering about "being murdered in our beds." Like the tales of the Mau Mau in Kenya when Africans did rise up.

FRIDAY JANUARY 30 One month. Seems much longer, due to, I'm sure, the amount of endorphins that have raced around my body ever since liftoff. The same sensation, I've read, as a person in love feels.

Had an interesting experience with medical folks yesterday. I had run out of the ointment that I use to control my psoriasis, but the druggist would only give me a small tube and the phone numbers of several "companies" of doctors. I called one and the receptionist was most obliging about arranging for the last appointment of the day with a Dr. Weim. The office was located across the street from a large dirt area of parked cars and buses and a few stalls, the most popular selling one-hundred-pound bags of potatoes; a large number of black people wandered around.

Inside, the clinic looked western and served a mixture of white and black patients; the only doctor I saw was mine, a young Dutch Afrikaner. The restaurants in Hermanus serve a wide variety of Europeans, but I don't believe I have seen a seated black person. The waitstaffs are integrated, which was not the case in Cape Town, and not true of the building crew next door: the occasional pale face always has either a tape measure or a roll of paper plans in one hand. It does appear, however, that at least one work crew boss is a skinny, tall-hatted, loquacious Zulu, I think. So many tribes, so many stereotypes to shed.

Breakfast outside again today with the spin drift curling up the mountains where yesterday we had followed chalky stone paths to the top. Hot sun, cooling breeze; split an omelet stuffed with tomato, mushrooms, feta with Sandy. Starter was my usual fruit and yogurt: banana, watermelon, cantaloupe, all fresh and sweet. I tried using local water in decaf last night after returning from an incredible meal of African beef and I'm sure that it, not the beef, set off my diarrhea this morning. Immediately hit it with an Imodium and if that doesn't take hold in half an hour, I'll do another. It's important since we are setting off on an all-day drive to the east and south — hope to get our first glimpse of the Indian Ocean.

Sandy was greatly pleased by our two hours of climbing in the fynbos hills yesterday and is out doing a short one on the beach path to keep the newfound firmness in her legs: she is a true hiker. I, too, enjoyed the exercise and the views of folding green heights against a deep sky and the peeks of ocean and our beach walk below. Up there walking in silence and beauty was where the idea of a steak fastened itself in my brain. Lisel had mentioned an excellent beef restaurant.

On our way out I enjoyed a short chat with an engaging couple from Jo'burg on a week's holiday. Our conversation followed the usual pattern of the man having been to the states on business and the woman playing the support role. When the subject of crime came up they both eagerly dove in with long stories about the slickness of con men at the ATMs. "Be particularly careful in Jo'burg," Dr. Weim, whom I liked a lot, had also gravely told me, "There's much more crime in the northern areas. "

He said to expect a great deal of rain there, as well. Rain and wild creatures have been in scarce supply, so I imagine we'll not only cope but enjoy. Actually I think this hustle—by our definition—across to the East Cape and then visiting in Jo'burg will foster a great longing for some flat indoor days.

SATURDAY JANUARY 31 ...Woke at 5:00 to a total soft blue scene. The lack of clouds presaged a simple gold ball rising, so I flopped back into dreamless sleep. Now after four cups of coffee, fruit and yogurt, croissant and jam, bit of ham and cheeses, I feel ready to face a few hours of what I anticipate to be a bustling tourist day in Hermanus. With luck the cooling fog will come all the way in and take some of the burn out of the sun. Although it was a definitely in-the-car day yesterday, my body feels as though it was much exposed.

Lunch on the back veranda of one of South Africa's oldest farms was a highlight, although standing on the southernmost tip of the continent can't be beat for drama. Before lunch we had our first taste of non-vineyard farmland: cattle and sheep in small clumps, and vast, often rolling fields tan with the stubble of mown wheat, barley, hay. As if a pause button on the video had been pressed, the strong African sky and endless pasture edged with a lace of umbrella trees seeped into me. Africa. Here. Now.

Art was displayed in the stable where the slick concrete of the floor had been intentionally imprinted by sheep hooves, and the thick walls whitewashed inside and out. The rather young blond wife of the current owner-manager told us that the boundary of these 25,000 acres had been enclosed by the traditional 1700s one-day's ride on horseback. Sandy asked if the land was still fertile and received a stiff farmer's reply: we take good care of our land. She has also set up this restaurant, B&B rooms, and the paintings are hers. The quiet is intense, the thick, twisted, shaggy tree trunks ancient, the suspension of time absolute. Is this the gold I seek?

SUNDAY FEBRUARY 1 An apt metaphor for this splendid temperature would be a god manipulating hot and cold spigots as one would a shower. "A bit too warm?" Okay, a twist of cold. "Now with that breeze I could add some hot." Done. And so, back and forth to keep the perfect balance: a bit of this, a dap of that. And perhaps on a more sophisticated model, a sliding scale for cloud cover.

We will be off to a winery for a one o'clock lunch, although breakfast still fills my belly.

Found our next accommodation, Grace Walk B&B, in Swellendam in a booklet from the Tour Site travel center last evening. Only R 600 a night. We did not opt for far out places near nature parks—we'll have enough of that at Inkasi. Besides, we don't want to get careless with safety.

Have shin length capris on for the first time: psoriases has retreated that far. Now I'll have to shave my legs again. A welcome chore, however.

THURSDAY FEBRUARY 5 *The Waves, Victoria Bay*

The Waves B&B is rightly named: fed by a easterly wind that must be over twenty mph, they roll and break only a porch, grass strip, and a few yards of shore rock away. Ian Campbell, the owner along with his wife Lisa, said that winds usually blow offshore. They rip over the towering hills that limit this town to one short street of B&Bs, a narrow oval beach. and a grassy spot for visitors who prefer it to sand. We have lucked out again, as we did last night—and the two nights before.

We left Hermanus and the ocean for Swellendam, not over an hour's drive on our slow journey east. The town is historic, full of restaurants and accommodations, but the quiet in the ad sold me, because if a place says nothing about that, it is no doubt on the main street and noisy. Quiet it was, but the room was minute, a condition that would have been a thorn except for the exterior: a patio under a red-leafed grape arbor, well-kept lawns and gardens, and a multitude of birds for Sandy to study and photograph. Especially the pin-tailed wydah whose magnificent tail, at least three times its body length, is a miracle of furious, functional flight.

After that delightful two-night stay—which included the Bontebok National Park and the excitement of our first wild antelope types—we headed out on the N2 highway again. Hoping for a place by the Indian Ocean, we turned down a long road of fynbos vegetation and found the Tour Site. Their bed and breakfast booklet seemed to showcase the four-star Buttercup B&B, and sure enough, Evelyn had one room left. Long steps led down to the most glorious sand beach, and I felt happy as a child as I strode along with soft white sand between my toes and the warm sun and cool breezes on my body. I did not swim at the mouth of the river, however: too fearful of strange skin-irritating unknowns. We did spread a luxurious towel, from our host's amazingly complete beach accoutrements against a dune and just drank in the scene with all our senses. Take-away ribs on the table in our lounge room completed our short stay in yet another paradise.

This morning, knowing we had to book ahead for weekends, I bought an hour at an Internet cafe. It was a frustrating experience, but we left with a fair idea of a good place, called from our car, and lo and behold they had this "garden cottage" vacant. So that was happily settled. It really helps that we can book three-and-four star places and still stay under US$100. In New Zealand we could not do that and therefore had to risk more disappointments. Now that we are used to luxury—and our present spot is surely an example of that—I wonder if we would be so pleased with our accommodations there.

FRIDAY FEBRUARY 6   Yes, we certainly struck gold at The Waves. I could never have imagined waking in such a setting. From the king-size bed we could look through the sheer white curtains that shielded the sunroom to the white rushing foam and the restless blue sea.

Sandy was out before six catching sunrise photos of a couple of fishermen on the jetty; I was groggy, guilty of reading from 3:15 a.m. to 5:15 to finish *Frieda and Mim*, probably the best South African novel so far.

The first young surfers arrived very early and for a couple hours crisp blond heads continued to pass by the windows, most moving at a brisk pace that we later learned is to loosen their leg muscles before getting on their boards. Lisa spoke of surfers as being rude, arrogant, and careless of their surroundings, as though all this was created just for their temporary use. After my in-bed coffee, I sat with Sandy in the very comfortable white upholstered chairs in the sunroom: Where's my *New York Times*? I asked.

Sandy joined Lisa on the concrete porch to help adjust the table away from the sun, and I heard them chatting as a sweet African woman set out placemats and silver. When we arrived yesterday Sandy had gotten paint from underneath the table on her shorts and Lisa was again apologizing, thanking her for not making a big fuss and handing her back her clean, unmarred shorts. Lisa asked if we traveled together often and I was pleasantly surprised to hear Sandy say that we had been partners for twenty years, adding, "It has worked very well."

Usually we mention to people whom we expect to be around for a while that we sold our house, we live in Maine now, and they get the idea of a long-term relationship, the nature of which they can imagine as they wish. I am more comfortable introducing her as my partner than she is and so this compromise works well. Anytime she drifts into playing "friend of the family," I am appalled.

This old Dutch-style whitewashed house is one of a kind along this line of maybe two dozen houses, side by each, pinched between hillside and ocean. Beach communities the world over have a similar feel, damp being one of them, and The Waves at water level is the worst yet. I am thankful our home cottage is high on a rocky shore and without the constant wind that this coast endures. The locals are unanimous in their dislike of it, and after eighteen hours here it is beginning to wear on us.

LATER. *Tsitsikamma Lodge*
"The garden of the garden route." Forest is certainly a new definition of garden for us from the northeast of the US, and we have been slow in realizing our mistake: there is not one "garden" on the garden route. Tsitsikamma is a national park and also the name of our just-off-the-highway—I'm amazed we can't hear traffic-—woodsy paradise. It is similar to an American 1920s-30s retreat: all buildings are made of notched logs and the huge dining hall is surrounded by thirty-five cabins connected by paved paths and little arched bridges. The vegetation is outstanding and each cabin has a small patio area with angular style Adirondack-chairs and a picnic table. Inside, giant trees wave above the skylights. We are still debating about eating in the lodge: US$27 for the two of us, but we really don't have the energy to try to find any other place; we long for the constant cool wind of Victoria Bay.

LATER. I've never seen a buffet dinner the likes of the one we just enjoyed. I wanted to eat much more than I could hold; the spread could have fed sixty and there were only about thirty there. Superior roast of beef and many side dishes we will never know the names or contents of.

SATURDAY FEBRUARY 7   *Tsitsikamma Lodge*
Eight-thirty at night. Cool at last. "Hottest day in ten years here," our ponytailed carpenter master-of-all-jobs told us at dinner. I had asked a receptionist at noon the temperature and she replied, "Damn HOT." Midthirties was the general consensus: that's midnineties Fahrenheit.

We had bravely set off on a trail walk at 9:00 this morning having no idea what was in store for us. At the end of a half hour we were at a stream, the bed of which was the trail for the next couple miles. Too rough for us. Took some woodsy photos—nothing spectacular in way of vegetation—and climbed back up to the sun-baked path. By that time even the dirt was hot.

Our room has a telephone and I did manage to find the home number for the place where we are staying in Port Elizabeth. Having seen nothing in the guide books that looked affordable between here and there—one hundred plus miles—I wanted to request Monday and Tuesday nights too. Good thing I called. We were not even booked in for Wednesday—our flight for Jo'burg leaves Thursday morning—but she moved somebody for us. She—a relative of some of the Inkasi people— gave us some names in St. Francis Bay; the first two were about US$200 a room, and the receptionist at the third, Sandals, said she had a room at R 675 per person. I said we couldn't go over 559 and the woman on duty said she'd have the manager call us back. I gave her our cell phone number, which we had never even heard ring before; it was a miracle we figured out what buttons to press without cutting her off. Well, it turned out that the manager was fine with US$112. So we are set there for two nights. Big relief, since we are barely able to move from the heat.

Bathing-suited bodies litter the pool's shady spots, and one man is standing up to his nipples with a book propped on the edge. It seemed cooler in our cabin with the fan going than outside in the shade, so I just lay on the bed and read and dozed the afternoon away. Now they say that it is raining in George to the west and if it does move here, it will break a two-month drought.

We are cheering it on.

HANDWRITTEN NOTES from a reception brochure: "Tsitsikamma is a Khoi word meaning 'place of abundant or sparkling water.' ... large tracts of indigenous forest, commercial plantation and Fynbos. Deep river gorges cleft the plateau, as they make their way down to the sea, creating spectacular waterfalls and deep kloofs." As in all commercial pamphlets, only businesses that pay get much notice, so

I checked guide books. Decided to go tomorrow to Storm River's "intimidating suspension bridge" and Monkeyland, that "restores the freedom of ex-captive primates." Day in an air-conditioned car sounds just right.

LATER Time in reception on Internet (US$3) and then beers on deck and inside for another terrific dinner. Loud night insects.

SUNDAY FEBRUARY 8. Good sightseeing. Sandy very comfortable driving now, although any entrances onto main roads still require the mantra: Left lane, left lane. Lots of exercise both places we stopped. The Storm River suspension bridge is long and beautiful, the Monkeyland bridge shorter but primitive, full of dips and sways and made a bit scary by ranger's insistence that a female go first, because baboons on the other side attack males entering their territory. All primates are free to roam the twelve-hectare (thirty-acre) forest, but we humans were kept on trails for our hour and a half trek. The residents, most here for life, feed both naturally and at platforms stocked while they sleep, but newcomers are caged and kept from hearing or seeing humans while being "dehumanized" from their former pet dependent status. In about six months they are released into the sanctuary. Complicated, this wild and free vs. tame idea.

After our people-filled day, we ordered a picnic dinner that a woman from the dining room kitchen carried over to our cabin in a basket. She unloaded dishes and hors d'oeuvre type food on the patio table. Three cold beers and glasses arrived on the second trip. Two weeks and we humans have become servant dependent. Scary.

TUESDAY FEBRUARY 10 *Sandals, St. Francis Bay*
Can't get into any sort of rhythm with this writing. We are either moving on during the morning, or there is no suitable desk, or if I try in the evening the light is not good and on this very small keyboard I make mistakes I can't even see to correct. I never really learned the numbers or punctuation marks, anyway.

On this bay every house is thatched; the more residential section across the cape looks like Florida with its canals, fancy boats, and luxury homes, whose dark gray thatching is as uniform and precious as money can make it. Sandals claims to be five star, but certainly this room is four, so really the reduced price is right. We have gotten some real bargains so a little over US$100 a night is no great loss. There are occasions, however, when certain credit cards won't go through and then having another source—bank card for ATM or another credit card— is truly necessary: at Abalone in Hermanus, for instance.

At the restaurant at Storm River Mouth we had just come off a strenuous number of steps up and down on the hour hike to and from the seventy-seven meter pedestrian bridge—across the gorge where river meets sea—and collapsed hot and weary into the shaded area of seating. We had ordered rather pricey, almost US$10, entrees along with our beer when their computers went down and no credit cards went through. So add that to the Traveler's Warning List, alongside the No American Express accepted here.

And here's one for the Safety Column. After we left Hermanus with its persistent high security, we kept getting more and more slack, until at Tsitsikamma we didn't even bother to ask about fences, let alone the fact that anyone could have wandered by, reached in our open window—a necessity because of the heat—and lifted this computer, or us if they were so inclined. The only warning we received here in St. Francis was from a gallery owner who said that since a developer had done in a huge swath of wild acreage nearby, monkeys had been forced into the suburbs and their offspring figured houses were part of their natural habitat. The inside of houses, that is. Now here—finally—comes the kicker: at the St. Francis post office we were told it was closed. Two men had robbed it at 11 a.m. From Ghana, they said. Our receptionist said that it had been robbed not six months ago by a couple of Nigerians. (We have heard foreigners blamed more than once.) As we walked back to Sandals in the dark from a delicious pizza at Endless Summer last evening, we joked about post office robbers jumping from the bushes. In Cape Town we certainly would not have laughed.

Sandy just came in from another futile attempt to mail those postcards and reported the post office closed until 1:00. One thief caught—there is only one long road out to Route 2—and if I wanted to see a scorpion, go up and look on the second step into the breakfast area. Inch plus and black. Moral: gear up for the unexpected.

When they let us in our room yesterday—2 p.m. latest check-in time yet—I called the travel agent, Mereike, who had made flight arrangements to Inkasi, about confirming reservations on Thursday. Not necessary on domestic flights, she said. Also, that no vacancy has opened up on Saturday February 28 flight to Jo'burg, so she would make a reservation at the International Hotel for Friday night. I said, no wait. When I got off the phone Sandy said, Do you realize we are fully booked? That is the last one in Africa. I was startled. It's

over? We did it? Of course, there are always possible flies—
scorpions?—in the ointment, as evidenced by the urgent e-mail
from Sue's father, Dennis Tutt, telling us to stay put at the arrival
gate until they arrived to meet us. Sue had told us her father is
almost blind, so his wife—Sue's mother had died—does all the
driving.

Well, of course our adventures are not over. Isn't Jo'burg rated
the most violent city in the world?

NOTES: Long sand beach walk: picnic and fun splashing in Indian
Ocean. Wonderful to get skin into the sun. Terrific breakers by
lighthouse.

WEDNESDAY, FEBRUARY 11 *Harbor B&B, Port Elizabeth*

Left St. Francis early and arrived at Addo National Park around
noon. In spite of drizzle we signed on for game drive in big—holds
fifteen— Land Rover, US$20 piece. It was worth it. Lots of relatively
tame elephants—more than four hundred roam this seventy-eight
square mile enclosure after being hunted down to eleven in 1931.
Babies, youngsters, herds of twenty or so of these amazingly huge
trunk-swinging beasts. Then there were the two-inch dung beetles
who are endangered and have the right of way on roads. Do the
elephants know that?

Sandy did well driving city highways to the tip of Port Elizabeth
and our elegant B&B one street away from beaches. Tea brought on
silver tray to an antique-stuffed sitting room. Fountains and pools
everywhere. We feared the cost of their recommended restaurant,
but it was a short drive, so—. It turned out to host tours and so was
chattery, but fine food for a moderate price. I am certainly glad
we're not here for more than overnight—too stiff and staged.
Tomorrow a big breakfast and an easy twenty-minute drive to the
airport.

NOTES. Thursday and Friday in Jo'burg.

Flew over Africa low enough to see the deep green, but unaware
that we would land two miles high. In domestic airport held tightly
to bag with Karen's computer nestled among my underwear. Quite
anxious until we spotted Vera and Dennis with a sign. Long drive
around city to get view of skyscrapers in this largest—next to
Cairo—city in Africa.

"Now don't be put off by this neighborhood we have to drive

through," Vera said, turning off the rushing highways into a black section just like the poor urban areas in the US. Dennis is a retired metallurgist; Vera worked all her life as a nurse in this city. They have a one-bedroom unit in a tidy lawn-and-tree-filled senior village subsidized by a long-ago visit from the Queen. The shock was the high wall with curls of barbed wire.

Vera devised clever arrangements for our comfort, but outside of sleeping and breakfast we were never there. She did marathon driving the next day to the Apartheid Museum and Lesedi Cultural Village. The former evoked strong feelings of separation and oppression — revealing photos. Our host's comment: "We were living here but not told all this was going on." The latter place — quite a long drive outside the city — presented demonstrations which included the click language. A walking tour featured five different tribes, giving us an incredible understanding of village life that we could not have come to on our own. The variety of types of houses, crafts, languages, body builds, hair, and clothing was all amazing. How did it come about that such different people existed in a relatively small area? During one of the evening dance exhibitions, Sandy and I both were chosen by large women in skirts, who twirled and whirled us about the floor. Such fun.

Saturday. Took plane down into low veld — Hoedspruit Airport. Merle was there, but no rental car for us for about thirty anxious minutes. Lunch in bush café by river — no hippos though. Her son Winston Wiggill owns it. It's all overwhelming.

SUNDAY FEBRUARY 15 *Inkasi Game Reserve* Don't pinch me. If this is all a dream I don't want to wake up. I want to continue to exist in this thatched house by the brown pond where warm wind has stirred ripples that move against the stark trunks of tall dead trees. The ripples mask the rings of rising fish and the dance of gold insects in the dawn light. The water is high due to the heavy and constant rains this summer, but those seem to have ended.

Indelible moment yesterday: followed Merle's car off the high grasslands down the grade to this park like setting and the sprawling cottage that is our home; met lanky, wide-Obama-smile George — who speaks English and is in charge of Inkasi, we think; two smiling brown women came down the path carrying trays of lunch — Julia and Leah. Merle had been vague, expecting our grasp of local arrangements to be a given.

Before dinner George took us on our first game drive — a misnomer for bird and animal watching — in a small, old Land Rover

over dusty roads that wind and loop across the grasslands of this former farm. After an hour or so he stopped on a high spot; the expanse was thrilling: the sky crystal and the sun a goblet of red as it sank behind an umbrella tree. To complete the perfect African scenario dozens of storks perched in awkward silhouettes against the dying light. Photos completed, the Land Rover bumped us home for our braai—grilled—dinner. We are alone, the only guests here in Paradise.

LATER. At the moment I'm barely functioning as my mind struggles against the urge to lie down again and lose myself in an earlier nap so shockingly ended. After my dawn bird-watching session—there are huge twig nests in these dead trees—instant coffee and fruit, we went off on an hour's stroll with George, who pointed out tracks of impala, rhino, guinea hens, giraffe, and named vegetation. The sun grew hot. On our return a cheerful Julia and Leah had the table set for us in the bomba: fruit, poached eggs, biscuits fresh from the oven, bacon, a new kind of mushroom, and tomato.

I showered, lay down on the bed under the fan George had just repaired and that was that until a male voice from the doorway dragged me up and into this semi-reality: we are lunching at Merle's with the Winston Wiggils at 12:30. He, along with Sue Wiggil's husband, Alic, own this farm. Sandy was no help at this forced, misbuttoned-blouse meeting, as she was in the pool at the time. I must lie down again and regroup a bit before I go on company behavior once more. The two days of constant contact with Vera and Dennis in Jo'burg is something I don't easily recover from. Some folks are energized by people, some, like me, depleted.

LATER. Lunch—Sunday dinner really—was pleasant. Merle is so easy and the two boys of the don't-speak-unless-spoken-to school were sweet; Winston is a bluff man of common sense politically, so that helped; his wife, a local schoolteacher, was absent. Upon returning home—courtesy of Winston who made the twenty-minute round trip between the adjoining properties—I sat down on the terrace in a lounge chair to review photos, but in a matter of minutes had to hand the camera to Sandy so I wouldn't doze off and drop it. It was hot, but not as bad as Tsitsikamma Lodge at ninety-five degrees, so more than that is at work: perhaps the fact that I am finally not visiting, but living in the midst Africa's wild animals. And we are alone for two weeks in a huge Out of Africa quality thatched house with suites at each end of a living room of hunting lodge proportions. The kitchen is off the terrace, although I doubt we'll use it much. Really a setup worth a thousand a night instead of US$60.

George took us for another game drive tonight and the outstanding animal moments were handsome water buck and eight giraffes — instant love, I could watch them forever. No buffalo to be found, although Sandy and George had a fine time birding. I was content to ride through the low veldt of lush grasses and scrubby trees with a vast, changing sky above. The heat of our morning stroll was replaced with soft breezes and a feeling of good will to all.

Two abstractions come to mind for this country, perhaps continent: abundance of life — the dirt road this morning busy with the prints of at least a dozen species that had used it during the night — and space. North America has space too, but it seems chopped by cities.

It is 8:30 and I'm falling asleep right here — best I move to the bed.

MONDAY FEBRUARY 16 We step from the glazed-by-nature gray stones of the floor, out the twin French doors, and onto the dining area of the wide porch that runs the length of our brown fieldstone cottage. The roof timbers and sticks topped with thatch leave only a five-foot high slit between it and the porch stone: beyond the brief lawn floats the dammed, river pond. From the small kitchen with the lion carving on the door Sandy brings lunch, setting it on the massive wooden dining table: yesterday's biscuit and what we think is a mango taken from a huge bowl of tropical fruit sitting beside the leather couch when we arrived. I'm full again, too full. Shopping in town, Hoedspruit, later this afternoon should provide us with better self-feeding choices: we will also buy food for Julia to cook for our big breakfasts and dinners.

This morning a driver picked us up at 8:00 and drove us the thirty-five minutes to the Cheetah Endangered Species Preserve, an upscale good-works place sponsored, I think, by Princess Michael of Kent. They are such beautiful, sleek-moving creatures. It was well worth the time for someone like us, tourists with little real knowledge of the cats of Africa, but the driver and van cost big bucks we did not need to spend; we had rented a car. Gerald, who manages Inkasi from Jo'burg for the Wiggills, was aware of that but did not cancel the pickups, but then, someone had to make judgments on what would be convenient, safe, and interesting for us. Also, I'm sure almost all tourists have much deeper pockets than we do. Looks like we will be on a tour every other day.

A couple strokes of thunder were all that disturbed me last night. The dawn rain was gentle and sunlight came before we had left for the preserve. The bare, peaked ridges of the gorgeous Drakensburg Mountains were, however, shrouded in come-and-go clouds. Whoops, there is another drumbeat from heaven. Perhaps we will be in for a downpour like those to the north of us had last night—all night. We have yet to be sopping wet, but I'm sure that will come. Will mosquitoes whine then? So far, nothing.

Rest time. So easy in this cool, dim, silent Isak Dinesen house.

TUESDAY FEBRUARY 17 Today—one of those labeled free on our list—everything feels close to being under control. Clothes stored; desk set up for writing against bedroom wall facing the pond; two good nights sleep; routine of Julia and Leah regarding meals and laundry (hand washed and ironed whenever we want) and cleaning (every day) understood; food of our own here, including plenty of milk and water.

Merle, now seventy-three, and her husband homesteaded this huge farm, some of which became Inkasi Game Preserve (6,000 acres) when in the 90s, I think, farming no longer provided a viable living. George, born and raised here, is in reality the on-site manager, although he and the women and their families live at least a mile from us.

So we will swallow bills we didn't expect and suffer occasional wrong choices, but that will not dilute our pleasure in this extraordinary place by the river dam, the mainstay of these safari weeks. It is all we had hoped for, and in many ways beyond even fantasies. Thankfully, beyond those of heat prostration and deadly mosquitoes.

Unfortunately, I fear to swim in the huge pool—half shaded by a thatched roof, half sunny—because of the delicate condition of my skin. Also, yesterday's mango liquefied my stomach contents to an extremely incontinent degree.

We love our solitude, our pleasures—Sandy must have already identified ten different bird residents of this pond—each other, and Africa. And our time with George. At six he led us into the still, gray, vast low veld. A giraffe gazed down on us from probably fifty yards away. I stopped and said, "Good morning," quietly amazed that there could be rapport between that creature fifteen feet tall with the long, powerful neck and benign face and my small self.

Later, George pointed out dark shapes that also watched us: motionless, inscrutable buffalo, part of the Inkasi herd of forty-two, safely distant. Bliss, pure bliss. To nap ...

WEDNESDAY FEBRUARY 18 It is early: the fish have just begun to rise to the black silhouettes of insects above them, the birds have quieted since the shell of morning cracked. Sandy had gotten the idea that our pickup this morning for the Moholoholo Sanctuary was arriving at five instead of eight, so we struggled between four and five to pull it all together and then pufffffff, so we sat by the dark water with another cup of instant. Now I'm at my desk and probably by the time we do leave my innards will not be so compulsive in their demands: I took an Imodium to make the drive endurable. Constipation is preferable to abject embarrassment.

Yesterday George wanted to make an earlier start on our evening drive. And what an animal time it turned out to be. The whole herd of buffalo, their thrust forward heads weighted by that massive stretch of don't-I-look-fierce horns, stared at us from about forty yards away. They would probably run from a stranger in a truck, George said. But he admires them and the reverse also seems true. At Addo National Park our driver had said the herd we were watching from about the same distance could reach us in three seconds if they decided to charge, but tourist talk is to be expected; most people like thrills. Personally I enjoy just us riding with George: his smile, his low voice and easy movements, his sure, non-show-off knowledge; I hope for a lot of it before folks move into the other cottage.

THURSDAY FEBRUARY 19 The gold today was in the grasses. At six a.m. dressed in my usual walking garb of safari pants and shirt, crew hat, and a fanny pack holding water with a bino case threaded on the strap, I followed George and Sandy, who were reviewing bird types, on our way to the crest of hill. The climbing sun had already painted an artist's scene of buttered grass and green umbrella trees and spotless blue heaven. Impala hesitated only a second before they began leaps and dashes to and fro, more in fun than fear. In the world according to George they had sought the sunshine to warm both their reddish hides and the grasses. "Too long in the wet grass bad for them. Their skin peel off the bone." Animals know these things, people don't have to shout at them, herd them, enclose them; they learn from their mothers, from watching others. I am definitely stuck in a "domesticated" world view, and cooperation, communication between intelligent wild things continues to startle me.

I asked if there were honey badgers here. "Yes. Cheeky animal. They fight with snakes." George laughed. "They get bitten and fall down and get up and start fighting again," thereby confirming what we had heard at Moholoholo Sanctuary for animals the day before. But George disagreed with another guide who had said the lion was slow to kill and the wild dog quick. "They [the dogs] will go at the running impala biting him here and here. Many bites. The lion breaks his neck." Many of George's stories are accompanied with gestures, often humorous, but his face was grave when he said it was very bad of the man teaching to tell us wrong things. But those "wrong things" had been what the guide had been most passionate about—do animals have hired lobbyists? Was this man a paid advocate for those trying to get the wild dogs on an endangered species list?

The Moholoholo Tour cost US$75 per person and I felt the time and money could have been better spent elsewhere. Rather a circuslike atmosphere with lots of raw meat and audience participation, plus endless stories of animal abuse. Our first close-up glimpse of the Drakensburg Mountains had been awesome, however, and our personal driver, who took different roads to and from the site, explained much about the local economy when I asked about the huge water-spraying arms in the corn fields and the people picking. When I fact-checked with him, he also said that the lion killed quick, the dogs "bled the animal to death."

It was also very hot and today promises to be even hotter. Yesterday I fell into two wonderful afternoon naps, but today we will be with Merle in our non-air-conditioned—well, we told Mereike cheap—1980 Rabbit rental driving to a Vera-recommended "factory" where silk is taken from cocoons and spun into scarves. I may purchase one for myself, one for Tee's graduation, and another for Sandy's birthday if she loves them. Like the Tutts were in Jo'burg, Merle is our insider guide and we pay for fees and meals; Sandy drives. Merle is a valuable resource and pleasant companion for us.

The air conditioner in this bedroom—large enough to hold a king bed, wardrobe, and long writing table—is an excellent, remote controlled one; all rooms, except bathrooms, have double exposure and fans. We have found a setting on it that is perfect for the entire night, although I sometimes pull up a soft mohair bright red blanket. Perhaps if these blankets are much cheaper here we should purchase one for Milbridge; both Maine and New Zealand prices are way high.

Last evening we sat silently in the Land Rover maybe twenty yards from the farm's extended white rhino family: they stared, we stared. On morning walks George had already shown us many places where they had rolled in the road. Their evaluations done, the sound of grazing began. The four-month-old baby stayed by his mother, who would snort if the other two females came too close. George explained that the baby "still on the teat." He is a boxy little fellow with a child's curiosity, but I noticed he did not approach his father—"a very nice big male," according to George—who after making all appropriate motions of protecting his family resumed his solitary munching. I did not, however, feel the connection to them that I had for the giraffes who had gathered to stare over the trees at us this morning. Perhaps I romanticize, but the sense of a non-verbal, motionless flow of mammal-to-mammal communication with them has remained. Probably it flows only one way, but maybe not. When I walk behind George I have the feeling he knows exactly what I'm doing and beyond that, thinking. A result, I suppose, of his amazing ability to sense animals: to see what we cannot, to smell their presence, to hear a lion miles away on the next preserve. A new, unsettling perspective: does the family of man actually extend beyond our species? Is sensing that kinship a faculty we have lost?

Which reminds me, I promised myself to write a lion cub card to Schoodie before our trip to town. No worries about him this year, thank goodness.

Tomorrow, Friday, is Kruger Park day. Ever since its establishment in 1898 Kruger has been a destination for the world traveler. Now larger than the state of Massachusetts, it is home to 147 mammal species, including twenty-one different antelope. Instead of an overnight stay, Gerald has arranged for an all-day private driver/guide; even though we are a near neighbor, its gates are miles to the north or south.

SATURDAY FEBRUARY 21 Dreamy calm. The rhythmic tic-creak of the ceiling fan, bird calls; no sound from the breeze. No effort to prepare, to do, to have the senses on high alert, to absorb—that was yesterday's game drive in Kruger Park.

The night before I had warned myself that it would be a pinnacle experience, that I would never after be the same. And, although that can be said of every day, especially those spent traveling, yesterday was unique: I had indeed been fully present in the heart of Africa.

Some moments were mystical, some awesome, some pulse-pounding.

An example of the latter was my first glimpse of a great African river, the Oliphant. A rush of brown water swept over the causeway that supported the road; a vehicle used for heavy roadwork was making its way slowly across. We had time to evaluate our situation: going around, backtracking, did not seem to be good options. Our driver-guide, Geoffrey, leaned out the small van's window as the chugging vehicle stopped beside us: the workman laughed in response to his worried questions and drove on.

"He was laughing," Geoffrey told us, "because I was afraid." We all were afraid: I of stalling and being trapped as the water rose to sweep us away. Sandy of the causeway being weakened and crumbling. Geoffrey of being eaten by crocodiles. I had thought of drowning—but yes! crocodiles ... We sat silent as the wheels entered the water, then came Sandy's quiet, encouraging words: There, you are past the deepest section. You've made it through the second. We're all right now. Applause from us all, including Geoffrey.

Then late in the day, his voice high, crying out: "We're in the middle of a herd of elephants!" Dead stop. Geoffrey, we had learned, was seldom surprised; he took in everything around us from nearby to a mile, two miles, away—instantly.

My mind scrambled. On the very near right a mother elephant with a baby at the teat opened wide her great ears, began to raise her trunk; on the left was the black wall of a giant male. Bits of elephant bodies, knees, stomachs, mud-smeared broadsides, shown through every thicket. We sat breathless, surrounded. The mother broke off her charge preparations, the others moved in slow elephant fashion toward a huge tusker who stood, intently watching us, from a few yards ahead on our right. He stepped back into the road, crossed. "They are headed for the river," Geoffrey said. Sure enough, an edge of water was only a hundred yards on our left. A white pickup truck appeared out of a riverside road just ahead of the leader.

A rumble, a big elephant belly noise. "He is angry at the truck," Godfrey said. The truck eased onto the pavement and down the road a short distance. We had heard stories—bush tales?—of elephant picking up vehicles and tossing them away.

The gray, creased-skin group, even the massive one tearing off bush on our left, moved once more in the direction of the side road. Those minutes had been very long, but like the river crossing, the seriousness of alternative outcomes made our day for peak excitement.

For mystical dream fulfillment we'd had a post-dawn opening act: stage bathed in low yellow dewy light, herds of impala and zebra grazing, running—impala sleek, fat zebra rumps shining, over the low veldt grasses; and then in the high heat of the day at our lunch stop, the wide Oliphant River meandering among sand bars, marsh grasses and hippo backs, leaping rocks as it spread its dragonlike form over the land. Our 6 a.m. to 6:29 p.m. —gates close at 6:30—drive over macadam and dirt roads covered less than half this vast park.

Extension of my growing absorption with life-is-one philosophy came with the awesome sighting of a cheetah. Two other tours, small carriers of fewer than ten people—numbers of daily entrants are limited—had discovered her first; Geoffrey parked us down at the dam bridge and we waited. Even with binoculars it was difficult to spot her across the water lying in the dappled shade of a fallen leafless tree. When the other people left we drove closer, and from this embankment I could with the aid of binos see her lolling on her side, beautiful face, mouth open and panting in the growing heat, and her rounded white underbelly. I asked if she was pregnant and Goffrey said it was possible; at the Cheetah Preserve we learned that pregnancy only shows five days before delivery: no bulges slow down this fastest animal on earth. Later George said that is what cheetahs look like when they have finished a full meal; his pantomime of her belly fit.

At least one prairie-dog-like creature—a suricate—stood upright in the dun grass beyond her. Finally she rose and began a slow walk up the slope in the direction of a huge cistern; Geoffrey's superior eyes followed her. The whole ten minutes had filled me with the type of spiritual experience some seek from cultures like the Maori, or Buddhist, or American Indian. A peaceful oneness with all life on this planet. It is easier for me now to conceptualize the beginnings of life here and the gradual evolution into the abundance of forms that cloak this land. No human-expressed doctrine, even simple animism, works for me. No need for rules of behavior or thought, no manmade artifacts or symbols, simply a felt *always was*. Perhaps this is the gold of Africa I sought.

Brought half my nine o'clock breakfast back from the bomba to our refrigerator to store along with half of Thursday's lunch at the Cotton Club.

SUNDAY FEBRUARY 22   Thinking about this elusive gold of oneness takes me back to Thursday. At Merle's before we left for the mountains, I asked her if I might have a closer visit with her baobab tree. She was pleased. "Last time we measured the girth," she said, "twenty-two adults held hands around it."

I was struck silent in its presence. Gray and nobbly, rising with rootlike arms running along the ground and more stretched heavy against the sky. How do words fit a miracle? A 2000-year-old miracle. I touched the smooth bark reverently in greeting, but who was I to assume equality with this living spirit? Great organs, choirs of hundreds, row on row of kneeling worshipers would not be the proper tribute. Truly, silence and a beating heart can be the only offering. I circled it, touching and breathing in its being. Two thousand years on earth.

Merle pointed to a stalactite object growing perhaps five feet tall beside the trunk and lifted a branch with a few green leaves. "This is new growth. It grows so slowly." Merle and her husband chose to build their farmhouse here by the baobab tree. In that half century it has barely changed except for that new growth. She and Sandy wandered off; I tried pointing the camera upward at yet another angle along its elephantine limbs, but I knew that its essence would not be captured. Before we leave Africa I need to return at least once more to feel that humble, awesome presence. Even more than the great Kauri tree in northern New Zealand, a seedling contemporary, Merle's baobab shows in its knobs and twists, stops and starts, the vicissitudes of its existence. One could do no better than to be buried here and share its soil, the symbolic soil of this planet's life.

LATER. Last night at ten when we got back from dinner at the nearby five-star Kapana Guest Lodge, catlike animal cries sounded from around our cottage. Hyena, George told us this morning. At the end of our two-hour walk, we paused at the far end of our pond while George read the signs of a huge thrashing fight between our pond's big crocodile and a hyena. "See, five or six more hyena sit here." He said if we had been awake with the air conditioner off and the windows open, we no doubt would have heard that battle, which apparently ended in a draw. Also, sometime in the night the rhino and her baby were here, baboon too. Tonight we will have to sit on the terrace and watch.

In spite of all our misgivings Sandy's first night drive—from Kapana to Inkasi—was without bad incident. Saw only one car in the thirty-minute drive. Very dark in Africa at night. Mysterious.

Earlier after our sundowner drink on a hilltop, our Land Rover sped across Kapana's 16,000 acres in a blackness that gave me another of those all-encompassing moments. Stars began to shine forth until the large sky was filled, edge to edge. Orion rode above our heads astride the clouds of the Milky Way—which our vehicle full of Brits had never seen before. Casper, our driver, stopped and pointed out the Southern Cross and how to determine true south. Enchanting.

There were some other pleasant moments in our 4 to 10 p.m. time there, but food bracketed the game-drive experience in what seemed to me like sideshow gimmicks to cover for the shallowness of the highly touted night-time game drive, our main interest in going. What we got was a Casper who knew only a few textbook facts— some wrong—from a Jo'burg guide school, and an old lion and several elephants who acted hand-fed tame, and who were located by radio contacts and rough racing across long distances. The vaulted "night" aspect yielded only one owl in a treetop. High tea, sundowner drinks—to be paid for after dinner—and a pretty good buffet back at the huge complex—water at extra charge—were hardly worth the US$75 per person.

The tourist-first profit motive took precedence for sure and I have my doubts about returning for the elephant ride on Monday morning. According to Casper—I sat next to him in front and quickly spotted his fondness for spinning a dramatic story—the reason for the announcement that none of our fleet of ten vehicles would be going beyond the river anytime today in order to avoid agitation of some already upset females was, he said, because of a sad incident. "A death in the family?" I threw out. "Yes. Their bull." "Who killed him?" Long pause. "We did." No one in back could hear us, indeed we had to edge close to hear each other's bumpy, wind-caught sentences, and in spurts he told the story. A few days ago an older elephant bull was shot for actually charging—not just threatening—tourists as they rode the tame elephants. The females of his family are very angry. In fact, they are now charging the tourist vehicles. He, Casper himself had been involved in one incident and had to perform a long, scary back-up. My misgivings are both moral and safety-wise.

It is another hot day, although I see the pond has dimmed to rippled brown. I wish we did not have to drive the half hour to Hoedspruit to shop, but Julia says she needs food for tonight and we must keep our part of the bargain. The pure silence here is beguiling and enervating. I do feel sorry for the people paying some huge sum per person over at Kampana Lodge. The very military dress of the game people—Casper wore his with Germanic stiffness—put me off too. All the drivers are young white boys, the spotters in the jump seats black.

I believe our last-week-in-South-Africa duties, such as my writing our obligations and plans on the calendar —e.g. call BA for flight confirmation from Jo'burg to Madrid—are also tightening my grip on our precious time.

TUESDAY FEBRUARY 24 Very long day yesterday. I heard George's voice as I wrote that. He would have drawn out the "very" and followed it with: "You come back all ..." completed with a pantomime of wiping forehead and slouching. Particularly after being with George's voice for an hour or more, I find myself using the word order and emphasis that he would. It is the same with Julia and Leah, although our mutual total language incomprehension makes our talking time with them quite short.

Alarm sounded at four and I woke excited that we would be riding on the back of elephants. The hour before leaving was not rushed, but we surely did not have our wits about us when we left without rain gear or jackets. Our driver, white of Portuguese descent, used the back gate into the vast Kampana preserve and consequently our forty-five minute drive was endless rattle and lurch. I stayed away from the chitchat and examined again this moral quandary of invading the elephant family's grief and anger. I had no doubt about which side held the power. If an elephant "misbehaved" enough to endanger a tourist, she would be shot. Probably my mixed emotions showed on my face when a stereotypical Brit colonial stood in front of a line of eight elephants, each ridden by a military-outfitted man from Zimbabwe and behind him an empty saddle with two sets of stirrups. The largest was the twelve-year-old male who had not reached full growth and certainly was not mature enough to become bull of the herd. Jambalaya, the original orphan and impetus for founding this preserve, had come front and center for an elephant show and tell: his obedience and docile nature had everyone smiling. I learned later that the saddles were all foam, no hard parts, and each made to fit the configurations of the individual elephant.

I was reassured by the fact that the men mounted behind their elephant's head had strong ties to elephants in general and the one they rode in particular. The sight of a gun in the hand of the short, stony-faced white officer and the too casual comment that they fired them occasionally to get the elephants "used to gunfire" deepened my moral qualms and lightened the security ones: no effort would be spared to avoid trouble and quash it if necessary. As we dozen or so riders were herded to a loading platform, I asked the colonial Brit if they had any spare ponchos. He solved that obvious lack by giving me his jacket. Jambalaya was led up beside the platform and the mounting procedure explained. Suddenly the little officer's stick pointed at me and something was said about getting on. I glanced around to see if someone had volunteered to go first, but the stick and impatient voice let me know the answer to my question, "Me?" was yes, you. Ah, the oldest on the safest elephant.

The ride was pleasant, less precarious than my   Thailand sensation of sitting in a lurching porch swing, just a huge rolling rhythm of one giant foot after another. I assumed my horse riding posture: head up, heels and hands down. There was no question about the hands: a soft tube instead of a saddle horn was the only grip and I had to lean slightly forward to hear the voice of my driver. In good English he imparted much information in a relaxed manner, but the haunting song of that Thai boy, heard from a hoodoo with Chuck more than a dozen years ago, will always accompany my elephant ride memories. The trail was gentle, the scenery fine, the air cool and devoid of mist. To my consternation I dropped the colonial's coat as I took it off, but the driver simply signaled Jambalaya to pick it up with his trunk and pass it over his head. What a thrill to accept a gift from not a hand but a trunk. I asked and learned that in Zimbabwe elephants are still used in agriculture, road work, and the timber industry.

Directly in front of Jambalaya's trunk walked a man with a DVD camera; next the colonial with the rifle. (George later told us yes, that type has a big bullet that could kill an elephant.) The colonial kept his eyes down as did the little officer in front of him. Both constantly searching for tracks that I was quite certain would not be lion, but disturbed female elephants. When I asked my driver about the bull that had been harassing the tourists, he seemed to either be ignorant or intentionally misleading. "Maybe you weren't on the ride that day," I said. He answered quickly, "Oh, I was there," followed by some meandering sentence I couldn't follow. "Sad thing," I said and quit. Last night George said that he would probably never hear anything about it. The night before, however, he had told us a story: a man was beating and beating the orphan, Jambalaya, with a stick until finally that little elephant picked him up and threw him against a tree and he was dead. George said his tribes people were afraid of elephants and would not work with them.

The afterglow of the ride was spoiled by a little boy lieutenant who was not going to let us out the gate because Sandy and I had not paid for the ride. The driver of the van used his influence to get us out, but the issue was not resolved until noontime when we managed to phone Gerald in Jo'burg from the top of our hill. "Oh," he said smoothly, "that was the only place that refused to take payment through the transportation company. That bill is about R 1100 apiece." I held my head in my hands, wondering why that message had never been conveyed to us, or had it and we had misunderstood? I gave him a credit card number I hoped would work. The driver had apologized for South Africa, saying, "We don't have some things ironed out here yet." Well, neither do we.

It was a similar experience when later in Hoedspruit we tried to pay our R 18,000 bill for Inkasi and all our trips — except the elephant ride — by, as requested, transferring money to their bank account at a Standard Bank. But for some reason they could not use my Capital One credit card or my Provident Bank debit card. The ATM would only give me R 1000 a day. But the ASBA bank two doors away said they could do that. However, by the time ASBA put it through, the Standard Bank would be closed for the day. "Okay," I said. "We'll take the money now and bring it in to Standard tomorrow."

The teller's eyes widened. "You can't do that. That is a lot of money. You don't know what might happen to it while you sleep."

The bank's unique system of doors let through only one or two people at a time; we were already over the shock of South African bank personnel being behind glass, perhaps bulletproof. But while we sleep? Then Merle's story of the murdered neighbor came to mind. We had been standing in her bedroom watching her point to a spot over the door "where anybody could get in." Then, rather calmly I thought, she told us that not long ago her nearest neighbor had been murdered in his bed, then went on to talk about Winston fixing her window lock.

Wireless at our regular Internet spot allowed us to confirm that there is still $6,000 in the Credit Union account that we have been drawing on and that my checking shows $5,000. Good to quickly scan family letters and find that all is well. And Schoodic in spite of a dip in taking fluids showed no signs of blockage. And we were right in not taking a hotel reservation in Jo'berg. A cancellation did come through and Mereike secured us tickets to Jo'berg on the Saturday flight. Yea!

LATER. Sandy is over at Merle's house taking tea. They could not make clear connections over the phone to plan tomorrow's lunch and boat trip, our last adventure trip of South Africa. Trust that the drive to the Eastgate Airport, the hour in the sky, and six hours in Jo'burg's airport will not be an adventure, just time to pass. So I'm at my table with my tea and the wind blowing in through the tops of the double Dutch doors, always a welcome visitor here. Although there were those times down on the coast where it felt like one who had overstayed. Clouds have remained, spreading their shield between land and summer sun. I still have on my safari jacket from the morning walk.

We started a half hour late, six-thirty, nevertheless relished coolness all the way. New tracks: rabbit and — leopard! From the first George said that he has seldom seen them so I had little hope, but now one is on our farm. "A nice big one." George's favorite expression of praise. (But he doesn't say that to me; he calls me "strong." He's pleased that I can walk for two hours, not quit partway up the first hill like some of the guests.)

A leopard ... If only the light for the Land Rover to use on a night drive had come through ... Perhaps the owners don't want the Land Rover on the roads at night: after the heavy rains of January they need scraping, and a grader will come soon. I hope it is that rather than some punishment for the last light going "missing," as in stolen. We'd gladly pay for a new one. Lot cheaper than Kampana ...

On the open plain, before starting down the road to home, the giraffe, blue wildebeest, rhino greeted us: "To have their photographs taken," as George would say.

We have been here long enough to feel that they and the herd of buffalo and white rhino family of five — they started with one couple — are ours. This subject came up the day we drove the fence line between Inkasi and the Karsie Game Preserve. They have taken down their fence and mingled with Kruger. George does not want this.

"One day you will have many animals. The next day no animals. All gone and you will never see them again." He added later, "Kruger always tell you what to do with your land. Do this. Do that." George had told us early on that Inkasi has no lions — they would kill too many impala — or elephants — we're too small, they would eat all the vegetation. He has talked of balance between all the living things, but he avoids the subject of culling although we know this goes on — and agree it is necessary if this game paradise for humans is to exist. I just don't want to picture George killing, but when questioned one evening as he was locking us up for the night, he did say, quite proudly, that all the skins on our stone floors are "from here. See, big blue wildebeest there ..."

Hanging on the tall, tight fence that encloses the yard where George, Leah, and Julia talk around a small fire every night are skulls of the antelope types that at first we found so confusing. The blue wildebeest is almost as ugly as a moose and has buffalo like horns. The male waterbuck's impressive horns are tall and lyre shaped. The kudu male's are long and triple spiraled. The mental chimes of Africa! Africa! rang, however, at Kruger where Kudu moms and young ones had gathered in the shade of small trees, their side stripes precisely matching the shadows. Antelope add a sense of light and freedom, grace and liveliness—bounds, leaps, gallops, whirls, jumps—to the whole veldt landscape, an astounding display of evolutionary adaptation.

While on the Karsie drive Sandy had said to George, "Inkasi is just right now." I agree. I've come to think even more strongly that the Big Five—elephant, lion, rhino, cape buffalo, leopard—is such an advertising tool that tourists feel they haven't been to Africa unless they can brag about seeing all of them. Originally, Big Five meant the animals most difficult to hunt on foot, but it is used now to push the average two-week tourist into an expensive one-day safari with the headline "Big Five!" Of course, a bunch of Land Rovers circling a feeding spot is a far cry from a month-long trek of Karen Blixen, writing as Isak Dinesen.

> ... *a herd of elephants ... pacing along as if they had an appointment at the end of the world. ... progression of the giraffe, in their queer, inimitable, vegetative gracefulness, as if it were not a herd of animals but a family of rare, long-stemmed, speckled gigantic flowers slowly advancing. ... royal lion, before sunrise, below a waning moon, ... drawing a dark wake in the silvery grass ...*

Geoffrey had said, "How about the Big Five of trees.? Marula, fig, baobab, lead, jacoberry." And certainly birds can be as awesome, like the secretary bird that we saw that day in Kruger and the hornbills and storks we have seen everywhere. But the leopard is one of the Big Five and I surely would love to glimpse him. However, cats, except cheetah, hunt at night.

The conversations we have had with Africans here run together in my mind, and some of the gems are probably lost for good. I do want to find time to try to reconstruct a few, perhaps in a large summary form. I can state rather simply, however, that my response to them has changed. In Cape Town my mind, poisoned by media reporting, leapt to conclusions: See a black man, hang on to your purse. Lock every door, prepare for the worst, including cruel, random murder. Now, I want to talk to Africans, get their opinions on their future, their children's future, their country's future.

For example, George has two boys, Lukens and little George, and a daughter. "I will let them decide what they want to do," George says. Lukens, twenty, can spot animals like his Daddy can and George is teaching him the names of trees. He can thatch houses and is learning to build them. He speaks and understands English: "Very well. Yes. They teach it in school."

I was quite disbelieving and then enraged at the way the only African at our dinner table at Kampana was absolutely ignored by the British family he had driven several hours to get there. A simple introduction might have salved my rising indignation. Since I was sitting beside him, I ignored the others' chatter and had a serious, intelligent conversation with him about animals as a commodity for viewing. He is afraid he is losing his Africa. When I left I took his hand and told him there were many of us with him, and he said something to let me know "people like you are appreciated."

At our bush lunch camp in Kruger, we expected Geoffrey to sit at our table, and were pleased he did not wander away with his burger. We talked politics, but he would not reveal his choice for South Africa's new president. Nobody has.

THURSDAY FEBRUARY 26 More frustrations. Yesterday we stopped at the bank in Hoedspruit prepared, we thought, to get the R 18,000 to pay off Inkasi's two-week bill and found out that a passport was necessary to do a credit card or bank debit. Our stupidity.

An earlier frustration occurred when we called to confirm flights with British Airways and they could not find our tickets by name. We were at the top of the hill and I hadn't thought to look up the ticket numbers. So, we stuffed any worries on that one, but another hill-top call was interrupted by a voice that said we were out of minutes. Well, we have to drive to town anyway for the money. Let's hope they sell Vodafone time there.

I did find the info on our Granada rental—at least the name of the house—so we'll get online to them at the hot spot and see if plans for pickup are firmly in place. Unfortunately, the sun has come out and the humidity is the heaviest it has been. And a nagging bit of diarrhea is still with me.

The 5 a.m. drive George had suggested was good: lots of animals standing in the bleary first light staring at us, particularly waterbucks—big fine animals so similar to our deer, but sporting a distinctive white ring around their rumps: "Sat down on a toilet seat while the paint was still wet," was Sandy's observation. Yesterday we had a good look at the tiny—probably forty pounds—gray duiker on Merle's property when we returned from our boat ride in the mountains. Which was magnificent. I'm still not sure what the huge dam and resulting lake is called—Merle made the reservations—but it should be on every tourist list. Or maybe not. The remoteness and silence are of an ethereal quality.

We ran out of time and had to abandon most of our lunch, under giant fig trees by a river, and race farther into the isolated valleys, then climb a windy mountain road similar to Cadillac in Bar Harbor. Sandy put the pedal to the metal, "with spirit" Merle was pleased to note, and we made the 3:00 p.m. boat, a barge type with a canopy and folding chairs. For an hour and a half twenty or so Swiss, Brits, and us putted beneath towering red cliffs while from the stern our African driver/guide told us what was what. Got a good look at hippo heads, but, told firmly these territorial monsters would probably bite hunks out of the bottom of our boat, did not venture close. Evidently, more people are killed by hippos each year than by any other form of wildlife.

After another of Julia and George's fine braaied dinners, I was fast asleep by nine. Tonight we are dining at Winston and Sally's; George will give us a night drive on the way home.

We did nap for an hour after an 8:30 breakfast, but I'm still droopy. Getting all this business stuff settled should help, so after a bit of peanut butter and milk, off we'll go.

FRIDAY FEBRUARY 27 Last full day at Inkasi. Writing at Joshmacs, Winston's bush cafe where we had hoped—vainly, it turned out—to find wireless. Merle brought us here for lunch after meeting our plane, and Sandy is photographing a red bird she saw then. We'll push on to Hoedspruit, in spite of both of us feeling not up to par, in order to read e-mail. We walked with George this morning—last one. Afterwards, we napped, showered, and ate, but the wim-wams persist.

LATER. Bett had sent Spain website address which had missed the transfer to this computer. The familiar photos and captions of our Granada rental ignited a happy flame for the place; our flight-weary selves will now have a happy ending to picture. Their letter re:

confirmation should reach us en route.

In mid-afternoon our pond is still noisy. Incidentally, the birds here do not sing: they talk, trill, cry, rasp, chortle, yammer; sometimes utter a sudden scream. One sounds like a bell, another a cell phone ring, a third the beep-beep of a truck backing up. Our song birds at home can generate a bustling feeling, and crows and jays certainly break any mellowness, but here the tone is staccato: cackles, rasps, creaks, squeaks, croaks, caws, chirps, squawks, sometimes in stereo.

Last night's braai at Merle's and her husband's original home was excellent in many ways. Sally, our hostess, lithe in her skirt, smiling and gracious, greeted us by the Land Rover and led us into the darkness; the boy Graham stopped me by a looming shape to show me the photos on his new camera. A huge silent hello came from the gray mass so broad that the edges of it could not fit in my vision. The boabab tree. I felt wrapped in its sphere and lingered after Graham had finished to properly greet this god of the earth. That done I walked toward a line of folding chairs facing a blazing wood fire. Beyond it arched the dark of the African night. I should live so long ...

SATURDAY FEBRUARY 28 Hoedspruit airport, a quite busy place today. By busy I mean there are probably over a dozen people here; it is very comfortable sitting under the fans inside. Outside, it is getting hot and is humid, but the morning of packing—the bane of travel—ended at last as it always does. Different for me, however, in that when George stood before us saying what good people and good guests we were, I teared up. He is the symbol of the Africa I have waited so long to see and now am leaving, perhaps forever.

Will quit writing in the interests of saving the battery for a time when it seems more necessary: namely the six hours in Jo'burg. On Sunday Heathrow will be rushed, Madrid lengthy, and Granada a question mark.

TUESDAY MARCH 3 *Boabdil House, Granada, Spain*
The rain in Spain ... But we are secure in our cottage. Beyond the narrow leaded window curtains of drops plummet, beating on the patio table, spring leaves; from the clothesline in front of the other whitewashed one-story flat hang sodden jeans and a sheet sags onto the puddled stone/concrete walkway. The tall wooden gate is black with wetness. This Albaicin district packs medieval charm into every square inch. Yesterday our misty up-hill lurches, both

north and lurches west, were made in an attempt to find what our Welcome! instructions had called "the nearest supermarket." It turned out to be forty feet wide with luscious fruits and veggies spilling over the sidewalk and fresh meat at the back. No English, no foreigners— except two young students—no familiar words on labels, credit cards accepted with a sigh. Someday when the sun comes out we'll have a field day in this riot of photo ops.

But today we must set out to find an ATM to pay off the rest of our eighteen-day rental fee. We have adequate heat—after a very uncomfortable first day—and the toys of civilization: fast Internet, CNN, and for me a compelling airport purchase: a Jodi Picoult novel. Life within our little casa is relaxing, not dull.

I never returned to writing after our thirty-six hours of flying and queuing began. Eight take-offs and landings, as measured by my gum supply, and at every airport a fruitless effort to connect to the Internet to check for a positive reply to our expectations to be safely escorted from Granada airport to rental house; it had been a month since our last contact with the owners.

Over a beer and descending night at the Jo'burg airport we had felt rather triumphant at what worldly travelers we'd become—that was the last time those particular emotions enveloped us. Our 777 flight to Heathrow over the dark heart of Africa was long—about nine hours –and cramped, but we did sleep some. My head-set has become a fulltime necessity for blocking out the wind roar and for enabling me to hear movies; despite many stops and starts I finished a comedy set in Barcelona. But I had forgotten to put a flashlight in my purse for dead-of-night reading and that was a bother—as had been losing one of my support travel socks at a security checkpoint when I pulled my computer from my hand luggage; and, earlier, a leaky pen created a Rorschach blot on my corduroy pants. The real troubles of the next day began at 5 a.m. when I politely asked for coffee. I'd been waiting patiently since 3:30 a.m. for that jolt into humanity. The very British all-business steward said, as though he had no comprehension what he was doing to my psyche, "Oh. Too late." Whatdoyamean, toolate?

I raged, quietly, to Sandy about leading a revolt of these several hundred of us incarcerated, bottom-line products. I thought of the New Hampshire residents who braved icy roads to find coffee the morning they woke to no electricity; there were rumors of long lines at Dunkin Donuts where honest-to-goodness hot coffee could be had. And here we sat like lobotomized robots after a night with fourteen inches between our noses and another's seat back, forced to stuff another desperate longing into a body already replete with full bladder and bowels.

No delays landing at London's Terminal 5, but we, particularly me, struggled on a long walk, toting our heavy carry-ons—Sandy's backpack held her twenty-pound veridite rhino—and not a coffee bar in sight. We had planned a bathroom stop and then a glorious sit-down with a steaming cup or two: a pleasant Sunday morning in London, but instead we had to focus on Terminal Connection signs as we trudged and rode escalators up and down until finally we were spat out in front of an open door with a Terminal 3 bus outside. A ten-minute ride later we were dumped at the far end of some warehouse; once inside we dodged, at last, into a sleazy bathroom. When we came out the railed-in walkway to security was packed with people: we slogged upward to find the end, up and around, up and around... Finally, reality stopped our bodies dead in their tracks—this is our line. But our murky minds blubbered, There's some mistake, this could not— No, it was true. A man in a blue suit was shouting and pointing for all Terminal 3 people to go to the end of the line and those bound for other terminals to hurry back down. They galloped past and we robot-walked to the end, joining this incredible mass of humanity standing stock still in a line that stretched forever. The blue-suited man was besieged with hysterical people afraid of missing their flight. "I'll keep an eye on you," he told them. Ha! we others smirked smugly, then I looked at my watch. Out of our three-hour wait only one was left. "We'll never make it," Sandy predicted. Two agents passed by and dispassionately agreed they'd "never seen it as bad as this." British accents were becoming an anathema to me.

Things got worse. In security Sandy's hand luggage was pulled off the line after being X-rayed. A beady-eyed Brit took over. Treating her black bag like a terrorist's treasure, he began unpacking it. To Sandy's remark that there was nothing in there, he replied, "That you know of. That's what scares me." When she reached to put the lens cover back on one of her cameras, he screamed, "Take your hands off! Don't touch anything!" We stood stunned as underpants flew by. A nutcase, our eyes agreed. When he had done everything but slit the seams of the bag, he studied the monitor once more and returned to sort through the tray of hard stuff. When he, for the third time, took a pair of reading glasses out of its case, he tapped an ear piece. "It looks just like a drill bit," he said and started to walk away. Sandy suggested—mildly, I thought—that his attitude could use improvement, and he did mutter something conciliatory.

Still wobbly from that brush with insanity, we were forced to drag ourselves and luggage through a New York long block of shops searching for our gate. The trail curved through store after store of glittering merchandise, and once we lost the gate signs so completely that we were surrounded by nothing but high-end Baby Care. How could they do this to people desperate to get to their airplane? Criminal, we muttered more than once, roundly cursing bottom-line capitalism. By the time we finally got out of the hustler's hustling we had the wrong gate number firmly in mind and collapsed there until things got too strange. We staggered back to check the big board.

We made our flight—just, but with no coffee. Once airborne I told Sandy that she was to grab the first flight attendant that came down the aisle and tell her there was a caffeine emergency case here. I'd been up for seven ghastly hours with no life-giving fluid passing my lips.

Upon landing at the vast, sleek steel and glass Madrid airport, I experienced again the futility of attempting to exercise free will in an airport. When on one of the interminable escalators I spotted a corridor of food and shops, we left the human pack and climbed some stairs to find it. Like a couple of rats we discovered many dead ends, but no other way out of the maze; we had to follow the leader. We retreated down, up, and around and this time did as we were told. Security had become a stop and go game, and this time it was Sandy's backpack pulled from the line. An excited attendant gathered others around the monitor pointing at—a what? When he unzipped it and laid the books and shoes aside, the only item remaining was the carefully bubble-wrapped and taped rhino. Sandy's explanation of Cape Town and the US$80 cost to ship made little impression. Another man was called in, Spanish flew—could they confiscate it? Not understanding what had transpired Sandy stood by her open pack until the agent got interested in another strange bundle and waved her on. I lost my expensive body lotion because the bottle held 200 ml—even though only half of it remained.

Occasionally, loudspeakers would proudly remind us that flights were not announced; we would have to watch the board to find our gate. We did—for hours. We rotated to different flight lounges and tried to get pesos at ATM machines, most of which were empty. One very irate well-dressed man informed me in brief English that he had called his bank and they were bringing money over. I did not wait; Jim had warned us about empty ATMs on Sundays. At last, a half hour before boarding, there was a change on the board—the flight would be delayed fifty minutes. Yet one more trip to information revealed that no, there was no gate number available. At least by now, we had been internally fortified by a marvelous veal stew, but not as yet mentally soothed by finding an Internet connection—in spite of numerous "Internet" locations--—to assure us that yes, we would be met at the Granada Airport.

We had no address to go to, no phone number to call, and what if the airport turned out to be like many small ones, completely shut down after the last plane of the day was in. And we do not speak nor understand a word of Spanish. In the terminal a resident had warned us to "be wary of the gypsies", did they emerge as darkness fell? It was late and grew later ...

LATER. E-mail to family
... so if no one was waiting we were at the mercy of the night and unknown cabbies. (And if we got a gypsy driver ...well, might as well be lost in Jo'berg. Every place has its bogeyman). But there was Antonio holding up a Sandy and Martha sign!! I came near to hugging his burly frame. And another miracle, Teresa was waiting at the square to help us haul baggage up the 48 steps which were spread over 100 yards of stone-in-concrete walkway.

The first locked gate is iron and leads to the narrow communal walk, the second is metal, and finally our own ornamental one and the green-shuttered door. We slept almost 12 hours.

Home now from supermarket the size of Portsmouth's Provisions on top of a New Zealand steep hill of cobblestones and a hot bowl of veggie soup and bread and glass of black coffee. Must nap ...

WEDNESDAY MARCH 4 *Dear family, Will continue with yesterday's letter at the point where I hit the draft key and boom it was gone, sent. Oh, well, the weather continues to be of the indoor variety—clocked another12 hours of sleep last nite. Woke only briefly once to read a bit of Washington Irving's* Tales of the Alhambra. *We have reservations for a tour Wed.—they only give out 7000 tickets a day. Also have picked out some inexpensive restaurants to try Moorish and Andalusia foods—Spanish ones will follow.*

Many are within a short walk, but we will stick w/afternoon hours. Our streets are so narrow an umbrella impedes a car passing. The direction a car may travel is regulated by stoplights which the walker cannot see. We never know whether to huddle against the left or right wall.

KATH Loved your letter today—ah, a ride and a warm bed at the end is the height of actual travel security. Thank you so much. 8 p.m. will be about 2 a.m. for us.

BRENT, JAMES, KATH, MARY, CHARLES, NATE. I do not have gifts for you yet. Thought Spanish more appropriate than African. Please send your thoughts.

BETT, BLAKE, RACH. Your animals refuse to get out of the bottom of the suitcase in the closet. They do not want to go out on their leashes until the temp is in the 80s — no chance of that.

Love, Mom, Mamar

THURSDAY MARCH 5 A shaft of sunshine around 10 a.m. hustled us off into the outside world. I had a really bad stomach on the walk to and from downtown and chills were still with me in late afternoon, so Sandy was forced by our lack of bottled water—my problem—and wine—her desire—to make the tricky climb to Cordovan Market alone. Here in Granada I was not concerned about her getting mugged, but hit by a car. All went well however. Again I slept twelve hours.

Today my body has been fine, but legs still resist the climbing. Nevertheless, blue sky and a plan to lunch at an inexpensive restaurant—courtesy of *Frommer's Seville, Granada & the Best of Andalusia*—got me showered and dressed. Earlier, I had gone to the supermarket with my nightie still on under my layers of clothes. The tropics linger in my marrow.

On the walkway beside the river sun hit my back—warm! I was warm! Although the thermometer must have only been 50F, that sun lifted our spirits and eyes upward. For days both have been down on the stony sidewalks; now the light slanting into the dozens of alleys made each worth a score of photographs. I want to stop every step and gaze: study roof tiles, or windows and balconies, or Moorish goods. We may never get beyond Granada.

As advertised, our lunch of Andalusia food was plentiful and good—all sort of stewed in clay dishes, heavy on veggies: spinach, lentils, chickpeas, peppers, squash, onion, but light on meat and carbs. The three courses: starter, main, and dessert or coffee was 8.50 euros, about US$11 each. At least twice as much as in South Africa. However, the coffee in a glass was probably the best since NH. We ate at three and still were not hungry at eight, but we did manage a bakery roll, with beautiful tomato and ham and cheese.

Contact with home and the *NY Times* has been most enjoyable, enhanced, as is CNN, by a language we can understand. Funny how different each phase of our time abroad has been and yet all pleasurable.

FRIDAY MARCH 6 Another ten-hour sleep night and didn't actually rise until after 10 a.m. Have decided this is similar to cave living, which still goes on around us and was very popular in Moorish times. Actually none of our walls are into the hillside, but they are made out of earthy materials and the west one has no windows. Around us flowers grow on roofs, the most luxuriant in gutters, but here and there is a whole little field with waving yellow blooms. In Inkasi we lived in a dark house, too, but that was a grass hut type. Tall Victorian-type windows distinguished the Cape Town domicile, but I'll bet the original cottages were low-browed and cave-cold. Of course, interior coolness is welcome in these climates. Sun will make a huge difference here and this weekend when the nubies—clouds—finally depart, we ought to have sun from late morning to sunset. At the moment I'm at this efficient, window-facing desk, set up with a big blanket on my lap and every bit of warm clothing I possess covering my arms and torso. No rain but maybe the temperature is still in the forties. We are heading for the shopping mall beyond the downtown area.

SABITICO MARCH 7 I washed my hair. A risky venture in a cold house with no hair dryer. But there is no doubt that it is warmer; 13C (mid-fifties F) according to the Internet. Thick clouds, but in our case warm interior air is more important than outdoor sun. Called our ex-Brit landlords—whom we met briefly when they picked up remainder of rent, more than we expected— regarding clean sheets and towels. The man was almost brusque: that's what that washing machine is there for. Yes, you hang it outside on that little metal rack. Fortunately, she grabbed the phone and said she would be over with clean sheets and towels on Monday. Obviously, Sandy says, he has never done a wash before. Our neighbors do leave laundry out until the rack collapses with the weight of the soaked garments; at present a sheet draped over a plastic chair is gathering debris from the shrubs.

We are trying to get over our pampered state, but abject poverty tactics are not in our book. Home cooking has reclaimed some of its glamour: last evening the chicken breasts were so plump that I cut a pocket into them and stuffed it with leek and crumbed biscotti crackers. Little spring artichokes were a taste delight. And ... ah, there is a smidge of blue in the sky.

"The Mall" turned out to be one big store. They had a machine to print digital photos but somehow their paper did not fit our pixels, so I'm giving up mailing out any. Bought a few postcards and after a long wait in a big post office, stamps. Found Vodafone stores, but decided just to go without buying a new cell and rely on Internet for accommodations. At our cottage there is a land phone that reaches all of Spain, and we don't anticipate having to make any panic calls as we did in South Africa. Besides, we don't speak the language. Everything feels very safe, but no way will I chance a walk to and from a flamenco spot that opens at 10:30 p.m. We are tourists, not dance experts and will probably end up at the no-entrance-charge-dinner-and-show up by the grocery store. That starts at 8 p.m.

Ah, blessed sun!

LUNES MARCH 9   I should write a book titled *Slow Travel*.

Yesterday after coming indoors from a marvelous full-sun day, I started exploring the web to decide what, when, where for the week between leaving here and the plane to London/Boston from Madrid. Neither Sandy nor I liked the two to three day skipping from city to city idea; too exhausting before the big hop to the US. I've also wondered if we should begin looking into must-see attractions in Granada. An urge to start checking off cathedrals and monuments is sorely lacking—as is the urge to do that in any other city. That's what tours do.

I did not notice this "problem" in New Zealand and South Africa; perhaps sightseeing is more European in nature. But then, there was Gerald's list of places, prepaid, on which we dutifully whirled about. On the other hand we are not here "just for the weather." That's what Audie said about her annual trips to Key West with Paul: We just sit on the balcony and read the newspapers. Apparently, even taking walks or eating in town did not interest them. Still, warm is the main criteria for us.

Sunday was a good example of our idea of Slow Travel. At 12:30—mornings are Internet, e-mail and my writing—we set off to stroll the narrow, up and down, curving alleys of our Albaicin district complete with overviews, one with a market even. By 2:30 we had doubled back and reached our lunch/dinner goal, the Carmen (large house with garden) Mirador de Morayma (*Frommer's* inexpensive). The tall metal gate was shut and we were unsure about ringing the bell; finally, we did and were ushered into a garden terrace with linen and sparkling glassware, black-suited waitstaff, and a few quiet local diners. (*Frommer's* had mixed up two restaurants, but outside menus had saved us from Expensive.) Two delightful hours later we left with a plastic box of leftover veal steak and breaded rib lamb chops. Fifty euro, which included beer and a Moorish tea.

We savored the remainder of the afternoon sun on the patio, dozing, writing postcards, looking over digital photos, and finally about six bringing in the laundry. Slow travel.

If we should ever decide to return to someplace, a country or even one particular rental, I'm sure we would call it wintering in _____. We have met a number of people who do that, the latest being the Brit who sat beside Sandy on the flight from South Africa to London. He and his wife have a condo in a non-tourist spot and have spent several months there for many years.

Is that any different for them than going to Florida for three months as most of the state of Maine does? Not really. The Brits have no tropical south, except their former colony. A different concept, however, from exploring the world, which is the basic push behind our travels. Measured exploring is surely not extreme. Well, I guess South Africa was riskier than most, and for some even an unfamiliar nighttime passage from bedroom to bathroom is too perilous. Those are the true hunker-down folk.

We got word from Barb today that Schoodic is still enjoying his life in Maine. Lots of ice and snow there and temps in 20's at night. Don't think I'm up for that.

THURSDAY MARCH 12   Tourist impressions.

The Cathedral. The Spaniards were famous for seeking gold, obsessive may not be too strong a word, that was entwined with exploration and conquest—often cruel and bloody. All governments seek a higher rationale for their existence and in the "teen" centuries that was most frequently an omnipotent God. The Catholic Church posited the saving of souls as its rationale. The Cathedral in Granada shouts that message through stained glass windows, statues, carvings of wood and plaster and gold. Indeed, the weight of that blare of gold seems to ground the vault of the ceilings and dome, as though to prove the point that gold was the earthly version of heaven, or paradoxically, a greed that man's soul must rise above. The walls appeared to tilt inward with the layer upon layer of straining ornate preciousness, to the point where humans might at any moment be crushed by it. Sitting dazed in a pew I stared at the overbalanced wall and saw it waver, heard the bolts begin to pull away from the plaster, saw the gold pipes quiver; the mass of it reached the tipping point, wavered, but its sheer size determined that its ponderous and then quickening descent was inevitable.

Alhambra. One of Europe's greatest attractions. I cannot recall seeing any gold at all. Its exterior boasts the raw power of stone: gigantic walls, towers, gates, bastions, buildings, all dwarfing humans, all singing of war. Only deep within do the honeycomb domes of the Muslims rise to seventh heaven and the name of Allah, endlessly written in the graceful stucco plaster, appear. No precious metal, only modest tile ties the graceful, delicate, soaring walls to earth.

The Christian heaven is a city of many mansions and streets of gold; the Muslim one is a garden of palm trees and shimmering water. Each is a hopeful dream fashioned by geography and climate: cold, rough mountains or burning desert.

The garden is certainly closer to the gold I seek.

TUESDAY MARCH 17 My computer time has been filled with arrangements. Finally, got everything to flow for this high season weekend; we'll be in places we want to be. Many choices I did not feel comfortable with. A true bargain in Jaen—60 and 50 euros a night including breakfast— resulted in more euros to spend in Cordoba which sent me to four-star and up. A compromise was necessary, however, when the art center B&B could only take us Sunday and Monday nights. We had them recommend others, who recommended others and we kept getting "All fulls" until finally one place gave us a citywide list of available rooms. Not sure I could have handled the search without that: it was after ten at night. Out of the list a quite acceptable one emerged.

We vacillated over city or airport hotel for our one-night Madrid stay. I was ready to settle for the Holiday Inn near the airport until I read the list of services more closely. Nothing about a shuttle to the airport or transportation to the city: we plan on seeing the Prada Museum on the afternoon we arrive from Cordoba. Whoops, forgot we need to get those train reservations ...

The agony that plagued us right up until 8:00 last evening was credit cards. We had been having trouble with Northeast Credit Union Visa card since the first of February, when they refused our bill of US$800 at the Hermanus B&B. American Express was not accepted there, as was the case with almost every place of business. So I whipped out my Capital One MasterCard and all was fine. This became a pattern: if the Visa did not work, try American Express, then the MasterCard which always worked. We knew that frequently the problem was with the charge setup at the business, so did not dive into checking the card itself.

Last week my Capital One was refused for a 16 euro purchase at a shop, sending us into low-grade panic. All our reservations were on Visa, which we preferred to use, backed by Mastercard believing it was a safe bet. I checked online and Capitol One had a restriction on my credit limit: the reason given was "card use that had not been finalized e.g. car rental." What are they talking about? But due to an error with the site I could not view my transaction sheet. I determined that Monday I would call the international number on the back of the card.

In the meantime Sandy e-mailed Northeast Credit and they said they would contact Visa first thing on Monday. She also wrote to American Express—her card had been rejected a couple more times—reminding them she was in Spain now. We were shocked out of our complacent waiting when the Madrid hotel booking company—I had found a good spot near the airport—informed us that our credit card number had been rejected. Knowing that at least one other reservation was being charged on Tuesday, we started chewing our fingernails. We cannot make national, only local, calls on our phone here, so I called Sarah, our host, and she gave us—this was on a Sunday—two places downtown that handled international calls. They were a healthy walk away and the sun was hot. I sent an e-mail to the Madrid Hotel explaining the situation and asking them to e-mail us if they wanted an alternative card number. They never replied. My e-mail to them was eventually returned undeliverable; evidently our e-mail had been misbehaving on Sunday afternoon.

Yesterday, Monday, we went to town and finally found a store that promised Internet and international calls. We wended our way through the aisles of a typical street-grocery and found the booth with the phone. After several tries and several trips to the man at the cash register, we gave up. The one up in Neuva Plaza was closed—it was after 2 p.m.—but I asked in the little grocery next door what time it reopened. The man shook his head and waved his hand to indicate "Enough—all done—no more." And finally we understood that it was never open anymore. I must tell Sarah.

Online there was no response from anyone except for the Madrid booking company e-mail, also returned as undeliverable. I decided to call the hotel from a street phone when we go downtown.

After dinner Visa responded. There had been a security emergency and they had sent out new cards to everyone: ours was, of course, returned because of the no-forwarding rule. No e-mail had reached us and no letter as far as we knew, but Hurray! The Credit Union was giving us ten days use, enough to get us back to the US and then to pick up a new card. And American Express came through with: Card fine now, enjoy your vacation in Spain.

From Capital One, an e-mail form letter extolling the virtues of their wonderful customer service and they would be sure to get back to us in seventy-two hours. Well, you know where they can go. ...

LATER. After an early lunch Sandy checked the guide books: one said the King's Chapel closed at 1:30 and opened at 3, the other said 1:00, reopening at 4, it was then noon. So with a clear mind I went to the patio to finish *Driving Over Lemons* by Chris Stewart; I had bought the sequel, *Parrot In The Pepper Tree,* yesterday. I had sat in full sun for lunch so I slipped around one side into half shade, thereby becoming a living example of the old saw: feet on ice, head by fire defines the mathematical term average: "On average I felt fine." The lack of humidity here permits that.

The main noise component of springtime patio sitting in Granada is music: endless burbling, trilling monologues by unseen birds bouncing about in the surrounding bushes, more distant doves and occasional snatches of the human variety. Sunday our young black-bearded neighbor and his two guests sat around his outdoor table singing while he played the guitar. Quite lovely. He has a lot of recording equipment, leading us to believe he may be longing to leave his day job where I assume he is today. Radios occasionally fill the music gap; not nearly as enchanting but easier listening surely than the commercial-filled rock stations favored by American house painters. Even buses grinding up the hill below and motor scooters whining are mellowed by distance. Bursts of castanet cluckings rise from the henyard of a huge salmon-pink-orange house, whose metal rooster weather vane is about on a par with the height of this patio.

Yesterday on an exploratory bus ride to the bus terminal we saw more evidence of why a guide book advised that noise was the biggest problem in selecting Granada accommodations. On our old side of town it invades the flats or hotel rooms hanging directly over busy roadways or snuggled close to bars, restaurants, markets, or flamenco spots; the modern side's would be big highways with big buses, strips of stores, and grids of car-laden streets. Those of us in the Albaicin and Sacromonte districts have the advantage of being nestled in pedestrian-only alleys behind thick walls of stone and stucco, the outside shielded by height and trees and blooming shrubs. No retirement village could match this for easing into heaven were it not for the fact that ancient legs could never manage the ups—or even the downs.

My seventy-six-year-old calves are now curved with muscle, but the upper legs moan for a ride up the last, long strenuous climb from riverside to our alleyway entrance. The steps from there I can manage with only one stop to catch my breath. Speaking of breathing, it is not unusual for the noontime air here to be laden with most delicious odors of braising meat and spices.

WEDNESDAY MARCH 18   Three small cities of the world have left a warm and familiar imprint on me: Dunedin, New Zealand, Cape Town, South Africa, and Granada, Spain. In each we carved out a section of town that became our own, ignoring the others except for quick bus or taxi rides; and in each the patio became the heart of home. Yesterday we did our last walk to town, returning in the waning sun of late afternoon. The royal chapel of Ferdinand and Isabella turned out to be a real gem and we toured slowly using the guide book. That will be left here for others as we are trying to lighten our hand luggage for bus travel.

Being dependent on public transportation makes leaving a place more of a chore: physically because of careful packing, and mentally because leaving when you have a car is ordinary. Tomorrow we psychologically become packages to be transported with other packages to the addresses on our labels.

THURSDAY MARCH 19 *Jaen, Spain*
I think I packed the computer while it was still on. Plugged it into this hotel plug and it lit up to my e-mail site. So, either it was dead because the battery was discharging, or I killed the whole machine because of no air circulation for twenty-four hours.

TUESDAY APRIL 7 *Maine cottage*
I must gather an orderly nook for calendars and guide books where handwritten notes and my imagination can fully recreate those last ten days in Spain, the quiet moments and the beauty, as well as the vivid shock of being robbed. Leaving Granada flowed quite smoothly. Up and out of the House Boabdil by 9:40 to bounce the luggage down the forty-seven steps to the Square where we waited for the taxi in a slant of sunlight. We arrived at the bus terminal early and Sandy did not understand that the driver was loading the 10:30 bus, not the 11:00 that our tickets were for. Exasperated, he waved us on and we stowed our own luggage in the grimy hold. The realization that this was the local bus delighted me. Each of the many donkey-narrow
white villages was a postcard of Spanish village life.

Like our hillside in Granada, the streets were squeezed by old buildings and filled with short people—it was Saturday—but the surrounds held only the monotony of brown earth and measured rows of olive-green trees, one hundred and fifty million of them, we later learned. Certainly centuries removed from the grandeur of the Alhambra and the bustle of modernity.

The feudal land system here—similar to what the colonial powers created in South Africa—has left ownership of these vast estates in the possession of a few families who reside mostly in Madrid: the people living here and caring for these groves remain peasant poor. There is a similar division here at our accommodation, a five-star business hotel and sports complex in Jaen. The paintings on the walls feature numerous variations of muted green groves marching up hillsides and down into valleys, but outside, this hot monotony is replaced by the vivid green of artificial turf soccer fields and bright blue tennis courts where lights blare and balls bounce until midnight.

Our landlord John in Granada had warned us that Jaen was not used to tourists, and I did find that my gut decision for the business center outside of town instead of something old in town was probably the correct one. Modern, efficient, shiny clean had a sudden appeal for us. In fact, we lazed away that whole first afternoon eating excellent food in the sunny gardens of a 24-hour café, shielded, it seemed, from traffic noise by plastic barriers that reduced it to a distant hum. The desk clerks were tolerant of our lack of Spanish, ordered a cab, and even went curbside to give explicit instructions to the driver to pick us up at 7:00 in the square where he had dropped us off. Maps had proved confusing and we were understandably nervous since the cathedral we wanted to visit was only one of many with similar names, all at an uncomfortably long walk from each other. The drive seemed to take forever and I was relieved to look up and recognize the towering façade of the guide book photograph. When our driver laughed as he pointed to a line of people snaking across the huge stone terrace and down the street, we thought he was amused by the number of tourists waiting for the 4 p.m. opening. After fifteen minutes in line, gawking up at the truly awesome towers, hearing only Spanish, and noting that many pushed strollers and loudly greeted family members with double cheek kisses finally convinced us—all of them were locals. Not a real tourist in sight.

Inside, the line disappeared behind some sort of altar; something very Catholic was going on. "Sandy, we don't want to be in this line," I said, quickly leading her off to the left. Great vaulted ceilings, of both Christian church and Muslim mosque, diminished us humans. Somewhere up there, almost beyond sight, hovered God and Allah, reducing us to a pittance of devout worshipers. I remember a highly intelligent high school student of mine saying, "I don't mind the idea of God, it's the worship thing. I can believe, but whoever said I had to worship?"

We skipped the side altars and wandered around the vastness — in one section a priest led a service — and left. The Jaen Cathedral was not a relic, a symbol, a history, it was a going concern, yet for me the Inquisition lurked in its shadows.

Outside, the line of not-tourists now tailed around the leafy corner; a huge electronic sign announced: Waiting time: 28 minutes. For what? our Protestant minds wondered. What is going on in there?

The narrow alleys we explored were much like Granada and although an owner of an art gallery — who actually spoke English — assured us that she had frequent American visitors, I had my doubts. This Spain belonged to the Spanish.

Back in the square the line stretched out of sight. We shifted nervously from corner to corner and I strangled stillborn the question of what we would do if the taxi didn't show: we had forgotten to bring the name and phone number of our hotel. At 7:05 we, like drowning people tossed a lifeline, dove into the taxi of our savior. We later were told all those people were kissing the feet of the statues of two saints in preparation for Holy Week. So literal a means of worship stunned and depressed me more than it should. Who did I think inhabited the world outside my comfort zone?

The cost — 26 euro round trip — the confusing information given by different guide books, desk clerks, and, to us, incomprehensible Spanish pamphlets left us extremely uneasy about another day in town. Consequently, on our return I made straight for the reception desk where Sandy had earlier established a friendly relationship with a young woman, Mari, who spoke some English.

My question, How much to hire a car for one day? was answered: Avis 74 euro and another for 54. I shook my head and she — often hesitating to find English words — talked of the wonders of seeing the castle on the hill at night "When the —" She consulted her little dictionary and found landscape and smiled. "When the landscape is the most beautiful." I suggested and she glumly agreed that the taxi fare there would be huge. Later she came to our room to give us the phone numbers for the car hires, explaining she would be off work tomorrow. A few minutes later we tracked her down and said we had a crazy idea to present. She laughed as she defined "crazy," but answered yes, she had a car, but no she could not be our driver for the day because of a planned trip to Malaga. What she did offer was a night drive up to the castle when she got off at 9 p.m.

Vivid moments of that trip remain. Chatting in her little car in the busy street outside her apartment building where she lives with her mother; her boyfriend's arrival on a motorcycle to join us; the traffic-filled round-and-round drive up the mountain to the shining golden castle.

This restored Muslim/Christian fortress was built in the twelfth and thirteenth centuries. The walkway between the sheer drop and massive stone towers was dimly lit, and, as we hurried back from standing by the great cross that shone across the valley, Mari took my arm and counted out any steps leading downward. The cross and the castle were, as Alhambra had been, bathed in an ochre glow that awakened stirrings of the powerful clash between religious faiths, thrusting me back to the safety of history when the future religion of all Europe hung on the tips of blood-soaked swords and within men's devious minds. That people should build such giant structures with interiors of such exquisite craftsmanship—half the building is now a Parador hotel—is indeed awe inspiring. So was the fact that these two pleasant young people, total strangers, would create such a marvelous evening for us. I would, Mari Paz Rodriguez said, hope that someone would do the same for me. Do onto others ...

I can easily imagine Europe as the old country, not only meaning the former home of immigrants, but physically old, and New Zealand and South Africa as new, untouched, virgin.

The next morning I woke very early feeling headachy and queasy. A couple hours later, I shut the slider to outside and almost immediately felt better. The horizon was thick with gray smog. We had seen open fires the day before, but perhaps this was something industrial. We did venture into the city again and finally found our goal: another fantastic bit of restored ancient history deep under a palace —the Baths of Ali. We walked on a thick plastic floor lit from below with a greenish glow, on top of low stone walls for pools of cool or tepid or hot water, on through succeeding rooms where eight centuries ago Arab men lounged safe from the torrid summer sun. It was ample justification for the subtitle, "Jaen: Inland Paradise," in the tourist book *Andalusia*, written by Ferando Olmedo. Yet I wondered, paradise for whom? In what century? "I came back home from Barcelona," Mari said. "That is a city—you can be anything there. This is a town." She and her fiancé, who teaches older people about computers, are painting a small house they have bought in a nearby village. Is another type of paradise in the making? I love young people.

THURSDAY APRIL 9 Cordoba, a city which reached its peak as a cultural center for Arabs, Jews, and Christians in the tenth century, had been a goal ever since Vera in Johannesburg told us with great sentiment about a youthful trip there with her father. Its inclusion in the Roman Empire fascinated me, and immediately after checking into our one-night B&B we found tangible evidence—a sunken circle of stone in a park. Greece and Rome featured in my studies right up through graduate school and touching the same stones they once had and literally walking in their footsteps sent shivers up my spine. The gardens themselves were disappointing: we found both them and the food lacking in flair, imagination. That evening we ventured into an upscale tapas bar in a little alley off a very busy square, but still ... Perhaps we never hit the right restaurants, but my lasting impression is either of hastily mixed leftovers from yesterday's menu or blocks of potato, meat, whatever.

Being in the lively city center on a Saturday night was, however, a real treat; the streets and alleys and squares and plazas seem laid out for just such public times: Boy and Girl Scout games in the largest plaza, streets crowded with couples, families with children— hundreds in strollers even at ten o'clock. A cathedral wedding provided a fashion show of Spaniards "dressed to the nines." The guests ranged from high class to mid-middle, and from old to young, and because they had to park heaven knows where and walk several blocks down a narrow pedestrian street to the church, I could stare openly from an outdoor ice cream shop at the pageant of an invitation-only Cordoba social event.

Unfortunately, on returning to our B&B we found the lobby stuffed with Spanish bus tourists, who then disappeared for dinner and returned to enjoy midnight room parties that reverberated up and down a three-story air shaft, which in the morning also acted as a megaphone for bathroom activities. Moving to the hotel Casa de los Azulejs, a reference to their omnipresent splendid tiles, was an awesome delight. A balcony of bedrooms looked down on a large, open courtyard of tall tropical plants, and off to one side was a book-lined library with a wi-fi computer. A strong woman carried our luggage up the broad stairs and into the exquisite furnishings of our upgraded, due to some repair in the courtyard, room. Windows overlooked a narrow street bright with flower boxes and pedestrians, and on the inside was a full-wall black fireplace that rose from floor to the eighteen foot-high ceilings. Ah, the art of necessity. This had been a gracious family home until its loving, exquisite conversion to a B&B and, occasionally, a venue for art shows. Stairs lead down from the courtyard to an indoor/outdoor restaurant; we lunched and lingered in a delightful patio of lemon, orange, and fig trees. Ah, the benes of five star.

Cordoba's mosque was as awesome as Alhambra. Once more, I found myself resenting the intrusion of altars on the magnificent open space—clunk instead of grace. Nevertheless, a forest of arched columns stretching down nineteen infinite aisles, the incredible arch upon arch and dome of the caliph nook and the Byzantine mosaics cannot be diminished—in spite of the Catholic propaganda of the tour pamphlet.

The day was warm and the walk long; I began to feel tourist-jaded, ready to head home, until we rounded another corner and found the leather shop—such artistry.

SATURDAY APRIL 11 *Cottage in Maine*
Snow in the air. We've given up on FairPoint, who took over a couple months ago, connecting our phone. Bought a good cell phone yesterday in Ellsworth. Of course we may have to go out in the front yard to get a signal. For e-mail we'll use the wireless at the library. Even third world countries do better than this. Back to Spain.

The two-hour high speed train to Madrid was a sheer delight in many ways. The comfort and quiet of car #10—smaller one at the end of the train—and the wide view of pastures and an occasional farm set on vast green plains like a child's toys caused me to meltdown in youthful memories and wish for a never ending ride. All the way to heaven, perhaps.

The Madrid train station with its botanical courtyard of giant tropical green, splashing fountains, and high arched ceilings continued my illusion, in spite of fuzzy memories of the terrorist mayhem here. All our luggage, with the aid of helpful technicians, fit into one big storage compartment, and we hurried out to the Pravdo Museum. At the sunny, peopled, traffic-filled junction of streets we paused: lunch first. We rejected an in-the-shadows sidewalk café as too chilly and too slow and laughingly headed for the McDonald's; I had convinced Sandy it would be good to Americanize our stomachs. We munched on cheeseburgers in a booth by the windows: I told her the guide book said there were no pockets of crime to avoid in Madrid because people flowed constantly in and out of every street. Then she went off to the bathroom, leaving her purse on the windowsill across from me; my purse lay beside me on the table as I bent over a city map.

A husky young man—American?—in a red jacket sat down in the booth between ours and the door. His nervous twisting around attracted my attention and I glanced over my shoulder at another young man talking on a cell phone; he seemed focused on me. I saw it mentally, before the physical action actually took place: the kid in the red jacket was going to grab Sandy's purse. I whirled, started up as he threw something over the purse and ran, me scattering chairs in hot pursuit, shouting, "Stop him! He stole a purse! Thief! Thief!" I pushed the waitress out the door in front of me, hoping she would shout in Spanish for the police. The last glimpse I had of the lime-green purse was under Red Jacket's arm as he and his buddy hurtled into traffic and across the wide street into the park.

We never saw a sign of any enforcer of the law as we hurried, harried and frustrated, three long blocks to the police station. I thought of Cape Town's lean, brown-eyed security men: it would have been a different scene there, no doubt ending with Red Jacket lying on the street felled by a long billy club. Definitely what he deserved. I was angry, Sandy calm and philosophical.

MONDAY APRIL 13 When we tell our story of a traveler's nightmare: stolen purse with passport, two billfolds, and camera a day before flying home, we end it by saying, "But everything went really well after that." A testament to the Madrid police and the US Embassy. At the station the police were prompt and pleasant, the report we filed was in English—any of Sandy's possessions that were recovered would be sent to the Embassy and then on to her US address. A policewoman went the extra mile by calling the embassy for us. She could not get through, but gave us information on how to get there by taxi.

On the way we stifled our pain over the loss of all our Spanish photos and toted up our blessings: it had happened not in some distant rural spot but minutes from the embassy; the ticket for the luggage storage was in my purse; I had enough cash to cover the taxi and a bank card with which to get more. Best of all we were not hurt: it was lucky I had not caught up with the thief— his elbow in my face could have done serious damage—or my lunging pursuit could have ended in a fall.

The embassy was secure, but not frustratingly so, and fortunately empty of petitioners at the moment. The man we spoke with had an easy, can-do attitude: his first question was if we had to catch a plane that afternoon. If we had I'm sure he would have gotten us there. His second question concerned credit cards: very speedy resolution there, and both Visa and American Express offered immediate help by sending cash through Western Union and overnight delivery of a temporary card. Fortunately, we did not need that: our plane confirmations were in the station locker. Sandy completed all the forms for a new one-year passport and two hours after the robbery we were on the street hailing a taxi to collect our luggage and head out of town.

The Clement Hotel was on a suburban street and featured the best in room comfort, including a silent! air/heat conditioner. We chose to eat where the desk clerk said they served American, rather than go the tapas route. A very good meal and conversation with Brit ex-pats at the next table proved a lively distraction from our troubled afternoon. We slept well and relaxed over a breakfast buffet of an interesting and tasty variety. I even slipped a couple rolls in my purse: we were not sure of food on the Iberian plane to London, and once there we had a tight schedule from terminal 3 to 5. The hotel shuttle van was free and in under ten minutes there we were, back in Madrid Airport, our loop through Andalusia complete.

It felt good to be heading home.

SUNDAY APRIL 28 Last evening Sandy, relaxing on the couch after an at-home, mosey-about day, said she had zips rising through her: "Tingles like a kid gets before Christmas." Due, she thought, to having time to look around, admire and enjoy all we have here, what both nature and our own efforts have created.

"Zips of happiness?" I asked. "More like a rush." "Like falling in love?" "Yes, but not sexual." It's true, we have found a new groove. A pattern of living and are not only content, but excited by it.

Off and on since our return, we have munched about in the field of "How has travel changed us?" and not come up with anything definitive beyond the new images in our heads: architecture in Spain, animals in Africa. Most surprising to her, she said, was the similarity to here. And it is true, like a fish that is called by a different name and cooked with different spices, but still a familiar white fish, firm but light. Of course, that is a metaphor easily expanded upon. Under the different skin, the different culture, humans are pretty much the same. Taken in a biological sense, very accurate—everyone's livers reside in the same place, and our DNA is a bit of this and that from here and there. Even geography has a common core now that the theory of tectonic plates is accepted.

In 1987 before embarking on my nationwide swings to interview women-loving women, I decided that I would not read up on the subject. I wanted to form my own conclusions from what I saw and heard, not try on the different theories and conclusions of others. In following that same policy with travel, I read only what is necessary to choose what to see, where to stay; definitely no GPS, nor videos, I want to be surprised.

The South African calendar on the wall in front of me is an example: the big color photo is a helicopter shot of the ridge of red rock leading to the precarious perch of the lighthouse at the Cape of Good Hope. My actual experience was a bus ride across miles of flat fynbos, the gradual rise of surrounding hills, and the final, "Up there? You have got to be kidding!" exclamation to see, after the steep funicular ride, stone steps rising and winding up and up to that red brick, white capped edifice. Contrary to the commercial slogan about not needing or wanting surprises when you travel, I do want them. I want to be startled, jolted by new facts into new thoughts, new connections—universals—about the earth and its inhabitants.

I believe that is the gold I seek.

FINANCIAL SUMMARY

DECEMBER 31-MARCH 24
    Nine weeks; 63 days in South Africa.
    Three weeks; 21 days in Spain
    Exchange rates. South Africa: 8 Rand=1 USD.
    Spain: .80 Euro=1 USD

Accommodations:
(One person, double accommodations, in USD)

	Average: $82 day	$3500
Food: Restaurants and Groceries		
	Average: $15 a day	$634
Transportation		
Air — International		$3250
Air — Domestic		$650
Car Rental (5 weeks)		$470
Bus, Train, Taxi		$250
Total:		$4620
Tours & Entertainment:		$775
TOTAL		$9300

We used American Express Travel Insurance again: 6 weeks for $36 for both of us. No Internet costs to speak of: it was provided with our accommodation almost everywhere. Book costs are included under tours and entertainment. We gave Barbara $5 a day for cat care, and the vet is providing the monthly bum trim free.

I did not separate the costs in South Africa from those in Spain, but generally the former was inexpensive, the latter expensive.

Not all our CD's made 5 percent this year, but close enough so that interest on my money easily covered the trip.

Entome, housekeeper, Capetown

Mt. Nelson Hotel, Capetown

Ostrich, Cape of Good Hope

Guide, Shireen & host, GG

Hermaus

Swellendam

Cape Agulhas

Lesedi Cultural Village, Johannesburg

Pond, Inkasi Wildlife Lodge, Hoedspruit

White rhino & baby, Inkasi Lodge

Buffalo, Inkasi Lodge

Guide, George, Inkasi Lodge

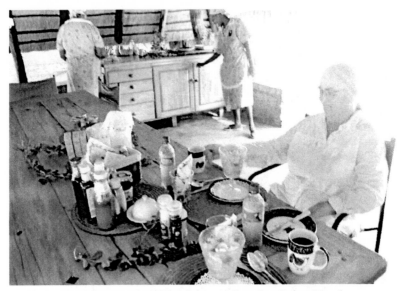

Julia, Leah & breakfast in Bomba, Inkasi Lodge

African Elephant, Kruger National Park

Baboons, Kruger National Park

Giraffe, Inkasi Lodge

AT THE ENDS OF THE EARTH:
ARGENTINA AND ANTARCTICA

"Everything wears an aspect of unreality. Icebergs hang upside-down in the sky, the land appears as layers of silvery or golden cloud, cloud banks look like land, and icebergs masquerade as islands."
—Ernest Shackleton, Antarctic explorer

"Wanderer, there is no road, the road is made by walking."
— Antonio Machado, Spanish poet

Andes view, Upsallata

Argentina

TUESDAY MAY 26 *cottage in Maine*

I saw a *New York Times* article titled: "Fishing at the End of the Earth in Argentina." The end of the earth … Even if planning had not already been underway for going to Jim's place this winter those words would have caught me. The romantic extreme of it: going to the ends of the earth. I had not thought of Argentina that way, had not heard of Ushuaia, the southernmost town in the world. But at 9 a.m. Central time, an hour from now, I'll find out if we will be going there. I'm a bit light- headed.

Last Saturday the mailbox held a University of Pennsylvania alumni travel brochure. The caption across an ice-littered blue sea was "Expedition to Antarctica Featuring the Deluxe *M.S. LeDiamant*, February 9 to 23, 2010."

Having company for the holiday weekend kept my wild imaginings at bay, but Sandy and I found time to rather solemnly agree that this tour had everything we wanted. Now it was Tuesday, time to commit. The least expensive staterooms—Category 6 Jade Deck forward—has limited availability, and who knows how many people received this brochure and when. Perhaps some had even been n pre-reserved. A total cost of $7,000 (including $500 of taxes) divided by 14 days equals $500 per person a day for a Number 5 mid-forward. A Number 6 with early booking is $6,300; $450 a day. All food and drink for the 12 days is included, but still that's at least three times our usual per day travel expenses. However, Jim has offered his little house way west of Buenos Aires rent-free for six weeks, so … Time to call Thomas Gohagan Tours.

We're in! I'm going to Antartica! Putting my money where my dreams are. Where's the champagne?

WEDNESDAY MAY 27 No champagne, but we let excitement run wild. Bett e-mailed congratulations, and added: "How will you pack for such extremes of temperature?" Brent wrote, "Wow! You will have been on every continent. Not many people can say that." I counted and he is right: South America and Antartica make all seven. Bagging continents at seventy-six! Wow! indeed.

While my adrenaline was getting an extra workout, there was, paradoxically, a rush of relief. Most of our three months of wintering-over plans for this year are set. In the seven months leading up to the big liftoff, we have only to complete a few weeks of arrangements and really nothing more. We have already given Jim money for some household improvements; for example, Nancy—she and Seba house-sit—said, "Jim, your mother has to have curtains!" So, this summer we can live in the present instead of bouncing along in puckerbrush, frantically trying to out-guess the future.

Yesterday I took a break from spading the garden and sprawled on the rocks where strong breezes and warm sun dropped me into a nap of all naps. I woke with a guilty start, but my body said, "It's okay, Martha, you can relax now. You've done it."

LATER. What "it" have I done? Maybe in leaving the tracks two years ago, I also left the train. Maybe experience has fashioned a new vehicle. One that has big tires and four-wheel drive for an easier ride over rough brush. Could that indicate a much-vaulted parallel synaptic path? New brain cells, new habits?

Perhaps humans have a built-in shedding regulator. Children shed favorite toys, babyish clothes, even pets and friends and finally parents. That's called growing up. For many people growing a next generation and shedding them also sets the following stage of weddings, grandchildren, and so on. Others make different decisions about who and what to shed and when. Live long enough and most everyone faces free-will years; which, it must be noted, sometimes their children, now experienced adults, once more usurp, this time as the caregivers.

Two years ago I had the opportunity to run my own train on or off the tracks with the concomitant responsibility for how it turned out. Is that what "Relax, Martha, you've done it" was all about? The new tracks I had scrambled to lay had not led my train over a cliff or into a swamp. Not yet, anyway.

THURSDAY MAY 28 E-mail from Cindy, my UNH Spanish teacher friend, in reply to my question about an audio system for learning Argentine Spanish.

Personally, I don't work much with real-world audio programs (that is, the world outside textbooks), but a friend / excellent prof. taught a course a few years ago using Rosetta Stone and thought it exceptional. As you've no doubt gathered, the key is listening ... you need lots of input to help with output (speaking). I also suggest reading vs. a straight study of grammar.

There are lots of basic readers out there ... the Lola Lago series is a hoot (start with Vacaciones al sol).

Jim has warned us that almost no one in his small town speaks any English. But he does have some friends there who do: Jessica in Buenos Aires; and in Capilla, his house-sitting couple and Tito, the former occupant. That is more than we had in Granada when we landed. We had felt helpless and quite alienated, particularly Sandy who enjoys daily chit-chat with neighbors and shopkeepers.

Jim, at fifty, found learning Spanish very difficult and I am so poor at "hearing" a different language that I have minuscule hopes. If I had had even a year of it in high school it would be a help—as my high school and college French did in Quebec. Sandy suggests we take Blake, who at sixteen already has had four years of Spanish. Not a bad idea.

Another raw day with temperatures that will barely crawl out of the forties. The whole garden, both flowers and veggies, is sitting in green plastic pots under the windows in the new west wing, warmed by any afternoon sun and the pilot of the hot water heater. Even on the back porch most shrivel with overnights in the thirties. Will perk our Ellsworth day up by taking Rhonda, our neighbor and first of the summer people with us and have lunch in Cleonice.

SATURDAY MAY 30 In pondering those thoughts of laying new tracks for my train, I realized that by changing the pattern of my life, I changed circumstances and therefore needed different skills. If, however, *Le Diamant* goes down to the bottom of the sea, I will be one of the "poor down below, where they'll be the first to go," according to the old song about the good ship *Titanic*, and all this learning will make little difference.

Except I will have been faithful to following my passion—learning—to the end.

TUESDAY JUNE 8 We picked up the mail on our way home from a double graduation party in Natick, MA: Tee's from the University of Maine two weeks ago and James from high school. A heavy 8x10 envelope bore a return address of Thomas P. Gohagan & Co. and was stamped Time Sensitive Material—our Antarctica packet had arrived.

Once settled in bed for the night, we took a hasty look through the contents of the quietly classic folder. There it was: *Reservation confirmation Expedition to Antarctica.* The remaining payment, $10,980 for two, is due by November 6, so is at this point irrelevant, as are the forms to fill out. On to the good stuff like clothing. I hadn't seen such specific directions since church camp in 1943 and I found it equally exciting. *Shipboard attire is casual. Suggested attire for the Captain's welcome and farewell receptions is "smart casual."* At age ten I had read: On Sundays girls wear Whites Only.

Shore excursions in Antarctica require that you step out of the Zodiac into cold Antarctic waters. Ah, now we're getting to the meat of it. We hurried on to Weather. *Antarctic Peninsula Daily High 45F, Daily Low 25F.* Humph, sounds like March in Maine.

The Stateroom Features list was lengthy and we were amused by the inclusion of phone, TV, DVD, VCR. Size etc. for Deck 6 room was missing, however; Sandy thinks it will resemble the Yodel place we rented for six hours in Heathrow: a big screen and a bed that converts to a couch. Could be.

Four pages of luggage and packing information that could be called handholding, or micromanaging for efficiency. The total effect was: don't worry or think, just do as you are told. But there were sample *photos of proper footwear* along with five online addresses and the search keyword: rubber boots. Gear freak Sandy has many happy hours ahead and predicts spending "hundreds." Already, while down in NH, she sneaked into Best Buy to check out this year's version of the camera snitched in Madrid.

Eyelids sagging, we laid aside a seven-page Expedition Manual, a five-page Travel Program Media Guide, and a fourteen-page Participant Guide.

I was awakened once by various boots tromping through my dream. So this is what tour traveling is like, I thought, and went back to sleep.

WEDNESDAY JUNE 10 While lunching on the rocks, a rarity this spring, Sandy, who had been reading packet material, mentioned how difficult it was to get in and out of rubber boats, citing the width of the sides and the unstable bottom for pushing off. She knows about such things and is always more aware of possible perils than I. I said it sounded like we'd have an experienced and attentive staff, adding that this was not a New Zealand outfit, nor would our fellow passengers be of the extreme adventure type. She muttered something about head in the sand and then said, "Well, you know, a physician has to approve your fitness before you can go." Really?

Wondering how Dr. Diane was going to decide our fitness, I looked up the form. Indeed, it listed *steep gangway, inflatable landing*

boats, uneven and slippery terrain. I raised an eyebrow: Yeah, well ...
In New Zealand we had managed the Routeburn Trek in '87, the
Bottom Bus tour scrambles in '08 and other climbs supervised and
unsupervised; the steep stairs to airplanes on the tarmac where I had
to ask a fellow passenger for help with my heavy carry-on bag; the
isolation of Inkasi. Even the life-imperiling climbs to the grocery
store in Granada.

I think of a tour in terms of a child in a car seat, strapped,
padded, safe.

FRIDAY JUNE 12 *Expect one to two inches more of rain downeast this
morning.* Probably the line storm between spring and summer. Let's
hope it won't mean a reversion to March weather, but just a payback
for the warm days that April borrowed from June. Old adages cover
every contingency.

Speaking of rough storms, Sandy's friend Elaine saw a
documentary of some Russian ship loading passengers into Zodiacs
under hair-raising Antarctic conditions. She passed her fright along
to Sandy, who has no great love of the sea and boats to begin with.
Well, last year before we left for South Africa Elaine had the blacks
rising up to slaughter whites in their beds, which sounds more
painful than a free fall into the briny depths of cold, black water —
perhaps sliding under an icepack for good measure. Elaine had
watched the program through to the end, a sign that it succeeded as
entertainment by keeping the tension high. Another difference
between virtual living and the real thing.

WEDNESDAY JUNE 24 *Hi Mom, If you have Google Earth on your
Mac, this should pinpoint the casita (cottage). If not, the Lat is 30 deg 51'
06.55" South and Long is 64 deg 31' 14.35 " West.*

*Geographically, Capilla del Monte lies on Ruta 38 NNW of Cordoba —
an hour and a half plus by taxi--on the west flank of the Sierras de Cordobas
(low mountain range. It is about 700 mi NW of Bs. Aires).*

Let me know if you find it,
Love
Jim

THURSDAY JUNE 25 Saw an eagle yesterday while sitting high on
the ledges eating lunch. This is not rare anymore. An immature one
has been hanging about for a couple of years now, seemingly always
busy on some errand or another. This time he veered, spiraled
upward, didn't stop, just kept that updraft under those broad,

steady wings. Up and up, smaller and smaller against a white cloud, finally disappearing into the glare. I thought, he's just having fun. And why not?

Sandy returned from a Portsmouth visit with the *Insight Guide: Argentina*. Awe-inspiring needle peaks on the cover. I imagined eagles on those updrafts. Or is it condors there?

FRIDAY JUNE 26   Two weeks since we've seen the sun—except for a half hour around five yesterday. The good news is that the last two days have been just clouds and fog. And warm so I got the snap peas staked, two more dahlias in larger pots, and Sandy weed-whacked the puff-ball dandelions. The Beauty bush Tina transplanted last fall has its first bloom, a welcome sign among all this jungle green.

Yesterday we got a letter from Merle Wiggill at Inkasi: our first personal contact from South Africa; we never heard from New Zealand people except arrangements with Cris Morrell for shipping the painting.

Dear Sandy & Martha

Very many thanks for the photo and the note – was pleased to hear from you – George Julia & Leah were so please to get the photos. Was good to see how appreciative they were. George is so proud of the fact that he is the father of a lovely boy. Showed him proudly to us. It's his second son. I think he had given up hope of having another son. I have just got back after a week spent in Kruger with my 2 sister & Allan (younger sister husband). We were so fortunate saw plenty of everything – leopard with kill in tree – baby (newborn) hyena's right next to the road & kid & lioness very busy also on the road. The weather here hasn't been too good. Windy (gale force) overcast & cold as a result nearly every one has flu –(myself included).

Sorry about your camera – Graham feels very important that he has been asked to take photo – we haven't had a chance to get there yet.

Looking forward to read a book about your travels Martha.

Love to you both

Merle

She included an e-mail address so we can keep in touch; will remind her that she is more than welcome to come visit us here when she is at her son's in Massachusetts. We'd have fun.

A couple of nights ago when Sandy and I were having warm milk and graham crackers to aid sleep after a Schoodic hair-ball attack, she said: "I'm having second thoughts about this cruise." My stomach lurched, but after she spoke of seasickness and how the Drake passage was one of the roughest in the world, I remembered she had just talked to Elaine. I listened, changed the subject, and we went to sleep. In the morning she said, "I'm all right now."

In Portsmouth on Tuesday we both got "new tooths" — one crown for Sandy, two for me, and Sandy had a physical. She passed over the health forms for the cruise company and Dr. Diane will fax them on closer to the November deadline.

In the waiting room I napped and started *Insight Guide: Argentina* — big place.

MONDAY JULY 6 Woke to sun instead of a tunnel of wet fog — perhaps this finest attribute of summer has at last arrived. Already house guests and summer friends and Baldwin Head neighbors fill the landscape and calendar; the garden has taken hold and the once glorious meadow-cloud of daisies and clover and buttercups is ready to be shorn to lawn. Argentina and Antarctica folders are lost amidst the coffee table piles of reading begun and put aside.

WEDNESDAY JULY 8 I woke in our South Wing encased, as usual for the last what, sixty days, in green tarp, green shades, and a humidity-pressed skull — it actually rained all night — but thankful that Sandy's and my robust health allows us to keep opening different doors. Even coffee was slow to disperse the weight of last night's reading about Muslims' Allah-induced anti-woman behavior in Barbara Grizzuti Harrison essay on Morocco. What I saw in Africa and Spain was so twenty first century sanitized, and further limited by my own ignorance, that I should not consider my impressions of Islam more valid than that of any white Christian tourist.

WEDNESDAY JULY 15 Morning sits quietly upon the earth — and sea. Also, my mind. Seems I've been in the grasp of human voices for a week; now summer silence wraps my head in lemon yellow and lazy green. Ah, the song sparrow calls, but that is fine. I may soon move to the porch and join her — and nap.

Jim is coming to Argentina with us in January: take a week to introduce us to his village and house. During his days here — with Ginger — he kept referring to "a challenge" and "third-world country." Apparently, South Africa was a warm-up for this trip.

No, don't mail down extra Antarctic clothes: "You may never see them again." No, don't rely on credit cards: "In Capilla del Monte only the high-end gift shop and restaurant will take them." No,

ATM machines are unreliable, especially during siesta. No, siesta lasts five hours: "From noon to five o'clock, the only store open is the hardware—until three."

I promised him that we would have a pretty good idea of the dates we'd need his cottage after we blocked out our areas of interest. He is going to rent another place for his tenants; they pay him no rent, but act as caretakers and he is very fond of them. Besides, he says, I have my own personal economic stimulus packages that I'm passing out around the world. A little here—he paid a considerable amount for all the shellfish we ate while they visited—a little there.

So, deck sitting with the Argentine books and a calendar are on the list for this week.

WEDNESDAY AUGUST 5 The Brown truck backed into the drive on Monday. My Overshoes had arrived. My first since grade school ones. shiny-red and made of real rubber. These are drab mushroom, but "super lightweight, waterproof and durable." Their lugged soles "employ an aggressive tread with high traction for cold, icy conditions ... flexible even at sub-zero temperatures." I pulled them on over my light hikers—they reached up to the bottom of my capris--and headed for the rocks. I looked pretty funny, but they performed well. Sandy pointed out the quick release strap over the instep; no going to the bottom with these full of water. She had gotten hers a couple of days before—$70. Today, maybe, will be another shoe box—another $70—Easy Spirit light blue and white walkers, mostly for the boat and plane.

I did rough out a plan so Jim could let his house sitters know when and for how long they would have to vacate. Three weeks at the beginning and three weeks at the end. The six weeks in the middle are for the cities of Cordoba, Mendoza, and Buenos Aires, the trip to Antarctica, and two weeks of wandering about the Patagonia region. He said fine, thereby freeing me to live in the Maine present that resembles monsoon season. Where is all this water coming from?

THURSDAY SEPTEMBER 17 We sat on the little porch in our old winter robes—red for me, forest green for Sandy—in the early sunshine, eating boiled egg and English muffins, exchanging occasional words about construction of porch ramp beside the new west wing, taking Schoodic to the vet's for his for monthly bum shave. When a morning breeze began to stir the cove, two loons stood on their tails and shook their wings in readiness to deal with eiders and grebes if they flew in. We, too, are on internal alert, looking southward—all the way to Antarctica.

Jim has found compatible flights through Buenos Aires to Cordoba. Round trip $1,063 each for Sandy and me. A lot better than the $3,000 plus to South Africa and Spain and $2,000 to New Zealand.

Jim's house sitters had sent a list of things to be done to his house before our arrival: window screens, curtains, bedroom ceiling fan. We will send him a gift of $600, our rent so to speak. Also, we discussed various options for getting the twenty or so books I will be reading while in country. Definitely no bookstore in Capilla. A book reading device seems to be the answer—Bett is looking into it as a family gift.

Also, we filled out the health forms for our Antarctica expedition: I had to mention mild heart attack in 1994 with no problems since, and Sandy her double knee replacement that certainly made her more able, not less. We both checked the Good Health box. Certainly, psoriasis is not a consideration at this point—all my skin has healed to perfection. Now, hopefully, my visit to Dr. Turner to check my left eye will show that my recent poor vision test was due to those drops, not deterioration from glaucoma. Dr. Diane's forms should be in the mail today; we don't have to fully pay for the cruise until November. That's another upcoming chore: we'll each be redistributing some $75,000 plus good interest from a mature CD next week. Lucky us amidst all these economic woes.

MONDAY SEPTEMBER 21 The morning sun shot over the window frame and hit my cheek, crawled to the corner of my eye—drenched in glaucoma drops—blurring my beloved room of wood and books into a gold haze. A high out over the Gulf of Maine holds steady, no clouds allowed. My birthday week—seventy-seven on Friday.

Reading *The Last Continent* has reminded me that we are not going to the South Pole with its forty-below-zero temperatures, but the Antarctica Peninsula where the temperatures are akin to Maine's. No need for clothes beyond our usual ones.

TUESDAY OCTOBER 6 Kitchen floor sanding and refinishing have resulted in a clean and glossy surface for our new, small biscuit-colored stove. The new gas line is connected, walls painted, and electricity scheduled for tomorrow. Probably the sensation of clean resonates the most: the stove and floor suffered from the irreversible collective crud of the ages.

Yesterday morning while the kitchen was already stuffed with four workmen, Dave put in a new south window and fixed the windy, cold gap in the front door. Also, a zest for getting some Spanish conversation under control has been ignited by an Adult Ed class at the local high school. After concluding the conversation with Jim over tickets: JFK to Santiago, then over the Andes to Cordoba, we tackled vowel pronunciation, colors, and numbers. Sandy will learn much more than I with my tin ear for sounds, but no matter, as long as one of us can make ourselves understood, our time in Argentina will be happier.

So, the goals of two years ago—winterizing this cottage and exploring the lands that rim Antarctica—are still on track and our lives speeding along on sheer delight.

SATURDAY OCTOBER 10 Speaking of speeding along ... The other evening as I read in my flannel nightshirt and red bathrobe, I had the sensation of a perfectly happy day. Not unusual, but what followed was. Instead of a te dum, te dum feeling of endless pleasure, I slammed into a wall of: It's going too fast, the end of it all is just around the next bend. I was sad, like knowing that vacation would be over the day after tomorrow. As with all my age peers, I suppose, knowledge of mortality has become a more frequent visitor over the last decade, but this sadness was different, as though the sounds of a lover packing her suitcase was just overhead.

On the flip side of that coin, I expelled a snort of laughter when I was editing my 2006 pages of this journal. "... and I do wonder if I've still got it to make even the first plane. Let alone the second or third. Certainly, we'll not do as we did in 1987: rise at three a.m., drive to Boston's Logan, spend twenty-four hours in a plane, land at Auckland, tour the city with a local, catch a flight for Christchurch, walk around town, have a drink in an upscale bar, a spot of dinner, and at dark curl up in a B&B bed. Never happen."

So what did we do in 2007? Up at 3 a.m., make our way to Logan in a snowstorm, toot around San Francisco's Union Square on New Year's afternoon, spend fourteen hours on a plane, land at Auckland, at Christchurch, at Dunedin, tour the area with our host, dine in a pub, and finally curl up in our bed-sit. Now how did that work? Go from Never happen to Yeah, this is fine?

Is it possible to get tougher between seventy-five and seventy-six? Did those months crammed full of climbing stairs, lugging boxes, Sandy's operation and recovery, making scary decisions, diving into uncharted waters, give us strength instead of a heart attack? Or were we riding the crest of success?

And last year we traveled from Hoedspruit to Johannesburg to London to Madrid to Granada and then what? Sixty-eight dark steps up to a strange home. Am I getting younger? My skin is new, my brain is grappling with Spanish, my body can still shovel dirt, rake gravel, paint a ceiling. ... What's the message here?

MONDAY OCTOBER 12 At least twenty years ago a local told me, "Ain't no prettier road than the Wyman Road in the fall. Don't need to go driving anywheres else." She was right. Maples and birch and dark evergreen, houses easy with themselves, are scattered on each side; the Narraguagus River on the right gradually widens either to gulp in or spit out the ocean's salty tide, and the woods on the left-- after leaping Route 1—flow northward, nearly uninhibited, to the Great North Woods, Hudson's Bay and the Arctic polar regions.

TUESDAY OCTOBER 20 Checks for $1000 for the flight from Logan to Cordoba are in the mail; the $5,250 we each still owe for the thirteen-day tour will go in two more weeks. The wait until the last minute seems prudent in the light of possible broken legs, onset of leprosy or some such. We'll take our chances with swine flu—this year's disease titillation.

Started Water, Ice & Stone by Bill Green last evening. He describes the world through chemical elements—different and thought provoking. *Yet all this talk about physical properties says nothing of water's dynamism, its splendid life upon Earth — its swift turning in storm and fog, its movement through rivers. No matter where it is, water is moving. It is always in passage, wanting to be elsewhere.* He tells how long it pauses: *nine days in the atmosphere, a few years in lakes. a few hundred years in groundwater, a few thousand years in oceans, more than ten thousand years in the ice cap of Antarctica.*

He is traveling to Antarctica's lakes near McMurdo, the American base, way south of where we'll be. *In Christchurch we stayed at the Windsor Hotel, a small bed-and-breakfast...* That line stopped me as dead, as did the one about water "wanting to be somewhere else" but for a different reason. The Windsor is where Sandy and I stayed overnight in 1987. I have grown used to having some connection to almost every place mentioned in the US, but this— Am I truly becoming a world traveler? A bit awesome.

THURSDAY OCTOBER 22 As I lay flat under the pile of blankets on the electric bed pad with a cup of good hot coffee steaming on my chest, penguins were in my thoughts. How excited Sandy and I were about staying in Dunedin with penguins on the peninsula; in Cape Town, the South African penguins were incidental to our tour; now in Antarctica we may actually interact with them. Nothing is ever as stirring as a First, whatever that happens to be. First bicycle. First kiss from a boy. First kiss from a woman. First infant. First glimpse of the Rocky Mountains. First call from an agent saying that your book has an offer from a publisher. I suppose it is the sudden burst, the soul-jarring accumulation of long conscious or unconscious longing.

Is that a reason for travel? The rocketing high of Firsts?

SUNDAY OCTOBER 24 *Rachel and I went to Barnes & Noble last night. They do not yet have their e-readers, called nook, but I picked up a little brochure that I will send you. They will have samples in the store after Thanksgiving. Depending on lag time in ordering, and I will check on that. I thought we might try to get over there as soon as you get down in December, so you can test drive one. Ginny has a Kindle, so you could see hers as well. My only concern, of course, is can we wait that long to order either.*

love
Bett

THURSDAY NOVEMBER 5 Sandy paused before handing me my coffee in bed this morning. "There is a white mist moving across Trafton. It doesn't act like fog—it must be snow." Indeed. A couple of hours of white drifting across the deep green of firs and spruces and pine, melting on the rich redgoldneedletan cap of the earth.

I have a deeper, literally, sense of the earth since playing the CD of a new neighbor, a seismologist from MIT. I listened to the clicks and rumbles and background sibiulating of our planet as it goes about its business of being. A bit scary to grapple with the idea that our only toehold in eternal black space is alive, with a mind—will? destiny?—of its own.

SATURDAY NOVEMBER 7   Interesting fact: The amount of money I have in CDs, $137,000 is almost exactly the same as I put away from the house sale in September of 2007. That means I have lived basically on just interest and $500 monthly Social Security.

I said to Sandy yesterday after we spent more on Antarctic clothing in Cadillac Sports, "If we had not sold the house when we did, I would be scared to death right now." And I meant scared of how we would be paying our household bills. Instead, I was buying waterproof mittens to go over my new silk/wool liner gloves, and a neck hugger to cover any gaps between silk undershirt and balaclava envelope hat, and a dry sack for camera and binoculars.

If we hadn't stretched when we did, we'd sure be hunkering now.

THURSDAY NOVEMBER 12 Gold sunrise, wrinkled-sheet sea, dozen grebes in close formation eyeing cavorting seals. November taking a calming breath.

SUNDAY NOVEMBER 22 *e-mail from Jim in Capilla*
My favorite part of the property is under the big tree in the garden. Tito and I were just out there talking. Even in the strongest heat of the day there is enough of a breeze to make it extremely comfortable. I found this true even in summer. In fact, it is preferable to being in the kitchen, which is fine too, but not as much of a breeze in there. You will learn that the people in Capilla are more sensitive to both heat and cold (except perhaps Tito) than we are. My guess is that is because there is less of a range of temps in Capilla than we are used to.

Which brings up the next question - chairs. There are wooden chairs in the kitchen with cushions that are easily moved about. There are more form-fitting thin plastic chairs which are extremely light. I see there is only one of those. There is an office chair in the living room to use at the computer (this is Seba's but I don't think he will use it while you are here).

Do you think the chair situation will be ok? Inside of course you can sit in the kitchen. There is only the two small tables and office chair in the living room (and a futon which is probably too low to the ground to be useful).

The gate and carport gate will likely not be done when you arrive. I have asked Seba to make sure the bedroom is painted though. Everything else should be in fine shape ... or certainly functional shape for your visit. They are still rationing water, but with our reserve barrel we can use even when the city is not supplying the water.

ok, to wash the dishes now.

TUESDAY DECEMBER 8 *first floor apartment, Hampton Beach*
Visits with Dr. Diane always leave me whirly. Zip, zip, zip. And yesterday's seemed worse than ever. This time Diane's focus was

our trip: vaccinations, altitude and seasickness; she had already submitted forms to our ship doctor.

Sandy and I had both brought our yellow immigration cards with us: added were generic flu shots and for me, a tetanus. Weight, 150, height 5'3", blood pressure 128/60. Diane scanned the blood work: cholesterol, perfect; thyroid, perfect—no B12 problems. Discussed seasickness patch and wrote new prescriptions for all meds. I was cautioned at sign-out that Portsmouth's HCA hospital--the office recently allied with them--would not be patient about waiting for Medicare to kick in for payment. Whoosh, off to the collection agency.

Teeth, eyes, internal organs. I suppose I should be thankful I have only three docs. Although I imagine Diane wrote on my chart "short-term memory?" I muffed a couple of items, but surely not enough to need a head shrink. It's only white-coat syndrome.

FRIDAY DECEMBER 18   The wind chill is below zero. I'm enjoying a slow quiet slog of writing Christmas charity checks, adding to the Kindle book list, and learning more about this Asus computer from a fat manual Karen gave us when she and Joyce met us for lunch in Exeter. We paid; she will take no money for the Asus, but we promised her photos of everything Darwin saw. Broad reading in *Rough Guide.*

MONDAY DECEMBER 28   When I laid down last night   and realized that our sheets and blanket would be gone tomorrow and in their place Gary's chlorinated ones, I actually clutched them Linus-like to my cheek. How ridiculous, my pragmatic, adventure-bound brain scolded, and reverted itself to considering all there was to do before leaving for the bus station on Thursday at 11:15 a.m. Not 3 a.m. — an advantage of flying due south.

SATURDAY JANUARY 3, 2010 *Capilla del Monte, Cordoba District, Argentina*   Snowflakes fell a few minutes after we boarded the C&J bus Wednesday. and in another few minutes we knew from the dense white that this could mean trouble: but, assuaged by two years of no-delay travel and forecasts of rain in NYC, we touched hands, smiled, and said, "We're on our way."

NOTES EN ROUTE. Logan Airport. What we were on our way to was a slide that would last for almost thirty-six hours.

Curbside wouldn't check us in because we're flying international beyond JFK. In line to get boarding pass one half hour—twice we've failed at self-help machines. Three-oh-five departure delayed until 3:44, then 4:56. Still in Boston, sitting in rockers to watch plows and more snow coming down. Excellent soup from cafe, oyster crackers from home, water; quiet--keep dozing off. Returned to café for a turkey pannier. Now 5:20—at JFK we'll have to hustle getting to LAN Terminal 4 for 8:00 flight. Hope for some coffee, have to keep going.

Jim called on his cell, joked that he'd put a foot in front of a tire to hold the plane for us.

Enplaned I. At last side by side, off and up we go. Been awake now for twelve hours.

Enplaned II. 10:30 p.m.—once more rolling toward a runway. Not toward Santiago as planned, but Buenos Aires. The near hysteria sequence that led to this is best left for telling later. We all made it—Sandy is behind me in another empty double seat, Jim eight rows back. Eight thousand five hundred miles, nine hours and forty-five minutes to go. I hope to eat and sleep. Legs, shoulders, heart, nerves appear sound.

LATER. *Jim's casita.*
I'm here. Open window with green, warm, and bird talk beyond. Whitewashed walls, five old ceiling beams, twirling fan. Three low wooden chests, two bed tables, woven orange spread over most excellent queen mattress. Our bags opened, but not emptied. Jim's charming casita.

He is walking Jessica back to the small B&B she owns here. Seba and Nancy are in living room on computers, Sandy in yard with bird book and binoculars. Dishes from chicken, rice, and fresh apricot lunch await washing. Jim's friends are handsome, intelligent, delightful people.

Slept twelve hours at night, two more after egg and potato breakfast. Now six o'clock—think I'm fading again.

SUNDAY JANUARY 3 Last evening I walked up Varaona Street. Dirt rutted by run off—green shoulders, drought must have broken. Homes on either side, mostly old brick with arched doorways, difficult to judge size and condition of inside, but some have new walls and are obviously restored. This reminds me of the last dirt road in Santa Fe where a friend's sister lived. I don't believe, however, this one is in danger of being paved: lot of green folks in Capilla. Seba and Nancy are a fine young example of immigrants from Buenos Aires searching for a simpler life: Seba's successful website is called Path to Bliss, geared to a new generation who believe that with the right attitude, good things will come. Having lived through so many variations of this philosophy, I feel like a breathing history book—but I don't say a word. It would not be fair; youth should dream and reach.

Also like New Mexico are the mountains to the east, not west. Seba says sandia means watermelon in Spanish and that yes, these mountains also turn that color at sunset. Most of the houses I've seen have a pleasant feel about them, but the low stone or brick or whitewash walls and gates signal private. Tito, a local aloe grower and sculptor who lived in this house for many years, is going to fashion a fine wooden gate for Jim.

On a longer walk with Jim and Sandy, I saw that houses are scarce beyond the bisecting dirt road, the climb steeper, and the mountains ever more revealed. The dominant mountain, Uritorco, is thought of as a place of special powers. In the last few decades tales of alien spaceship landings have been revived and add to the magical allure for tourist and immigrant alike. Indeed, there's plenty of room for a saucer up there. The young woman who cared for us during the Cordoba airport search for the security man who had to release our bags from a locked room and re-X-ray them, said she climbed to Uritorco's formidable rocky top, ate her food, fell asleep. and woke hungry and cold. She swung one arm back and forth—"Nothing, Nothing had happened"—and looked at us with a puckish smile and raised eyebrow. I like this country and its people.

At the top of Varaona Road the mountains, even a jagged-tooth second layer, were clamped in solid majesty against the graying sky: on the lower flanks sprinkled house lights collected in a bright pool at the farthest end of the valley. None of Jim's evocative, descriptive letters could come close to this, this being here, standing in the road gazing and waiting ... for what? The forces to gather?

LATER. Chuck, after hearing from Jim of our travel travails, wrote longingly of the days "when flying was fun." Having heard the nostalgia beat of "the good old days" too many times before, I wondered about the specifics. His answers would probably have been more adventure oriented than those of the Brit in Madrid who riffed on those fun flying days. What he implied was: when only people of my class could afford to fly.

Today Americans fly to get places, just as they used to ride on canal boats and stage coaches. which were not all that much fun either. But perhaps even back then the ticket sellers insisted that getting there is half the fun.

It was and is an adventure, however; as Titia put it, a testing by circumstance. We had several circumstances thrown at us between Hampton Beach and Jim's casita. Number one: Landing late—7:00—at Kennedy to catch our 8:00 international flight. Two: A fifteen minute—timing for the elderly unlisted—walk to the air train that would carry us to Terminal 4. Asking an employee for a handcart elicited only a don't-see-one response, so we bowed our heads and did our best. I would pull Sandy's heavy roll-along to the entrance to escalators and then trade for my heavy soft-side; at the end we'd switch again. Up and down and around and around, finally to face air trains on either side, both labeled Track 8—no other signs. Number three: We dithered, jumped on the standing one. Seemed like a long, long ride. Panic mode. Was this it? Terminal 4 at last? Now where? People, signs, but where did we get a boarding pass? The agent at Logan had not given us them for the whole trip. High grade PANIC.

Number 4. There! Sandy shouted and pointed way to the end-- Row 8. We bolted. The line was long. I almost literally grabbed a loose airline person and with my ultra-red face shoved into her stony one squawked, "My flight leaves in twenty minutes. If I'm not at the gate—" She started in on the "Lateness is your fault, not ours" spiel. We fled to security. I repeated the scene in HYSTERIA mode. Nothing. On an elevator, I believe, at 7:50 Sandy called Jim—he had gotten his luggage off, the plane had already pushed back.

Sandy and I lifted our bags one more time and trudged back to the LAN desk, where a nice lady did look rather stricken when she looked up the next flight to Santiago—not tonight, not tomorrow, but Saturday. Wait! There is an American at 10:50—to Buenos Aires. Jim arrived looking a bit wild himself.

Once he was with us at least my bag toting was over—my heart had come through. Back we went to the air train, back to American Airlines desk. A good soul made out new tickets for us on the 10:50 and said we could pick up our luggage in Cordoba. Will it be safe? I asked, remembering I had no shrink-wrap, no lock like Sandy, only a strap on the big one, nothing on the little one. "We can hope," he said.

Back Jim went to LAN to grab his bags and get an AA ticket. We were booked all the way through with them, so we were their problem--Jim was not.

Sandy and I made our way through security and on to the gate. Again what had seemed like a long wait quickly evaporated into a nervous, Where's Jim? Sandy checked to make sure our cell was on ring and I went to the desk to see if we could get seats together. Boarding call came over the speaker. People surged out of their seats—my glances toward the door became more frequent. Sandy handed me the phone: "They want $3000 for a ticket," Jim said. There was a long rattle of Spanish—back and forth the voices went—"Hang on, Mom, I think I got a deal"—more rattling—"Okay, I'm heading for Security, but don't board."

The agent explained to us that the plane was nearly empty so Sandy and I had double seats, one behind the other: More room to stretch out.

"Where's Jim sitting?" I asked him.

"We'll put him near you—then he can move anywhere to sleep."

Another agent stepped away from the line and said to me, "You'd better board, we're closing the flight."

"You can't. It's still twenty minutes to take-off."

He raised an eyebrow in mock surprise. "But we have a long way to go—all the way to Buenos Aires."

"But you can't go without Jim."

"Okay. We will hold the plane for Jim. Where is he?"

Yet another agent put down his phone. "He's left security. On his way."

Our man watched the door at the back of the room. As a truly harried Jim emerged he shouted, "Hurry, Jim. Hurry! Your mother is waiting for you."

Jim ran past us and shoved his boarding pass at the waiting agent.

"See," the agent said, "he is willing to leave without you. Hurry, catch him."

We hurried. A short easy hurry this time. Circumstances had been defeated by a Plan B, but did we pass the test: Stay calm and carry on? I don't think so.

MONDAY JANUARY 4 Noon. A bit more eased into life at Casita Jim.

WEDNESDAY JANUARY 6 Accommodations in Ushuaia at the place recommended by a friend of Jim's mother who works there secured for February 22, 23, 24. Had given up when Jim's computer here gave the same can't-find message I had continually gotten before. And no reply yesterday, but this morning Jim found an e-mail his virus screen had stopped: a charming letter from Carlos, $135 a night w/buffet breakfast for three nights. Sent off Visa number so just await confirmation. This bodes well for all our online traveling stays, as did last night's search through Ushuaia Tourist website that resulted in an informative update on all local places. And maybe our Spanish dictionary will carry us through the websites written only in Spanish.

Can't believe I'm going to have to get my safari jacket to put on over my blouse. Yesterday we got home from a pleasurable introduction to the town and I retreated to the bedroom, took off all my clothes, and quietly died. When hunger hit we staggered up for peaches and cheese and then died once more. Jim went off to the river with assorted friends and Sandy and I finally got as far as the living room for tea at 4:30. Full consciousness came a half hour later, and Jim cooked a big dinner of boned chicken thighs to complete the comeback.

Sitting in the garden after dinner—Jessica and her toddler ate with us--Sandy and I watched lightning flare like far-off fireworks. Jim said the rain was many miles to the south and seldom moved on to Capilla. This time it did—at 2 a.m. Howling winds, beating trees, then bursting rain. Jim apparently experienced it all with Palu the cat, and Sandy tended to our window and doors that were banging and rattling. I slept, aware, but motionless. This morning Jim wore a sweatshirt on his walk to shop for tonight's three guests—or is it four? By the time he leaves Saturday we will be saying hola, como esta? once a block.

Body report. Ankles and feet swelled during flight, normal in a couple days. No added aches and pains from extra long trip; in fact, my night leg cramps have disappeared and Sandy reports improved movement all over. So no problems from heat, humidity, or altitude—although we're higher than any other trip.

The almost constant breezes and changing skies are similar to New Zealand and South Africa, making Jim's plans for building a triple story gazebo for mountain, storm and star gazing in one corner of his garden seem apt. He will meet with his architect tomorrow to see if he agrees with a triangular shape fitting into the two existing brick walls.

The breeze also creates captivating sights and sounds: the giant aquaribay, a sacred and protected tree, swishes its spreading willowy arms in more of a waltz than a tango; and the mora, rustling lord of garden shade, is usually dressed in squawking parakeets. None today and I wonder why.

SATURDAY JANUARY 8 Long time away from this record of impressions and wonderings, a condition due mostly to my stupidity with the computer--too embarrassing to reveal the problem, the anguish, and the simple solution. Also the days have been busy with in-the-moment activities of cooking, cleaning, talking with Jim's friends. He left at 7 a.m. for his twenty-seven hour flight—has to land in Ecuador in order to avoid the worst of possible flight charges. Feel bad that he lost so much money for doing such a good deed. He has been a great host too: we feel quite in control of the casita and the town and ready to simply follow the rhythms of summer. Our bodies and minds have absorbed the week of healing—in spite of Sandy's brief cold—and I love to have my limbs bared to the air and sun, albeit with an SPF 30 sunblock.

While I was roaming in some other mode of this unfathomable machine, before the miracle occurred that put me and the computer on the same path, I wrote of the different objectives of travel, as I believe I have in other sections. This type of musing will probably occur even more frequently on this last trip of our original schedule. Of course, warmth and sun always were front and center as objectives, and New Zealand, South Africa, and Argentina have all lived up to their superb reputations. This is our first mountain climate, but it is much like the Pacific island and the tip of the African continent: sunny, breezy, changeable, and almost always tolerable temperatures. That was a goal and it has been achieved. Sandy is out under the mora tree—certainly the most private patio we have had, although a child's in-the-pool noises leap over the brick wall. I will make up the new tea and go out. Am hoping for orange pekoe but reading Spanish box labels was not covered in class. Yesterday we made tea from the leaves of a bush in the garden—not bad.

SUNDAY JANUARY 10 "Sundays are for taking out splinters." Credit that saying to Sandy's old farmer neighbor, Wyman. It is a fine adage to play with either by trying modern substitutions for splinter, or grand metaphors, or basic values. Example: "I won't work, I'll quit," declared the young employee in the Milbridge hardware store. "Sundays are for church and football."

This year our day and time are almost the same as home's, but a January Sunday in Capilla del Monte is quite different. "Welcome to paradise," Sandy said when I struggled awake at eight o'clock. Indeed: silence, sunshine, and gusts of wind streaming in through the new gold curtains; and with the second cup of coffee—still instant—we ate tiny Tostitos dabbed with Seba's mother's jelly. After refreshing our pattern of intimacy we ate peaches and cream, then showered and mixed a bowl of lettuce, tomato, avocado, chard stems, carrot, and rice and sausage leftovers to eat in the shade of the Big Tree. Hmm, call it basic values day.

Yesterday the temperatures climbed into the nineties and will do so again today, so if we walk anywhere it will be much later; besides, our desire to see other people has been satiated for the time being by the variety of folks we have met.

Perhaps to prove "splinters" can also arrive on Sundays, the washing machine—which draws its water from a hose outside and outflows it into the bathtub—refuses to start.

TUESDAY JANUARY 12 I feel on top of the world today. The cooling effect of a sharp night storm; solid sleep until nine; a hearty breakfast of corn flakes with peaches and milk, a biscuit from the bakery. and half a hard-boiled egg. We then leisurely prepped for a hike up Varaona Street. We paused for scenery, photo ops, and from the higher reaches, binocular surveys of possible villas and downtown; the population has grown to about 20,000. Conditioned by the hilly mile walks to and from town, my lower extremities never tired, my lungs never grabbed for oxygen, and even though the sun was almost overhead a taut breeze cooled my skin. The road, we discovered, leads to the trailhead to Uritorco Mountain. That has, according to our tourist map, Energia, Naturaliza y Misterio Maravilla Natural. Today's buzz words: energy, natural, mysterious, marvel, and another natural. A few pickup trucks, motor scooters, and a horseman leading a spare mount passed, but today the dust is minimal. Truck traffic we presumed was due to an elaborate estancia being rebuilt—built? renovated?—on top of a hill quite a way past the point where the other residences peter out. Stays at these sheep/cattle ranches are pricey, i.e., US$100 to 300 per person. And that is a comment on the economy in Capilla. Jim has always spoken of it as a "poor town," but I doubted that definition as soon as I saw the shops downtown. The locals may be poor, but there is tourist money here. Also to be considered is our different milieus: mine Milbridge, his Manhattan and northern New Jersey.

The other side of town where Jessica has her rental house is dense with stolid middle class, and some of those and upper middle class sprinkle our walk to town; farther to the east along the rio is some pure wealth, perhaps due to the low prices here compared with, say, Buenos Aires. The infrastructure is, I agree, dirt—literally--poor, and seeing a horse pulling a cart of wilted vegetables along the main street and the abundance of rusted cars, some with no mufflers, favor Jim's definition. However, Sandy pointed out that old cars can be repaired by mechanics lacking elaborate digital machines, and compared to South Africa where the vast majority of the population—read, black Africans—own no car at all, it makes sense. As do horses and dirt roads for them to trot on. Yesterday when we turned the corner onto Varaona, a boy of perhaps ten came trotting along on his fine looking horse. Seeing us gawking he put on a grown-up face, kicked his bare, stirrup-less heels against her ribs, and pulled back on the reins which pushed his little rear firmly into the brightly colored blanket. The horse pranced, the boy's impassive face inwardly glowed; he could not, however, resist a backward grin and another prance before trotting off down the rio road. Cultural charm is often a backward glance.

Using the word rio instead of river is perhaps demeaning, but I, an American, cannot grace this trickle, this tiny creek which can be crossed in one light jump—Sandy's description—as a river. Even what ran along the edge of my grade school red-dog—aka, mill slag--playground required a plank bridge and was not accorded stream status. It was a creek. Rivers ran through the heart of Pittsburgh: the wide Monongahela, the green Allegheny, the mighty brown Ohio, carrying on their broad backs barges of coal, limestone, and iron ore to feed the fiery blast furnaces of World War II's Arsenal of Democracy. But then I have yet to see the Rio Calabalumba in full spate.

This two-hour up and down walk set up our confidence for what is to come. Good feeling.

THURSDAY JANUARY 14 Early, I guess it was about six, I lay listening for a sense of the land, the place. Dogs across the river continued their seemingly eternal chorus. The yappy one next door added Me! Me! Me's; the true guard dogs across the street did not. A cock crowed. A bird—dove? parrot?--seemed to be clearing her throat, and the kiskadee announced his name. Human presence was felt only in silence, a heavy, sleepy weight infusing my body with lethargy. I turned, edged my back closer to Sandy's warmth--no hurried trip to town necessary this morning--and slept.

I began today's Kindle reading by completing an Andrea Barrett; moving on to dip into *Too Much Happiness*, delicious Alice Munro stories more in the style of her early ones; and *The Little School*, short memory pieces by Argentine women who survived the disappearances of the '80s. Decided to start Ben Yagoda's *Memoir,* a history of the genre. Having been involved in some fierce arguments regarding the "truth" of same, I thought a historical perspective might bring enlightenment. Well . . . I'll restrict my ruminations to my present writing.

In the strict how-to sense--e.g., there are many options on how to build a chair, but basically the human body should be able to sit without danger on the finished product—I am dedicated to passing on to the reader what my senses, filtered through my brain, have shaped into "truth." The fact that I have in Capilla drunk water delivered by truck in water-cooler-sized bottles, and have washed dishes and my teeth in tap water without resorting to Zantac, Imodium, or the prescription pills for severe diarrhea, or ended up in the hospital, is something I would not lie about, or embellish, or offer the generalization that "You don't have to worry about the water in Argentina" as a PR person might. This is a "what I did and these were the results" type of narrative.

I have no underlining theory or practice to promote. If our cruise ship should go down in the Drake Passage, I will have no chance to comment on the good or bad of that outcome, nor am I preparing the reader for one conclusion or the other by any foreshadowing or stacking of evidence. How could I? I don't know it.

In fiction the writer creates a life for a character, often writing pages of stuff that will never see the light of a final draft, but some of it will be either directly or indirectly revealed through the actions, decisions, and thoughts of that character. I think a memoirist would have to do the same by showing or telling of the filters through which he or she views the world. To my high school anthropology students I presented these filters as: physical body structure, cultural attitudes and customs, family environment, and unique personal experiences. In this memoir I have occasionally narrated glimpses of my filters that possibly add relevance to this tale of late-life travel adventure and ignored those that would not—such as childhood pain in the dentist chair—or those that are nonexistent—such as weekly Catholic confession.

Not infrequently, I have quit reading memoirs because I do not want to be in the company of the writer. Hopefully, that list does not include the usual prejudices of his or her foreignness, but rather, for instance, a man who slyly disparages his older parents; or a woman who, looking back on her life, still cries *pity me!* Others might, but I do not wish to. Anymore than I ever tolerated a crude television personality in my living room. Life is too short. Especially at seventy-seven.

Our third perfect day in a row. But if our wireless comes back from wherever it has wandered, I will have to stay seated here working on reservations—my first choice for a Cordoba hotel was full.

FRIDAY JANUARY 15 Our days here have established a de-dum rhythm. Probably more like my original thoughts of what wintering-over someplace might be like. Ordinary days when reflection dominated action.

SUNDAY JANUARY 17 This Sunday morning while lying in the golden bedroom undistracted by revving of cars or child-thin voices, I considered the minutia of this different environment. Dirt roads, for example. The dust is soft and now deep--no rain for a week—therefore human footfalls cannot be heard, not solitary, not groups, and only the faintest plop of shod hooves: trail rides into the mountains begin at a corral situated just beyond the beautiful, extensive grounds of the labor union vacation compound in the next block. Car tires, however, crackle as though crushing a surface of eggs, or gravel. I thought the cause was speed until I listened closely to a motor scooter rush by: no egg/gravel sound, only motor. Weight, I concluded, weight and motion. I will refrain from banal similes with modern life.

Bird calls are brief, no underlying song of cicadas, but there is an insect we first thought was a screamer bird, then something mechanical. Its courting cry begins with a clickity-clack of body parts loud enough to be heard twenty yards away. Faster, faster until is become like a wet finger rubbed around the rim of a crystal glass: piercing, soaring and reaching now maybe a hundred yards, maybe more. Once I heard an answering call. A question for Nancy and Seba when our paths cross again.

Then there are the dogs. Many run free, most bark. These dog packs, usually three or four of assorted size and muttdom, do not seem interested in humans. They have their own canine world of things to do and amigos to do them with. Most trot smartly with tails---short, long, feathery, or ropelike—high; their coats are unkempt and mouths open.

The most startling free-dog sighting occurred one evening just as traffic in town was picking up. Sandy and I were at a small curbside table when down this main street—empty at the moment—hurtled three dogs, small, medium, and large abreast, and occupying all the space between cars parked on left and right. Faster and faster, laughing and urging each other on.

Now, a pause for driving minutia. Capilla lacks red lights, stop or yield signs, and one-way signs, although apparently some streets are. Faster drivers, usually in shiny VWs and other European makes, pass slower old Fords and Chevy's with a blast of the horn. The former are hybrids in the sense that they can run on either gasoline or bottled gas; it is possible to choose one or the other to buy at the same gas station. Confusing, especially to Americans who believe they are at the forefront of every innovation.

An add-on minutia: last week the labor union estate hosted the gas station attendants of Argentina--or perhaps only Cordoba province, attendance was slight. I should also include what locals tell us: Argentines drive fast and take a morbid enjoyment in reporting the most grisly accident details over TV, radio, and newspapers as though they were sporting events; Tito, who drives a motorbike, was badly hurt in one a couple months ago. Cars wear sidescrapes, bumper dents, missing windows—even missing hoods—like badges of honor.

So, anyway, here are these three dogs pell-melling down the street past our table, toward The Roof which shades a block of the fancier shops; Sandy faces that way, I have a view of their starting line. I don't turn to watch what happens at the corner, just listen for breaks and squeals. Nothing. A couple minutes later the dogs are back for another try, and given the still empty expanse across the side street and on under The Roof, they jubilantly start another gallop. This time cars interfere and they chase them, barking and snapping at their tires. Then back again, tongues lolling, to race off at some starting signal only they can hear. A faster driver surprises the little one in the middle, who tries to maneuver from in front of the fender to bite at the tire. I imagine the dog knocked on his back and the terrible, stomach-churning cries of humans, but no. No sounds at all, the car with its pale driver passes. No dog lies in the street. All three of them are gone. Sandy asks, "What happened? I thought that woman at the next table was going to faint." "No wonder," I said.

Another dog, a handsome brindle of nose-table height, is staring at me with enormous liquid brown eyes and tall ears erect as pointed tents. Not a whisker twitches. His eyes—and nose— ignore our pizza, and steadfastly gaze into mine. A minute, two minutes, who knows? I blink but do not feed. At an empty table a man carefully maneuvers a chair to within reach of it without waking the dog sleeping underneath.

LATER. Today is an unmitigated scorcher, in the hundreds I guess. No one is about. Even Palu and the sleep-in-the-sun dogs are not to be seen. It beats with horrific force on my unhated head, determined, I guess, to smash me into a puddle with all possible speed. This morning we—noting the lack of breeze as an ominous signal—went native, cooking a noon meal of noodles with sausage bits, tomato, grated cheese, and generous portions of the chard that had waved from Sandy's backpack on the walk home last evening. We ate in the deep shade of Jim's tree, with a short glass of red wine and tall ice waters. I washed up "the tin dishes," as Chuck's Maine farm mother would have said, and quit. Afternoon will be spent on the bed under the fan, the next meal will be in the evening, probably in town. where we'll see if any hotel responded to our e-mails for reservations. It is odd to look forward to darkness.

In Maine and New Hampshire we treasure the sun, crowd into it winter and summer, exposing as much of our bodies as is bearable. Well, the fisherman don't; their knees and elbows are white for life. We build houses with windows facing south, with sunroofs to grab that gold. In Argentina they worship shade. Lines at ATMs play hopscotch: a clump of people under a tree--bare space—a thin line tight along a shadowed wall. So it goes here, as in South Africa.

A tad more town minutia. When we emerged from the restaurant on Friday evening at 9:45, the street was filled with tables and chairs, a walkway ran down the middle. People abounded. Realizing that the second half of the Argentine population had been released from work for their two weeks of summer vacation, we decided not to risk sharing the narrow, dark dirt roads with loose tourists in cars. The remise—taxi—ride was, pretty wild, in itself, what with the young driver's blood up, stimulated, we guessed, by the lovely, calm young woman who had graciously invited us to share her taxi. Then last evening, Saturday, the town was setting up for a music and lights show and people, especially the women, were dressed for street dancing and dining. As we lay in bed an hour later the music began—and the power failed.

Under the minutia heading, I must not forget an early culture shock—trash disposal. Plastic bags of garbage are hung outside houses on fences, whatever. A neighbor has a fancy wire basket on a post; in our case it's a ten-penny nail driven into a telegraph pole. Sandy asked Jim, "So they pick up on Mondays?" No, most every day, was the reply. Any time is also true, the midnight one being our most spectacular so far.

TUESDAY JANUARY 19 Woke from a siesta to hear voices in Spanish passing along the road outside. I watched the breeze give the curtains life, stretched and lolled in the knowledge that, our shopping completed, the rest of this day holds nothing but tea and a sweet in the garden, reading a story from Kindle, perhaps a Jill McCorkle, perhaps an Alice Munro, a supper of leftovers on lettuce. Will I recall this ease as the best gift of all the getting ready and going to foreign parts, or will it be the sights of Cordoba, or Mendoza, the Andes or Buenos Aires?

More transitory will be the accomplishment-satisfactions: securing a great spot in Mendoza, another in Cordoba, and a flight from Mendoza to BA—finally went to Orbitz. And solving the cultural riddle of where to buy tissues for nose-blowing, a magnet of Uritorco mountain to mail to Nate on his twenty-fourth birthday, or having Daniel, the big, handsome bass player and carpenter, find us a ride to Cordoba: "Don't worry." His tone was avuncular. "I will arrange it for you, don't worry."

San Luis and Upsallata accommodations are not yet finalized— maybe we'll chance a cell phone call. At any rate, I feel good and yesterday, while the wind howled in the tiles and thunder rolled, we did a dry run on packing for this month and a half on the road. We'll make it by using only one big bag, two carry-ons.

We spent two hours on Friday, Saturday, Monday, and Tuesday scowling at our little computer in City Cafe, drinking lemonade, or beer, or coffee in an attempt to secure these online bookings. Their website glitches and our running out of battery necessitated the daily returns. Hope this throwing around of credit card numbers does not result in a misuse and a cancellation. Walks to town—a hilly mile each way—are tied into taking and dropping off laundry, and shopping for trip items like nuts and dried fruit. Soon, thanks once more to a favorable exchange rate, we'll be nestled in the caring hands of four-and five-star hotels. The cruise ship to Antarctica will rate a six, I'm sure.

Missed minutia: the sky. Like New Zealand and South Africa no jet trails, no pollution to dim it, and here the mountains on both east and west are breeders of hypnotic cloud formations that the winds lash every which way. Often it simply burns a pure hot blue.

The language. Much effort, some progress.

Lost. My beloved Gap hat.

LATER. Now we are out of gas for stove-top and water heater. Tried to call Tito on Jim's cell, which we are supposed to use on the road for reservations, etc. All I got was a torrent of Spanish. What? What did you say? Are you a person or machine?

At least hard boiled eggs are cooked ...

THURSDAY JANUARY 21 In the garden. No breeze moves the cloud behind which the sun is resting, perhaps napping--it is deep siesta time. No dogs, no cars, no human voice, only a couple of gravely-throated doves and one twitterer. Ah, the muffler-less car of the musician across the road has arrived home, so Sandy will be going over with the cat food for his son to feed Palu. We leave tomorrow at three for Cordoba. A two-hour trip, but Daniel's friend says only 190 pesos; US $47.50. Perhaps no air conditioning? No muffler? We are launching ourselves on what we hope is a firm carpet of trust. Not only in Daniel, but that the first hotel will help us along to the next one.

Had that trust shaken yesterday when I called the Amerian Hotel in San Luis. I had carefully worked out a script, but from the beginning it looked ominous. "Habler usted ignlesh?" "No." No offer to fetch someone who did, no attempt to help by asking questions that I was prepared to answer in the best Spanish I could muster. At the point where I thought I should give a credit card number I still was not sure he had said a room was available. I hung up.

The breeze is stirring, but the sun is still asleep behind the gray duvet hovering over Uritorco. The child next door is up from her nap and splashing in the pool; her dog yaps. Plenty of flies. Not as bad as last night while we ate our sidewalk pizza with anchovies, which we blame for a bout of early diarrhea.

Sandy and I dusted and swept and wiped down floors this morning, bringing life to Jim's fabulous wood. Also washed out a last few things in a bucket: we'd picked up the laundry yesterday. Bathroom and kitchen floor tiles will be mopped before bed. It is comfortable to know we will be returning here for most of March. Right now six weeks of not being sure of the quality of our bed and board is a bit, what shall I say—stressful?

MONDAY JANUARY 25 *highway between Cordoba and San Luis*

On computer. From our seats high above the road I just saw a river, a lake? A rarity in this basically dry land. Since eight-thirty this morning it has been corn fields and some other short plant stretching across this flat valley to the Cordoba Sierras. A vast pleasant sea of green that our stately ship moves through. The AC hums with assurance and road noises are mild, except now when branches scrape the rooftop as we enter a little village; perhaps we are stopping. Much too early for lunch and we carry our own bathroom with us—just like a plane except the trip up the aisle and down the stairs is more akin to an old-fashioned train, or perhaps a ship in unsettled seas? Good practice. Maybe some of our fifty or so sleeping fellow passengers will disembark here. Yes, all asleep in their semi recliner seats. Very cool and only 85 pesos ($22.50) each for this day-long trip.

Do have a reservation for the next three nights in a hotel/casino, part of the Amerian chain. Looks Victorian in the brochure and I'm sure English will be spoken. Our Spanish is still very bashful,

Cordoba was fun. The Amerian hotel there gave us a renovated suite—a definite up-grade in black, white and red décor with chrome furniture—on the tenth floor high above the all-night whirl of traffic and people. Knowing that these folks have no concept that night is for sleeping, I'd asked for a room above the fourth floor. Every day we made tracks back to our dim cool room and white sheets no later than 1 p.m. and stayed there—tea from room service—until six when we went forth to hunt food. Late openings and high prices continually sent us back to the hotel's Golden Restaurant.

The last night we ate tenderloin beef, pink and melt in your mouth, and real vegetables. I'm so sick of nothing but tomato and lettuce. This feast was accompanied by an excellent 50 peso bottle of red wine. Even before the wine, though, the waiter and another fellow, who was practicing his English--so he said--were quite captivated by Sandy's smile and twinkle, and we narrowly averted having them in our room at midnight with a bottle of champagne, ready to give massages. The best line by these young blades was "Us two and you two, si?" I almost dropped off the bench. Whee! I guess they thought, here's a couple of retired American teachers looking for a good time—we'll play the gigolo roles. Room 1008? Sign here. I had my name half written before Sandy said—that's not the bill! We left a good tip, as always, went to an art show down Hippolyta Diagonal, and before we retired put the door stop alarm in place.

Good thing we didn't have hangovers because we took a remise at nine to check out the bus terminal for tickets. It was quite a scene, slow snakes of yellow cabs outside, inside huge numbers of people in lines and boarding huge buses. We did succeed in finding the right floor and right gate in spite of our poor Spanish and secured the last two seats together for today's ride.

Back to the fields: corn in tassel and maybe potatoes in bloom here. Perhaps higher rainfall, or irrigation? The line of mountains has dwindled in the blue haze. I had trouble convincing people in Capilla that I preferred the bus to plane because I could see the countryside. Besides, how many other days do I get where the program is eight daylight hours in perfect comfort—the seat back angled, the cushion soft and the seat wide, as is the window—to simply read and doze.

LATER Am enjoying *The Help* on my Kindle. Lunch is iffy: nada? a restaurant? a box lunch?

At 2 p.m. a half-hour stop—we rushed for food.

TUESDAY JANUARY 26 Losing a city is not easy to do, but with a wrong assumption we managed it. The Amerian Hotel brochure, plucked from the elevator in Cordoba, listed "Amerian Palace Hotel Casino/ Villa Mercedes/ San Luis" and the features sounded good. Discouraged with other efforts to secure a place in San Luis, I asked our obliging desk clerk to call for us. He did and turned the phone over to me for, I assumed, a credit card number. However, the gentleman at the other end merely said all was arranged and hung up.

Immediately after arriving in the San Luis terminal we bought tickets on to Mendoza on Thursday morning. The taxi driver seemed uncertain when I showed him the hotel address, but the old men on the bench gave him advice and off we went. We unloaded the bags in a plaza, paid the driver who pointed us down what looked like a mall of shops as the police hurried his taxi away from the curb. Puzzled by the street names and seeing no sign, we reluctantly trundled our bags where he had pointed and into a hotel which did not seem right. An extreme stroke of luck put a pleasant English-speaking man behind the desk. I showed him the brochure. He said we were in the wrong city. The Amerian Palace was in Villa Mercedes, 100 km away. Good thing the desk was holding me up.

After my siege of shocked sputtering he told us a taxi was ready to take us back to the bus station. Sandy and I were of a like mind and said we wanted a taxi to Mercedes. Within five minutes the desk clerk produced Pablo, a friend of a friend. Pablo hoisted all the bags out the back door and into a car that had seen many better years in Florida, USA.

As we sped out of town, Sandy panicked about the direction we were headed and tried to call the hotel, but our cell had run out of minutes. Pablo assured us as best he could that Mercedes lay to the southeast, not west toward Mendoza. The English-speaking desk clerk had explained to me that San Luis was the name of the province, and Villa meant village, not a big house, so I was pretty sure—only pretty sure—that the hour drive would put us where our reservation was. Traveling without knowledge of the local language is like traveling deaf.

Pablo, all windows open, rushed us on and on into the heart and glowering heat of a land I could only compare to Kansas. The entrance to town was miles of industrial park and some quite ordinary streets. Only the desk clerk's smile and handshake and "Mercedes is nice, very small but nice," kept me sane. My first glimpse of the Amerian Palace lobby with its eternally racing rows of yellow light bulbs, slot room just behind the door and dice table to the rear did nothing to reassure me.

Now, at 10:30 a.m. I am okay, even looking forward to our stay. The room has become familiar and certainly has good points, the food in the restaurant—a rare hunk of sirloin and roasted vegetables!—was the best we have had. My view out the window was of a busy crossroads sans red lights, four-way stop or yield signs, or a policeman. With the addition of pedestrians—children, strollers, dogs, bunches of young people—it was a game of chicken the likes of which I had never seen before. Sandy's back was to all this mad action and to her my sudden shoulder shudders must have resembled severe Parkinson's.

The AC works and the windows open. Last night the total dark and silence of this little town with all its trees, was indeed "very small but nice." Also comforting was breakfast, chosen from the buffet selections and served in our room. I am ready to join Sandy who is waiting in the park just outside the door.

WEDNESDAY JANUARY 27 I believe *Rough Guide* said there was not much to do in San Luis but relax, and that is doubly true for Mercedes. Hopefully, the effect will be to push the dark eye circles from the middle of my face up to where they belong.

Because of our adventurous arrival the town has a Wizard of Oz feel: corn fields, hot sun, quiet—fortunately no yippy Toto—a saturation of ordinary. Our window view is the tops of green trees; the six-block walk back and forth to the end of the "commercial" district is shaded by huge plane trees with blotchy sycamore trunks.

Like in my grandmother's midforties Carlisle, Pennsylvania, people of all ages and stations in life ride bikes, the drivers of cars are polite, and a horse-drawn cart picks up the trash.

A woman reading on a bench in our plaza park told us in a mixture of Spanish and English that she is a teacher and moved from Buenos Aires to San Luis and then to Mercedes for what sounded like "to escape the traffic." She typified what we have come to define as Argentine pleasant. Polite, patient, generous with help and smiles. I have no wish to visit Europe again. Sandy agrees. We couldn't think of any nationality that we would want to stay among. New Zealanders, Africans—at least those in South Africa—and the folks here are all more than easy, they are a joy. I smart thinking of some Americans with their curt ways, some dour, some unseeing, some rushed, some leering and scary. Perhaps we will find them in Buenos Aires ...

At present we are happy to be confined to our comfortable four-star room from eleven to six with the pleasures of writing and reading; even the chore of hunting for accommodations is so easy from this chair and desk in our own silent, cool room. Last night after a dinner of pork for Sandy and fish for me—both excellent—we retired to our room at ten to find Australian Open Tennis on the big TV screen. I made it to midnight when Venus Williams lost, but then my eyes shut until eight this morning. We had room service bring coffee in bed—what's not to like? Indeed...

THURSDAY JANUARY 28 *on the bus*
Quite jiggly and the movie Julius Caesar is on DVD—well, for us here in the top deck front seat, sound only, blasting our peace with the ring of sword on sword, grunts, and death rattles. The fields to the east and south of San Luis were cultivated; here is shrub. Nothing hinders our wide-screen view: a straight road into the haze where the Andes lurk.

It is eleven, we've been up since six—an air-conditioned taxi brought us to San Luis bus station—but all has rolled along smoothly so fatigue has not set in. Due to arrive in Mendoza about two, in the midst of the afternoon heat. It will be three more days of relaxation, don't expect much else.

No roads run off this highway. Only telephone wires, tree wires, and a wire fence nailed to sticks. Plenty of sun and wind—olive trees of Spain come to mind—but agua, one of the few Spanish words that my brain has integrated, is probably the reason for this wild expanse. The sign says 200 km from our destination, the red wine capital of Argentina. They must have water there.

FRIDAY JANUARY 29 *Mendoza*

We spend time not planning meals, but when we will eat next. This is sometimes demanded by others, sometimes by our own hunger. For example, yesterday we ate only peanuts, crackers, and M&Ms between the hours of 6:30a.m. and 7 p.m. After arrival we stayed in our new room—the description in *Rough Guide* was apt: "Small, but comfortable"— admiring the ridge of the Andes from our large west-facing window, then descended to the elegant lobby to locate an Internet connection, and to talk to the English-speaking desk person about a tour bus on Monday to see the mountains and on its return trip drop us at Valle Andes for three days. We will return here Thursday night. At last we crossed the tiled walk under the grape arbor to the restaurant operated by our Aconcagua Hotel.

Big surprise. We were handed the lunch menu and our wineglasses were removed from the table. Wine and dinner, our black-clad waiter explained, was not until eight. Not the impression we'd gleaned at the desk. So beer and a hot sandwich of fried eggs, cheese, and pork was dinner. We fell asleep with Sandy's head on my shoulder watching tennis: Bill Murray, the ever hopeful, won several sets. At seven-thirty this morning we called room service for coffee in our room—it never appeared, so after my eyes had absorbed their newly prescribed double dose of drops down we went to an excellent buffet and a long stroll around the streets of shops and restaurants. The other determinate of our days is heat: here, overwhelming heat. The streets and parks are marvelously shaded by magnificent plane trees, and in some places the three foot deep stone gutters have a bit of running water. However, I have not succeeded in replacing my Gap hat although I came close this morning. My Molasses Pond baseball cap intended for Antarctica is quite warm, and one with Aconcagua Mt. 6959m is not quite suited to my white hair and rotund middle. These Argentine women are slim and tan and lovely; I am more than content to look the granny.

By noon, however, anyplace not air-conditioned was unbearable and snacking out of the frig in our room is not dietarily sound, nor cheap. I confidently told Sandy that I planned a cool drink and web mail at the lobby bar, before retiring for siesta. Another surprise. The lobby bar was closed and we were directed to the restaurant for our cool drink. Once there and confronted by the lunch menu we ordered appetizers: excellent Roquefort cheese and fresh arugula plus agua and cafe filled me. Now at 4:30 we are prepared to eat at a nice place we spotted this morning that apparently begins serving dinner at eight.

So we will continue to plan and fail and confuse our stomachs, but we have had—and anticipate more—excellent food in this quite charming city.

MONDAY FEBRUARY 1   *Hotel Valle Andino, Upsallata*
This morning I entered the Andes Mountains. Like time-speeded photos they sprout from scrub desert, sudden and small, then quickly grow to peaks. The straight, flat road begins to twist and climb hills dressed in meadow colors: green with white and gold polka dot flowers. Higher until they close about the bus, these in-your-face mountains of sharp black rock, slides of red and tan and yellow dirt. They forbid like rows of soldiers' sharp bayonets; they loom, press ever closer as the needle of Sandy's altimeter rises: three thousand, four thousand: lean, volcanic basalt twisted into Grimm Brothers pen and ink horrors. Five thousand, six. Mile after mile of vertical painted-desert wonder. Charles Darwin, who saw this from train windows in the 1830s, wrote in the *Voyage of the Beagle: Red, purple, green and quite white sedimentary rocks, alternating with black lavas broken up and thrown into all kinds of disorder, by masses of porphyry, of every shade, from dark brown to the brightest lilac. It really resembles those pretty sections which geologists make of the inside of the earth.* How right he was.

The mountains made a historical ruin of that railroad: glacial waters caught behind a gigantic ice jam broke loose and scoured the valley floor of the little stations—one every 10 km—and buried the iron rails. Repairs that took years were then undone by avalanches of snow hurtling from cone-shaped funnels, by slides of land and rock, by floods. Today the Alta Montana highway faces the same enemies, and I wonder if one day people traveling by plane between Chile and Argentina will look down and reminisce about the scars left by this road, abandoned to the force of these immense waiting-to-strike creatures.

Beyond ten thousand feet they taunt and leer, they crowd and threaten with boulders poised above our heads. From Mendoza we had seen them lost in dust, stirred by the wind called Sonda. I imagine the sting of it, the howl, the darkness. I imagine them deep in winter snow like the eternal snows of Aconcagua now rising beyond the windows, the tallest mountain of this continent of tall mountains, the tallest outside the Himalayas. Imagine glaciers, blizzards, white-outs, skiers black dots of insanity. In the cemetery for climbers lie the one hundred and thirteen lost to Aconcagua wiles. I see what is beneath its snow and ice packs and wonder if this is what a bare Antarctica looks like.

We reach the pass, the line between the east or west flow of the glacial streams. While our guide speaks in Spanish I feel the road shift to dirt under the bus tires. Before us a narrow strip of dun snake launches itself up in ever higher switchbacks. Our tires hang on edges with no support but the thin air of straight drops. Ten thousand, one more, then twelve, thirteen thousand. Why are we doing this? Why are any of these vans and cars doing this? I can certainly get through the rest of my life without gazing on the Christ of the Andes. Stop! We do, but only to let another bus pitch and grind downward. My head floats.

At 12,500 feet we disembark: I hang on to the railing until one foot is firmly planted on the ground. The wind is pushy, nasty. For two pesos we use the bano with toilet paper, freely photograph Monumento al Cristo Redentor formed from melted-down cannon and other weapons of wars with Chile. A current of satisfaction swims through me: one more great adventure, one more step in knowing the planet we live on. It is fearsome, this unfinished sphere. I sense the rumble, the mighty voice on that seismographic CD, and know we live here at its whim and our peril.

It was a day in the land of wondrous strange.

TUESDAY FEBRUARY 2 *Upsallata*

The tall Lombardy poplars move like dancers, but although their line is straight, each exercises to her own music. The backdrop is white clouds rising on the hot dry air, outlining the tops of the Andean peaks. In front of me sprinklers blow willy-nilly over the spacious back lawn; skinny boys dive into the pool.

After our initial shocks of bunk beds, chipped paint, and Spanish debacles over choosing dinner from a spoken menu, we are quite enjoying ourselves. In this oasis we have found cool nights and silence, unique "camp" birds, and in the village this morning I at last found a replacement for my Gap hat. Beige, woven, wider brim, a perfect fit and perfect for the streets of Buenos Aires. Yesterday, on the trip down from the grim peaks, our tour bus stopped at a turn-of-the-last-century sulfur springs spa—buried by a landslide in 1965. I deserted the group for a big spread of what was called Inca items, and on the rack of shoulder bags found a woven pack of guanaco wool, well made and with secure fasteners. It will be my purse on the flight to Ushuaia, allowing me to carry much more. So there, shopping complete except for Tee's wedding.

Sunday in Mendoza had been a day of happiness—inspired no

doubt by a solid sleep and cooler temperatures. It held a bit of all the things we treasure when wintering-over away: intimacy, a good breakfast, easy strolls through the four plazas, lunch at Florencia seated next to a jolly wine-drinking Dutchman and his partner, a dancer and dealer in towels and bed linens in, of all places, Mercedes. She could not speak English, but her raised eyebrows and rolled eyes conveyed a lot. To use a cliché—we hit it off. Waiters, recognizing us from our lengthy beef assido dinner, smiled and chatted as they tended couples and families—perhaps fifty—seated at long umbrella-shaded tables; musicians played pan flutes and guitar. Argentines eat so much and enjoy it so much. Lacking the energy to return that hot evening, we waited until after eight and strolled across hotel garden. Dinner was exquisite: a bowl of marvelous risotto flavored with a vegetable broth and herbs, topped with a whole trout—pink and tasty. By ten we were in bed: on the floor below the young and beautiful bikini people still lingered by the terrace pool.

The wind is blustery now, causing a great whooshing among these trees and, as in Capilla, dust is everywhere. I'm ready to take on the Big Apple of Argentina.

SATURDAY FEBRUARY 6 *Amerian Park Hotel, Buenos Aires*

Yesterday's trip was a normal hop by plane from Mendoza to here, an airport we'd already been through; the trip the day before was surreal: a two-hour taxi ride down from our 8,000 foot perch of Upsallata. The scenery was wild and fierce and incomparably gorgeous; the speed hair-raising. A couple of times in college when the driver was drunk, speeding, and any suggestion that he might like to … ah … let someone else drive only made matters worse, I had distracted myself by kissing my date. This time, eyes wide, I focused on swinging my head from side to side: would we crash into that magnificent cliff wall, hit that oncoming bus, tumble into the beauty of the glacial reservoir? I was more curious than panicked. He was not drunk, simply Argentinean.

I should make a correction. Our plane flight was not normal, more of a lesson in: What you worry about will not happen, but what you don't will. We had for probably two hours juggled possessions—even abandoned some, like my water shoes, to the waste basket—in an effort to make the eleven-pound hand luggage and thirty-two pound checked luggage requirement on the flight from Mendoza. We got it right down to the tenth of a pound according to our hand-held scale. We zipped through airport check-in with no problem, and quite self-satisfied went upstairs and ordered a pizza. I pulled my boarding pass and passport out of my pocket to restore them to my leather case. "Where's mine?" Sandy asked. Well, that started the ball rolling. We only had one boarding pass—made out to Robert Lawson. While an agent made her a new one, Sandy came back up to the delicious pizza I was already into and announced she'd been told I was to look very carefully because I must have my boarding pass. I think both of us thought the other had slipped a gear, but no, when I went down and told the woman I absolutely did not have it, she glanced toward the man who had made them originally, marched over, and searched the floor. The guy was standing on it. She brushed off the footprint and I went back up to another slice of pizza. No need to spell out the morals to that story.

On Tuesday February ninth our tour fellow people will be boarding their planes in the US; their return is on the morning of the twenty-third making this a fourteen day tour. Eleven nights will be on the ship that sails from Ushuaia. Sandy and I will move from here Wednesday to take advantage of our reserved room at the Marriott Plaza for two nights.

However, last night we learned that a big east coast snowstorm may change—or even end—some people's plans. A woman from Washington D.C. said she flew out two days early to meet her tour. Said the airline was eager to change her ticket with no charge. Good tip. And she went on to tell another one—we were in the hotel restaurant. When her cab from the international airport dropped her here, she looked in the truck and saw sticking out from under the tire iron a bit of color. "Isn't that my cosmetic bag?" she asked the driver. "Where? Where? No it couldn't be." A swat with her hiking stick—she is seventy-five—convinced the driver to allow her to pull out her cosmetic bag, the contents of which spilled from an already slit side. Since the desk clerks inside did not report it to the police, she vowed to do so herself in the morning—she knew the cab's number. "I wasn't born yesterday." We passed on Jim's tip of not getting out and shutting the door, so the taxi could take off with all the luggage. Jim had managed to run the guy down in slow traffic, but us ... doubtful.

Not letting down your guard when you hit big cities should— since Madrid—have been engraved in blood on our foreheads, but we have now tightened our grip. On our walk around town this morning I wore Jim's leg money purse with my wedding dress cash in it. And we walked very fast past McDonald's.

That reminds me of another caution. Our guide book said: "Buenos Aires lends itself perfectly to aimless wandering and its mostly ordered grid pattern makes it fairly easy to orient yourself." Key words: "mostly" and "fairly." Sandy and I, armed with a good map with print large enough to read, learned once more that our sense of direction is quite reliable—except where parks and circles are concerned. This morning despite directions from a woman in an information booth right beside Plaza de Mayo, we lost Santa Fe Street and never did find it again. I discovered while having lunch, a Viennese coffee loaded with ice cream and cream, that the corner street sign above me had two absolutely unfamiliar names. The waiter located us on our map and yet we will probably never figure out how we got there. We plan on a taxi to take us to the area our desk clerk circled as better shops. A friend in Capilla had also mentioned the pedestrian Florida Street, but it seemed to me a place where a tourist could really be hustled.

We had our afternoon tea brought by room service; tonight we will dine at "Al Carbon: Best Grilled Steaks are Argentine." The business card is stamped by the hotel for a free glass of champagne. The meal will be pricy, no doubt, but the exchange rate holds at almost 4 to 1.

SUNDAY FEBRUARY 7 We like our near the top room and take long siestas. Standing at the windows we can see the Rio de la Plata and the ship traffic back and forth to Uruguay and out to sea. The breakfast room overhangs the lobby; we eat leisurely and well. The location with its fascinating architecture, blend of old and new buildings, bustling and quiet is perfect. Rain, yes, but no pollution, thank goodness.

Last night, Saturday, we returned to the same restaurant: it opens at seven-thirty and we were there, comfortable in the emptiness. And remained comfortable when people arrived: three American women, a lone Argentine woman, two couples, two men, a man and woman—the woman was French and chose the wine—two men, two other American women. As I think I've said before, the feel of this whole country is companionable, one of good will.

TUESDAY FEBRUARY 9 Sandy and I went to Bullrich—a unique-in-my-experience example of upscale stores housed in a glamorous old two-story circular building. Being just in the idea stage of looking for something to wear to Tee's wedding, we window-shopped around both levels of the rotunda, then around again to briefly scan some racks inside. I did try on a gray top that Sandy pronounced tacky—price does not dictate class. What they really spend money on here are the accessories: shoes, purses, belts, jewelry, items that have never attracted me. We lunched at tables set on the rotunda floor--a personal pizza cut in half and two bottles of agua; Sandy photographed the magnificent surroundings and I gawked at the slim, at least trim, and well-dressed shoppers.

It is necessary to lighten our luggage in order to get it on the flight to Ushuaia and I am crossing my fingers and packing a box to mail to Capilla. Not wedding clothes, just two pairs of shoes to put us under the eleven-pound hand luggage limit. Tonight we'll repack for the brief taxi drive—10:30 a.m. checkout--to the Marriott Plaza. Our Antarctica tour group is to assemble mid-afternoon.

Lunch today was at 2:00 in the courtyard of the convent of the sisters of Santa Catalina. The huge trees dripped pink or red flowers as they waved in a cooling breeze above the whitewashed walls of arches and narrow black windows. The clientele scattered at shady tables were all Puertanoes, residents of the port, as was the lone non-English-speaking waitress. Nothing on the blackboard menu was anything we recognized, and since the minimum for a la carte was 53 pesos, I simply said the two words I recognized--risotto and calamari--and soon our dos especials of the day were set in motion. Truly a meal descended from heaven.

Farmer's Truck, Mercedes

Glacier Perito Moreno

Christina, Ushaia   Tablita Restaurant, El Calafate

Jim's Casita, Capilla

Jim Barrett, host, Capilla

Golden-billed Saltator, Capilla

Tito and Pelu, Capilla

Seba & Nancy, Capilla

Oil vendor & Mariano, San Marcos

Daniel, Capilla

Cordoba

Ushuaia

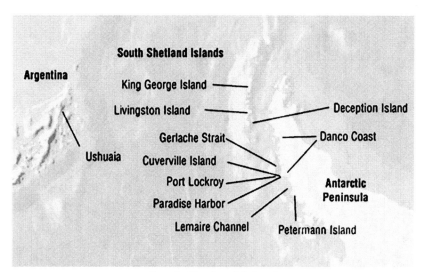

South Shetland Islands

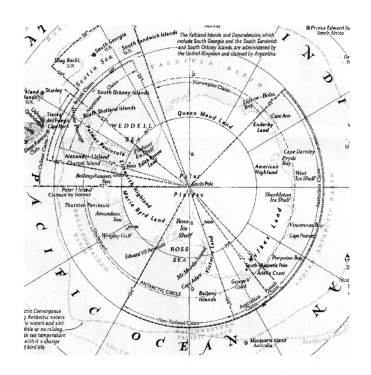

Antarctica

WEDNESDAY FEBRUARY 11   *Plaza Hotel, Buenos Aires*

I woke to a nightmare. Sandy was standing by the window frowning at the Antarctic trip folder. "What's the date today?" I paused to think. "The ninth." "Well, look at this." I looked. It said we flew to Ushuaia on the ninth. This morning.

My brain rushed and snapped. My hand reached for the phone. 6:30. Maybe there was time to catch them at the Marriott. Dear god, how could I have ... All of the correspondence was in Capilla—none of it here. My voice crackled, the pause was heavy, then a blessed: "That tour checks in this afternoon."

The trip folder was dated 2009. The 2010 was in my luggage. How on earth—? Never mind. I lay back and shut my eyes.

LATER. We moved the few blocks by taxi. Now we descend to the wine and cheese reception to mingle with our fellow travelers to Antarctica.

THURSDAY FEBRUARY 12 Last night I lay back and said to the ceiling, "Mother, I made it to the Plaza." The Buenos Aires Marriott Plaza, but nonetheless the Plaza. Touches of the long gone days when the city aspired to be the Paris of South America remain. High ceilings, fine furniture, rugs with real wool pile. A couple of good pasta dinners from room service—just like in the movies of my youth. A bed with six pillows, and a bay window whose floor to ceiling gold drapes provided a secluded 3 a.m. bathroom detour, where I contemplated the lighted windows across the street where men and women sat at their computers. Stockbrokers?

But. No wi-fi in the rooms, and a lobby often so crammed with people and luggage it resembles a five-star bus station. The Amerian in Cordoba, those South African B&B's, and Annabelle's in New Zealand, of course, suited me better.

The bus tour of the city was fine; we used our room service privileges for dinner again. Sandy is down at the desk settling the bill of incidentals, the bags to be checked are ready to zip and set in the hall, heavy clothes are lying ready for us to don at 4:30 a.m. We are to be downstairs at 5 to grab coffee and a snack, then it's off for the bus and into the air southward at 7:30. To the ends of the earth, as I wrote to the family. Indeed. High Adventure. At seventy-seven. Not all the way to the South Pole where time stops—literally—but close enough. Do our bodies slow to match the earth's fall in rotation from spin to crawl?

EDITING NOTE. Some later additions were made to the ten days of shipboard entries.

FRIDAY FEBRUARY 12 At 5:30 a.m.—we were on the early flight-- eager to get started and impatient at lingering about in the reception room after a too-scanty breakfast, we picked up our box lunches and made for the lobby: I think we were first on the first bus. The airport was familiar, the waiting at the gate was familiar, the final attempts in the lavatory familiar, but underneath it all ran a sensation of, This is it! We are on our way to board a ship bound for the last continent.

But first was Ushuaia, the southernmost city on the planet. The flight down had been included in our original price and now a free tour. Standing outside the bus that would take us around the national park—we were many hours ahead of the second flight—I felt rain, but it was not raining. I asked the local guide and she told me rain was like that here. Some form of snow? of sleet? I asked, but our different climate backgrounds prevented us from coming to any commonality except *wet*. The park was a treat: mountains, a lake we walked beside, new types of vegetation, a bird that certainly looked like a condor but the guide said was a black vulture. A much longer walk across low, marshy land—more birds—to a photo op at the end of Ruta 40, the famous north-south road up the western spine of this giant county. Invercargill in New Zealand, Cape of Good Hope in South Africa, and now here: Antarctica encircled.

The buses unloaded us by the harbor—a mountainous cruise ship was at the dock but none resembling ours—for two free hours in town. First: marvelous postcards to mail from Antarctica—if we can land; second, search for a good lunch place in this two-main-street town squeezed between the Andes and Beagle Channel. "Wait," I said to Sandy as we left the restaurant. "This looks familiar. From the Internet." Indeed. Large metal letters spelled Capapallo. Our hotel. Without pausing to figure out which one of the stores across the street was Christiana's—the mother of Jim's friend who had recommended the Capapallo—we joined the vaguely familiar faces milling around harborside gazing at our ship, which appeared much less dramatic than the brochure photo of it floating in an icy bay.

The month in hot, dusty Argentina made cold, wind-swept Ushuaia seem foreign, but at least it was land, not the totally foreign environment of a ship riding unfathomable seas. As a poet might put it: my skin jumped with goose-bumps, my mind with sparks of awe.

Dressed in cords, light hikers, and a polartec jacket, guanaco sack over my shoulder, I strode between rows of white-suited sailors toward an open door. A tall, handsome young man with sufficient braid to be the captain shook my hand and said, Welcome. Inside someone pressed a warm washcloth into my hand—which I found still there when I entered our cabin—and a small man—Filipino?—scurried back and forth along the hall. I had told him cabin #330, which did not exist, but Sandy said #303 and there we were, the likes of which I had only seen in movies. A queen bed under two big portholes. I was delighted. "And look." I knelt on the bed, rested my arms on the shelf. "I can see everything." On the left side were two comfortable chairs and a little table with a big mirror above it and a bathroom plenty big enough to turn around in. Opposite it on the right was a long double closet, a desktop over two sets of drawers, and above a screen for in-house use or DVDs.

That was it, home for ten nights, not in the bowels of the ship, but on the same deck as the dining room. Maybe they couldn't fill the ship and had bumped us up. Jan our agency guide had jokingly—seriously?—said she could offer us a suite on the top deck with the French passengers. Others had informed us that the passenger lists mailed to them had only three or four alumni, maybe one, from colleges across the US and Canada: three from Penn and one of those had canceled because their flight was caught up in the Philadelphia snowstorm. So much for the notion of "alumni groupies." The economy is worse than anyone is letting on.

Outside El Club, one floor—deck—up, we tried on the gift parkas for size; they are a great red with all the pockets and zippers and cords of first-rate sportswear. We and the two women in the cabin across from us went in the club with its wonderful soft chairs and couches in bright red, small tables with tiered plates of cookies, and spacious windows on each side. I beat a hasty retreat from the bar when asked for my room number and joined the others for free tea. Five o'clock European time is not for wine, but having been on an adrenaline high for twelve hours, it certainly felt like time to me. If I were a real drinker I would have taken the fancy cocktail the bartender suggested.

In the cabin I opted for stretching out on the bed, not quite the Plaza but certainly adequate, while Sandy stored her clothes. A nap was not to be an option, however. A male voice burst into our room; Sandy bent her ear to the speaker above the desk op, trying to make out what he said. Half was in French, the English version heavily accented. With help from milling people in the hallway we understood: Abandon Ship drill. We found our life jackets, struggled to get them on over our parkas, affixed yellow stickers, and reported to the deck with the swimming pool. And it was a drill, efficient, serious. The yellow group's boat would be the first one swung out and down. Into my mind popped a photo: penguins in a line on a cliff, their next action to be determined by whether the first one to hit the water was eaten by a sea leopard. At the later briefing, our ship tour director, a truly fine comedian, said, "Perhaps the custom of learning how to abandon a ship before it sails should be incorporated into marriage contracts."

The next PA announcement I remember was: "The captain invites you to the decks to view leaving the harbor of Ushuaia," but we, in our classy red parkas, were already on the uppermost deck, Observation, taking pictures of spectacular shafts of light cast on parts of the flat town, water, and mountains by an insipid yellow sunset. Even though it was chilly Sandy and I, as is our habit, waited at various levels and rails until we were positive we were moving into the Beagle Channel. This resulted in a late arrival at the Captain's Reception.

Young ladies in long dresses quickly greeted us outside the doors to the auditorium cum café—our French captain was already speaking—and settled us into a couch at the back. Champagne floated by on a waiter's expert hand. We glanced about, relieved to see a wide variety of clothing; months before we had chosen from catalogues our "casual clothes suitable for the occasion." We clicked glasses. Underway to Antarctica.

Through speeches and eavesdropping on people around us we learned that this would be the last cruise of the *Diamant* to Antarctica, but whether this was because of the new restrictions to be placed on cruise ships for the next season remained a question. Our ice-master for this cruise was the former captain; rumor had it that Captain Marchesseau was "recovering" from being kidnapped by Somali. My confidence sloshed up and down.

Le Diamant is the biggest ship I have ever been on and certainly the most luxurious—the ferry to Grand Manan being the next in line … At dinner we learned just how fancy. Tables for eight, six, four, or two were nicely spaced around a big room; each person, usually accompanied by a cabinmate, sat wherever he or she wished. Sandy and I, the bewildered first-timers, were gently moved toward a partially filled round table of six, to be soon joined by Nicholas, our Russian leader who had told us at the briefing to knock the adjective "soft" off the word "expedition"; and John Silva, a Brit bird expert and "generalist." The large, calligraphic menu was not to choose from, but to let us know what we would be having for the various courses: soup, salad, fish, meat, dessert. Bottles of wine, French, of course, hovered and we chose either red or white; thereafter our glasses were never empty. Later Sandy commented on that and the amazing efficiencies of the huge staff of waiters who presented the food, impeccably, at the perfect temperature, be it hot or cold. The linens, the array of silver, the comfort of the chairs—all was perfection. I do recall picking up my dessert spoon for my soup. Ah well ... I could plausibly blame that on this middle of the night attempt to be conversationally adept.

In our room the porthole framed a dark sea and a darker strip of coastline. The Beagle Channel, named for the ship Charles Darwin sailed on, cuts eastward from Ushuaia past Tierra del Fuego to the Atlantic Ocean. No tumultuous convergence yet and the prediction was for calm seas. With a seasickness patch securely pasted behind my ear, I dropped into a dead sleep. My first bathroom trip was rather precarious even though the rocking of the bed—berth?—had forewarned me. Before exhausted sleep reclaimed me I whispered the words Sandy and I had exchanged before we shut our eyes: Do you believe where we are?

SATURDAY FEBRUARY 13 *shipboard Drake Passage*
Wind: force 4-5 (calculated by mathematical formula using wind speed)
Sea: Calm
Air Temp: 6C (43F)
Water: 6.1C

In a white rubber circle on the front of my parka is a map: the profile of Antarctica that resembles the head and shoulders of a buffalo facing west. Its horn—actually about 500 km in length-- curves toward the tip of South America; knifelike New Zealand floats a good distance from its chin and throat; the bulk of Africa hangs above its hump. Cape Horn, a small island lying off the channel, marks the start of that the stormy Drake Passage, the convergence. Crossing it will take thirty-six hours, more or less.

About halfway across is the Antarctic convergence--where cold and warm waters agitated by currents, winds, and gravity meet. It lies between the latitudes of the roaring 40s and howling 50s; even farther southward are the screaming 60s and the Antarctic circle. In summer this southern ocean is often turbulent, and in winter more than half of it freezes to a depth of a meter or more. Stonehouse in *The Last Continent* suggests, *"If you really cannot cope with violent movements at sea, think twice before booking an Antarctic cruise: there are much cheaper ways of making yourself miserable."*

Little remains in my memory about the first day at sea except that I hovered between queasiness and believing that if I did not put something in my stomach, preferably saltine crackers, in the next five minutes I was going to succumb to heaving over the rail, as those folks in the glass-bottomed boat did off Key Largo; or for that matter, those in the cabin of an Irish ferry crossing to the Aran Isles. Thwarted on the cracker mission, at lunch I popped a hard roll into Sandy's purse for security.

Of course, in the usual rhythm of my life in the seventies, the day after such intense activity would definitely be a flat day and this, both literally and figuratively, was not. We passengers needed distraction from lurching stomachs, sloshing body fluids in general, and we got it. Being on Deck 5 in the Grand Salon listening to and laughing with our Robin Williamsesque tour guide coach us on Zodiac behavior gave relief, as did a few brisk turns about the decks, and tea, cookies, and live music in El Club. Lunch and breakfast were staggeringly extravagant buffets, the likes of which I had never imagined. I had a healthy nap, but reading and computer use were no-no's because of the supposed discord between fixed eyes and those gyrating body fluids.

The word is we'll be berthed in the South Shetland Islands by nightfall.

SUNDAY FEBRUARY 14 *M.S, Diamant, Southern Shetland Islands,*
   Sunrise 4 a.m. Sunset 10:50 p.m.

Noon position Deception Is., where I set foot — both--on the ashy sands of Antarctica, the last, or lost, continent.
   Wind: Nil force 0
   Sea: Calm
   Air Temp: 2C (36F)
   Water: .5C (33F)
   Landings: Baily Head 1:50 p.m.
          Whaler's Bay 4:30 p.m.

Getting there was tense. Well, I should start at the beginning. Last night in his briefing on our destination, Nicholas, who is a totally in-command speaker, deep voice, easy humor, direct this-is-the-way-it-is style, told us that this first landing was the toughest we would face, but possible for all. Now, mind you, there were some 200 of us neophytes who had never seen a Zodiac up close, let alone boarded one, ridden across a stretch of freezing-point water, and disembarked into same water on slippery stones. Probably most listened with their hands clasped tightly as I did, pale, serious, determined, yet with an I-can-always-say-no simmering in the backs of our ancient fight-or-flight brain cells.

"On this beach"--envision Nicholas's height, the beard, the muscled leanness—"the waves can create a powerful backwash." Maybe others besides Sandy and I knew just how powerful an ocean can be, but we exchanged a raised eyebrow look. He went on in this tone for quite a while, and my eyebrows went up again at "walk to the beach as quickly as you can and up the rise so that any backwash cannot reach you." Right. Walk in new boots, in water how deep? And how far? How steep is that rise? "If the waves are coming in too strong, we cannot go, but otherwise it is safe for everyone. Everyone can go. It is a beautiful place. It is too bad this is your first landing. This being the hardest one. But then after, you can relax." He smiled but I didn't. Was he playing mind games with us, building it up to be the worst so it would seem easy if we succeeded? At that point I probably rested my chin in one palm and stared skeptically.

Our tour director did become serious over directions for how to safely get out of a Zodiac. "Always sit on the edge back to the shore. Lift your legs up, swing them over the side and drop into the water. We will help you." Darn right you will.

Then the expedition's whale expert, who did resemble one, came on stage and did a comic version of same. I laughed along with everyone else, but later I told the Gohagan tour guide, Jan, "Not my first choice for a landing with slippery rocks and backwash." I did not elaborate by adding "... and red parkas floating pack-up like a landing on a WWII beachhead." Yesterday Sandy had found the deck where the Zodiacs were being checked over—one motor seemed to have a problem—but much to our relief we discovered that the sides were made of hard rubber, mitigating our worries about wiggling our way over the side. This morning we reported to El Club to vacuum all the seams of our outer clothing. They are serious about not contaminating this continent that has never supported an indigenous population, but what about all those

Europeans who messed around there for a couple of centuries?

Baily Head, our initiation landing, is on the outer arm of Deception Island, one of the Shetland Islands off the Palmer (Antarctic) Peninsula. The Yellow Group was scheduled to disembark at 1:50 p.m., third out of the four landing parties. Instructions by the Robin Williams voice drilled through the PA speakers. At 1:40 he finished with the Green Group, and started on the Yellows, screwing into our heads the idea that we simultaneously must hurry and suit up yet not arrive in the club lounge too early. I tried to be methodical: silk undershirt and tights, turtleneck and polartec pants—whoops, off with the pants—silk socks, wool socks, hikers—whoops, on with pants, hikers, high boots, waterproof pants. Stand up. Polartec jacket, parka—whoops, back up, off with parka—fanny pack with water bottle, clip on that belt the waterproof bag holding camera and big sunglasses, okay, parka on, ski mittens in one pocket, tissues in another—Whoa. Neck hugger first. Parka off, on again. Life jacket. How in the hell does this thing . . . Yellow group. Yellow Group, go to the club. Blue group get dressed. Our steward was in the hall helping get arms through straps, front clips fastened. My parka zipper refused to work. Yellow Group go to the club now. Yellow group. I found Velcro strips for my jacket, zipper be damned. Sandy tried to snap my life jacket and swore. The hall was empty. My hat! I jammed on my Molasses Pond visor cap with the Duluth trading center attachment for ears—I'd completely forgotten my balaclava. Blue Group to club. Blue group go to the club now. Dear god ... Sandy and I ran down the hall, up two flights of stairs, through the blur of red and out onto the landing. We slumped in sweaty relief. People were still waiting to descend the stairs. There stood Pat and Shirley, a couple we had met at the opening reception—yellows. Thank god. For the cold air too. No one looked calm. My mouth was dry as a bone.

The line shuffled forward. ID swiped. A flight of perhaps twenty-five white metal steps, railing on both sides, so many things to consider: steepness in these untried boots, grip of silk gloves on railing, plastic tub of disinfectant at the bottom to step in, rope guide across to the outdoors and another flight down to the Zodiac. I could see there were two men helping people step up on the side of it and two more inside helping them down. Red parkas already perched on either side. Don't make a fool of yourself. Okay. Down. Too slow— keep up. Now. Step up. Grab those strong wrists. Down and in. Sit. I reached back and gripped the rope looped along the side. Takeoff might be rough.

Nothing was rough. Not the trip over, not getting out with two competent arms on the other side to steady me. Not walking up the rise. I planted myself like a flag and gazed around at the largest rookery of Chinstrap penguins on the Antarctic Peninsula: some 200,000 who stood like small figurines arranged from the black sand beach to the high ridge. Eighty-five red-parka'ed humans hiked up among them, then disappeared over the other side. Sandy and I had chosen to penguin watch and then go by ship around into this caldera. During some eruption--the latest was 1969--one wall had collapsed to let in seawater — and ships.

Perfecto. So perfect an outing, in fact, that my brain stored everything and stamped it: open later.

Smooth docking beside ship's loading platform. Up a wooden step placed on the firm bottom, and, in the wrist grip of men on the platform, up onto the firm side of the Zodiac and down. No stagger, no stumble. Climb the stairs, rub both booted feet against scrubbers in plastic tubs, step in disinfectant bath, climb the final stairs, sit on a bench. No need for a boot V to help kick off the wellies most people wore — just a simple snap of the instep tab, yank on the Velcro top, one kick of a heel against the other toe, and there. Shoes already on, boots in hand, I entered Le Club and was handed a cup of hot beef bouillon.

Yes, I am tired — thank goodness I did not attempt that two and a half hour trek, which probably would take a great deal more time and effort than advertised, nor even a climb to the top of the bowl.

LATER. I have a new love — blue-green icebergs. The first came into view this morning — a giant flat-top with a mammoth, ribbed azure cave where a seal swam, and where on an ice porch a dozen chinstrap penguins gathered, infinitesimal against the mysterious, cavernous mouth. The color, I was told, is from air bubbles impacted as the glacier forms, to appear in the broken off iceberg as a miraculous form of heaven. Alive, the bergs force their magnificent presence upon me like those massive old trees, the kauri and the baobab. The wonder of it. Later Sandy overheard one of the shop women say she had been on the ship four years and never seen one as beautiful as that. We circled it two or three times.

In another hour –about 5 p.m. — I will suit up again to land at the site of an old whaling station. The *Diamant* will slide carefully through Neptune's Bellows into the volcanic lake, now calm and devoid of commercial activity — except for the flow of bundled tourists. Beginning in the 1800s it was a refuge from storms and icebergs, then fur sealers came, and finally in the 1900s factory ships that boiled whale blubber into oil. Those humans left detritus: a giant rusted tank, an artifact of boiling down the stripped carcass; remains of scientific stations, an airplane hanger. ... Hopefully we leave no trace. I will not swim in the hot springs under the sand.

Just turned to catch the porthole view. There are killer whales out there somewhere, but I will wait to go on deck until we are entering the round wet eye of the old volcano. Feeling much better since the Drake Passage is behind us. The day has been an exceptionally welcoming one, but now gray has taken over—except for those sculptured, visionary bergs shining with inner light. There is always the possibility that the weather will turn and these are the only landings we will get—just like with Maine and fog—so I will push on and sleep soundly tonight as I have every night here on shipboard. We skip the entertainments and go straight to bed after dinner, about 9:30.

The floating life is an odd one. No complaints, however, with crew of 100 to serve us 179 passengers. I think I'll go up to Deck 4 and some tea.

LATER. Plays of light on water spectacular. Elephant seals stretched on the beach were a most amazing sight. They are huge, ponderous like their namesake, and seemingly unaware of their massive strength. Thank goodness, they were not lively or cared one whit about us invasive two-legged creatures. They simply lolled, their weird proboscis rising and falling with their breaths, must be relatives of manatees. Huge dark fur seals sat like dogs and in contrast the white-fronted little penguins were, like water itself, always on the move, talking, hurrying, changing.

MONDAY FEBRUARY 15 *off Gourdin Island*

Wind: SW force 3
Sea: calm
Air temp: 4 degrees (39F)
Water: 1.5 C (33F)
Landing: Gourdin Island 8 a.m.
Sunrise 4 a.m.; Sunset 10 p.m.

In the dark of the short night, the ship carried us across the Bansfield Strait to the very tip of the Antarctic Peninsula, and this morning at eight we stood on this island with a clear, brilliant sun casting its crooked light on the rocky, guano-thick shorefront. I could have stayed and looked for days: at the distant icebergs, the flat blue water and everywhere penguins: the gentoo (papua), chinstrap, and our friend from New Zealand, the adelie. This summer's babies hang out in groups, new black feathers glistening, apparently waiting for some adult to lead them to a safe launching spot. Soon they will swim off and not return. Loners and late-bloomers waterlogged by unshed down are often picked off by giant petrels, but tens of thousands survive to live as sea creatures. Most adults are done molting and they too will be gone, giving the rookeries over to eight months of wind and ice.

Sandy climbed partway up a tall hill of rock chunks but I barely moved, moored among the penguins in an attempt to shuck my alien status. Down by the landing people were looking, pointing toward the other end of the small cove. A furious splashing. A thick serpent-like neck thrashing, whapping a dark body against the surface. Disappearing. Rising again. I either heard, or imagined, the beat of that penguin hitting the water again and again. Whap. Whap. Whap. A Zodiac set off for the scene. I wandered over, careful to give the right of way to, usually, an adult penguin and three young ones making a running break for the water, or is it a harassed parent fleeing demanding kids? I could not see the aftermath of the killing, but was told the seal somehow removes the penguin meat, leaving the feathered carcass as litter. I caught a ride on the next Zodiac and we idled beside the ice floe where the leopard seal, silvery and spotted, lolled, quite friendly looking except for the blood on its whiskered face. Red also streaked the calm blue water. These lone hunters will often adopt a rookery for the season, snatching, when hunger strikes, a young penguin returning from the sea.

This afternoon our ship will seek sea ice and tubular icebergs under the guidance of our Ice Master. Apparently, these weather conditions are extraordinary, making all these wonders accessible to us. So far every landing has been easy, and our waterproof pants and boots have not allowed in a drop of moisture.

Antarctica's vast, immutable presence diminishes us, penguin and human, to what we actually are, small and transitory specks not worthy of note by these massive glaciers, which are more knowing than the eye of a leopard seal, more birthed from the planet, it seems, than descended from the sky, more ancient than time itself. I suspect my remaining life will be divided into pre-and post-Antarctica segments.

My immediate hope, however, is that once used to ship living and the schedules we keep, I will feel rested.

LATER The sea is the dominate blue, thicker than the sky which is about two hours from sunset. Icebergs abound: car-sized growlers, smaller bergy bits, and break-offs from those called bitty bits. Or at least that is the terminology on the *Diamant*.

Orcas, killer whales, have been sighted on the starboard side: Sandy is on deck, I stayed in our room with the starboard view and saw a bit of action. Whales do symbolize this part of the world, and their massive bulk is fitting in this massive emptiness. Our evening expedition took us out into the ice pack, another symbol, where I actually disembarked the Zodiac to stand on the flat surface of a "table" tubular ice floe. It was moving with the sea and rotating, and the ice was thickening: the horizon resembled a city of white and gray block buildings, a nature city. None of the residents, multitudinous penguins, seals—leopard, Weddell, and crabeater— whales, or rare birds would attempt to improve upon it: only that arrogant mammal, the human, would even think of it. But we are not residents, merely red penguins tromping about on this temporary bit of real estate, taking photos for alumni magazines, driving snow golf balls, shouting like kids at recess. Like the sea, the ice will bear no memory of our passing: wind and snow will quickly erase every trace.

The weather has continued perfect, but we were turned back from exploring the sound leading to the Weddell Sea by early forming pack-ice. So, in addition to the intentions of the clouds— grays, pinks, blacks, whites—that arch above the mountains, ice and water also determine when and where we travel. And then there is the human element: sometimes I think we are on a Disney cruise full of surprises to make us passengers squeal with delight or gasp with fear. However, Jan, who has a basic honesty about her, told us that on her last cruise it rained every single day, and apparently the one last week had howling 90 *kph* winds and angry surf that prevented most landings. But Jan also has used the word surprise more than once. Why am I so cynical about the use of crowd control devices? After all, isn't that what we teachers do? Maybe it is the shock of not controlling, but being controlled.

TUESDAY FEBRUARY 16 Noon: *Livingston Is., S. Shetland Islands*

Wind: SW force 6
Sea: Choppy
Air Temp. 7 C (45F)
Water: 3.0 C (37F)
Landings: Half Moon Is. 9:15 a.m.
Hannah Point 2:45 p.m.

A real struggle this morning to suit up for yet another embarkment to another beautiful landing spot. A shower and breakfast did not push my enthusiasm, but I went anyway, and it was a scene so filled with otherness and mystery that missing it would have been a major loss. The smell of the penguin colony preceded landing, but they were scattered enough so that our little climb to the ridge brought freshness and buoyancy to the dry air. Half Moon Island is small and nestles in the curve of the Livingston Mountains, which tower beyond a shingle beach thick with penguins and seals, and a thin strip of calm water. The sky's responsibility is special effects and it put on a great show. Of course, a line of sharp snow-covered mountains is a joy in itself, but sudden brilliant white spotlights, moving shadows, and the pink tint that hovers over waters and horizon create a painted, evolving abstract: Antarctica.

Probably high 30s, little breeze: I could have sat and watched for hours.

The hot chicken bouillon ladled out in Le Club made a perfect elevenses, but it is once again time to fling oneself into the excesses of the buffet: it is pasta party day.

LATER The walk this afternoon from our landing spot up and over to a beach to see fossils of plants now found in New Zealand was really too long—probably a mile in black sand along the side of a two-thousand-foot high dune. Clouds had moved in, slapping a thick layer of gray over everything except the fierce black of jagged finger-pointing mountains ahead—and the ubiquitous red parkas of all four groups. We Yellows marched single file, and that was okay except that I could not raise my eyes for fear of slipping and it was a long way—probably a hundred feet—down. Then we met the Greens marching our way, necessitating that one of us get off the path. I happened to be first in line and had to decide if I should climb a step up, or take a step down. No longer just a slogger, too hot in my neck hugger and clumsy in all my gear, I now had responsibility—ugh. In this environment Sandy always led, but, although I didn't dare to turn and look around and look, I knew she was far back in the line. I stepped up on the slope. If I slipped at least someone would have a chance to grab me on the way by.

Lots of stragglers in ones or twos came at me. Unless they looked dottery, I stayed on the path and let them adjust. I made it without falling, but also without grace.

Done in and nerve-wracked, I never walked the extra distances across the vast beach to see the fossils or the krill—the shrimp that is the basic component of the Antarctic food chain—washed up on the outer shore. Sandy reported petrified wood from Gondwana forests, both fossilized vegetation and live moss beds, plus the flora of gray-green lichens; a huge whale skeleton and nesting giant petrels were an added bonus.

My final discomfort was the Zodiac trip back to the boat against some pretty high swells—a real fanny whacker of a ride.

Whenever we disembark and stride, boots in hand, into Le Club I'm reminded of a friend's flying days in Vietnam. When in the pilot's seat of a Hercules cargo plane, Tom was at war; when at the base in Saigon, he was playing tennis in spotless whites at a French club. We as an *expedition* experience that same sensation—proud of our efforts in the field, but more at home in the club room: plush seats, hot soup. At seven o'clock the briefing will tell us what tomorrow has to offer. Actually, more worrisome to me is rough seas arousing that punky feeling.

WEDNESDAY FEBRUARY 17   noon: Foyn Harbor, Wilhelmina Bay

Wind: SSW force 3
Sea: choppy
Air temp: 7C (37F)
Water: 3.6C (38F)
Visibility continues good
Zodiac cruise among Enterprise Islands: 8 a.m.
Whale cruise on Diamant: afternoon

Just finished a room service dinner American style: a simple chicken sandwich, lentil soup, fresh fruit. Lunch had been a surprise!

We climbed to the swimming pool deck. It was set up for a cruise on the Mediterranean, but the diners wore red parkas and the shiny blue bay was edged with white mountains and carved-by-nature icebergs. What a scene for a "barbeque" of sirloin with twenty other dishes to choose from. Such a festive air—we shared a table with a French couple—that I had two glasses of white wine and one of our pastry chef's beyond-this-world desserts.

This morning's Zodiac runaround was the most spectacular symphony of sculpture. The clouds here do not seem to know proper cloud behavior: they run wild all over the landscape and in whatever clothes they choose. In fact, nothing here seems to have been properly tamed. The cool dry air allows nothing to decay, to disappear. All remains, such as a rusted whaling factory ship, oak barrels, wooden dories, are literally frozen in time. In Africa the wildlife, giraffes, rhinos, monkeys, were part of the everyday scene; here it is penguins, seals of all kinds, and whales. In both places humans seem extraneous, walk-on extras in a movie the narrative of which has nothing to do with them. We are merely red dots moving across water, over rocks and black sands, small, incidental creatures. I imagine wandering in space must feel like this.

I am surfeited by too much rich food, too many people I must converse with, and too much beyond-belief beauty.

THURSDAY FEBRUARY 18 *Antarctic (Palmer) Peninsula – Port Charcot, Gonzalez Videla*

> *Wind: Calm*
> *Sea: Calm*
> *Air Temp: 6C (43F)*
> *Water: 2.9C (37F)*
> *Landings: Port Charcot, British Station 8:30 a.m.*
> *Paradise Bay, Chilean Station Gonzales Videla 4 p.m.*

The cold is in the wind. The ambient air temperature remains mild, but all wind comes off the ice caps and is absolutely bone chilling. In the Arctic it blows from the gulf stream, so is more moderate. The water is also deeply cold—barely above freezing—so these two forces are ever ready to assail unprotected human flesh. Penguins have six layers of feathers beginning with down and they are totally waterproofed. I feel like a molting penguin today, helpless until my protective coat is restored. It is about nine-thirty and the ship is deserted, everyone is off in Zodiacs rubbing shoulders with icebergs. I look out at the threatening gray sea littered with alabaster ice and feel the need for thick walls, even thick blankets. Tomorrow will be our last day for disembarkments and I will go out then before the queasiness of the Drake begins. It has been long enough, this strangeness of shipboard life: I crave the familiar and silence.

There are some interesting and surprisingly active older — seventies and eighties — folks on board: women who do long distance biking, hike mountains, and fly planes. Some people's company we have enjoyed at several meals, but by now have reached the limits of transitory relationships. Harvey and Phyllis, a famous cardiologist and his wife, probably know most about our lives — Phyllis asks questions and listens to answers — and our meals together have been intellectually stimulating. Pat and Shirley are casual familiars. The Taiwanese engineers from LA are fun, as is Margot and her eighty-five year-old mother from Austin, Texas: conversations are lively but not superficial. Carol from across the hall continues to be excellent company. Most came gradually to the realization that Sandy and I are partners — we certainly do nothing to hide it — and the story of our travels, in this very traveled group, seems to be generally known and is frequently introduced into conversations by strangers. So it is not that we are uneasy with the people on board, it is merely that I have had little time alone to absorb what is happening.

These happenings are not isolated but layered. There is the basic novelty of life aboard a luxury ship and an on-stage quality to meals; there is the tension of the suiting up and a murmuring undercurrent of uncertainty: Where we are going? What mind-shaking marvels will we see? Often the layers collapse into simultaneous physical, emotional, mental adjustments. I look forward to some sort of drop into oblivion in Ushuaia.

I am secreted in the little library off in the corner of Deck 5 in the bow of the ship. Outside icebergs roam. This morning six Zodiacs had to — just wanted to? — herd one away from the ship by pushing their heads against its icy sides.

Silence, a chance to reflect, is a force I feel as strongly as hunger, or physical fatigue, or sleep-deprivation. This hour up here surrounded by books, lulled by the orderly passage of time is untangling knots and loops, allowing frayed ends to unite with the whole, restoring my ability to behave as social creature. More icebergs: one with snowy sinuous curves; another's cliffs and slopes are a breathless blue; a small one with the head of a seahorse rides like a forgotten toy in a fancy pool. Inside a jolt. On the stairs men of color are on their knees furiously polishing every inch of brass railing and whisking spotless the red carpeting. While I wander in idleness. For me an unresolved enigma. Shouldn't I be helping?

LATER. As the ship emptied midafternoon and Sandy set off for the Chilean station, I had second thoughts and had to give myself a stern talking to. Lunchtime reports of falls on guano-slick rocks at Port Charot had bolstered my resolve not to go by reminding me of how unsteady I am on unfamiliar ground — a chipped elbow or even a sprained ankle could make the rest of our stay impossible. But if tomorrow's embarkation is canceled … Shut up! Think how good you'll feel tomorrow morning.

Sandy and I had napped before lunch and spent the early afternoon on the observation deck with a few others who, considering the amazing scenery, were calm, inward-focused. We were down visiting the bridge when our whale spotter let out a giant cry of "Orca whales!" naming some type infrequently seen. They come to this bay to feed on the humpbacks, improbable as that sounds. I'd heard that the orcas, weighing only a quarter as much as the thirty-something ton humpbacks, hunt in packs, circling their victim and dashing in and out to grab a bite. The PA announcement brought flocks of humans who raced back and forth chasing fins and blows. The parallel actions, whales and humans, was disturbing or humorous, I couldn't decide which. I did join the photo frenzy, but for my best shots forgot to remove the lens cap. …

Nevertheless the awesome beauty of the hour-long passage out of this bay with sheer glaciers on either side, boulders high above or seemingly close enough to touch, the *Diamant's* path narrowed by ice and curves, inspired bubbling joy. It is impossible to believe that so much wonder can be continued day after day, resulting in one of those "you have to have been there" experiences that words, even photos, will fail to convey to others. Of course, part of what we have seen may be credited to the exceptionally fine weather and the energy expended by those in charge of the expedition phase of our trip, but the glory of it could not have been concealed by any circumstances. Time for a lie-down before the bustle of the evening commences.

LATER. I woke thinking of age. Would it have been better if I had taken this trip at forty? Well, sure, physical and mental powers are sharper at forty, but there is a question of money and time — and perhaps guilt at leaving children or ailing parents. Plus the fact that I was forty in 1972. Did they even run cruises then? I know the Argentine Navy ran patrols, but I believe that was a long time before the free-red-parka crowd. Both Phyllis and Margot's mother have taken days off from expeditions; in fact, Phyllis did not leave her room for twenty-four hours. Probably overload happens on tours of art, architecture, and poets-of-the-lake-district too—and not only to the elderly.

One woman said she was going home to tell her son to re-finance his house, sell the truck, farm out the kids if he had to: But go see Antarctica now! I think she is more concerned about global warming melting the glaciers and pollution ruining the seas than his age. And maybe us older folk have a viewpoint on all this stark and ancient scenery that surpasses the value of what a forty-or fifty-year-old Margo sees and feels as she devours every aspect in whirlwind motion. Perhaps being closer to that final crossing of the bar allows us to feel more kinship with the eternity presented by this vast, ageless land.

FRIDAY FEBRUARY 19   Noon: Neumayer Channel

> *Wind: SW Force 4*
> *Sea: choppy*
> *Air Temp: 4C (39F)*
> *Water: 3C (37F)*
> *Sunrise 4:25 a.m.; Sunset 10:10 p.m.*
> *Landings: Port Lockroy 9 a.m.*
> *Neko Bay 1:39 p.m.*

At the shipboard briefing this morning the base commander at Port Lockroy turned out to be not a straight and narrow military type, but a jolly Brit woman in lively colors. She described the environmental dos and don'ts of our landing, then to enthusiastic applause announced that this station established in 1944 for military reasons was for the first time ever "manned" completely by women. With a comic's timing she explained that when it became necessary under the Antarctic treaty for the stations in this triangle of Antarctica to establish legitimacy, purely political occupation being forbidden, the Argentines and Chileans took to having children born there. We British, she said, of course, "took a different path—and established a post office!" Whoops of laughter and more applause. We knew all our postcards were in sacks waiting to be ferried over to receive the treasured "British Antarctic Territory Port Lockroy" postmark. She advised us to bring euros, pounds, dollars, or credit cards to "relieve your pent up souvenir desires."

I spent most of my time absorbing the living museum part of the station: framed photos of British royalty, food in cans, bulky communications equipment, and makeshift furniture. All reminders from the days of deadly German submarines up until the 1960s. Although science is still conducted there, the station receives 15,000 visitors a season—one or two cruise ships a day—and hand-stamps 80,000 pieces of mail.

LATER. Neko Harbor was a nook of perfection stashed off to one side of a fiord lined with sheer, ice-covered mountain ridges. Everyone except a man with crutches and a helper—I guess the one who had fallen on that first day hike—trudged on up the, to my mind, rather daunting slope, shedding clothing as they went; I sat down. Comfortable rocks were in short supply, but I had secured a good one right off the trail and piled Sandy's and my parkas beside me.

Gentoo penguins, as idled by the sun as I, dotted the beach in both directions. They stood, mostly silent, on ice patches or in run-off streams like retirees cooling their feet on a too hot Florida day. The sheeted waters of the cove lay still, content to reflect the glory around them. I shifted to watch the glacier that poured in a wide swath, like quick-frozen vanilla ice cream, across the hillside, its edge sinking into a light blue mirror reaching, apparently, to middle earth. It gleamed in the hot sun. We had been warned to stay up along the crest of the gray beach shingle because a "calving" could occur, the tall slice of glacier causing an instant massive wave. For a long time I held the camera with one finger on the button, but any action was auditory, not visual: creaks and groans issued from deep inside. A penguin came and stood beside me.

The restless clouds shifted the sun's rays across crystalline water, sculptured ice, and sturdy rock in sweeps and blasts. I tried to collect and focus all my senses, stamping my brain with this last hour in Antarctica.

SATURDAY FEBRUARY 20   *Midway Drake Channel Passage*

> *Wind: SW force 5-6*
> *Sea: moderate*
> *Visibility: poor*
> *Air Temp. 6C (43F)*
> *Water: 4C (39F)*
> *Sunrise: 5:05 a.m. Sunset 9:40 p.m.*

The ship dips and rises but since I'm sitting in bed, its effect is more like a rocking chair—padded--than a tossing about, which occurs when trying to move down the hall or navigate between tables in the breakfast room. I am attempting not to look at the monitor. Yesterday after we returned from our last landing I put on the patch, and apparently it had the effect of mitigating any unpleasantness by the time we—six of us stateroom neighbors—rose from dinner and lurched laughing down the hallway. I had forgotten not to drink wine, so my sway was enhanced and I sort of dove onto the bed, into my nightie, and under the snuggly duvet.

SUNDAY FEBRUARY   *21 Beagle Channel*

> *Wind: NW force 2*
> *Sea: Calm*
> *Air temp: 11C (52F)*
> *Water: 9.2 C (48F)*

Our last boat day. I'm not sorry about that in more ways than one. First, ship travel deprives me of freedom of movement—I can't make it stop or go in a different direction. I realize that this is psychological. A defect? Perhaps an innate desire not to be constrained? In addition, I prefer my bed to stay in one spot and not go hither and thither with me. I recall Anne Morrow Lindberg writing of a simple home that could be carried on one's back, and I liked the concept when camping. Different story when on a cruise ship with a couple hundred—make that three hundred—people on it. In a campground or hotel each person departs carrying her own shell on her back. I suppose this is a privacy issue. A big problem for me is that both my privacy and control are invaded by a daily log with times to be here and there, and those voices--Big Brother comes to mind--over the PA system: the captain's nasal "humm," the tour guide's bark. Why am I so prickly when most people seem to relax and enjoy it?

Also, I am ready to stop dressing in full gear, doing something exhausting, undressing, and feeling wiped out. But—and it is a big but—what I have seen and felt here I never want to lose. I have done it, now I shall treasure it. Time to go forth.

Eduardo Shaw, the expedition leader who gave a marvelous lecture on Shackleton's journey, has helped us with our going forth by literally mapping out what we should see in the next two weeks. He also answered my gnawing question of "Where is Patagonia?" by pointing northwestward from the Tierra del Fuego Peninsula/Island to up around Mendoza. That was a surprise. There has to be, however, some blank time before we physically begin all that. Hopefully Ushuaia will give us a break in the action, return us to parts of life that are familiar.

I am not looking forward to all this hoopla over the captain's dinner, a gala farewell, this evening. Pack and be gone would be much better. Besides, we had a perfect ending this morning. Cape Horn.

I couldn't even find it—a tiny island named Homos by its Dutch discoverer—on our big Argentina map, but I've read about its storms and shipwrecks all my life. The rocky shape of a rhino's horn rose from the sea while we happy creatures milled about on the deck in the morning sun; dramatic loudspeaker music heightened the spell. Cameras were everywhere.

Placid seas allowed us to land, and I stood—boots on the ground, as they say—atop this storied island gazing toward Antarctica: a fitting exclamation point to a journey to the bottom of the globe. The trip had not been about the ship, the food, the people we met, but what lay over the horizon. Even when I was actually looking at it, or walking on it, a sense of disbelief hovered. What mind can conceive of the earth's rotation slowing and slowing until it disappears? Who believes in zero?

Sorting it out, as the Brits would say, will take some time. When the concepts gel and details become sharp, I'm confident words will follow. At present they are as mysteriously elusive as the shapes and shadows of ice, clouds, snow packs, and peaks of the last continent.

The following accounts of daily events on shipboard were fleshed out and the following written during that sorting process in March.

Cape Horn was a thrill, no doubt about that. On the narrow beach sat a table of champagne glasses, which made me wonder if this landing was another PR surprise. But no matter, I was here where I never expected to be. The 150 straight up steps reminded me of New Zealand and I did not hesitate to commit myself. The wind was nil, the sun blaring, and the balaclava that I had worn, afraid that my peaked hat would blow off, was an encumbrance. However, my polartec jacket, ski mittens, and neck hugger were back in the cabin—thanks to Sandy having spotted green vegetation and splashes of flower color.

At the top Sandy visited the lighthouse and walked partway to a metal sculpture whose open edges framed an albatross—more like the noble royal ones of New Zealand than the rather puny Antarctic ones—a tribute to those lost to the sea as they rounded the Horn. Somewhere they were giving our passports a Chilean stamp. I stayed beside a marker to Captain Fitzroy of the *HMS Beagle*, listened to John Silva talk, and asked questions. Interestingly, of all the questions I asked over the ten days I don't remember exactly what they were or what I was told. Probably they became part of the mush that some call a muse.

Going down the steps was easy and the ship that had once looked so foreign now signaled Home. Off we went, our last trip by Zodiac.

These sturdy, inflatable, hard-floored, boats had become my favorite way of seeing the shore, up close where my aging eyes could catch the details of birds and seals, crannies and snow cliffs without having to watch my footing every second. They seated ten, had three separate air chambers, and powerful outboard motors. The driver stood and steered, an expedition member almost always sat in the bow, ready to answer questions and suggest routes to the driver. If I was in the stern by the outboard motor where I had to strain to hear his voice, I would usually shift my body and fade into intimacy with water, a heavy cold blue; and ice, shades of blue, green, or brilliant white; and pink slopes, sometimes striped with green.

On our longest Zodiac ride we had slid away from the ship at 8 a.m. sharp to explore the Foyn Harbor, a former whaling center. At our approach orca whales, tired of boat play, sank back into their chosen kingdom. Now familiar with the Zodiac and crew—it was Wednesday, our fourth day of expeditions—and untroubled by littered pack ice, I had no qualms about heading across a longer stretch of water toward a sunlit snowy peak, where amazingly, we landed. We churned about on slippery rocks—I had to ask for a leader's arm—guessing that the point was simply to get our boots on the ground. I envied the woman who did climb straight up, lie on the top making snow angels, then slid all the way back down. I would have loved the feel of that. We happily continued putting along the shore, the guide giving fascinating details about the snow algae and birds--petrels and shearwaters—and about seals: Weddells sleeping in snow above the beaches, fur seals romping, crabeaters swimming, lofting themselves onto bergies. We were riding across the surface of their dining table that held their live eats: fish, krill, etc. Near a rusted whale factory ship, a yacht from Tasmania rocked peacefully at anchor.

Monday's trip into the pack ice had been, for lack of a more apt metaphor, a horse of a different color. Not without its tension. I admit to loving the sight and sound of ice bumping and cracking against our sides as we plowed toward the table-top tabular iceberg already sprinkled with a clutch of us red penguins. I silently congratulated our Ice Master on finding and coordinating a visit, one rarely afforded to visiting tourists we were told, and of course the weather gods. As we approached, our boat driver throttled down and although pack ice surrounded us, she seemed quite casual in her driving. We halted with a jolt that made me grab the safety line. Going down under the ice would be a cold, silent, terrifying way to die.

Efforts to free us from a piece of underwater ice jammed under the propeller seemed a bit lame—a short wooden paddle wielded by the guide in the bow failed. He radioed over a small white Zodiac; a man stood at the wheel riding the bucking creature like a lobsterman out of Stonington. After maneuvering about he found a stretch of ice he could plow through to reach us.

For ten minutes or so all us red parka folks sat relaxed, chatting or watching—either oblivious to any danger, or in the grip of elementary school fire drill tapes: don't run! don't talk! don't push! One fellow stood and continued his trip recording, speaking calmly and quietly: "A large piece of ice has become lodged under our propeller and someone is coming to pull us out." No one up on the ice paid any attention to our small drama. and indeed after a couple of missed rope tosses, we were towed to open water and motored around the berg under our own power.

Landing had its own excitement. Our Zodiac positioned itself opposite a slick slope that the advance team had probably worn into the edge of the berg. Full power on. Charge! Men on the ice grabbed the boat before we slid back, although that might have been even more fun. We inched our fannies uphill toward the bow, then one by one swung our legs over. With minimal help I jumped—and there I was. On top of a football-field-sized piece of ice that rotated while moving along at about four mph. Nicholas towered at center ice, smiling proudly and enjoining us to enjoy ourselves. I thought perhaps our large, handsome Indonesian waiter would appear to serve drinks at this revolving restaurant. No, but a golf club appeared, snow balls shot skyward, and photo taking reached a frenzy. Sandy and I even got roped into pretending we were Ohio State grads: I recall I was the *I* and Sandy one of the *Os*.

We all knew the Shakleton story; indeed, the evening before our Robin Williams tour guide had thrown out several good lines about pack ice and having to winter over. I noticed the usual bundle of emergency equipment was not in evidence and the sun was low. Having just experienced one of those odd combinations of events that can make for a serious situation, I grew nervous. Was that a white scum of ice crystals forming out there, beyond where the Zodiacs lingered, their drivers watching us play? Nicholas, in a booming voice, was urging us to relax and have a good time, but when I saw a Zodiac rush up onto that icy ramp and prepare to load, I started in that direction. Sandy seemed oblivious of my intent and I had to walk over and tell her directly: I want to be on that boat. I want to get out of here. We did. But that night at briefing Nicholas apologized for being a little tardy with the last Zodiac, or something like that, and I, of course, assumed that I had been right—it was time to leave the pack ice behind. Accidents happen when there is a confluence of small unexpected events. On the way back we had had motor failure and had to be towed the last fifty yards.

Day after day, I'd wandered among hundreds of penguins who swayed from foot to foot, flippers thrust back for balance as they went about their business. Their clumsiness often caused spills, as did deliberate jumps where they would pitch forward from a pile of rocks flat onto their round tummies and bounce back up. In the water, however, their dark underwater shapes moved swiftly, elegantly.

Millions, maybe thirty or forty million, years ago they probably were gulls, as *The Last Continent* suggests, but then as the advancing ice denuded vegetation, they'd forsaken the air for the sea. Conversely, the mighty albatross became king of the air. One's wings became thin flippers, the other's a magnificent flying propellant. No god came to their freezing land and pointing, said, You go down, you go up. More mysterious, more marvelous than legend was their adaptation and survival.

Penguins are birds, but seals are mammals. The fur seal shares the ancestry of polar bears and dogs. Sea lions are kin to fur seals, but prefer more northerly, warmer waters than Antartica, where, like the fur seal, they were hunted to near extinction for their pelts. Out on the Tierra del Fuego, east of Ushuaia, a factory business of killing seal lions for their hides foundered, and thousands of them were left to rot by the battered old buildings. (*Fire Walking* by Federico Ezequiel Garguilo.) I don't know about hair seals' ancestry. Maybe an overweight pig fell in the water one day. Take a look at a three-to-four ton male southern elephant seal, the only one who molts, and it does seem possible that obesity is the cause or result of their migration into the sea, where they instantly can move with weightless abandon.

Another deeply felt Zodiac trip happened at the end of that last long sunny afternoon at Neko Harbor. Our Zodiac, instead of heading straight for the ship, veered toward the glacier, whose bulk, tall as the wall of a many-storied building, filled one end of the small cove. Although I was a bit leery of a huge section breaking off and forcing us to ride a tsunami, the warm blue silence and knowledge that this was the last time I would ever do this lulled me like an infant in a womb.

We motored slowly along—incredible beauty below, above and in every direction—rousing my deepest sensation of, I am here. Me. I am for these few moments of my life floating in waters that touch the Antarctic circle. Had the kid I once was, daydreaming of my life ahead, ever imagined this? Well, probably yes, my world was wide, and to travel it in imagination and in reality are perhaps more twinned than we realize.

We paused to watch a young leopard seal who had hauled herself out on a small ice floe. She seemed to smile as she rubbed her blubbery back against the glistening white. Other types of hair seals, also cute and deceptively friendly looking, brought positive human anthro-pomorphism to the fore; contrariwise, even the smell of a dozen elephant seals sprawled en masse like three-ton slugs belching, slithering, and squirming offended us. Our smiles of affinity for the young, lithe creature we watched sunning herself in spite of possible sunburn and enjoying a good massage demonstrated the strength of shared bonds. The penguin blood on her whiskered cheek that binoculars revealed struck me as simply a shared oxymoron.

I ruminated on another side of that coin later. The warnings from home had been: "Don't get near a leopard seal, a woman was killed ..." I remember the courage it took me to canoe an alligator-filled

river in Florida. Those great jaws, being eaten alive under water ...
The woman who rented the canoes, however, had said, "Haven't lost
anyone yet. Our alligators are well fed." Yet I had wondered, as we
paddled past those unfathomable eyes: When might I become food?
What circumstances would it take? Wading birds had stood fishing
next to those alligators; here, there were penguins swimming in the
same cove as the seals who eat them for snacks; now a dozen of us
floated within thirty feet of a "killer." Makes me wonder about them
... about us.

As I said, I had difficulty remembering the sights of Antarctica;
sounds were even worse, non-existent in fact. Neither Sandy nor I
could recall if penguins made any noise at all, then offered wild
guesses at possibilities. Finally Google came up with answers,
recordings in fact: surprise! they sound like birds. Once prompted
we recalled their squawks, clucks, and brays; their chortles, whistles,
and trumpets. And with eyes closed a human would know if they
were squabbling, muttering, agitated, or calling their children for
dinner—incredibly, every chick can pick out its parent's voice from
hundreds of others. One or two hundred thousand penguins can
raise quite a rumpus, but I never found it annoying. On a rocky
ledge in Canada a thousand massed gannet voices sent me literally
over the hill, but the constant, uneven buzz of these amazing little
fellows, spread far and wide over beaches and slopes, added
warmth to the gray desolation of the Shetlands.

On shipboard noises, particularly human voices, were constant,
except on the Thursday I skipped the expeditions. That silence was
lovely. So was the day we recrossed the Drake and discovered the
bikes in the empty exercise room. Sounds from the windy sea were
dimmed by tall windows, and we cycled away as though riding
across it, warm, unencumbered by red parkas. I hated the sound of
the PA, enjoyed the afternoon music in Le Club, and felt a sailor's
thrill when the rasp of the anchor chain grated underneath our
stateroom. Mornings we usually managed to avoid dining room pre-
coffee chatter, and at all times voices that carried arrogance,
smugness, or merely hot air.

When people back home ask if Antarctica changed my life, I will
reply, as Sandy does: Not so much changed, as enlarged. With Gaia
firmly in the center. That concept of planet-centered control and
balance had surfaced briefly in the 80s, and I was drawn to it now
not so much as an intellectual answer to the human question of,
who's in charge, but because I had felt it.

TUESDAY FEBRUARY 23 *Ushuaia, Argentin* An enormous switch from the extraordinary to the ordinary. I now walk on sidewalks, see people I have not seen before, eat food without a French sauce, sleep in a bed in a room that is in a building set on land. My body has taken sharp notice of these differences. Sometimes I stagger on the flat floor; my foot rises at every threshold to step over an impediment that is not there. Last night I slept soundly for twelve hours; my mind, however, is cloudy, struggling to awaken when it is already awake. The eleven days on shipboard are tucked in some corner not to be rummaged in just yet. The present is just that, the moment. Although we have diligently investigated tours and future destinations, listened to professionals at the information center, tour operators, airline officials, we've committed to nothing, made no decisions. We will meet Christina, Jim's friend's mother, for lunch today at one. This evening or tomorrow we'll again cross the street to her shop, Inca Rose, to buy little stone penguins for gifts for women at home--the men will get End of the World T-shirts--and I will wear my wedding shawl to see if we can come up with a necklace to enhance it. That's it for planning, except that we'll eat in our room again—a sandwich to go with the red wine and cookies we bought yesterday.

LATER. Fortunately both of us are in the same semi-stupor state, vaguely confident that before checkout on Thursday some plans will have drifted from our shadowy brains. Right now we have no desire to experience anything beyond this town, this street, this room.

Our functions have been limited to receiving and sending e-mails, and enjoying a terrific barbequed lamb buffet lunch with Christiana. We have also showered and applied lotion to skin dried out on shipboard; and reveled in the humid, cool air outside. The weather here doesn't change when you round a corner, the season does. The sun has been out since two adding a cheery yellow to our view. So, we float, we procrastinate, we wonder when will and curiosity might stir us to action.

FRIDAY FEBRUARY 26 *El Calafate, Southern Andes, Patagonia*

Silence is priceless. Maybe tops the list of my most highly valued life possessions. That was reinforced when I stepped into this room at El Quijote in El Calafate. Silence and spaciousness. Even Jim's bare bones bedroom does not have this much space—I guess I had accepted the shipboard cabin as a temporary adventure. Crackle of poplar leaves beyond the open window is the only noise, and the only boundary of my thoughts.

In Ushuaia we never did recover enough to do more than the necessities: buy gifts, mail excess poundage to Capilla, find restaurants, buy jewelry for Tee's wedding, and sleep. Well, we did make a couple of smart/lucky travel decisions. One was waiting at the Areolineas office to buy plane tickets; a travel agent had wanted a higher price at an inconvenient time. Another triumph was making a cell phone call—two hours before takeoff—to a five-star in Calafate. When I heard the totally unaffordable price for a three day stay, I fell silent. Then stammered a bit. "Wait just a moment, please," the clerk said. The moment passed, she returned. "If you pay cash I can give you a forty-percent discount." "Cash?" I may have shouted. "Yes. Si. No problem." The reason? It was Thursday and on Monday their rates would be slashed because the whole country would be back at school or work.

Even on this clear, crisp morning I'm plagued by a shroud of slipperiness, a desire to lie down and fade away. We plan nothing but walking and looking today, perhaps a lake cruise tomorrow. Lago Argentino is the third largest lake in South America and so deep, its temperature maintains a constant 8 C (46.4F)—no boats, no swimmers. What season are we in? To the west are glaciers and ice packs; east toward the airport is stark and dry like the US badlands; town streets are mellow with summer shade. At least my skin is recovering.

Body report. Loggy but adequate, some morning diarrhea, touch of Sandy's sore throat, and occasional lightheadedness, which is disconcerting. A nagging mental downer is the critical condition of our friend Joyce--partner of Karen who lent me this computer. Her only complaint when we all lunched together in December was weakness. A diagnosis resulted in a couple emergency surgeries and now kidney failure.

Time to dress—how I've loved a morning naked under my bathrobe!—so the maid can clean, and Sandy should be back soon from her bird walk by the marsh.

SUNDAY FEBRUARY 28 A week ago I was climbing the 150 steps to the top of Cape Horn, symbol of the mightiest of sea storms. Yesterday I climbed on broad steel gratings down and up 60 meters, 180 feet, beside the symbol of Andean might, the Perito Moreno glacier. Earlier I had stood on the deck of a catamaran beneath that mass of crevices and blue caves, awestruck by its glowing power;

some twenty hours later a shift in plates, an 8.8 quake, shook the Chilean coast. What unimaginable, cosmic violence could be spawned by even a tremor beneath the huge growling icescape of Perito Moreno?

That is what I have seen, what I will carry home. The touch of power that seems beyond the mind of humans to fashion in any form: science or art, mathematics or words. Michelangelo had the finger of God touch man, not the core of the planet. Indeed, humans seek to define their spiritual longings in tribal beginnings, the planet being merely a quickly sketched neighborhood, a Garden of Eden, the back of a turtle. Yet all of human existence is a shallow comma scratched on the face of earth. Physical elemental forces are as far beyond ours as the galaxies are above the moon. Why should one cold ball of reflected light grasp an instant of notice in the dark infinity of space? Why should a speck of a mammal be noted on the stage of this timeless earth? That way lies despair, holy men would cry, whereas I sense only power and glory.

Not until this morning did I make any reckoning of how long it has been since we left our ship. I guess time had in some fashion been locked up—frozen? Perhaps eventually those eleven days will make sense in normal terms; perhaps there is no sense to be made. Just as Joyce's death two days ago makes no "sense," no matter the myths and judgments and terrors we bring to it. Karen wrote of her peaceful passing: "Amazing Grace" for music, Tennyson's "Crossing of the Bar" for poetry. That is what the human mind seeks in mysteries: soaring calm, the quieting of the tempest, green pastures. I am coming to understand, not just intellectually know, that humans are inexorably bound to what I saw yesterday: frozen millennia of snow and ice splitting in crescendo roars into megaton towers of ice that slice toward milky water as both it and we ride this uneasy, grinding crust.

Today the air is filled with dusty howls of Patagonian wind—our first real taste, literally, of that force of nature. We breakfasted leisurely inside windows of sparkling sun and flowers, and not until one-thirty did we shove open the glass doors and scamper down to the main street for Sandy's quiche and my pumpkin soup. I can't hear it now: I'm with my tiny computer in an elegant interior corridor; Sandy is in the room watching the Olympics while nursing her cold.

On the way back from our tour yesterday I asked our guide about the enormous number of new hotels/motels and many more under construction here. Thinking of our virtually empty place I asked,

"Are they filled?" "Every room" was the proud reply. I then asked our desk clerk about this, and she told me the Quijote would close for the winter at the end of the month. "Only a few stay open past summer vacation time." We had already learned from the airport taxi man that the Calafate boom had begun about seven years before. I asked him why here and he replied—his English was sketchy—it was wild, not built up, closer to nature. Yes, and last year they completed paving the 80 km highway to the glacier. The tourists liked it, but the once abundant herds of guanaco, graceful kin to llamas, had fled to the interior. "You won't see a single one," our tour guide said.

Flight tickets to Bariloche secure for tomorrow, and I'm struggling to find an appealing accommodation without the aid of any information save Internet marketing. Considering our lack of drive, the added hours of travel going east to the ocean and then back became a self-evident bad idea, but how we will spend the days until our scheduled arrival in Capilla on Monday, March 8, is a real puzzle. The searching, let alone the reservation process, is full of surprises and adventures. Jim reported a "tremblie" of this good earth far north of Capilla—guess we won't travel from Bariloche to Cordoba that way.

MONDAY MARCH 1 The wind was down, as were Sandy's cold symptoms, so we walked to the lagoon, cameras in hand. The town is attempting to preserve and make tourist friendly the area where the river meets Lago Argentino. There is a circle of concrete seating for music—now graffiti sprayed—and a wide, paved road and sidewalk with private development limited to the non-water side. Already one building is going up. I hope the developers checked the plans out with the wildlife, or it will be gone like the guanacos. At present the scene is a feast of green marsh grass, interlaced with wind-ruffled water where a few unfenced, untethered horses feed; quantities of shore birds, often a different species every square foot, bob and flutter; and in deeper water the incredible pink of flamingoes flash. Binoculars raised I saw, for the first time in the wild, these unselfconscious fashion models of the feathered universe preen, feed, and fly, brilliant round middles hung on a skinny pole of legs and neck and beak. How many wonders of the world are there to see?

Calafate is still mainly a one-street town, but that street with its long parklike median is bursting with succulent food. Pizza, pasta, beef, and lamb grilled at the tables of La Tablitta with its marvelous white-tablecloth ambiance, diverse clientele, and handsome Argentine waitstaff. Both coming and going we have wandered in and out of clever shops, stopped to smell the roses in a little park, and seen some startlingly short, stocky native people who make unique hangings from the inner fiber of a certain tree bark. In a craft fair on a side street a man played a recorderlike tube of an ancient root. implanting a haunting sound in my usually tone-deaf brain.

WEDNESDAY MARCH 3 *San Carlos de Bariloche*
I ran out of puff in Bariloche. The warning signs were apparent: lack of enthusiasm for any accommodations which ended with a last minute "I can't remember why I bypassed this one the first time," and a tired click on reservations. This set me up for increasing uneasiness when the airport taxi drove through the less than stellar outskirts of this much touted tourist destination, and then meltdown when the driver pulled to the curb across from a trash-filled lot and wall of graffiti. The unswept entryway, empty dark downstairs, lone frazzled woman who dragged our bags up the steps to the desk, and sickly-sweet air freshener that blasted from a small hot room with no ceiling fan liquefied my bones. Granted, Quijote had been an exemplary five-star, but this was rated four and felt like a three. Sandy looked around and asked, "How soon can we book out of this place?" I sighed. "We're in for two nights."

We are now on our third day and everything looks all right. Our urge to escape was quickly paralyzed by no desire to see or do one more thing. Totally jaded. That helped reduce the town to a bland: okay, German immigrants from Chile saw the tourist potential in this lake and mountain setting and built a town for them after the park was formed in 1937, resulting in today's holiday tourist destination amidst the jumble of high-rise hotels and exploding population. So what?

An upswing began yesterday when we discovered that there was an express sleeper bus from here to Cordoba. Of course, we told ourselves, that's the answer: a twenty-four hour rolling bed for the entire thousand kilometer trip to Jim's. A lot easier than slogging away on the Internet to find several buses and accommodations. A long, diverse tour of the mild lakes and blue mountains outside of town further lifted our drooping spirits—maybe we could just find a place out there until Sunday, then hop on the bus north and east.

This morning, however, we woke flat and stayed flat until almost ten—check-out time—leaving no option but to sign up for another night before staggering into the breakfast room, empty except for the honeymooners. Still groggy after eggs, sausage, and three cups of pathetic coffee, I dragged myself to the hotel computer in the wild hope that somewhere out there in web land was a woodsy place that would set our hearts leaping again. There was. A cabin at the Estancia del Carmen will only cost 390 pesos ($97.50) a night. I phoned; they had a vacant cabin, a restaurant, and the host would call a cab to pick us up at 4:00 for the twenty-minute drive. Another call: the express bus still had two sleeper seats that would be sold to the first comer.

Arms swinging, we fast-walked the dozen scorching blocks to the ticket office and yes! –they're still available. We would leave Sunday, arrive Monday. Our cell phone died at the end of a call to Daniel in Capilla giving him the time when Mariano should pick us up in Cordoba. Squeezed out of the crowded narrow office into the heat of the streets, we zigzagged about in search of a phone store where someone spoke English and did not try to sell us a new phone. A man fixed ours but we were never sure how.

Discovered a bookstore with good local writers in English: Sandy needs something to read during our twenty-four hour bus captivity. Also renewed the challenge of Spanish supermarket shopping to buy breakfast and lunch supplies for three days. For dinner we'll rely on the restaurant—hope it is not too pricey.

It was not easy, but it is a deal done—emphasis on done. No regrets over leaving town—and the reserved bed here—for the mountains.

LATER. It is now almost four and a faint breeze off the great glacial lake is stirring the white curtains. A couple more adventures are on tap. Can't wait!

THURSDAY MARCH 4   *Estancia del Carmen outside Bariloche*
The picture window frames green beech, different from home, trees and either a cedar or cypress, but the featured show is, as usual in these climes, the clouds of the day, or I should say minute. Their shifting variety requires constant watching, making this a bad spot for writing. Plus, the bright sun obliterates the monitor. Nevertheless, for the time being I'm glued. A powerful thunderhead has roiled up on one edge of this ridgeline of the southern Andes and now another, even darker, is making a race of it from behind the cedar. International skiers continue their training here in this land's winter months; the drop is precipitous, easy to imagine it deep in white powder. If we have more lightning tonight, what a show.

Paula, a former Buenos Aires resident who manages this place with her husband, was among those we heard expressing sharp displeasure with this summer's unpleasant weather. Reminds me of a Maine tourist-dependent business person. In fact this area is very like Mount Desert Island's steep, forested slopes falling into deep water; these, however, are glacier-fed lakes. From here to the Atlantic must be a good 600 kilometers. Also, this area has the aura of mountain fastness—and stillness. Our estancia was constructed like America's lodges in the thirties, or Tsitsikamma in South Africa—perhaps any worldwide: bulky log cabins with panoramic picture windows, minus the cutesy European flower boxes.

Maybe we'll walk to the lodge now and buy a bottle of red to have with cheese and crackers while we wait out the tick-down to eight o'clock dinner. I adore the silence and being alone with Sandy.

FRIDAY MARCH 5 The sun has just now brightened the trees. It is noon. All morning mists and clouds have played up and down the mountains, but we stayed in the dim bedroom under a wool blanket just being people, not world travelers—or explorers.

SATURDAY MARCH 6 Brilliant morning. Today the treetops lit up about eight, and now at ten the ground is splotchy with shade. I was stunned yesterday afternoon by the clarity with which I could see our granite neighbor: ravines, faint tracks, possible niches fit for human feet. It was like looking through binoculars. I have not had this kind of vision since—well, maybe never: I got glasses at seven. A few days ago my eyes were so blurry that by evening I could not even read.

Is it due to the mountain air devoid of pollutants, including dust? Or my relaxed state? Or ... In the mirror I see eyes with white whites, not red, and the brown of them is steady and alive. Very little droop to the left eyelid. Perhaps like the miracle of new skin last year, I am getting new eyes? The fact that I can see this little monitor extremely well may be due to the perfect lighting here on the eating table—or ...

I mentioned to Sandy as we lay in bed this morning, enjoying the unique luxury of a good cup of coffee in the quiet of our "own" bedroom, that in these lands of the southern hemisphere we do not have winter aches and pains. In Milbridge some part of her anatomy is usually hurtful: with me it is legs or lower back. Is it warmth, or dryness, or the unique cool dry of Patagonia? I'm full of questions this morning. Probably because we are not "doing anything," and I have time to reflect and speculate. Taking stock as it were, which I missed so on the Antarctica trip. There, if I had a few moments lying on the bed when I was not obsessed by watching for whales or something out the portholes, I either fell asleep or was stuffed stupid with lassitude. I could not collect my thoughts—or my body either, for that matter. Both just longed for oblivion. But here, with the last arrangements made, I have regained a brain capable of looking back or even ahead and at peace with now.

More body report: skin has remained soft and unblemished, calf muscles are hard and round, hair normal, breasts and tummy full as ever. No aches, no colds, no headaches, an occasional call for an imodium tablet, mind clear. In all our bopping around for fifty days we have not forgotten anything—except two nights ago my packet of leftover steak, which was charmingly restored to me by our waitress, hair flying, running down the street after us.

SUNDAY MARCH 7   *sleeper bus traveling from Beriloche to Cordoba*
The highly dramatic scenery that kept our heads twisting from side to side for the first hundred kilometers out of Bariloche has dwindled to flat, high plateau scrub. Altitude has dropped from 3,000 feet to 1,800. I guess we have lost the Andes for good, but how I have loved being in them. These southern ones were more familiar—evergreens reaching down to lakes—but nevertheless startling in their majesty. Strange uprisings of rock, or perhaps formed by other softer materials eroding, has been a most notable feature, strongly reminding me of the Wyoming landscape of *My Friend Flicka*. Must check out geology. The flat blue buttes lining the western horizon might precede a sudden drop of this road into a ravine; the map shows water ahead. I was reminded, however, that lakes are not sea level when Sandy's altimeter reading beside Bariloche's wind-whipped glacier lake read 3,000 feet. A steamer travels through this chain of high-altitude lakes taking tourists across the Chilean border.

The seats we have rented for twenty-four hours on this bus cost 394 pesos and are worth every penny, although the unstoppable movie sound tape is driving me whacko. Three empty seats are scattered about the twelve in the lower deck of this monster; the four singles on the right side are all occupied by older ladies. Up front is the cockpit for two drivers and a steward; behind that a bathroom and stairs to and from the upper deck, where the seats are even cheaper but not reclining. The engine is in back and we are in the last double, so when we fully recline the seats to sleep, our heads will be over no one's feet and there are no noticeable fumes. I am especially fortunate in that—whoops, the guy in front of Sandy shifted to the window and put his seat back, reducing my space to slightly more than arm's length even though I am partially reclined too. After dark I will pull down the footrest over my carry-on bag and wool shoulder bag and turn my face to the window. Whether I sleep or not seems, right now, immaterial. It is six and the steward just delivered a snack and coffee, so I feel motivated to visit the lavatory. Hope it is as clean as the rest of this accommodation is. I should figure out the value of my space here versus that in an airplane—of course if I figured in miles per hour .

MONDAY MARCH 8 *Cordoba Provincia*
Woke at sunrise to flat and green, and tasseled corn.

TUESDAY MARCH 9 *Capilla casita* The computer battery died on me yesterday, but I will continue those thoughts.
The bus arrangement for sleeping worked out quite well. It is amazing how the body shuts down its need for a bathroom when it realizes access is not available. I did not have to consciously say to it: Look, no way can I step over Sandy's legs and the reclined head of the guy in front of her, so forget it. I didn't see anyone else up either; I was awake a good while watching a lightning show and later, stars over the black landscape. No streetlights, no car lights, only sudden gulps of brilliance and noise when another monster bus passed from the opposite direction.
With daylight not only were there cornfields, but what I guess were potatoes, and under the tall poplars whitewashed estancias and towns with big farm equipment stores, dusty roads, and parrillas that serve grilled meat and usually pasta. It all fits so well with my reading of Nora Mackinnon's, *An Estancia in Patagonia.* Mackinnon is British, a bit older than I, who married a farm manager employed in the Brits' huge system of sheep and cattle raising in Patagonia. Argentina was never a colony of Britain, but as in New Zealand and South Africa, British immigrants believed in the mission of "bringing civilization" to an almost empty land and a scattered primitive people. Amassing wealth was another goal, the result of which is still hugely felt. Mackinnon's narrative includes some good history and she writes well.
On the two-hour taxi ride into the high country from Cordoba, Mariano, our driver, told us that the land had received a lot of rain,

but still needed more to get through the coming dry season. The hills that gradually became mountains were startlingly green. Grass was thick where none had been two months before; indeed, the land seemed a happy one. Small butterflies greeted us as we stepped out in front of Jim's casita, birds sang, and the garden was overrun with plants. As a first-time traveler I would have said, I like this place. It is friendly, pretty, and as we found out during last night's ten-hour sleep, cool. This morning it continues that way with clouds graying the sky, but purple, rose, and white morning glories light the garden. Palu, the cat, looks handsome and Seba gave Sandy strict warnings: one feeding a day! They had greeted us with smiles and cheek hugs and then were off to a rental somewhere in town. The house is clean and ours. I am content although still dopey.

WEDNESDAY MARCH 10 My day so far—it is 2:30—has reflected the tarnished gray sky and air humid enough to clog my sinuses. This afternoon even the birds, so chatty this morning, have fallen into dumbness. Sandy and I did the same after lunch, each flipping a bit of the orange spread over our shoulders as our breathing lengthened into sleep. We did not do so well at sleeping last night, even resorted to warm milk around midnight, but like the birds had seemed quite our old selves after two cups of good, strong plunger-carafe coffee. Caffeine-zest has a short life span, however.

I would like to write of dogs, the cause of our sleep disruption last night. I have written before about the dog societies here, how they populate the towns like the sacred cows of India and act as a chorus of accusation to any who pass their property: humans are judged guilty of felonious intent without the slightest evidence. Yesterday Sandy went into the street to hang our plastic bag of trash on the telephone pole and the resident dogs of the three surrounding houses—five dogs in all—cried thief, thief, in voices ranging from bass to operatic soprano, and even brought Palu to the opening in our whitewashed wall.

Now, neither of us have ever seen Palu on the walkway that leads from the garden to that opening, let alone boldly looking around it. Nor have we ever seen any dog even as close as the other side of the brick garden wall. Most are either fenced in or are property dogs, who may step into the street that borders their land—public property—but never beyond. Yesterday, Sandy watched the big buff weimaraner across the street prance and greet a passing dog friend who tried to entice her to "Come with me, I'm going to the river," by doing a chase-me dance. The weimaraner did one in her yard and the road dog joined her for one go-round, but then trotted off, leaving her floppy-eared in a clear state of doggy dejection. As Palu must know, it is a complex society.

At our mountain retreat outside Beriloche, Paula said, "Dogs arrive." We saw at least five regulars plus a floating community. One cat. A small female with orange and white tortoise shell markings. Maybe our cabin, number 9, was hers, for she showed up along with our luggage and insisted that she lived there—inside. Sandy would lift her gently out the door and I would bark and be stern. Neither worked, and so we reluctantly gave up any hope of fresh air from an open door or window—which she could slip through nicely. At dinner Sandy asked the waiter to wrap the leftover chicken "for the gato." By the second night we'd learned she had three month-old kittens, although she looked like one herself; she ate her bit of venison and noodles under the steady stars.

On our last afternoon there, we were sitting facing the granite wall, watching climbers and condors, when a terrified yipping arose. Around the side of the manager's cabin two large dogs dashed hell-bent with one small cat hot on their heels. The yelping dog kept going through our yard, but the bigger one slowed and that kitty was in his face in an instant. The dog was clearly cowed; nevertheless, she moved right in and gave him one terrific belt on the muzzle. He ran as hard as he could. She watched them out of sight, and I could swear she smirked and dusted her front paws one against the other, then turned, little tail erect, and marched back the way she had come.

Humans are peripheral in this other Argentine society.

THURSDAY MARCH 11 Three weeks from today we will land in Santiago, then Miami, then Boston. Unlike last year in Spain we have time to look ahead and think about getting the phone, electricity, etc. turned on in Milbridge, and organize thoughts of accountant and eye doc visits in Portsmouth. Tee's wedding is on April 17.

Once again the cool gray sky makes a fine background for the bursting colors of morning glories and some other brilliant yellow and fuchsia weeds. Just finished a second bowl of corn flakes and milk—how did I live without it? But then how did we live with a fifty-cent-sized spider residing in the bottom of the toothbrush cup at our mountain camp? And speaking of those creatures, some type of them has built nests on the ceiling and walls of our bedroom here. At first our attitude was: no way am I dealing with them, we'll have to hire someone. Second thought: we'll call Tito and borrow his shop vac. Of course, with some reflection I realized he would have no idea what were even talking about—shop vac? So today after a lie-down and tea, I found a rake type thing, tied an old cloth over it, clapped my sun hat on, and, like my mother before me, went after them. Of the dozen or so I hurried outside on the cloth, probably 89 percent lived—they are more like daddy long legs than spiders that bite, making my feelings more kindly.

I think I'll allow the experiences in Ushuaia, Calafate, and Bariloche to take proper residence in my brain before I revisit my journal of Antarctica. Probably deal with the emotional and intellectual side first and then reread what I have written; next read the log blog online and the daily newsletter placed on our bed every evening; lastly view the hundreds of photos. I suppose any needed details of shipboard life: food, people, etc. can be worked in. I turned quickly away from Sandy's camera the day she went back too far in reviewing Bariloche and a shot of the great Horn came up; I need care in approaching these ghosts, this still unbelievable idea: Antarctica, you were in Antarctica.

FRIDAY MARCH 12 Half an inch of rain in Pelu's dish   this morning, garden green-drippy, sky gray-drippy, crickets cooing to crickets.

Sandy was up at eleven last night tending to windows; I never stirred, in fact, she had to put a hand on my ribs to make sure I was breathing. We woke and snuggled at 6:15. E-mailed Bett to have phone and electric turned on March 29 and asked price of night in new motel next to her. We arrive in Boston at 10:15 a.m. but fear driving north on that day might be dangerous, especially since we will be awakened ungodly early to prepare for change of planes in Miami.

Have lots of good food on hand, anticipate arrival of water truck, so probably will do a laid-back day—literally, since there is no place to sit inside except hard straight-backs and the wonderful bed.

SUNDAY MARCH 14 Propped on the bed, limbs relaxed, and tummy full of yogurt with walnuts from the garden and a local pear, a cinnamon-sugar-currant pastry, and good coffee. I skimmed my Antarctica entries. Carping about my dopey mental and physical state seems more central than descriptions of the land and its emotional impact. Would tape recording have been better? Too banal and clichéd, probably, and then there is for me the almost impossible task of transcribing accurately.   When doing the 125 taped interviews for *Invisible Lives*, it would sometimes take three tries before I overcame my instant mental editing and quoted accurately.

I won't look back again because Capilla-type interruptions of low-level emergency status keep slamming me into the here and now. Sandy just boomed into the room, "beside herself" as she put it, because the washing machine refused to start when it had a few days ago. Well, at least Nancy is in town and can come over, maybe to spot some small mistake. Seba did get our Internet working—the problem was a couple of letters missing in the hook-up name we had. Let's hope the washing machine is as easy. We have gotten used to having a corps of people look after our every need; the shock of being responsible makes us whirly.

FRIDAY MARCH 19 Our days are like nuggets. Small, smooth bits of gold dipped in green, separate yet so much the same. Occasionally, especially at 3 a.m., I am anxious, due, I think, to those fifty-four days of prep-time, deadline, moving forward—now this hiatus. The first year in New Zealand we were exploring the island of Waiheke right up to departure time. And in Spain on top of a wild week of sightseeing, came the robbery and all those airports and planes to deal with. But this March all motion ceased on the ninth, as though I hit the last page of a book that can't be closed. At Tee's wedding shower Kath told the women, "The grandmother is still in the southern provinces."

Each day someone comes by: Daniel to put up the new shelves in the hall, Tito with a bag full of aloe cream to sell, day before yesterday Seba and Nancy to do a wash—Sandy explained we'd been using the Laundromat; they said they'd call someone. Yesterday it was Seba's Buenos Aires parents for a delightful visit in the garden. She is small like Seba with his arresting blue eyes, or rather he with hers. I'm sure if we had a language in common we would have planned a longer get-together, perhaps to talk of our sons' close friendship. Yesterday the smiling young gas delivery man came, today the water man is due. These guys are all so good-looking, it's no wonder Sandy has erotic dreams.

Another short cloudburst this morning; the wet garden blooms even brighter when the sun finds a hole of blue between white or gray clouds. I bought a pair of garden gloves and weed when the mood strikes. Seba's mother pointed out more walnuts that are ripe: I gathered all I could reach and cleared some weeds underneath so we can find any that drop. Sandy is engrossed in reading two books, the Patagonia one and on my Kindle, *The Help*. I am half-done *Factory Girls*, an eye opener on the migrant women in China.

Ant traffic on the knothole-pocked grape vine that twists diagonally across one small pane of the window in front of me is nonexistent this morning, perhaps a bridge washed out. A yellow butterfly nudges in vain at the tightly closed blossoms of the four o'clock flower bushes — called ladies of the night here. Beyond, in the huge dripping arms of the mora tree, green parakeets flutter. If the water man comes before the stores close at noon, we'll walk to town and shop.

SATURDAY MARCH 20 Last evening at the end of a dark, airless day the wind whipped up the greenery, banished the gray, and Sandy and I strode out, up Varaona Road to the hilltop. Stiff calf and thigh muscles were brief and energy flowed as though I, too, was being swept clean by the breeze; the slopes and pinnacles of sandia sunset colors and the playful clouds heightened my sense of well-being. According to Sandy I slept right through a 3 a.m. tumult of barking dogs as a horse and rider went by; at 6:15 I woke rested. My sight remains sharp. Is my post-Antarctica hunker-down stage complete?

SUNDAY MARCH 21 Ten days before the flight and home ties are growing. Even details — like a pumpkin pancake breakfast with Margaret at Bett's — are set. And I've spent a lot of time today peering at this small monitor catching up with American news, mostly political.

MONDAY MARCH 22 The Health Care bill did pass — hopefully a step toward a more equal America. Focus on home was deepened by news of a boy in Rachel's class killed in a car accident, those awful what if's ... And Margaret's e-mail was filled with longing to fly free herself, but more major surgery for her ninety-something mother-in-law and the ballast of partner and dog keep her grounded. In my reply I granted that my loved ones — ballast — were healthy and independent, keeping me on an even keel wherever I choose to roam. Fortunate me.

Every day conversations with Sandy move the Antarctica experience a bit more into reality.

THURSDAY MARCH 25 Am a little shocked at extent of memory losses when recalling those days at sea. The emotional side is sharp, evident in the writing, but the where's and when's and what's definitely lacking. For example, yesterday, in my additions to what I wrote at the time, I attempted to add some facts about penguins and seals. It took Sandy's reading aloud from *The Last Continent* to set me straight:

"*After breeding the mature animals [southern elephant seals] molt … a spectacular never to be forgotten.*" Right, never forgotten, but I had called them leopard seals. Scary.

It has long been my habit to read detailed material after an interview or a trip, not only to avoid prejudicing my senses with what others see and believe, but to give a broader scope to my limited first-hand observations. The Antarctica photos and the daily online blogs will be invaluable; probably the lecture material and extemporaneous Q and A's with the expedition leaders is lost forever.

FRIDAY MARCH 27 Another day of polished air: high 60s, low seventies. How silly to leave this In his book *Memoir* Ben Yagoda wrote of the failing memory of the elderly. About five years ago my tendency to blend events, be vague on chronological order, exaggerated itself to the point where others were constantly disagreeing with me. A friend said she simply gave all past occurrences a generic time line of "seven years ago." It works for me too. And the older I get the less it seems to matter, comparable perhaps to one's blurred, semi-awake states enjoyed between dozings.

When I decided to write about the life choices I made at seventy-five, the term memoir did not, I believe, enter the picture. I thought in terms of an account, a true rendering of the events of my seventy-fifth year. I would do it "on pulse" as May Sarton had, not exactly a Line a Day diary or random journal, but an accounting of decisions made, actions taken, reactions to results, and so on. And that plan carried over into what has become a travel memoir.

Given my rather drifty memory, a wise decision, even perhaps an absolutely necessary one. If I were to set out this April to write about that decision year of 2007 and the three following adventures, I would have to submit to the tedium of detailed notes, or the ease of sweeping generalities, or integrate everything around certain themes that in hindsight I thought were important. Perhaps I'd quit out of boredom, or fictionalize to make a better story. I could emphasize how smart or stupid I had been to build a more exciting narrator. Marketing ideas might dip it into the glossy stain of a twelve-step this is how you do it inspirational book. That would violate my fundamental belief that there are as many paths as there are people.

LATER. Kath e-mailed that James was in a fender bender accident, but after police etc., he resumed his drive to work. On Interstate 93 his hood flew up, breaking the windshield. He is not hurt.

WEDNESDAY APRIL 14 *Cottage in Maine*

Back in my cozy east bedroom. Windows tightly shut, oil-filled heater raising the ambient air from forty something to 70F. Back on the northeast US power grid. Must be about a month since my last entry, but I did complete my additions to the Antarctica days while in Argentina's verdant palace of sunshine—300 days a year of it. Here the only colors are muted evergreens, a tentative April sky, and two daffodils. But unlike the last couple of years there has been sun, and except for the South Wing the cottage and dooryard are in order. All familiar, all the way we think it ought to be. Familiar has its own comforts, perhaps more appreciated for having been out exploring. That word again. Exploring. I think I have gotten a better handle on it now. Can divide it into several types. One is the wow! I never knew this existed. Of course, I had no idea how it should look, so I'd just gawk in amazement. A case in point would be that holiday cabin in the southern Andes beside an immense wall of rock in a town I had never heard of. It did not confirm or disappoint: it was simply there, newborn to me. A surprise. Blundering into the unknown is certainly one aspect of exploring. Another, I suppose, is achieving a goal, like the explorers who set out to reach the South Pole. The so- called bucket lists are goals. A big hurrah when achieved, disappointment at not. My goals tend to be broader: Can a woman past seventy find warm, comfortable, interesting places to live for three months every winter?An example of a third possible type of exploring is climbing to the top of the great Horn, or standing at the Cape of Good Hope. I had read about them, seen photographs, and through fiction books emotionally imagined them. That opens the door for a letdown or heightened excitement. In the broadest sense, curiosity, the desire to explore to find out something, has, the experts say, been a key in the development of the human species. In elementary school my two close friends and I would say things like: "Let's explore the hill beyond the big boys' ball field." We had never been there, although we had gone to probably six years of school beside it. We had no reports on what it was like, only what our imaginations spewed forth—and that was always plentiful and tinged with danger. What we found was a deep split in the ground opened, we guessed, by blasting in a coal mine underneath; and a ledge of copperhead snake babies. When on hot summer days we said, "Let's bike to Little Joe's for pop," we were well acquainted with a particularly dangerous curve, and the sight of the caps of orange, grape, and cream soda bottles bobbing in deep cool water. Excitement lay in choosing and buying from a meager allowance, and that we were forbidden by our parents to go there. They said it was because of the curve, but we knew the real worry was the big boys who hung out in Little Joe's.

When I said to our Antarctic shipmates, "We are going to explore Patagonia," I did not even know where Patagonia began and ended, let alone what we would find.

SATURDAY MAY 22 Last weekend turned out to be a memory trip for Sandy who had entered her decade of being seventy on the 20th. We stood by New Hampshire's Little Bay and watched red kayaks carry Joyce's ashes and those of her beloved dog who had died several months before her out on the blue water. Ten or so members of the Lubberland Yacht Club of Durham Point Road, pretty stiff in the knees now, were there along with a couple dozen others to boldly recite: "I must go down to the seas again to the vagrant gypsy life … " My throat closed when it came to "…. And a quiet sleep and a sweet dream when the long trick's over."

The vagrant gypsy life is perhaps what we all have here on this swirling bit of matter. These groaning, shifting plates that merely give the illusion of terra firma. These rearing mountains and towering glaciers, these spreading seas and indiscriminate winds.

I turned away from the babble of voices clustered around the food tables and started toward the wharf and the lakelike lap of water against the pilings.

"So." A hearty voice from behind stopped me. "Where will it be next winter?" I turned, smiled, tried to place her. "Find a favorite to go back to?"

"Well, we …"

"Sandy says she felt most comfortable in New Zealand." The woman was tall, her face a blank against the low sun. "I don't think—"

"Your son's probably. Can't beat free."

"We're travelers," I said, probably too abruptly because she muttered something about food and turned away.

"Nice to see you again," I called and she waved without looking back. What had I said? We're travelers? What did that mean?

I think I had said it before in some hot country on a morning thick with humidity when buses were charging in and out of their stalls; every seat in the waiting room occupied by silent people gazing into the distance, hands clenched around purses or parcels, small children or luggage. An overeager B&B host kept suggesting a return visit until finally, out of awkwardness more than conviction, I stated,

"We won't be back. We're travelers."

He stared puzzled. "But —"

I shook my head, no. I did not add: There is no road, the road is made by walking. That thought came later.

When a Maine islander has gone to the mainland, he speaks of being "off-home." He may be buying a week's groceries or staying in town with his mother for the winter. Four years ago Sandy and I were not sure about selling our house, about committing to living off-home. Driving into the puckerbrush is what I believe I called it then. We did sell and since then two more decisions evolved: one, we will not move permanently out of the country, nor even spend every winter in the same place. Two, we are not done slow traveling yet. We will continue to seek out rentals in different countries and live the culture, so to speak. Checking off places or activities on someone else's must-see list does not interest us. Perhaps when we have a permanent winter spot—a Portsmouth apartment most likely—we will take two- or three-week tours to far lands every year in addition to at least four months in Milbridge.

For the last three years our search for favorable exchange rates and warm climate have led us to the lands that circle Antarctica. Dunedin in New Zealand, Cape Town in South Africa, Ushuaia in Argentina are all relatives and neighbors, so to speak, of Antartica, the core of the supercontinent Gondwana, that once stretched mild and lush from the south pole to the equator. I am speaking lightly here in tens of millions of years. We even crossed the Drake Channel whose opening allowed the circumpolar current to wrap Antarctica in its frigid embrace. There are, however, lots of Gondawanan pieces left to visit.

Glimmering in what we call space whirl truly off-home travel spots that one day marketing agents will dub unspoiled, authentic. No doubt I'll miss that. But in the meantime …

FINANCIAL SUMMARY

December 31 - April 1 11 weeks; 93 days
Exchange rate: US $1.00=approximately 4 Argentine pesos
As in my other financial summaries these figures represent my costs—a bus ticket, for example—or half a shared expense—e.g., a hotel room.

I found it impossible to separate food and accommodation expenditures. For the fourteen days of the Antarctica tour, both were included in the total cost. For three nights in Upsallata both room and three meals a day were included in our total bill.

During the six weeks in Capilla we paid no rent and ate no meals in restaurants, beyond an occasional pizza. Grocery costs were low. For example in US dollars:

> mid-price bottle of wine $6.75; mid-size
> Hellmann's mayonnaise $1.44;
> one pound coffee $3.89; four rolls toilet paper
> $2.04; six slices ham $2.60.

For thirty-eight nights out of forty the accommodation price included a full restaurant breakfast—often quite elaborate. We bought the larger size of bottled water to drink in the room. In Capilla we had two water cooler size bottles—for both drinking and cooking—delivered for US $5 a week.

Combined accommodation and food costs	$4,050
Transportation Costs Air:	
International round-trip Boston-Cordoba, Argentina	$1,060
3 domestic Argentinean flights	$600
Bus: 3 trips (1 overnight, 2 daytime)	$260
Taxi: 6 long distance (100 km each)	$270
Many local	$40
Total	$2,230
Entry Fee into Argentina	$130
Tours in Argentina: 4 (averaging five hours)	$60

Originally, I invested all money from the sale of the house in CDs of varying time spans. During the first two years the average remained 5 percent then rates dropped. Fortunately, the bulk of my money has been in a 5 year (60 month) CD that has remained at 5.35 percent interest.

Cabin #303, Le Diamant

French ship, M.S. Le Diamant

Blue-cave Iceberg & Chin-strap Penguins

Orca Whales

Elephant Seals and Penguin

Leopard Seal

Gentoo Penguins

Tubular Ice Floe

Sirloin Barbeque, Deck 5

Hallway of Boots, Le Diamant

Young Gentoo Penguin

Whaling Dory, Early 1900s

Zodiac Ride, Ice Pack

Zodiac Tour

Mutant Gentoo Mother

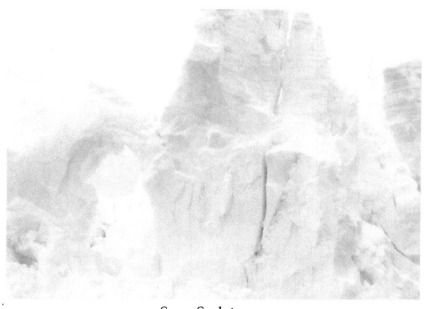

Snow Sculptures

Fur Seals

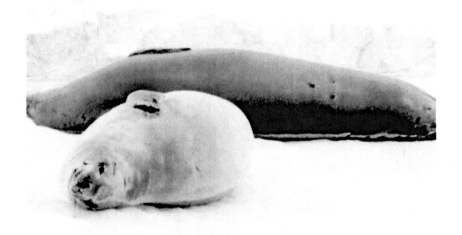

Crabeater and Weddell Seals

Leopard Seal

Sandy, Ridge Top, Neko Harbor

COMPARISON OF OVERALL COSTS FOR FOOD, ACCOMMODATIONS, AND BOTH INTERNATIONAL AND DOMESTIC TRANSPORTATION ON ALL TRIPS*

New Zealand 93 days: $ 8,300
          Daily average: $90

South Africa & Spain 86 days: $8,600
          Daily average: $100

Argentina 79 days: $6,500
          Daily average: $82

Antarctica tour 14 days: $6,650
(included 2 nights in Buenos Aires
& round-trip flight to Ushuaia)
          Daily average: $475

*In each of these trips international flight costs and our personal styles of living varied considerably. The text provides details necessary for any valid comparison.

ACKNOWLEDGEMENTS

This book, indeed the whole marvelous travel adventure, would not have taken place without the shared vision and beneficial involvement of Sandy, my life partner, who was there for every laugh and wide-eyed wonder.

My three grown children were also companions, although, except for Jim's brief trip to Argentina with us, their only contact was sporadic e-mail. They respected the decisions I made and offered assistance both tangible and intangible; for that I will always be grateful. Brent and Kath's generous assistance with comings and goings from Logan Airport are lovingly remembered.

My daughter Bett's constant, invaluable help extended to the crafting of the book itself. She and our mutual friend, Margaret Sofio, labored long and well: plowing, planting, and weeding the manuscript for six years.

My thanks for support extends to many: grandchildren, Chuck, friends in both Milbridge and Portsmouth. And to all our overseas hosts, I am sincere and confident when saying: I will never forget you.

CPSIA information can be obtained
at www.ICGtesting.com
Printed in the USA
FFOW04n1508170414
4888FF